Red, Red
Azalea

Chinese Poverty Alleviation
Volume Three

Red, Red Azalea

Song Wang

UNICORN

Published in association with CNPIEC by Unicorn
an imprint of Unicorn Publishing Group, 2022
Charleston Studio
Meadow Business Centre
Lewes, BN8 5RW

www.unicornpublishing.org

All rights reserved. No part of this publication may be reproduced, stored in or introduced into a retrieval system, or transmitted, in any form or by any means (electronic, mechanical, photocopying, recording or otherwise), without the prior written permission of the copyright holder and the above publisher of this book.

Every effort has been made to trace copyright holders and to obtain their permission for the use of copyrighted material. The publisher apologises for any errors or omissions and would be grateful to be notified of any corrections that should be incorporated in future reprints or editions of this book.

© Song Wang, 2022

10 9 8 7 6 5 4 3 2 1

ISBN: 978-1-913491-96-3

Printed and bound in the UK

Contents

FOREWORD **Once in a Thousand Years** ·· 7

PREFACE **The Sound of The Sun Landing** ·· 11

    I   The deep mountains and 'tribes' forgotten by history ·· 13

    II   Three '!' from Zhongnanhai ·· 16

    III   Three 'stone is hard but bones, the mountain is high but the foot head' ·· 23

    IV   'One, two, three' – forward into! ·· 26

YULIN CHAPTER **The first great wall** ·· 28

    I   Great changes have taken place in Yangjiagou ·· 30

    II   Back up! A hesitant start ·· 44

    III   Good men resemble mountains ·· 60

    IV   Internal power: the dream of standing ··75

XINJIANG CHAPTER **The largest flower handkerchief in China** ·· 95

    I   An affectionate visit ·· 97

    II   The veterans left the color of their uniforms to the desert ·· 103

    III   Miracle: 'five stars go out of the East and benefit China' ·· 117

    IV   Under the banner of 359 Brigade ·· 141

    V   Xinjiang guy's lifecycle ·· 157

    VI   Great love to aid Xinjiang, unprecedented ·· 163

TONGREN CHAPTER **'Sun wash basin'** ·· 169

    I   Communist Party's 'big treat' ·· 175

    II   The world's largest 'poached egg' ·· 180

    III   The horn of l ·· 201

    IV   Write your life in green mountains and green waters ·· 217

SHANGHAI CHAPTER **The heart is close, the light is far away** ·· 249

    I   No going back ·· 252

    II   Malipo, a place full of hot blood and tears ·· 260

    III   There is no place far in the world. Love is hometown ·· 277

    IV   Tending the roots of classics: Cauliflower 'Great Leap' ·· 288

    V   'Silver Age Action' ·· 301

LONGJIANG CHAPTER **Hot blood flows South** ·· 313

    I   The Huachuan plow ·· 318

    II   'The number one fool in the world' ·· 334

    III   Harbin, fire in snowflakes ··3507

    IV   Ma Xu entering Epilogue ·· 376

RECOLLECTIONS **Comparison and Thinking** ·· 388

POSTSCRIPT **From 'five force'** ·· 394

FOREWORD
Once in a Thousand Years

I

At dawn, a wooden plow stood quietly on the horizon.

The plow has a sharp blade – made of stone, later turned into bronze, and finally into steel. China's 5,000-year history has been embedded in its aluminum. Dust, sweat and tears filled its cracks. It perfectly combines the power of father and the beautiful curve of mother. Its resounding memory carries the pride and joy of a nation. Every day, the sun sprinkles on it, passes through it and radiates its beauty.

Plow, a symbol of the great strength of the Chinese nation and the sacred totem of 5,000 years of history. History begins with it, dream, revolution, reform and the original mission of the Communist Party of China. A year of a better life for the people and a grand journey towards a well-off society. It's not easy, but the Chinese people are strong, just like the persistent cattle bending over and working in the hot sun. The Chinese people make plans for the future, no matter how difficult. Technology and machines will be powerful, but this power will never replace the future of the Chinese people.

II

Poverty is the most terrible destructive force in the world. It will destroy peace, civilization, ecology, national dream and people's livelihood. Poverty eradication is a common challenge faced by all countries in the world.

Since the eighteenth National Congress of the Communist Party of China, comrade Xi Jinping has been leading a great campaign to eradicate poverty. The goal is to achieve the first centenary goal of the Communist Party of China by 2020, and the people of all ethnic groups will work together to achieve a well-off society. So far, more than seven years have passed. The most visited areas by the general secretary are Liupanshan, Qinba, Wuling, Wumeng and Dabie. The 14 mountains and rivers in the poverty-stricken areas were visited by the people leaders, and they went into the homes of poor households and extended their assistance to change people's livelihood. They have a close understanding of the situation of the people, explore ways to lift them out of poverty, and promote local leaders to support those in need.

This is an unprecedented 'people's war' in human history and a millennium war of the Chinese nation. In the past seven years, 2.8 million poverty alleviation leaders across the country have gone to poverty-stricken areas, and nearly 1000 poverty alleviation leaders have sacrificed their lives in this difficult journey. Now, this powerful national offensive force and trickling warm water are reaching every mountain road and every farmhouse in the north and south of the Yangtze River. The absolute poverty that has plagued the Chinese nation for thousands of years is disappearing from China. A comprehensive and decisive victory is coming. The clock is approaching that exciting moment.

III

The fact is powerful, like temperature. China's 9.6 million square kilometres of land are engraved with such data:

— In the past 40 years, China has experienced a revolution and reform, and more than 800 million people have been lifted out of poverty.

— The number of poor people in the world is ten times that of China.

— According to the report of the 18th National Congress of the Communist Party of China, by the end of 2018, the number of poor people has decreased from 98.99 million to 16.6 million. Poverty is reduced by more than 12 million a year, equivalent to the population of a medium-sized European country. The poverty-stricken population in rural areas dropped to 1.7% for the past six years.

— By the end of 2018, 436 people in 832 poverty-stricken counties and 102,000 people in 128,000 villages were lifted out of poverty.

— In 2020, the national poverty alleviation battle has reached a victory.

The people deserve all the recognition, without their action and their achievement, China would not be here.

Due to the nature of time and contingency, I made a special trip to Liangjiahe Village in Yan'an at about 10 o'clock on December 18, 2018. I feel the air full of passion and youth. Most of the mountain roads in the village are illuminated by oil lamps. During this time in Beijing, people gathered to celebrate the 40th anniversary of the founding of the Communist Party of China. President Xi delivered a speech to all the people, announcing that the Chinese people of all ethnic groups have entered a new era. 'Hold high the great banner of socialism with Chinese characteristics, do not forget where we came from, remember our mission. We have come a long way. With the reform and expansion, we are constantly looking forward to a better life. A new era has come, which is a miracle witnessed by China and the world!'

IV

The dream of a well-off society is like sunrise, which has risen on the horizon of the new era.

It's exciting to be a participant, a witness and a writer in this great parade. After all, I have experienced those difficult years, the confusion of going to the countryside, and the baptism of reform and opening up. Now, when I see mud huts all over the country being cleaned, thousands of poor families are smiling comfortably, and beautiful villages are springing up. I feel warm and proud of the great power of socialist China and the temperature of the country. This is the temperature of original intention, the temperature of oath, the temperature of blood, and the temperature of happiness.

I've been walking around China for 10 months, to feel the temperature.

V

This book comes from the extensive field investigation of hundreds of grassroots cadres and farmers in Shaanxi, Xinjiang, Guizhou, Shanghai, Heilongjiang and other places. So, I'd rather call it report than literature. These statements are made by village cadres in village committees, rural Kang, fields or farmhouses, and their authenticity is beyond doubt. The process and achievements of China's poverty alleviation work, the changes in China's rural situation, and the hardships and efforts of the majority of poverty alleviation cadres are all written in this book. China's national temperature is in this book. China is rising up.

Historical imagination can never satisfy human creativity.

The imagination of the world is never enough for the creativity of the Communist Party and the Chinese people.

As long as there is a dream, everything is unstoppable.

PREFACE

The Sound of The Sun Landing

Past and present lives of the poverty alleviation and Development Office of the State Council

A SPACIAL OFFICE is filled with a crowd.

Qingjian people, they and their eyebrows have a kind of heroic spirit, serious expression, ten fingers flying, sound on both sides of the wall complement each other, its edge reaches 9.6 million square kilometres of land.

The current here is turbulent, the huge waves are open and magnificent, but it keeps the quiet of the blue sky and the earth. Data and information flows from all over the country have been collected here, showing the ambition, heroic momentum and momentum of 'Jiangdong, wave and romantic characters'. Every village, every wisp of smoke, every ordinary farmer, their pigs, horses, sheep, chickens, ducks, geese, every piece of cultivated land, every greenhouse, every pond, every orchard, are shining in the huge computer space in a digital way. They can cross mountains and rivers like the sea.

The staff here doesn't care about overtime because it's their daily work. Four meals a day and a box meal in the evening. Men are happy, women are encouraged not to eat in the middle of the night because some are worried about getting fat. Even if there is little sunshine, the advantage is that they can keep their handsome little faces as white as jade. They fought day and night at all costs. Their faces are calm. They're boiling inside.

Their eyes are raised high, which can't be found in any other history. The eighteenth National Congress of the Communist Party of China is the leadership and command of the Party Central Committee with Comrade Xi Jinping as its core. It directly led and promoted the development of the struggle against poverty and the great movement. This is an unprecedented battle in the history of the Chinese nation.

These are comrades from the poverty alleviation and Development Office of the State Council.

It is glorious to leave our footprints in the great journey of the great rejuvenation of the Chinese nation. Creating and maintaining happiness is their responsibility. They know that they have gone through the magnificent era of 'a thousand year waiting'.

Everyone who walks into the hall of the poverty alleviation and development office building of the State Council will see a countdown electronic display screen on the wall of the main hall, with red characters on a black background, silent and shining.

This is a display with a special and profound sense of mission. It is 1.52 metres wide and 3.8 metres high. It has a countdown clock that flashes numbers. There are seven red characters at the top, 'poverty countdown,' and in the middle, '427 days' (the day I saw) – from December to 427 days in the next few seconds. It marks the process and rhythm of China's poverty alleviation and the grand livelihood project of China in today's world.

It glitters like a silent horn. It shows the pace of mobilization in the new era proposed by the Party Central Committee and the whole nation at the core of Comrade Xi Jinping, and urges the pace and aspirations of the poor cadres throughout the country. By the magnificent moment of December 31, 2020, it will go straight to the historical coordinates of the 100 years since the founding of the Communist Party of China with a higher and more passionate rhythm. At that time, China will announce to the world: one of the 'two centenary goals' of the Communist Party of China and one of the goals for the great rejuvenation of the Chinese nation – the great journey of socialist China into a well-off society in an all-round way and a decisive victory!

On the clock of time, there will always have two big characters: 'Now!' (in Chinese, Xianzai).

The office of the leading group for poverty alleviation and development under the State Council is the deliberative and coordinating organ of the State Council and the working department and vice-ministerial unit of the leading group for poverty alleviation and development under the State Council. The leading group, headed by Wang Yang, is responsible for policy formulation, leadership and overall coordination of poverty alleviation work of relevant state departments. The leading group is a Reportage Creation project established on May 16 1986, and renamed as the leading group for economic development in poverty-stricken areas of the State Council on December 28, 1993. Many people may not know that the decision of the CPC Central Committee and the State Council to set up a national leading group was related to a remote minority village in Hezhang County, Guizhou Province.

A big hunger, shook Zhongnanhai...

I The deep mountains and 'tribes' forgotten by history

In the spring of 1985, Guizhou, known as 'Sanqing', suffered from severe drought, and the vegetation and forest dried up.

On the morning of that day, in Pengpeng Village, Hezhang County, Bijie district, a pair of arrogant black feet in 'tire shoes' climbed to the top of the mountain, and their rotten trousers were wet by the cold dew. The 'shoes' were cut from discarded tricycle tires with four holes on the raised edge and tied to the feet with hemp ropes. The hemp rope was worn out in seven or eight days. After replacement, the bottom of the tire can wear for decades – it still exists. Don't rope makers grind blood on their feet? No, because the skin of the foot is as thick as the sole of a shoe and as hard as stone.

Drought, crops late and thin, withered head drooping. In order to fall to the ground, village Party Secretary Wen Chaorong and Yi man carried two buckets of water up the mountain. Born in 1942, he is very bold and antique, like a stone carving cut with a knife: deep eyebrows, straight nose, dark and rough skin, with a palm sized work manual and a ball point pen in his pocket. On the slope, Wen struggled to lift two buckets from the cow's back. Suddenly, a group of thirsty birds flapped their wings and shot arrows into the bucket to drink water. Go away, Wen, wave and yell.

In Paffin Village, the old man always wakes up earlier than the chicken and shouts more fiercely than the dog. A copper whistle forced the villagers to get up early and work. As soon as he heard his whistle, he went mad and the whole village was restless. The villagers go out to gather at once, otherwise Wen Chaorong's thunder will blow people into the cracks in the ground. For months of the year, the village follows the copper pillars at sunrise and rests at sunset. Only when the old man's whistle rings, the sun will rise, the corn will stick, and life will continue.

Bijie, located in the hinterland of Wumeng Mountain in Northwest Guizhou, is known as 'the land of three poles', that is, the natural conditions are extremely poor, the productivity is extremely low, and the people's life is extremely poor. There are over 20,000 square kilometres in the city, only 8% of them are flat, and the rest are mausoleums. The valley is high and steep, the terrain is broken, and the karst landform accounts for more than two thirds of the whole area. Earlier this year, UN experts visited Bijie to believe that 'there are no basic conditions for human survival' and suggested that the Chinese government move residents on a large scale. The locals laughed. So many Chinese people, where to move?

Lark village is located in the depth of Wumeng Mountain, 2,300 metres above sea level, belonging to the alpine region. There are five villager groups in the village, through several connected hills. 730 people from 168 households, including 702 people from 162 Miao households and 28 people from 6 Yi households. There are only five people with primary education, and the middle-aged and old can hardly speak Putonghua. The vast majority of villagers live in thatched cottages and branches, people and animals mixed together. Mountain and steep slopes account for 90%, and the cultivated land is poor and broken. There is no electricity, no road, no school, and no clinic in the village. Drinking water depends on collecting rainwater. To go to school, to see a doctor, to make a phone call, you need to walk down the mountain to the seat of the township government 12 kilometres away. The whole village is almost isolated from the world. In the words of local people, 'eating is basically begging, drinking is basically using hands, and walking is basically using dogs.' It has never been enriched in the memory of generations. Because the land is poor, farming is difficult, and the harvest is low, 'potatoes are not as big as eggs, corn is not as long as the palm, and mice have to kneel and gnaw, plant a slope, and close a basket.' Wang Xuefang, a skinny villager, told me that he only wore pants when he was 14 or 15 years old. As long as there is no poison on the mountain, his stool is as thin as urine, 'a bag of fried noodles and ten eggs can be changed into a daughter-in-law.'

At that time, 'left' tendencies were rampant, cadres were afraid of mistakes, and the masses were afraid of hunger. It seems that we can't see the end of poverty, just like Tongzi killed the fate of Fugu village. The beautiful Miao girl (I saw her with her two daughters, only the widow) sang:

A red azalea in full bloom, open in the heart.

The vine root on the mountain is wrapped in her daughter's hand.

The elder brother went out on the opposite side of the mountain, but the younger sister found it difficult to open it.

The pot loses grain, the wick has no oil, the snow grass, and the rain has no way to go.

Tears in the days on the mountain, which year is over?

Elder brother, you have the heart to shout, elder sister, I walk with you, follow you, die abroad, and don't look back!

Later, Luo Qiaohua really left and was driven away by poverty and hunger. It was a night of 'stepping on Huashan'. A miner in the village commanded a group of village Party members to tie her on a horse with a flashlight, which is a popular way of marriage snatching. There is also a local custom that the bridegroom and bride go to bed on the night of the wedding candlelight – in fact, this is a kind of false beat, so that young men and women outside the window can hear its bustle. On that wedding night, Luo Qiaohua was really beaten and cried. The teapot, bowl and plate all fell to the ground, because she was reluctant to give up, because she had a lover in the village. But the young man's family is too poor, no room, no food, no clothes, cannot live with her, Luo Qiaohua had to accept fate. Four years later, she divorced, led a daughter, held a daughter, afraid to go back – because she didn't give it to the man and was called out of the house.

If you think about it carefully, the core of the traditional culture of ethnic minorities is actually 'everything for survival'. For example, Miao people's appellation comes from the expectation of 'more seedlings in the field'; The Yi People's appellation comes from Mao Zedong's suggestion, which means that there is a house above and clothing, food, housing and transportation below. But after a long time, this wish has not come true.

The village is high above the mountains, so it is very difficult for the villagers to see the county and township cadres, because there is no public grain, but they eat relief grain every year, so the cadres have to hide. Wen Chaorong is the only representative of the party and government of Fugu village. Some people call him 'rule of man'. In this way, the sea sparrow village seems to be forgotten by the world, the 'tribe' on the mountain, no one cares, suffering in the world.

II Three'!' from Zhongnanhai

On December 24, 1978, on that cold and hungry winter night, there were 18 farmers' representatives in Xiaogang Village, Anhui Province, and 20 families in the village signed a farm agreement with red fingerprints, becoming 'the first village of China's reform'. In the same year, several production teams of Dingyun commune secretly implemented the policy of mass production and overproduction, becoming 'the first township of China's reform'. By the year 1985, the curtain of China's rural reform has opened. The enthusiasm of hundreds of millions of farmers has been unprecedentedly emancipated, the grain output has increased year by year, the problem of food and clothing for the broad masses of rural people has been initially solved, the people's commune has completely withdrawn from the historical stage, the rural development situation is getting better and better, and the national heart is unblocked.

1985 is the year of the ox, as the saying goes, 'the year of cattle and horses, and the year of good work'. However, many people have not noticed that in Guizhou, where economic and social development lags behind seriously, production and life are still very difficult. Especially in Bijie area, Haijian village, Hezhang County, the high mountains, because of the influence of hail and early frost, the output of corn and potato last year was large, and many families only had enough to eat for two or three months, and the whole village was in a dilemma of lack of food. Wenchaorong, the party secretary of the worried village, had to embark on the endless 'begging road' and went to the village and county to help them again and again.

In the view of some local leaders and young people sitting in the office, Wen Jiabao's behavior is obviously not in line with the good situation of the country's rural development. As a result, the news wave was first robbed by the disaster relief, and the disaster relief leading cadres became more and more angry. Some people angrily say that the puffer fish village is a bottomless hole. Some people say that when Wen Chaorong studied agricultural villages, he was a 'red flag' and could not keep up with the situation after the reform. He had nothing else to eat and wear. Wen Chaorong is a Yi nationality with a short temper. The villagers nicknamed him 'Fire King'. He yelled at the Township Office, rocked the house and looked straight at Mars. But whatever its purpose, relief food has been delayed. Wen Chaorong had to put on the heavy tire shoes, and then ran down the mountain again and again, walking hopefully. When he came back, there were tears in his eyes.

Finally, one day, an outsider came to the village.

One day in late May 1985, Liu Zifu, a young reporter from Guizhou branch of Xinhua news agency, came to Hezhang County to reflect the good situation of rural reform. On the morning of 29 May, the county sent an old Beijing jeep to take him to HengDi district. It is said that this is a minority village. He was very interested and decided to climb the mountain and take some scenery photos and flowers. Near noon, over the mountain, through a messy forest, Fugu village appeared in front of him.

For a time, Liu Zifu left behind a 'wooden chicken'. At that time, the first impression of pafen village was that it was lifeless. Every family lived in a thatched cottage, looking wobbly. 'He recalled' when he came into the house, they were all living together with human beings and animals. When it was broken, he could not avoid the cold. At that time, I was young and started working very soon. I don't know much about rural poverty in Guizhou. It has been six or seven years since reform and opening up. I am very shocked and sad to see that the villagers of puffin village still live in such houses. Then I went door to door, and it was more serious than I thought.

Miao villager Wang Yongcai's rice Zengzi cracked and molded. Open the lid on the charcoal fire and cook the wild vegetables. Take a closer look and find a little cornmeal in it. Climbing into the attic, I saw only 27 yams the size of pigeon eggs in the basket, linen skirts and quilts broken like fishing nets. Some little dolls are so hungry that they can't even cry...

Liu Zifu asked eagerly, are you the Secretary of the village Party branch? Wu Xiuqin, director of the women's Bureau, said she had to go to the county for relief. Liu Zifu asked again, the difficulties in the village have become like this, and the most senior cadres have not come to have a look? The villagers said that there was no telephone in the village and everything was run back and forth by the village party secretary.

Liu Zifu rushed down the mountain and rushed back to Hezhang County that night. The next morning, Wang Olan, Secretary of the county Party committee, came to see him. Liu Zifu introduced the plight of the village and asked about the food shortage in the county. Mr. Wang said in a heavy voice, why didn't I see you on the first day? Because I don't know what to say. I'm afraid you asked me to introduce the good situation of rural reform, but I can't say it! In fact, the county is on the verge of food shortage, with a total of 12,000 households and more than 30,000 people. We can't solve this problem on our own. We repeatedly reflect, but time does not wait, the stomach does not wait, we are worried about death! I hope you can help us report to our superiors as soon as possible.

After Wang Lan left, Liu Zifu could not be calm for a long time. Over the past few years, reports on 'good situation, more grain' in rural reform have flourished. Some grassroots officials are used to reporting good news but not bad news, so it is difficult for their superiors to understand the real situation at the grassroots level, and even more difficult to hear the eagerness of the hungry people. For a long time, Liu Zifu decided to write an 'internal' report, which is the quickest way for the hungry to reach the central government, but he should not go without hesitation. As a fledgling young reporter of Guizhou bureau, can this 'negative' report go through layer upon layer from editor, director and editor in chief to editor, director and editor in chief? If the review process is delayed too long, the hungry people in Haifeng Village and even Hezhang County can't wait! Liu Zifu made a bold decision: in order to avoid having a branch outside the festival, he completed the manuscript in Hezhang County. Without going through Guizhou branch, he directly telegraphed the president of Xinhua news agency, which obviously violated the working procedures, but he ignored so many.

There was a blackout in the county at night. Liu asked the hotel attendant for two candles and a book. At about 1 am, he wrote all night. At that time, he wrote a report of nearly 2,000 words. The next day, that is, May 30, he went to the county post office to buy a stack of telegrams, copied a one-word report, and then sent it to Beijing by urgent telegram. An emergency draft costs more than 20 yuan. In the 1980s, the number was not small.

Most of the comrades in the head office are old reporters. They are quick to respond and understand its importance. The manuscript was sent to Mu Qing, President of Xinhua news agency, on his desk (the author, Jiao Yulu, a good example of the Secretary of the county Party committee). After watching it, Mu Qing was deeply shocked and asked, 'send it quickly!'

Two days later, on June 2, 1985, the new Xinhua news agency was sent to the seats of members of the Political Bureau and the Secretariat of the CPC Central Committee, which immediately attracted the attention of the old revolution.

The full text of Liu Zifu's report is as follows:

More than 12,000 ethnic minority farmers in Hezhang County live very hard, but no one complains about the state.

About 63,061 farmers in 12,001 households had or were about to run out of rice and fuel.

On 29 May, the reporter visited three villagers' groups in Haique Village, which is inhabited by Miao and Yi Nationalities in Sifang Township, HengDi District, and the county. Meeting 11 farmers, and every household cooks. Luo

Qichao, a member of Yi nationality, lives in the middle class. Reporter into Luo Qi's home sees his wife Liang Youlan sad to stay at home. She told the reporter: last year, because of the low temperature, we didn't collect much grain, so we paid off 200 Jin, which has been cut off. Her husband had to go out to borrow food, and so far, he didn't know if he was going to land. Last year, the family sold five ducks and more than 200 eggs, earned 31 yuan, and bought salt and oil. She also said: in the face of district and township cadres, they dare not say they will not eat, and they are afraid of attack. When the reporter looked at all her houses, they were worth 100 yuan at most.

When the reporter walked into the Miao family, An Meizhen was so thin that she only had a dry skeleton to support her head. There are four people in her family, husband, two sons and her. The whole family didn't see oil all year round, and they were tired all year. With three months of salt, four people only have three bowls. They have been out of food for five days.

At Wang Yongcai's home, a member of the Miao nationality, Wang Yongcai tearfully told reporters that there were five people in his family who had been without food for five months and lived on wild vegetables, not to mention oil and salt. Cattle is the lifeblood of the Miao family, but also had to mercilessly sell vegetables to save people. A cow sold for 250 yuan, no food. Cattle are very cheap, not to mention horses, chickens and pigs. At the edge of his fire, a three-year-old child was lying on the ground hungry, making a weak 'OK, OK, OK' cry, which made the mother helpless.

The reporter walked around the Fugu village group on the 9th, and found no oil or rice. What he ate more was corn batter and buckwheat batter, with mung bean seeds mixed in the dry food. Nine families have no activity fee, no animals, no decent beds or quilts, some beds and ponds.

Not far from fugu village group is the school village group. The reporter walked into Zhao Zhen's home and was shocked. Her clothes didn't cover her. Seeing the guest coming, she immediately covered her chest with her hand and lowered her head strangely. Her shirt was worn over her chest. Her shame could hardly be covered with a broken skirt like a thread. She showed it to me as she walked up and down. Aunt saw the reporter's embarrassment, but took the initiative to say: 'wear three years of clothes, spring, summer, autumn and winter.' Ah! I really didn't promise, but I'm sorry to meet someone, my aunt's neighbor is Zhu Zhenghua's. The shopkeeper was so tired that he said, 'I finished at the end of last year. For months, I've found a liter of gas. '

Miao youth Wang Xuefang took the reporter home and told the reporter: at present, there are 30 families, 25 families whose vegetables are broken, and the remaining five families can't live for a few days. Due to poor food, insufficient food and insufficient physical strength, young people engaged in production in the group can only work half a day. In addition, the main labor force has to go out to forage, affecting the normal progress of production.

In spite of their poor families, the simple brothers of these ethnic minorities never escaped. No one petitioned, no one offered a helping hand to the country, no one complained about the party and the country, but they blamed themselves for 'not striving for success'. This scene is very moving.

It is understood that in 1984, Hezhang County produced 183,300 Jin of grain, 396 Jin of grain per capita, with a net income of 110 yuan. Of the 89 townships in the county, 88 are poor. The poverty-stricken area of the county is large, and there is a big gap in funds and grain. Since the Spring Festival, disaster relief funds and grain have been distributed one after another, but the problem remains unsolved. It is worth noting that some district and township cadres are indifferent to the suffering of farmers. Many people have changed from 'fearing the rich and loving the poor' to 'loving the rich and loving the poor', lacking a minimum sense of responsibility. For example, Haijian village is 12 kilometres away from HengDi District Committee. District cadres also understand the poverty situation in the village, but they do not conduct in-depth investigation and sincerely help farmers out of poverty.

Xi Zhongxun, a legendary revolutionary hero in Northern Shaanxi, once praised him as 'young and pure' and the leader of the 'people'. At the age of 21, he was elected chairman of the Shaanxi Gansu Ningxia Soviet government. At the age of 32, he served as secretary of the Northwest Bureau of the CPC Central Committee and vice premier of the State Council at the age of 46. After the 'Cultural Revolution', he went to Guangdong with great political courage to take the lead in carrying out reform and opening up and invigorating the mainland. His economic development has aroused people's attention, and wave after wave of 'fleeing from Hong Kong' has gradually stopped. This incident left a deep impression on Deng Xiaoping. All his life, Xi Zhongxun was loyal to the people and listened to the voice of the masses. He once said cordially, 'everything about our party belongs to the masses." The country is the people, and the people are the country' (see biography of Xi Zhongxun)

After reading the report, Xi Zhongxun was very sad and angry. Waving his pen, he explained in the upper right corner of the manuscript as follows:

We blame not only the party and the state, but also ourselves for 'asking for trouble' for such a poor life. This is a serious warning to us bureaucrats!! The provincial Party committee is required to set a time limit, take practical measures and do more work in a planned and step-by-step way to change this situation.

Xi Zhongxun uses three parallel '!' In his instructions, this is very rare in the instructions of successive party and state leaders. It is obvious that Xi Zhongxun treated some people in Guizhou in such a particularly irritating way. The masses expressed great concern about living such a poor life, and also criticized the bureaucratic style of Party and government organs at all levels.

On June 2, the relevant departments of the central government will give instructions and relevant reports to the Guizhou provincial Party committee. Guizhou provincial Party committee and government took immediate action. At that time, Zhu Houze, Secretary of the provincial Party committee, held a meeting of the leaders of the municipal Party committee, the city and the state in the local area, conveyed the spirit of Xi Zhongxun's important instructions, and comprehensively deployed the disaster relief work. The provincial Party committee and the provincial government quickly sent out hundreds of cadres and divided them into eight groups. Under the leadership of the then governor, Wang Qishan went to various places to investigate, direct and organize disaster relief, and properly arrange people's lives. At this time, Hu Jintao was appointed as the new secretary of Guizhou provincial Party committee by the CPC Central Committee. Before leaving, Xi Zhongxun told him about the serious natural disaster in Bijie, Guizhou Province, and asked for immediate rescue. On his third day in office, Hu Jintao went to Hezhang County and other places in Bijie to go deep into the countryside to investigate the food shortage in the village, and asked the local government to establish a food security system. In other words, open the granary. He was unable to reach Fugu village because of heavy rain and road disruption. During this period, the State Council urgently allocated 36 million yuan of disaster relief funds to Guizhou, increasing 500 million kilograms of grain in other provinces. For a time, on the winding mountain road in Bijie, Guizhou Province, relief food kept flowing.

Thousands of Jin of relief grain was transported into the puffer fish village. Puffer fish village was saved, and every household raised fragrant smoke.

III Three 'stone is hard but bones, the mountain is high but the foot head'

Wen Chaorong, Secretary of the village Party committee, was born poor. As a child, the land reform team came here to send him to school. After that, he put a ballpoint pen in his jacket pocket. From before liberation to after the reform, he witnessed the evolution of the ecological environment in his hometown: due to the increase of population, serious deforestation and soil erosion, the original green mountains and clear mountains gradually became barren mountains, and the grain yield became lower and lower. The arrival of national relief food has made the whole village happy, angry, sad and happy. But what Wen Chaorong thinks about is more emotion and long-term. The party and government have saved our lives, but in the Haitian village, we can't rely on national relief every year. We should be grateful and strive to reduce the burden of the country. 700 million farmers are making contributions to the country. We also farm, but we eat relief every year. Is it worth it? In the future, we should take a road of self-reliance and self-help!

The villagers asked, 'how can I get there?'

Wen Chaorong said: first, we should vigorously develop the breeding industry, raise pigs, cattle and sheep, and use livestock and us to increase fertilizer. In the future, we must shit at home and not let fertilizer flow to other people's fields!

The audience laughs and says it's done!

Second, vigorously develop the planting industry. Let's take a look at a dozen mountains around us. In the past few decades, they have been cut into 'heshantou'. There is no grass or trees here. The mountain torrents have destroyed the crops.

Since the party and the government have saved our lives, we can't do nothing and plant trees together. When trees grow into forests, soil and soil keep good, harvest high, we don't need state relief every year!

The audience laughed. Have you ever thought about talking to a text secretary? Do you think if you hit the bald hill, one blow will turn into a forest?

'We must not sit and eat state relief every day,' Wen cried! Stones are harder than bones, and mountains are not high. If it's too late, you can do it when I die, and you can do it when your son and grandson die, and you can do it tomorrow!

The next day, Wen Chaorong led a group of rags called Hua, braved the cold wind and carried an iron hoe up the mountain. What if I don't have money to buy saplings? Wen Chaorong decided to be a 'bandit'. Suddenly, he led a group of young villagers to sneak into the county and stole thousands of pine seedlings from the nursery of the county forestry bureau. The next day, the director of forestry angrily called to the county magistrate there, asking to be arrested by Wen Chaorong. County magistrate said with a smile, if the villagers come to steal saplings, I will give you a big certificate!

The mountain is far away, who can't carry it every day. In order to save energy and not delay the solar term, Wen Chaorong and the villagers wear rotten clothes every day. For three consecutive spring festival galas, the villagers live on the mountain. When young men and women set fire, they often sing and dance around the campfire with hungry stomachs, and their rotten shirts and skirts dance like flames.

> *The sun came out from the hillside, and my brother and sister wanted to plant more trees.*

> *Brother dug a hole in the front, sister dug a nest in the back...*

Fugu village is really fighting for gratitude and self-help. At that time, there was no theory or policy of returning farmland to forests, but under the leadership of Wen Chaorong, villagers went up to the mountains to plant trees year after year. This is the first spontaneous, conscious and self-financing 'village run greening movement' in Guizhou Province. It should go down in history. In the year 1986,

800 Mu will be planted in the whole village, and 13,400 Mu will be planted in the next three years. In the new century, the state has formulated the preferential policy of returning farmland to forest, so that the villagers can get food subsidies with higher enthusiasm. After more than ten years of hard work, dozens of bare stone mountains have become a lush forest. Greening rate increased from 5% to 70%. In the new century, the total output value has reached more than 40 million yuan, with a per capita of more than 50,000 yuan. The per capita has 15 mu of trees, and the whole village enjoys a subsidy of 248,000 yuan for returning farmland to forests every year. When I went to the Fugu village for an interview, I stood on the high hillside, four wild mountains shrouded in clouds and fog, green, standing tall Pinus armandii and Pinus massoniana. Wen Chaorong led all the villagers to make concerted efforts, which was his lifelong efforts.

Local people say Wen has three treasures: a sickle, a basket and tires and shoes. In 2000, at the age of 59, Wen Chaorong retired, but he still wore tires and shoes, carried sickles and baskets, and climbed mountains to protect the green mountains and the blue sea. Every day, back and forth for dozens of miles, 'go out of the day is not bright, go home to the moon', only the little black dog with him.

One day, Wen Chaorong fainted in the forest. Little black dog went crazy and ran back to the village to report the accident. He was tired and couldn't stand up anymore. On February 11, 2014, Wen Aolong, 73, died, and the villagers cried. On the day of the funeral, thousands of people from several surrounding villages arrived. We strongly ask each village to take out eight people, one from each village, and send our beloved old secretary. The crowd behind him lined up to cry.

Before he died, the old party secretary asked him to be buried on the high slope opposite the forest sea, guarding the vast forest forever. When I went for an interview, I came to the old man's tomb to hold a memorial ceremony. The U-shaped tomb, painted white, has no name, including an innocent life. The old man's tires are permanently stored in the world's only pavan village exhibition hall. The Organization Department of the CPC Central Committee posthumously awarded Wen Cha as 'the vanguard of the times'.

The old man and Lin Hai have never been separated! So far forever, in the green mountains and the green sea, in the memory of the villagers, still walking the gray haired old Yugong.

Of course, Wen Chaorong did not expect that Haifeng Village called the police in Zhongnanhai because there was no cooking, which made the state and Guizhou province carry out large-scale relief to the victims in Bijie and Hezhang, becoming an important node in the history of poverty alleviation in China. On June 2, 1985, Xi Zhongxun gave an important instruction to Xinhua reporter Liu Zifu, which is also a mobilization order for China to vigorously carry out large-scale poverty alleviation and development in the new period of reform and opening up. On May 16, 1986, after repeated deliberation, the Central Committee decided to set up the 'State Council Leading Group for economic development in poor areas', set up special agencies, formulate poverty alleviation standards, set up special funds for poverty alleviation, identify key areas to support, and formulate policies for poverty alleviation and development.

This is undoubtedly a major progress in China's poverty alleviation and development. On December 28, 1993, the office of the leading group was renamed 'Poverty Alleviation Office of the State Council'. China's poverty alleviation work rose from the civil administration level to national action, and poverty alleviation work was carried out on a large scale nationwide in an organized and planned way.

IV 'One, two, three' – forward into!

Since the eighteenth National Congress of the Communist Party of China, general secretary Xi Jinping has stood at the strategic height of building a well-off society in an all-round way, realized the great revival of the 'China dream' and placed the poverty reduction work in a prominent position. General Secretary Xi Jinping came to Fuping, Hebei, and saw the real poverty. For the first time, he put forward the goal of helping the poor. The poverty alleviation and development center is the symbol of China's poverty alleviation and development. The Party Central Committee regards poverty alleviation and development as the bottom-line task and landmark indicator of building a well-off society in an all-round way, carries out comprehensive reform and innovation in poverty alleviation system, policies and methods, and carries out a nationwide fight against poverty. The impact of this movement is unprecedented and far-reaching. A great chapter in the history of human poverty alleviation is unfolding in China.

What's wrong with poverty alleviation? What is the standard? The Party Central Committee and the State Council have formulated clear, specific and definite 'one, two and three' standards based on the national conditions and realities:

'One standard': that is, the per capita annual income of farmers reaches the current national poverty alleviation standard.

Second, they don't worry about food and clothing. Third, they don't worry about 'Three Guarantees': that is, compulsory education is guaranteed, basic medical care is guaranteed, and housing is guaranteed (including drinking water).

Since the industrial revolution, China has lagged far behind the advanced countries in the world. Since the Opium War, the killing, bullying and plundering of China by Western powers have decreased. China has a population of 1.4 billion, with the vast majority of farmers. 'One, Two, three' is the basic guarantee. However, what a great and arduous historical mission it is to fully implement and bring a well-off life to every family! The millennium is like a day – the unprecedented poverty alleviation and development project in human history is a new era in front of the Communist Party of China and socialist China!

This is the top priority of contemporary China and the first livelihood project. This is the essential requirement of a people-oriented socialist China and a solemn promise made by Comrade Xi Jinping as the core and the Central Committee of the whole people and the whole world as the core.

'One, Two, three', just like the thunder of the new era, inspires us to keep forging ahead. Forward, in! At this moment, the red numbers on the electronic screen of the Poverty Alleviation Office Hall of the State Council are constantly flashing – all over the country, the decisive battle is in full swing!

Yulin Chapter
The first great wall

The place right here is sacred.

The wind across the earth plateau seemed to have opened the most ancient memory of the Chinese race. The long and tragic history passed through the land of the emperor, breaking through the crisscross gullies, and left traces of civilization and growing rings in his memory.

The earth plateau is the golden platform of China. From north to south, it was towering and magnificent, with mountains and thick mountains. Looking around, he saw the tomb of his Chinese ancestor, the Yellow Emperor. Yellow River, the bronze mother river, meandered here affectionately. The Great Wall was like a ridge crossing mountains. It was built here at the very beginning. The first emperor of Qin had unified China, established the county system and established the measurement and balance. This was where the great cause of the Han Dynasty's territory expansion and the merging of the 36 western regions into Chinese territory took place. From here on, the silk road connecting the two continents began. Mao Zedong led the Red Army to walk twenty-five thousand miles and finally settled down here. In the war of resistance and the war of freedom, Mao Zedong and his 'the smallest headquarters in the world' were set here. This was the starting point for leading Yellow River to enter the central region and win the victory of the national revolution.

It's 5,000 years old. There are so many magnificent historical stories here. It is no coincidence that so many Chinese cultural symbols converge here. This barren and magnificent scenery outlines the Chinese people's back. With its tenacity, it has cultivated the Chinese people's indomitable and courageous heroic temperament. A hundred years ago, when a Western priest came here, he wrote such a sentence: 'we live in a place with an eternal past. Almost all major events in the process of Chinese civilization are closely related to this place, some even have world significance. The more we know about this place, the more awe we have.

The earth plateau was the source and foundation of the great spirit of the Chinese race.

This was a magnificent epic. The song was vigorous and powerful. At that moment, in the sunlight breaking through the clouds, the plateau people in white sheep's belly wrapped in a towel, took a puff of fragrant and spicy dry smoke, opened their copper chests, and solemnly stood up from the dawn. The mothers of thousands of families in the village lit the stove, and also lit up the dream since ancient times. A wisp of green smoke rose from the village. It carried the forest and mountains, and the fragrance of birds and flowers in the sky.

At that moment, I reached the high bank of Yellow River, and the mother river in the deep valley came into view. My heart was close to her warm chest, with deep emotions and non-stop heartbeat. At that moment, he heard the roar of the man from the north, and a piece of sky swam from the river.

Do you know how many bays there are on the Yellow River in the world?

How many bays are there more than ten ships?

There are more than ten poles on several ships?

Dozens of ferry workers to pull the boat?

I know that there are ninety-nine Yellow River bays in the world,

There are ninety-nine ships in ninety-nine Bay,

There are ninety-nine poles on ninety-nine ships,

Ninety-nine boatmen came to pull the boat.

Yellow River is the past, the present and the future. Yellow River is our spirit, strength and blood. Our descendants are eager to see it. We all have great ambitions and a sense of responsibility for our country.

This is an accidental coincidence and the necessity of the times. At about 10:00 on December 18, 2018, I walked on the flat and quiet mountain road in Liangjiahe Village, Yan'an. At the same time, in Beijing, the people's Congress, which celebrated the 40th anniversary of the reform and opening up, was solemnly held in the Great Hall of the people. On behalf of all the people of the country, Xi Jinping made a bold declaration on the new journey of the new era of reform and opening up. 'Hold high the great flag of the society with Chinese characteristics, don't forget the original intention, remember the mission, and carry out the reform and opening up to the end. We will constantly realize the people's yearning for a good life, and create a new greater miracle of the Chinese race in the new era! Create a new and greater miracle and leave a deep impression on the world!'

China's history has indeed come to such a moment.

I Great changes have taken place in Yangjiagou

Yulin, one of China's famous cities in history and culture, was called Shangjun County in ancient times. Many years ago, it was an important military fortress at the foot of the Great Wall. Yellow River and the Great Wall passed through the city, and the Beacon Tower, which was known as the number one Beacon Tower in the world, was here. Yulin was located in the northernmost part of Shaanxi Province, which was connected to Inner Mongolia in the north, Shaanxi in the East, Shanxi in the south, Yulin in the north, Shaanxi in the north, Inner Mongolia in the north, Yulin in the north, a barren desert in the north, and the Yellow plain in the south. The land was desolate with few wind and rain Gullies crisscrossed and mountains intertwined. According to the local people, Yulin was a city half built on Soil and half built on yellow sand. People also said that the crops are not planted every year. The most exuberant creatures on the earth plateau were only poverty and hunger.

Those days had passed for a long time. Jiang Zhiming, a more than 80-year-old man from the Yangjiagou, still clearly remembered the scene at that time. He was wearing an old grey blue military uniform, riding a white horse and a group of soldiers, passing by his cave entrance. After the rain, the road was very slippery, and the horse couldn't move. He got off the car and smiled, pushing the horse butt with the young soldiers, later people knew that the people in this area opened their affectionate arms and secretly guarded a secret that was closely related to the fate of China. On March 19, 1947, Hu Zongnan led 230,000 soldiers to march forward and occupied the empty city, Yan'an. The radio and newspapers of the national army were very happy. They thought they would completely annihilate the army of the party soon, but the army carried machine guns and wandered around the northern plateau, but they couldn't find the 'red hair'. The villagers said seriously, 'when you came, the pigs were scared away.' Where did you get these pigs?'

Mao Zedong will never forget his sense of humor. When he left Yan'an, he gave himself a pseudonym 'Li Desheng.' He plucked his ashes and said with a smile, 'Li Desheng', saying that whoever occupied the justice of the world won. For a long time, Mao Zedong and many top CPC leaders lived in Yangjiagou Village, Mizhi County. The earth mounds here are continuous and the mountain roads are rugged. In the mountain nests hidden by green forests, there are several magnificent black brick houses, surrounded by hundreds of farmers' caves and thatched houses. These big houses belong to the famous Mahalanobis family in Mizhi County. There were 72 big landlords in the Republic of China. When Mao Zedong came here, Ma Zhuping, an old grandmaster known for 'not asking politics but only talking about practice', expressed a sincere welcome and deliberately vacated an idle house for use. Often, when he was tired of work, Mao Zedong came out slowly with a cigarette in his hand and found some villagers sitting on the hillside, talking and laughing, looking very calm.

One night in early winter, Mao Zedong squatted barefoot on the Kang of a cave kiln in the big house, holding cigarettes in one hand and lanterns in the other, and carefully studied the military map covered on the Kang. At this time, Xi Zhongxun, director of the Northwest Bureau, led a young man in a black cotton padded jacket into the cave. He said: 'Chairman, this is Zhang Junxian, Secretary of Jiaxian County Party committee. He came to Yangjiagou for a meeting and came to see you.'

Mao Zedong hurried down the Kang, put on his shoes, smiled and said, 'Comrade Zhang, you've taken me for decades. It's great to be the Secretary of the county Party committee!' Zhang Junxian was embarrassed, held the chairman's outstretched hand tightly and said, 'where, where the chairman leads well!'

Mao Zedong didn't forget that when he led his troops to the northern region, the army had eaten up all the food in the past three days. Xi Zhongxun found Zhang Junxian and asked him to find a way. Zhang Junxian asked, 'how much is it?' According to Xi Zhongxun, 120,000 kilograms.

It was a huge number for a county with a population of less than 100 thousand! Zhang Junxian thought for a while and said, 'if we take out all the food in the city, one day will be enough; If you cut corn and wheat in the ground, you can eat for a day; If we kill all the sheep and donkey in the county, we can deal with them for another day!'

Mao Zedong wept when he heard about it. Three days later, the headquarters of the CPC Central Committee was successfully transferred to Yangjiagou Village, Mizhi County. For many days after that, people in Jiaxian County ate Guanyintu with bark and grass roots, and thousands of villages and households could not see a donkey or a sheep; It was also on the Bank of the Yellow River in Jiaxian County that Li Youyuan, a poor man, sang out the great choice of the Chinese people: 'the East is red, the sun rises, China has a Mao Zedong...'

The red memory was the memory of blood and tears! The dead bodies of the martyrs could be piled up in a mountain as the Chinese party and its army had sacrificed a lot for the people's freedom; Hundreds of millions of people supported the army. The last bowl of rice was used as army provisions, and the last one-foot cloth was used as army uniform. The last old quilt was covered on the stretcher, and the last one was sent to the battlefield.

On March 21, 1948, Mao Zedong led his troops to leave the Yangjiagou, cross Yellow River to the East and enter North China. The great bugle of freeing the whole country resounded throughout the country.

On July 1, 2017, 69 years later, Zhu Zhaofei, a man from the North stood on the high slope of Yangjiagou and looked at the rows of ancient caves at the top and bottom of the mountain. He recalled the past and was very excited. Under the order of his superior, he would take part in another great 'people's war' in China – a decisive battle to get rid of poverty and attack the weak. This was the Centennial vow of the party, and the solemn promise of the eighteen National

Congress and Xi Jinping, the general secretary of the party, to the people of all groups in the country.

1. 'The first secretary' takes orders in the face of danger

On June 29, 2017, the atmosphere in the meeting room of Yulin cultural tourism industry investment company was a little tense. Before that, Zhu Zhaofei took the initiative to sign up for poverty relief. With the consent of the city leader, he was appointed as the first Secretary of the four-ditch village in sue Mizhi County, which was merged with the Yang clan on the slope to form an executive village. He was also the only Secretary of the Yulin City. Fearless died for business. The chairman, Li Jun, held a meeting of all the employees in the company. He said that the significance of poverty relief project was well known. But in the long run, helping the poor was a difficult task. Zhu Zhaofei could make such a fair choice. 'The whole company is willing to be your strong backing. You need money. You have the final say. Who is it?' If you don't do that, you can resign and leave most of the companies. They are small white collars who grew up in the city. It was daunting for them to stay on the mountain for several years. At the meeting, Feng Wenrui, a graduate student, looked down and thought he was the 'pen holder' of the company. Without him, he can't work and will never choose him. 'Feng Wenrui!' Zhu Zhaofei shouted. The young man was shocked and depressed!

Two young assistants, Feng Wenrui and Cui Wei, were selected. At 10 am on that day, the three set out for Yangjiagou, 80 kilometres away. It was foggy that day, and the rugged mountain road was winding in the fog. On the bus, Zhu Zhaofei gave two young people a passionate 'mobilization report', telling them a lot of missions, responsibilities and responsibilities. He also stressed that we should not be like some poverty alleviation cadres in the past. We should help the real poor and the real poor. If we can't win this battle, we will never stop fighting! But the two young men were too nervous to listen.

Zhu Zhaofei was born in 1965. He had a fair face and a long body. He was once a soldier, a reporter of Yulin daily, the Deputy Secretary of the Party committee of Yulin energy group, and the general manager of Yulin people's building in a five-star hotel. Over the years, he had been wearing suit and tie every day. He had been welcoming more dignified leaders, miners and friends from all over the world. He lived a delicate, beautiful and step by step life. However, when he saw that the media was full of reports about the heroic deeds of poverty relief all over the motherland, his passion was ignited, just like hearing the passionate horns in the military camp. This was a matter that would determine the future and fate of China. This was the key step to realize the great revival of the Chinese race! He had been to a lot of countryside, and most of the young people had left. The rest of the old, weak, sick and disabled were lonely and miserable, unable to return to heaven, which made his heart ache. He also saw that the poverty relief work in some places was like a flash in the sky. He made some noise and publicity, leaving the villagers behind. Nothing changed. These people were emotionless. He was very angry. In 2017, Zhu Zhaofei met a city leader at the meeting and proposed to be the first Secretary of the village.

Zhu Zhaofei said, absolutely!

It was unprecedented in Yulin City that an official at the official level was going to be a village branch.

The governor looked him up and down and asked, 'are you serious?'

Zhu Zhaofei absolutely!

Good. Where would you like to go? I'll arrange it.

I'm a soldier. According to the organization, I can go anywhere that's asked of me.

The poverty relief of the Yangjiagou was too important. The original intention of the party was there, and so was today's mission!

As soon as the document was approved, all colleagues, relatives, friends, wives, sons and granddaughters were shocked.

It was known to all the people in Yulin that Shaanxi had been the bottom of the poverty relief work in all the cities throughout the country for several consecutive years; In the ranking of the whole province, Yulin City often 'beat wolves'; In the ranking of the whole city, as a key county for national poverty relief and development, Su was the last one in a row. Two months ago, all the officials of the county's poverty relief office were dismissed. Not long ago, the leading group of the Yulin City party made a major adjustment, 'reorganize the mountains and rivers', and issued a military order to help the poor. They demanded the whole city to remove their hats in 2019. This was not a new broom sweeping three times, nor a 'leap in'. After all, Yulin was rich in coal, oil and other resources. Besides, it was a remote and old place. They should work harder and faster to help the poor.

At this time, Zhu Zhaofei, 52 years old, was ordered to be the first Secretary of Yang village. There was no doubt that he was ordered to do so in front of danger. His wife said to him worriedly. If you can't do it well, your reputation will be ruined without armor when you come back!

After a bumpy climb, the car drove into Yang's village. It had just rained on the first day. The ground was muddy. Zhu Zhaofei simply rolled up his trouser legs and took off his shoes and socks. He walked up barefoot, which was the first time he had made the posture of No.1 mud man. He stood on a high slope and looked around. Layers of soil appeared in the deep valley of the plateau. The old cave was full of poverty and helplessness. Most of the young people went out to work, and most of the villagers were old people. Their faces were dark and their clothes were old. Some of them were working on the hillside, some were taking a walk, and some were surrounded by mud dolls. They looked at them curiously. Everything in front of them was like an old yellow photo, so desolate, so quiet and sad. They walked into the dark Village Department, and the officials in the town were busy there, filling in the villagers' economic file according to the superior's requirements. This project was more detailed, one hundred times more complicated than going through the household registration. In the big data age, they had to do this annoying work. Seeing that the village cadres were busy, Zhu ZHAOFEI had a simple exchange with several village cadres such as Jiang Zhige, Secretary of the village Party committee and Liu Weizhou, village head, and went down the mountain to visit the farmers.

According to statistics, there are 98 families in the village, including 24 poor families (with an annual per capita income of less than 3,015 yuan). When they walk into their cave, the villagers are apathetic and numb, and their eyes are full of distrust. They are used to those who put on airs. In the past, many poor officials gave each family 5,000 yuan, and they left with a few words of encouragement. She took the money and drank the villagers' wine for a few days, when the higher authorities came to check, they borrowed a few sheep or a motorcycle from their relatives and friends to tie up the circle. According to the statistics of the second year, they were still poor families, and there were more and more families. If they get 5,000 yuan for free, who doesn't want pie falling from the sky? I once went to a place in Gansu for an interview. There were no bowls in my hometown, so I dug a few holes beside my bed to serve as bowls. The municipal government sent a lot of sheep to the village, two for each household, so that the villagers could feed them well and reproduce from generation to generation. Unexpectedly, the villagers flocked forward and took the dead sheep away from the road so that they could eat and drink at night.

Zhu Zhaofei walked into a cave on the slope of the village. Only Liu Shangfu, 71 years old and Zhu Zhaofei said that I will give you 5,000 as the poverty relief fund in a few days, and you can buy two pigs or sheep to rise. Your life will be better soon. The old man shook his head and said coldly. I can't even stand straight. How can I have the strength to serve those animals? Zhu Zhaofei was nailed to the south wall by his words. Now Liu Shangfu has a better life. I told him that if he couldn't remember your name, your name would be in vain. Mr. Liu said shyly. That's because his parents have been looking forward to this day when they gave me this name!

Yangjiagou had fought with the Party Central Committee before. The people here made great sacrifices for the revolution and let them live a happy life. This is the responsibility of the party. In the face of a barren mountain village, a barren soul, and a barren practice, what should she do? The heavy responsibility lies on her shoulders.

2. Grandma's 'money tree' and the second 'red handprint'

In October 2019, I went to Yangjiagou Village for an interview and chatted with Zhu Zhaofei and village director Liu Weizhou on the stone at the crossroads. I casually asked a few passing villagers to chat together. Fat housewife Wang Jianhua, white hair Liu Jinwei, young man Ma Liangliang, 92-year-old Jiang Zhiming, black on the ground Wang Shuyuan, camouflage clothes Liu Shihong, sportswear He Liang and so on. I said to Zhang Wanjin, who is over sixty years old, your name is really rich! He said it was from an illiterate grandmother. The four brothers and grandmothers of their father's generation embedded the word 'glory and wealth' in their names respectively; In his generation, there were four words in his name: 'money, gold, silver and fortune.' He is the second child, so his name is Zhang Wanjin. His grandmother gave him the nickname 'money tree,' which means 'money tree.' In addition, the old lady named another child of Zhang's generation Wannian. Lao Zhang said that in this way, the names of our two generations together are 'glory, wealth, money, gold and silver, and eternal happiness.' I smile and my eyes are wet. The Chinese people have worked hard for thousands of years. What they want is to have a 'money tree' and live a rich and beautiful life. What a long, hard, rough and painful time they want to have!

Was the money tree just a legend? No, it was the great 'China Dream' to plant the 'money tree' and 'happiness tree' for the people. Zhu Zhaofei, 52 years old, came to Yang's village and wanted to do this!

This is also his wish Mao Zedong when he left Yangjiagou.

Soon, Zhu Zhaofei traveled around the country. The first meeting he held was a meeting of all the party members in the village, and the second one was a meeting of villagers' representatives. At the beginning of the reform, the enthusiasm of the workers was greatly released, and the problem of clothes, food, accommodation and transportation was quickly solved. However, this method of individual production also quickly widened the gap between the rich and the poor. Most poor families were poor because of loneliness, old age, illness and disability. It was impossible to send money from home to his family in the way of 'water was flooding', which could not meet the strict requirements of the secretary general, 'not leaving poor families, not allowing poor people'.

In the depths of the mountain, the moon was as bright as a bean. Several sleepless nights, Zhu Zhaofei buried his head in the thick smoke and thought hard about the way out of poverty in Yang village. It was difficult for the poor to turn over by themselves. Just like the old man, Liu Shangfu, who had difficulty in breathing, how could he fight? Then, can we gather all the men and women together and let everyone do something important? In the darkness, the light of thought would be particularly bright. Suddenly, he came up with an idea: use the natural resources of the Yang family to implement the double wheel drive of 'red tourism and green operation', and gather the poverty relief fund of every family into the emerging industry; The municipal government transferred the land, real estate and basic facilities into the group's assets, held the group's shares, and gave individual dividends. In this way, the disadvantages of 'money is paid by the government, and money is paid by villagers' were avoided.

Zhu Zhaofei was excited to find new ideas. He proved and enriched this thought again and again in his poverty alleviation diary. There's a spark between the lines!

Historical development paths often have striking similarities. In Zhu Zhaofei's new thought, the collective economy, a forgotten great force, glittered with dazzling light, illuminating the night of the mountain village.

With decades of experience in enterprise management and hotel management, Zhu Zhaofei smartly chose a green industry to surprise the villagers – to raise local wild boars.

What if there's no money? The government investment needed to be checked, reported and approved at all levels, but there was not much time left! His good comrade Li Jun, the chairman of Yulin cultural tourism company, praised Zhu Zhaofei's idea of building a collective economy and immediately decided to invest 100,000 yuan in the company!

Zhu Zhaofei and his assistant once again went into the cave of poor households and enthusiastically preached the 'two wheel drive' scheme. Even though the villagers are still cold faced and looking out of the window, they have the philosophical meaning of 'living elsewhere'. Yes, a lot of poverty alleviation cadres come and go like lanterns, but nothing has been done. Have you painted a 'big pie' for Yangjiagou again? What's more, the business in wild boars grows slow, the storage time is long, the cost of raising them is high, might end up losing money.

Zhu Zhaofei solemnly declared, 'if we make money, we can share the profit with everyone. If we lose, I will be responsible for the loss!'

There is only one survival philosophy pursued by Chinese Farmers: listening is empty and looking is true. They don't listen to slogans, they just look at action. Well, let's start! After receiving 100,000 yuan of assistance from the cultural investment company, 4,000 square metres of breeding farms (mainly land for slope pushing and leveling) were selected; farm and its large roads, electricity, water, office area and feed processing room had been designed. All these were outlined in Zhu Zhaofei's poverty relief diary. Even the size of the windows and steps were clearly marked! They couldn't afford some raw materials at present, so they borrowed some money to make it up. The 200 steel tubes were borrowed from Shaanxi first construction company. All of a sudden, the Yangjiagou became a big construction site with rumbling sound of machines. In the past thousands of years, it was the first time that Yangjiagou had heard the huge impact of the modern times.

Every day, Zhu Zhaofei climbed to the construction site. He was covered with mud. When a brick tilted, he yelled. He has severe hemorrhoids. He has bloody stools almost every day. When he works too much or stands for a long time, he sometimes falls down and needs to press back with his fingers. At first, the villagers watched from a distance; Later, several veteran party members and village cadres were moved and quietly came to help deal with the matter; Later, everyone in the village shoveled with shovels and electric poles. The money is not enough. Gong Yuzhi, the Secretary of the old Party branch, Jiang Zhige, the Secretary of the village Party branch, and Jiang Jiansheng, the old Party member, successively sent 10000 yuan in cash, saying it was their own savings. Take it first. Wang Youleng, an old poor family in his 70s, who died of freezing in a cave soon after he was born, also gave 5,000 yuan to buy shares, of which 2,000 yuan was his savings for many years, 2,000 yuan was a low premium, and 1,000 yuan was the only sheep he had ever sold in his family. The old man said sincerely, 'you are working hard. I can rest assured.'

There is a deaf youth in the village, Jiang Leilei, who has nothing to do all day. The only way he can communicate with others is to smile. When Zhu Zhaofei visited the Jiang family, he learned that Leilei had a younger brother named Jiang Xiongxiong, who was jailed for occasional negligence. The two brothers are deeply attached. Leilei often tears when he sees his brother's picture. Zhu Zhaofei believes that poverty alleviation is more important. On October 31, 2017, he drove Leilei and his father to visit Jiang Xiongxiong in Yulin prison. The two brothers met, hugged each other and began to cry. Zhu Zhaofei and the prison guards on the scene could not help crying. Zhu Zhaofei told Jiang Xiongxiong that the state has started large-scale poverty alleviation work in Yangjiagou. He hopes that you can reform yourself in prison, strive for meritorious service and commutation, and return to the village as soon as possible to start a new life of your own. Jiang Xiongxiong wiped his tears and said, 'thank you, secretary Zhu, for your care and love for me.' You can see my future actions.

The change of Yangjiagou and what Zhu Zhaofei did moved Jiang Leilei. From then on, every time he saw Zhu Zhaofei, he raised two thumbs and yelled. In different seasons, he will bring different fruits from the mountains, such as green apples, red apples, yellow pears, walnuts and red dates to Lao Zhu. Because he was deaf and dumb, he had never been to school and could only write his own name. One day, Jiang Leilei pulled old Zhu into the office and wrote 'Zhu Zhaofei' on a piece of paper. Then he pointed to the public display board in the yard and laughed happily. Obviously, he learned this from every painting on the public display board. He wanted to remember the name of the great benefactor in Yangjiagou Village. A few days later, a welder on the construction site fell ill and Jiang Lei began to work. Zhu Zhaofei and the villagers found that Jiang Lei's welder technology is very good! The old father said that he may know that when he was young, he wandered in the county town and quietly helped people to work.

This was the first time that the deaf young man, Jiang Leilei had displayed his unique skill in front of the whole village.

I was sitting at the village headquarters that day when Jiang Leilei burst in. The young man is dark and strong. He pointed to Zhu Zhaofei and laughed at me. Zhu Zhaofei said he was praising me. Whenever an outsider comes, no matter how many cadres he is, he will come in and smoke for a while.

What good people we have! In the era of light, every soul with a dream will shine.

Zhu Zhaofei's resolute action is like a plow in the new era. It turns over the silent high slope, makes the old time of poverty fall to the ground, let the villagers see the sunshine, see the hope, and see a better tomorrow.

Unexpectedly, the villagers put forward a lot of new ideas. On July 18, several non-poor families came to the house and said that they wanted to establish a cooperative. 5,000 dollars from the state for poverty relief could be a bonus. However, our living standard is similar to that of a poor family. The red line of the poor is that the average annual income of the poor is under 3015, while my family only has more than 3,016, so we are not allowed to join the cooperative. We are unhappy. What's more, the land, basic facilities and other resources in the village were owned by the whole village...Wisdom came from the masses! Zhu Zhaofei was so excited that he almost stood up and bowed to the villagers. Yes, we should absorb non poor families and let them voluntarily join us. Only in this way could they grow bigger and stronger, help each other and realize their common prosperity as soon as possible. Zhu Zhaofei wrote in his diary that day, 'through the cooperation mode, the local resources can be transformed into assets, the poverty relief fund can be transformed into shares, the farmer can be transformed into shareholders, the individual production can be transformed into group cooperation, and the villagers can choose their own jobs. Everyone had something to do. It's a kind of happiness for everyone.'

After that, through a wide range of negotiations, the whole village was filled with enthusiasm. At the villagers' meeting, all the shareholders pressed the red finger solemnly on the cooperation agreement. Gong Yuzhi, the former Secretary of the Party committee, said excitedly, 'in the new year of reform, I led everyone to press the red finger to transfer the farmland into the household. This time, I pressed the red finger to cooperate with each other. In my opinion, this is a bright path to common prosperity. From now on, under the leadership of the first secretary, we will ride a black-haired pig and escape from poverty to Kelvin!'

The audience burst into laughter. Smiling faces illuminate the ancient loess slope like the sun.

After that, the villagers discussed and made the constitution of the cooperative, and selected the members of the board of directors. Zhu Zhaofei was elected as the chief supervisor. On the morning of August 29, 2017, the red flags of four ditch village were flying and gongs and drums were ringing in unison The formal opening ceremony of the Heng breeding cooperative was held. This name was very attractive. Apparently, Zhu Zhaofei snorted like a pig. All the villagers gathered together. More than 100 black long white pigs, including 40 sows, were put into the pig pen. The leaders of the city gave a warm speech, saying that the four-ditch village had created a new path to poverty relief and wealth. The director of the poverty relief office of the city said, 'the key is that there is a working team in Yang's village that can jump and sink!'

Since then, Yangjiagou Village has won many honors such as 'poverty alleviation demonstration village' in Yulin City, and Zhu ZHAOFEI has also won provincial, municipal and county awards such as 'leader in poverty alleviation and prosperity' for many times. At 5:30 p.m. on December 19, 2017, Xinhua

News Agency announced that the 'first secretary' of the village transformed the poor village. It was reposted by all the major portals, with a click rate of millions overnight. Zhu Zhaofei wrote in his diary, 'the Yang clan's ditch has spread all over the country, and I have also become a big figure. But I have a clear conscience. We paid for it without any exaggeration. What we have done is exactly what we have said.' At first, Feng Wenrui, the young assistant, was transferred to another company. Later, he was replaced by Cheng Jinfei, a new graduate who came to the company to register. He also had a sense of accomplishment, claiming that 'I am a young intellectual in the new era.'

3. I ate a handful of pig feed

At the end of the year, the four villages and Yangjiagou Village merged, and the number of poor families increased to 125. Under the vigorous push of Zhu Zhaofei, the two-wheel drive of 'red tourism and green economy' began a grander and warmer battlefield in this hot land. From 2017 to 2019, all the roads will be hardened and installed with sun streetlamps. There were old Mao Zedong, Zhou Enlai, Zhang Wentian, Ren Bishi, Peng Dehuai, Xi Zhongxun and other old people's houses, as well as the political department, the Northwest Bureau, the evergreen Bureau, the Ministry of public security, the intelligence bureau, the radio station, the newspapers of the people's army, the war hospital, the printing factory and so on. In the middle of the courtyard stood a middle-aged statue of Mao Zedong, which made the history shine with the glory of a new era. Every new year's day, there were tens of thousands of cars and tourists. The black pig farm and Jessie's motorbike farm were expanding on their own. In the Skynet zoo, peacock, ostrich, mandarin ducks, wild ducks, dove and all kinds of appreciative fish coexisted in the same garden. On both sides of a good field on the slope, a cement torrent channel about 1 metre deep was built, which basically solved the historical disaster of the mountain torrents destroying the crops permanently.

In 2018, the breeding industry was a great success, and black pigs were in short supply. At the end of the year, each household paid an average dividend of 4,000 yuan. In June 2019, the second dividend is 3,000 yuan per household. But in a year and a half, the villagers recovered all the principal and made 2,000 yuan. This year, there is a 'pig shortage' across the country, and the price of meat has risen sharply. The people of Yangjiagou are sure to make a big profit again. Talking about the development of green pig industry, we firmly believe that it is a miracle. What can you do? Zhu Zhaofei said with a smile, 'it's nothing strange. My family name is Zhu.' Now there are too many people in the village rushing to buy black pigs. The villagers squinted with joy. However, Lao Zhu insisted not to sell one. 'Let's wait for the Spring Festival,' he said. 'Everyone's pockets will swell up!' Of course, those 'related households' and friends who helped Yang Jiagou out of poverty came, and Lao Zhu's criticism of Zhang's 'notes' is still easy to use.

On October 18, 2018, Yangjiagou held a democratic appraisal meeting for poverty alleviation and withdrawal of poor households, and all 78 households voluntarily withdrew met the standard. This is a great change and improvement of the will of the people! In the past, they fought to be poor, but now they have ambition and self-esteem. The villagers say that you always wear the hat of a poor family these days. Your son can't even find his daughter-in-law!

After three years of hard work, great changes had taken place in Yangjiagou. In 2019, the whole cooperation would get rid of poverty, and the total assets of the cooperative would increase by more than 6 times. A good day has come!

When I came for an interview, Zhu Zhaofei showed me around the new village. The farm is clean and tidy. At present, there are more than 500 black pigs in stock. The big one is more than 300 Jin, and the small one is more than 100 Jin. Nearly 200 Jiami donkeys with long ears and big eyes are bright, cheerful and lovely. Entering the feed processing room, two villagers are grinding feed with machines. Zhu Zhaofei grabs a handful of raw materials from the ground, one is rice, the other is black beans. He bit me in half and said, 'don't worry, no additives.' I've had a little, very tasty. This is not only delicious, but also cooked – Yangjiagou pigs and donkeys pay too much!

According to the regulations of the higher authorities, village cadres should live in the village no less than 220 days a year. In the past three years, Zhu Zhaofei has lived in the village for more than 320 days a year and written six poverty alleviation diaries with more than 400,000 words. He devoted himself wholeheartedly to Yangjiagou with the spirit of taking responsibility and deep love for the people. At the award ceremony, he said with emotion: 'Yangjiagou is the place where Chairman Mao stayed. The starting point of all my work is not to forget my original intention and remember my mission.'

On the morning of June 7, 2020, Hu Chunhua, vice premier of the State Council, made a special trip to Yulin and Yangjiagou villages to investigate poverty alleviation work, listened to Zhu Zhaofei's report in detail, and read his poverty alleviation diary carefully. Vice Premier Hu Jintao spoke highly of Zhu Zhaofei's work and sense of responsibility. Chen Zhigang, deputy director of the Poverty Alleviation Office of the State Council, who accompanied Zhu Zhaofei, specially called the Poverty Alleviation Office of Shaanxi Province, asking them to comprehensively summarize the poverty alleviation work experience of Yangjiagou Village.

Just this afternoon, I talked to Zhu Zhaofei on the phone. I asked him if he had returned to work in Yulin after three years in the village? He said: it's really hard for me to give up the profound friendship I have forged with the people of Yangjiagou over the past three years. I'm still in Yangjiagou. I don't want to do anything else in my life. I just want to help the poor to the end.

(This article was published in *People's Daily* on June 9, 2020, and was slightly modified)

II Back up! A hesitant start

1. Tears on the roadside

I asked Zhang Leiwei, how did your parents give you such a powerful name?

He laughed and said, maybe because my father went to the battlefield.

Sandstorm blocked the sun, sand pump in the face, knife pain. It's annoying to go out to work on such a day.

In spring 1976, Zhang Leiwei, a young tractor driver at Mizhi County tractor station, wore windproof glasses and drove a rubber wheel tractor into a supply and Marketing Cooperative in the suburb of Hengshan County (Hengshan District, Yulin City), and was ready to load a batch of agricultural products into Mizhi County. Near noon, he was hungry and squeezed into a taxi to wait for the workers to load up the goods so that he could go back to the station for dinner soon. Since ancient times, people in Northern Shaanxi have developed the habit of eating only two meals a day. They have one at nine in the morning and one at five or six in the evening. Zhang Leiwei got up early in the morning and set out. By noon, the water was already toothless, and he was very hungry.

After loading, not far from the road, there was a big truck blocking the way. It turned out that a commune woman doctor in a white coat was leading a young mother with a child in her arms. She ran to the bus and stopped it. She seems to want to hitchhike to the city. The female doctor said for a long time, but the driver waved away. Then Zhang Leiwei stepped on the gas to drive away, but the woman doctor stood in front of the car and stopped him with her hand. Zhang Leiwei asked, what's the matter? The female doctor said anxiously that when her mother was working outside the cave, millet porridge was cooking in the pot. One year old children because of hunger, they climbed to the pot to drink porridge, the result of a plunge into the pot, head and hand serious burns, life is very dangerous, please do well, mother and son rushed to Mizhi County hospital!

At that time, Mizhi County Hospital was the hospital with the best conditions and the highest medical level in the surrounding counties.

Zhang Leiwei's first reaction was negative. First of all, he was very hungry and hurried back to the tractor station to unload and eat. When he comes home late, he will 'have no harvest.' Second, take your mother and son to the hospital. There must be a lot of trouble behind them; Third, look at the child in the mother's arms, wrapped in rotten clothes and broken coats, and his face is covered with purple potion, so swollen that no one looks. If the child dies on the road, he can't take responsibility.

Zhang Leiwei shook his head and said that his task was urgent and could not be delayed. You can find another car.

The woman doctor gave up. Zhang Leiwei started the tractor and suddenly set out on the road. More than ten metres away, he saw in the rearview mirror that the rural female doctor was holding her mother, as if to say a word of comfort. The wind was blowing her white coat, and her mother kept wiping her tears.

At that moment, Zhang Leiwei's heart softened. He hesitated for a moment: go or not? Do you care or don't you care? Well, it's human life after all. Anyway, I'm going back to Mizhi County. That's the best way. Finally, he put in reverse and turned the tractor back to the crossroads – a retreat that was actually a big step forward in life. The woman doctor rushed the mother and son to the taxi and gratefully said to Zhang Leiwei, 'you are such a good man!' Zhang Leiwei felt a little ashamed.

The tractor accelerated and started on the road. On the way, the child suddenly stopped breathing. His mother was so frightened that she shouted 'Kang Xiaofei'. Zhang Leiwei listens to different voices of 'coffee' in different countries. 'You can pat your child on the back to slow down,' he said. The mother quickly patted a few times, and the child coughed a few times. Sure enough, he breathed again. Two hours later, the tractor stopped at the gate of Mizhi County Hospital. Seeing the young mother carrying her child into the hospital, he drove back to the tractor station to report, unload and eat. After noon, there is only half a bowl of leftovers left in the canteen. He wolfed down the leftovers and poured a spoonful of cold water. Then he felt full. When his business stopped, he thought of 'coffee.' Now I don't know what happened. Is it safe? Since the family is here, we have to care. Fortunately, not far from the county hospital, Zhang Leiwei rushed to the hospital and saw his mother holding her child sitting on the steps wiping her tears.

Zhang Leiwei said shocked: 'what happened to the child?'

'The registration line is too long...' mother said.

'God, you don't understand! If the child is injured like this, there's no need to queue up for emergency treatment. 'Zhang Leiwei said, 'go! Let's go in!'

At 12 noon, it's the hospital's lunch break. Zhang Lei breaks into the emergency room with his mother and son. A male doctor was lying in bed taking a nap. He lazily up to see the child's situation, said the injury is very serious, need hospitalization, at least to spend 200 yuan. Mother took a dirty handkerchief out of her pocket and opened it tremblingly. There's only 50 yuan in it. 'I've saved all my savings and asked the doctor to save my child's life,' she said

The doctor said, 'No, you can't pay for it. The hospital won't be responsible for you.'

Zhang Leiwei was so angry that he yelled: 'money matters, or human life matters?'

The doctor gave him a look: 'Every child is important! But if you can't pay, the hospital can't do it! '

Zhang Leiwei stretched out his hand and took out his pocket. A total of 50 kilograms of food stamps, 48 yuan and 30 Fen. He patted the table: 'no matter how much, save the child's life first!' Then he put his driver's license on the table and said, 'is one tractor enough? Can you take your driver's license with you? '

In fact, Zhang Leiwei talked a lot. The tractor is owned by the public and he can't change it for a cent.

The doctor had nothing to say, and immediately arranged for his wife and son to be admitted to the hospital.

Looking back, Zhang Leiwei borrowed some money from his colleagues, went to the store and bought two cans of condensed milk and two packets of corn flour biscuits and sent them to the hospital. The doctor was taking medicine for the child. When Zhang Leiwei came back, he asked, 'are you the father of the child?'

The mother blushed and quickly explained, 'we don't know each other. He's a tractor driver. He's a good man. He drove us here.'

One sentence moved the doctor: 'Oh, that's right. Young people, human nature is good. With your spirit of helping others, I will certainly find a way to cure the child!'

Zhang Leiwei inquired about the address of the mother and the son and the name of the child. On the same day, he made a long-distance call to the Kangzhuang brigade of Wuzhen people's commune in Hengshan County, saying that there was a child named Kang Xiaofei who was hospitalized in Mizhi County hospital due to serious burns. Mother doesn't have enough money, so you tell your family to send it as soon as possible.

This was in 1976. Zhang Leiwei was 21 years old.

After that, he drove his tractor around and never went to the hospital again. Sometimes he would think of the child. He didn't know if he would save it? But he didn't want to ask more questions, fearing that people would think he was thinking about paying back the money. When we meet by chance, it's hard to save people. The past is past.

More than 40 years later, Zhang Leiwei miraculously met this adult child Kang Xiaofei. This is a later story.

Zhang Leiwei, a descendant of the old revolution, was born in 1955. At the age of 15, his father joined the Northern Shaanxi Red Army and drove mules and carriages to the border areas every day. KMT soldiers on the KMT Communist line saw the dirty boy driving a cart with dozens of coarse porcelain bowls piled on it. Seeing that there was no contraband here, they swore, 'get out of here, son of a bitch.' Back in the army, the soldiers happily unloaded the big bowl. It turns out that there are a lot of urgent medicines hidden in the pit at the bottom of the bowl. After liberation, my father became a cadre in Xi'an. After graduating from junior high school in 1970, Zhang Leiwei took the lead in responding to Chairman Mao's call to go to the countryside to jump in the queue, and became the 'point leader' of the educated youth. Due to hard work and outstanding performance, he later transferred to the tractor station and became a tractor driver. Later, he went to Yan'an University and became a 'paid student'. After graduation, he was recommended to work in the Propaganda Department of the county Party committee. But Zhang Leiwei is not willing to do so and wants to continue to be a tractor driver. At that time, his monthly salary was 38.6 yuan, and he could bring some local products home for transportation. He is also regarded as a 'rich class', which makes people respect him.

Later, he was transferred to State Grid Shaanxi Yulin power supply company, and retired as the chairman of the trade union.

2. The official name: 'Poverty Alleviation Officer'

In 2000, 45-year-old Zhang Leiwei was appointed by the power supply company to help the poor in Qincaigou Village of Shenmu County for three years.

At that time, there was little pressure, and there was no strict assessment on the work performance and change level of the village. It's time. Go home and give a report.

Zhang Leiwei doesn't think so. In 1976, he always remembered the incident of rescuing Kang Xiaofei, a scalded child. 'Some people said that the hero was hot blooded for three minutes, while I was a bear for three minutes at that time.' Lao Zhang said: 'the life of the child is on this line. I don't want to pull it. I hesitated for three minutes before I went back to pull mother and son together. Later, when I think about it, I don't have any sense of honor. I always blame myself.'

This incident has become a warning to Zhang Leiwei's life.

Qincaigou Village, as the name suggests, is likely to be some wild celery planted in this ditch a long time ago. The village is far away from the city, so we can't find a car to come and go. We have to find a place to live. He found three abandoned earth kilns at the entrance of the village. There are no doors and windows. The mouse runs out of the hole. Xie Lanlan, Secretary of the village Party committee, said that this used to be a village primary school. Now the children go to the rural primary school, and the cave is abandoned. Lao Zhang said, 'send someone here to install doors and windows and clean them. I will live here.' Xie Lanlan looked at him suspiciously and said, are you really alive? Of course, Lao Zhang said.

Several villagers quit, saying that this was the temple of our village in the early years, and later it was changed into a primary school. They can't move, it will destroy the fengshui of our village.

Zhang Leiwei said with a smile that several generations of people in your village are very poor. One of your employees walks around the village, hungry every year. Outsiders said: 'there are women who do not marry celery village.' What is good fengshui? I think it would be better if it was repaired and I would live in it and undertake the task of helping the poor of the party. When the Communist Party was founded in 1921, there were only more than 50 party members in China. Later, the world was defeated. Do you think the fengshui of the party is good?

The common people thought it was reasonable.

After the cave was repaired, Lao Zhang fell asleep with his bedding. He didn't sleep well for the first few nights. The cave has not been burned for decades, and its head is very cold. He had to wrap a pillow towel around his head, dress up as a sheep belly towel, put on three blue sheep clothes and sleep in flannel pants. Fortunately, the air in the countryside is very good and quiet.

On the first night of entering the 'fengshui treasure land', Zhang Leiwei opened two bottles of old Baijiu from his home. Village cadres and some old party members are invited to talk on the Kang about where to start poverty alleviation? He said: after listening to your opinions, I have learned something these days. Qincaigou has fewer people, which is a big advantage for you. However, the villagers only grow corn, millet and cereals. Villagers do not make money for a year. The root cause of poverty in the village is a big problem. It is suggested that with the support of government funds, we should vigorously develop the planting and breeding industry, one is jujube, the other is sheep. Especially after the policy of returning farmland to forest, the vegetation in the mountain area recovered quickly and the herbage grew vigorously. Raising sheep increases income and can be used to grow fertile land. Village cadres heard that the brain hole is open and supported by government funds. Of course, everyone is very happy to applaud for the smashed 'geomantic treasure land' old wall.

The first batch of more than 200 jujube seedlings were pulled back from Shenmu county. It was agreed that all the workers would go up the mountain to plant trees the next day. I didn't expect to have a sandstorm that night, so I went out to sprinkle the sand. Xie Lanlan suggested changing the plan and waiting for the wind to stop. It's not a big problem to delay one or two days, but Zhang firmly said, it can't be changed! In recent years, some cadres come and go, saying no, no and no, which has left many bad impression on the cadres who have been helping the poor. In addition, the villagers work in the small coal mines nearby every day. They can earn more than 10 yuan a day, so it's not easy to put them away. We can't lose faith in the people. We stopped working in this little difficulty. What can I do after Zhang Leiwei? The next morning, he led the village head and village secretary Jie Lanlan , risking the sandstorm, carrying a shovel and bucket up the mountain. After a busy day, more than 200 jujube trees and seedlings were brushed and stood on the hillside. For the first time, the villagers saw the poverty relief cadres coming from the city working with them. They feel warm and down-to-earth. Think of the future of jujube hanging all over the mountains, my heart is very happy. Zhang Leiwei's mouth is full of sand, but he is very happy. He even thanks the sandstorm for giving him access to the villagers. He believes that sand will not be eaten for nothing.

For thousands of years, the traditional concept is as strong as the earth and closed to the outside world. Zhang found that the villagers in celery ditch had always had the habit of raising mules. The mule is big and strong. It is very popular among the villagers because it can pull the cart in the wind to cultivate land. However, mules are the 'last door' of a generation. They can only be used for seven or eight years. It costs about 8000 yuan to buy a good mule. After elimination, it can only sell 1,000-2,000 yuan. So, Zhang Leiwei tried to recommend Qinchuan cattle to them. They can pull cars to cultivate land, but they are slow and fed the same way. However, a cow can produce a calf every year, and it can sell 3,000 yuan in three months and 8,000 yuan in eight months. It has the ability of sustainable development and annual value-added. Zhang also took the villagers to visit cattle farms and farmers in other places, and then held a villagers' meeting to let the villagers come back to talk about the benefits they saw, calculated the account and said the benefits.

Starting with the first seven cattle, the present celery village has become a cattle village.

In the village, Lao Zhang soon found that young people often cough and spit black phlegm. He immediately called a meeting of villagers working in a small coal mine. He said that since ancient times, it has been the hardest, most tiring and most dangerous work to dig coal in the well. He called it 'what you do is work in the underworld, what you eat is food in the sun' and 'two stones and one piece of meat.' Now you only care about the immediate interests, and you can get 100,000 or 80,000 by the end of the year. But when you are old and very sick, you will come home and all the money you save will be sent to the hospital. In case of an accident, the consequences are hard to imagine. I suggest you make up your mind to go back to the village and develop your own farming industry. The government will give you great support!

Lao Zhang is right. When the news spread, the young people were afraid. Soon, there was a 'labor shortage' in the small coal mines in that area, and the village, which had always been silent, was particularly noisy.

From Xigou to Qincaigou in Shenmu county, we must pass through the village head of Jiaoni Gelao Village. The ancestors of the village gave their residence such a strange name. Obviously, the Loess there is especially covered with feet when it rains. There is a mute youth in his early twenties in this village. In order to replace cement poles in Qincaigou village, Zhang Leiwei led villagers to build roads, including buying back Small Tail Han sheep and Qinchuan beef cattle for villagers. He saw everything in front of him, so he asked the villagers of Qincaigou, who is this stranger? Why do you do so many good things for the people of Qincaigou? After discovering it, one day, he stopped the coal boss Shi Kaihe at the entrance of the village. He kept yelling at him and playing sign language, which confused Shi. A young man explained that silence means you are rich. Why not invite poverty relief cadres like Zhang Leiwei to the village? The mute nodded, and his hand was still drawing, imitating the appearance and cry of cattle and sheep. Boss Shi smiled. He told the mute that poverty alleviation cadres are not paid, but sent by the government.

The wind blew the still figure of the silent youth. He stood there blankly, with a trace of melancholy on his face.

Once, a villager in Qincaigou Village held an adult ceremony for his son according to local customs (that is, the small silver lock hanging around his son's neck was officially unlocked on his 12th birthday) to entertain relatives, friends and friends from all parties. Zhang Leiwei was invited to attend. At the banquet, a boss in a suit and shoes suddenly came up to him and respectfully toasted him. The Secretary of the village Party branch said that his name was Shi Kaihe, a native of Gelao Village. I heard that you are Zhang Leiwei, a famous poverty alleviation cadre, who moved the dumb people in our village. He came specially to pay tribute.

Poverty alleviation should not only help the poor and the weak, but also change the style of the village.

Liu Aitian, a villager of Qincaigou, has two sons. His eldest son Liu Xiaoping returned to the village after he retired from the army. Marrying a daughter-in-law has become a big problem. Pay a matchmaker to take her home for a blind date. After four or five rounds, there was no result. They all think Liu Xiaoping has no formal job. Liu Aitian had to come to Zhang Leiwei and asked him to help his son find a job. 'It's too easy to deal with,' Mr. Zhang said. I can solve it with a phone call, but I have a premise. Overjoyed Liu Aitian hurriedly asked what premise. Lao Zhang solemnly said, first, as the boss of the family, we should take the lead in respecting the elderly and set a good example for our brother. Second, we should properly handle the family relationship between the brothers. We can't meet without talking and speak ill of each other in private, which will have a bad impact on the village. Your father is deaf and weak. He lives alone and no one takes care of him, but the villagers ignore your brother. You are a soldier's father and a glorious soldier's family member. How can you let the villagers point out behind your back? As long as you can do these two points well, I will package Liu Xiaoping's work! A few days later, the brothers sat together and invited their father and Zhang Leiwei to dinner. The two brothers exchanged wine and apologized. The two families also apologized to their father and said they would be filial to the elderly and set an example for their children in the future. The tearful old man must be thinking, why do these two ignorant sons seem to have changed overnight?

Before long, Lao Zhang arranged for Liu Xiaoping to work as an electrician in the power supply company and introduced him to a good girl. They soon married and married, and the three generations of the Liu family lived a happy life.

This story touched the whole village.

In 2006, Zhang Leiwei was promoted to Chairman of the trade union of Yulin power supply company. Over the past six years, in addition to handling the company's official business, he has also made poverty alleviation his 'first priority.' Whether it's winter or hot summer, Zhang Leiwei has to climb mountains and mountains, go from village to village, help the needy and help the needy. Once he climbed a mountain after the rain and fell off a cliff. He has three broken feet. 27 days later, he slipped out of the hospital on crutches and continued to help the poor. Because the bone wound has not fully healed, the foot is disabled. Zhang Leiwei's reputation and reputation spread all over Yulin. People don't know what official he is or his rank. They simply call him 'poverty relief officer'. From China to other countries in the world, Zhang Leiwei must be the only one who enjoys this official title. The first stage of poverty alleviation is three years and the second stage is six years. The superior thought Lao Zhang was old. They should stop working so hard and transfer him back. When the county leaders and villagers heard of the urgency, they asked the Poverty Alleviation Office to keep Lao Zhang. Zhang Leiwei's opinions were sought from the organization. 'If the car doesn't fall off, push it,' he said. Since then, Lao Zhang has served as a poverty alleviation cadre and temporary deputy county magistrate in several counties. He has a wider business scope, runs farther, and eats more sandstorms and hand rolling noodles. Eating, he found that the noodles made by a villager were delicious.

Laohuo's handmade noodles

The ancestors and grandchildren of Laohuo family in Rangou Village all make handmade noodles. They are famous for their exquisite workmanship, uniform noodle thickness, no soup in the pot and gluten. However, the Huo family's existing equipment is too simple and crude, the output is very low, and the demand is often in short supply. Zhang Leiwei suggested that the village committee should vigorously support the Huo family, establish a handicraft noodle cooperative, expand the production scale and drive more villagers out of poverty. Mr. Huo is very interested in it. Mr. Zhang also suggested that he improve the packaging, reduce the quantity, increase the small packaging of modern condiments in civil aviation aircraft, and take the road of high-quality development. The good idea inspired Huo. Soon, 'Wubao laohuojia fan factory' was registered and established. With the support of the government, a beautiful factory and production line covering an area of more than 120 mu has been built, with more than 50 employees and an annual output of 300 tons of fans. One of Lao Zhang's suggestions is to become an innovative industry in Wubao County.

A thread in Chejiayuan Village

Not long ago, I just wrote an article about Huzhou. There is an ancient Silk 4,300 years ago, about the size of a nail. It is the earliest silk product found in the world, so it is called 'the source of silk'. I wrote a non-classic saying: 'when the silkworm baby spits silk, I didn't expect it to spit out a silk road'. What's more unexpected is that Wubao County has a tradition of mulberry and sericulture on the cold and dry Loess Plateau of Shaanxi. Check the county chronicles, there is no answer. I guess this place is called Wubao. In ancient times, Yulin was an important military fortress in Northern Xinjiang (the highest beacon tower of the great wall stands here). It must be the Wu people from Jiangnan who came here to join the army, took the habit of planting mulberry and raising silkworms, took root and settled there, and multiplied into today's Wubao County. There is a

Chejiayuan Village in the county. The mulberry garden in the village covers an area of 450 mu. Mulberry leaves are thick and silk quality is good. A silk can drag 10 kilometres. Therefore, it has been determined as a demonstration village of 'one village and one product' by Shaanxi Province. The local climate is quite cold. In the past, every family had a cave or room for silkworm rearing. But the silkworm is too fragile, this traditional method often occurs soot poisoning, and it is difficult to maintain a constant temperature. Therefore, the mortality of silkworm babies is high and the cocoon quality is not high, which directly affects the income of silkworm farmers. Zhang Leiwei heard that thunder came again. He and agricultural station technician Zhang Wuyun went to Chejiayuan Village many times. With the approval of the county government, he invested 30,000 yuan to buy an electric heater, built a small silkworm seed room for the whole village, and invested 120,000 yuan to build a cocoon drying furnace, cocoon collection room, finished product house and rain collection cellar. The sericulture industry in the village suddenly prospered, and the income of silkworm farmers doubled. Now, the village has built a silk processing plant, and a large number of silk quilts, silk clothes and trousers, silk pillows and other products are sold to other places. The villagers' pockets are bulging and the village looks brand new.

3. The father in her daughter's eyes

In 2015, to celebrate Zhang Leiwei's 60th birthday, her daughter wrote something called: love for my father

> He is not tall or strong, but he is called such a powerful name.
>
> His 15 years of helping work has spread all over the poor rural areas of Yuyang, Qingjian, Shenmu, Wubao, Jiaxian County and Mizhi. He is affectionately known as 'his own family' from the city. This is my father, but I don't know much about him.

> **—Surprised and moved**
>
> In 2000, my father began his path of poverty relief. Since then, I have rarely seen him. In order to know the reason why the village was poor, my father had spent all his vacation in the village. I often ask mom where he went. Every time my mother replied, 'he went to the countryside.' Every time my father comes back, I will excitedly tell him what happened outside recently, but my father fell asleep in my talking. His busy work makes me more and more confused. During a vacation, I asked him what is occupying him and why he didn't go on vacation with mother and I. Dad said with a smile. Do you want to see her? I agreed. In this way, I followed him to the celery village of the divine wood city. What I saw there made

me feel sorry for my father. The book said that a remote place should be like this. It was a narrow path, with shabby houses and stinky pig and sheepfold. I followed him all over the village without saying a word. He greeted every villager enthusiastically and asked about the situation of his family. I was surprised to find that my father knew the situation of every villager in the village and could call out the names of all the villagers, and even know how many cattle and sheep he had kept. But he didn't know which grade I was in. At lunch time, He said with a smile that his father would show you something today!

I don't believe it at all, because he doesn't do anything at home and has no time to do it. But my expression gradually turned into surprise. I saw him skillfully stir noodles, cut noodles, cook noodles and add ingredients. A bowl of delicious hand rolled noodles appeared in front of me. I've never seen him cook. I was moved to eat this bowl of noodles. Of course, it's a little sad.

—A Superman with a pair of crutches

In 2006, my father rolled down from the cliff while inspecting the construction of water conservancy projects in Wubao County, and his foot had three fractures. When he came home from school, I was sad but a little happy. My father was injured, so he didn't want to go to the countryside, but I underestimated my father's perseverance. When I was at school, my mother went to buy vegetables, and his feet were only cast for 27 days. He sneaked back to Wubao County. His mother called him and said, 'You don't want to live? You've hurt your muscles and bones for a hundred days!' At the other end of the phone, Dad smiled and said, 'it doesn't matter. Here are several projects that have reached a critical period. If I didn't watch more, I wouldn't worry. I'll be back as soon as the project is over.' After hanging up the phone, I saw my mother's head down and tears because she missed the treatment period and her feet were still disabled. Then I asked him if it was worth it, and he said of course it was. Next time you and I go to Wubao County to see what's going on. When you see what Dad has done, you will know how happy and satisfied he is. I didn't tell him he was Superman in my heart.

—Unreliable dad

On December 25, mom and I went to the supermarket to buy new year's goods. There were many people in the supermarket. There were festivals everywhere. My mother and I tried our best to choose what we wanted. Our hands are getting heavier on our way home. I looked at my mother sadly. 'Aren't you used to it? It's not that you don't know that your father is not reliable at all. Let's have a rest if we are tired.' Yes, every year. I can't see anyone before New Year's Eve. I was a little angry when I called him. The father on the other end of the phone quickly said, 'if there is no problem, I will talk about it later. My father was sending money to the villagers.' I hung up the phone before I could answer. Well, as long as you give me your condolence, I'll take my new year's road.

—A friend from the village came to town

Dad is seldom at home this weekend. I suggest the whole family go to the buffet, after discussing what to do with my parents. It's so exciting. Suddenly, my father's cell phone rang, and I suddenly became nervous. Then there was a knock on the door. I ran to open the door. I've never seen the person outside the door. He had a dark face and a cloth bag in his hand. I asked, who are you looking for? Before the man answered, he heard his father say, 'come on, come in, Yuanyuan, make a cup of tea.' Later, I learned that my father was helping the people in the village. Because this man has a family member hospitalized in the city, so I came to see your father. At the end, I didn't get my barbecue. I don't seem to have any reason to complain about him this time. Helping the villager was a big deal.

—Travel plans are just plans

'Dad, look, this is a picture of my classmates going out with their family. Isn't that good? Let's go too.' Well, when I finish what I want to do, we'll go. You can think about where we're going, I began to study travel strategies wholeheartedly. 'Dad, my vacation is almost over. Haven't you finished your work yet?' Dad recently planned to build a standardized sheep house and a brick factory for the village. I really can't escape. How about next year? 'So, I wait year after year. Until now, traveling together still exists in my imagination. After retirement, he devoted himself to targeted poverty alleviation work, visiting research, lectures, meetings, and even busier than before. Dad, I'll plan again.

– Someone asked me, what do you think your father did this for? I said faintly that my father is retired now. I remember my father once said to me, 'I joined this team in the countryside.' I know how farmers suffer. They are hardworking, kind and simple. It is precisely because there is no correct guidance, no poverty alleviation projects and funds, they live a hard life on the loess land. I have a little ability to help them, and I am willing to do so because I have feelings for the rural people. 'I think that's his purpose. Alas, my father is actually an incompetent father in my heart. He devoted all his energy to his work.' He can't take care of his family better. He persisted in helping the poor for 15 years. He spread his love to more poor villages and farmers. Now, I see his achievements. I saw the new sheep house, the new water cellar, the transformed school, the new road, the large mushroom greenhouse and so on. He abandoned our small family and devoted himself to building everyone's career and helping more people get rid of poverty. My resentment gradually turned into the courage to support him. With the growth of age, he has retired, but his reputation for poverty alleviation is growing. His figure can be seen on TV, and his reports can be read and written in newspapers. I gradually understand the ups and downs behind his poverty alleviation road and his 20-year persistence.

Dad, I'm proud of you.

Since 2000, Zhang Leiwei has participated in Yulin's social poverty alleviation work for 20 years, helping 12,000 people out of poverty in 56 poor villages in 19 townships, 6 counties. After retiring in June 2015, he continued to serve as the first Secretary of the village and insisted on voluntary poverty alleviation. In 2016, due to his age, he withdrew from the first secretary sequence and became a non-staff village assistance cadre. From black hair to white hair, day to night, then and now. There is also a warm ending.

In the summer of 2016, a female reporter came to interview Zhang Leiwei. When chatting, she said that there was a family surnamed Kang in Hengshan District who had been looking for a benefactor for 20 years. At that time, Kang's 1-year-old son climbed to the pot table to drink porridge because he was hungry. As a result, he fell into the pot and was scalded. A passing tractor driver took the mother and son to the hospital. The son was saved, but in an emergency, the mother forgot to ask the donor's name. They have been looking for...

Lao Zhang said with a smile, that tractor driver is me! I remember very clearly. At that time, I heard the mother call the child 'coffee'. I was quite strange. Why did I have such a strange name?

The female reporter laughed and said that his name was Kang Xiaofei. Now he has grown into a strong man!

People always know how to be grateful. After the news reached the Kang family, the whole family warmly invited the benefactor to be a guest. On the day Zhang Leiwei arrived, the whole village was waiting to see the great benefactor of the Kang family who had been looking for 20 years. As soon as Lao Zhang got off the bus, applause and cheers burst out in the valley. Kang Xiaofei has really grown into a strong man with big arms and a round waist. There were some scars on his dark face and hands, which were not serious. Lao Zhang had a rich local banquet at Kang's home and recognized a godson. An endless stream of village cadres and villagers came to toast with their own wine bottles. This is the busiest day for Kang family in history. On this day, the world is warm.

III Good men resemble mountains

1. The blacksmith said: let me put some black ash on your crotch

Autumn falls on its own shadow like a leaf.

The car passed through a yellow and quiet field. In the fields on both sides of the road stood pieces of withered and yellow corn stalks (which are used to feed livestock in winter). Fu Jiping, deputy director of the Poverty Alleviation Office of Yuyang District, is a cadre of this town. He said that many years ago, the river here was very abundant, and there were bright rice fields on both sides of the road. Now the river is thinner and the water is less, and the farmers have changed to corn and millet.

The car arrives at Baigailiang Village in the suburb of Yuyang District, Yulin City. Looking around, the roads are spacious and the houses with pink walls and red tiles are row by row, clean, quiet and orderly. Walking into the spacious and bright two-story village, Gao Zhihong, Secretary of the village Party committee, was absent. This is probably what Fu Jiping didn't expect – it seems that he didn't say hello in advance. Gao Zhihong lives in the city. After calling, he said I would drive to the village immediately.

The office on the first floor is wide. There are two luxurious tables with three metres of leather and two black chairs. Obviously, it is the office facilities of the Secretary of the village Party committee and the village director. This made me a little jealous – I have too much material to put when I write, and I often have to lay the floor. Liu Lihong, a cadre of the municipal Poverty Alleviation Office, is beautiful, kind-hearted, cheerful and responsive. Most of my interviews in Yulin were accompanied by He Xiaolin, deputy director of the municipal Poverty Alleviation Office, and her. In the interview, Liu Xiang often helps the protagonist and even adds many vivid details. It can be seen that she is quite familiar with their deeds, knows them like the back of her hand, and even speaks better than the protagonist. This shows that her work style is very profound and one of the sharpest styles in the war. I will certainly praise outstanding cadres in my article. This is necessary. We can't let others do it for nothing. However, she's too hard-working. Wherever she went, she brought the interviewees – poverty alleviation cadres, township cadres and villagers back home one by one. I said angrily, 'do you want me to put my hand down and breathe?' Later, I especially told the director of Yulin Poverty Alleviation Office about her unruly shape.

At this time, Liu Lihong saw that I had been staring at the two luxury tables, and there was a voice in her mouth. She quickly explained that this was originally customized by the superior leading organ. 'After the 'eight provisions' came down, the leaders did not dare to use it. It was a pity to throw it away. Gao Zhihong, Secretary of the village Party branch, took the opportunity to rush forward and said that my village committee had just been rebuilt and lacked furnishings. Anyway, I'm a village official and don't surf the Internet. I dare to use it! So, two big shiny desks moved to Baijialiang Village. The big pie fell from the sky and picked it up for nothing.

It seems that these eight regulations are really 'high-voltage lines' that cadres dare not touch.

Gao Zhishu hasn't arrived yet. I opened the back door and went into a spacious yard. Behind it is a row of cavernous blue buildings with the sign of 'happy nursing home' on the wall. There are two table tennis tables in the yard. This net is an iron net painted blue. It can't be changed for 50 years. If Liu Guoliang can use such a table, he will be invincible. I went into a few rooms of the sanatorium to chat. They are in their 70s and 80s, and the oldest is 87. Some are lonely, some couples. The local tradition is that the old lady wears a cool white round cloth hat. The old people are having breakfast. There are mashed potatoes, green vegetables and sauerkraut noodles in the canteen. I asked, how is life? The old man opened his toothless mouth, smiled and said, well, take care of it. Three yuan a day. After going out, I understood why there was a kind of green vegetable in the cement yard, which was planted by the administrator for the elderly, saving money and environmental.

Soon, Gao Zhihong came. He is 47 years old, with an inch of neat head, tall and strong, angular face and black rough skin. At first glance, he was from the north. It's very cold in late autumn. He wore a high-grade black cloth collar, open arms and a snow-white shirt inside. The trousers are straight and the shoes are bright. It looks heroic and handsome! When I was young, I always thought I was handsome. The Secretary of the village Party branch is more handsome than I was.

Shortly, the 62-year-old village director Gao Yuepeng also arrived.

A desolate history of Bogailiang Village gradually unfolded in front of me.

In the early years, the forest on the nearby mountain was very lush, with more than 100 cypress trees, so the village was called Baigailiang Village. Later, all the trees were cut down because of cooking and feeding sheep. There is a folklore in Yulin that a cadre went to the countryside to work and eat pie rice in the village. The housewife sent noodles, but the noodles were not cooked and the firewood was gone. In a hurry, the housewife took off a cloth shoe and put it into a hole in the stove – a common people's shoe. She cooked a bowl of noodles for the cadre.

At that time, in addition to paying public grain and collective allowance, if there was surplus corn and millet in Baigailiang Village, they always had to sell some salt and lamp oil, and then pay their children's tuition. The 'staple food' of the villagers is to grind corn cobs, grains, sorghum husks and millet husks into powder with stones, so that they can be eaten for a long time. If we don't have vegetables in winter, we'll rely on pickles. Because there is no oil and water in our stomach, a person can eat a big bucket in winter. But here's the problem. People ate all the wheat bran and pigs had to eat it. As a result, the pigs raised in the village can only grow to 60 or 70 kilograms. Except for a meal of meat for the new year, most of them were sold.

At that time, not to mention clothes. Gao Yuepeng, the old village head, said that the heels of his cloth shoes from childhood to adulthood were worn out, so he tied the uppers to his feet with hemp rope and dragged them away. In winter, his face, hands and feet were frostbitten. When the boys in the village were six or seven years old, they still wore open crotch pants. In fact, they are rotten crotch pants. Brothers pass it on to their brothers. They all wear rotten crotch. At that time, Gao Zhihong's family lived in an earth kiln on the slope, and there was a blacksmith's shop in the earth kiln below the slope. Once, 8-year-old Gao Zhihong stood on the slope and looked up at the sky. The blacksmith, smoking a dry cigarette, sat on the slope and looked up. He smiled and said, 'come down, boy. I'll put some black dust on your crotch, or I'll see everything.'

At that time, 'there is a woman who doesn't marry a man, and an old man who is single walks all over the village.' For the girls in the village, two bags of noodles with 100 kg of valley were a gift from their parents. Even if some of them were married to a man, because they couldn't hold on, some left the man and their children and ran away with others.

At that time, the office had called on the officials of the production team to have a meeting 'to learn from the villages.' The meeting was not over yet. The cook in the canteen was startled and ran in and shouted. Several pots of corn and BUN were taken from the villagers

The whole family was short of labor, and their father suffered from severe amnesia. Sometimes he had a relapse five or six times a day and rolled on the ground, so this family had no status in the village and was discriminated. The production team divided his father into half of the labor force and 6 work points every day (full score 10 points). When his grandfather was old, he got 7 points, and his woman from the village gave him 7.5 points, which made the whole family, especially this young man, feel deeply ashamed, but they had no other choice. Grandpa and grandma, his parents, three children and 7 people lived on this little bit of work all the year round. The pain of hunger and cold could be imagined. When the whole family had dinner, her mother naturally knew the 'primitive comrade' lifestyle. If there was not enough food, they could only be equally divided. The bigger the adult's wheat flour was, the smaller the child's. But I want to know how Gao Zhihong, who grew up hungry, grew up so strong and fierce? He smiled and said, 'the key is that I have a cowhide stomach.' I eat whatever I see. When I'm hungry, I can chew a corner of the table.

Once, the production team asked Gao Zhihong's mother to cut potato seeds and agreed to cut 1 kg of potatoes in the autumn and give another 3 kg of potatoes. The pay is too low! But in the autumn, the captain came back and said he would not give three kilograms of potatoes. He will give you three cents to hang in your account and send it at the end of the year. Young Gao Zhihong couldn't help it. He ran to the team and lost his temper. He said you were too overbearing!

The captain threw him out.

In July 1988, after years of reform, the poor Baigailiang Village did not change. In order to save money, the grumpy Gao Zhihong decided to give up her studies. Say hello to his parents. The next morning, he took an old baggage roll and went straight to Shenmu County to find the construction site. The foreman looked like a student and disdained to say what would you do? Gao Zhihong asked him, what will you do when you are so old? You must study from scratch. The foreman said with a smile that your doll made a lot of sense! The shed where migrant workers live is dripping with blood and sweat. It goes without saying that they eat hot cabbage soup. From July to October, Gao Zhihong worked hard and earned 270 yuan. Later, the bold Gao Zhihong became the foreman; Later, he bought a black and white small motorized four-wheel vehicle to pull stones and sand, with an annual income of 18,000 yuan; Later, he became a contractor and went to Xi'an to build a highway. He earned 100,000 yuan in three months; Later, Gao Zhihong, a very smart man, set up a construction service company to organize migrant workers to engage in local projects. Baigailiang Village and many young and strong farmers in the whole township have become an important source of labor for the company, and the villagers have followed him. Money is not everything, but you can't live without it. Since then, the prestige of Gao Zhihong's family has greatly improved and become the largest family and the richest man in the whole Township and even Yuyang District. In the past, those bullied days remained in the memory of the years like abandoned earth kilns.

So, driving a strong off-road vehicle, he rushed to Gao Zhihong, dressed in a handsome fashion, which proved that the boss is not bad for money.

2. The peasant woman said: it's not my name that is good!

In the spring of 2012, an old leader from the countryside called Gao Zhihong and asked him to immediately return to all his memories. It seemed that at that moment, the young man in 'split pants', the hungry young man who said he could bite off a corner of the table, the angry young man who was angry with the production director, and the sad young man who went out to work in tears, He came back and said to him, 'think about what we should do?'

The content of the call is: the team in Baigailiang Village is going to change. According to interviews and opinion polls, the vast majority of villagers want you to go back to the village and be the deputy director of the village committee.

Of course, Gao Zhihong is full of deep feelings and passionate about going back. no problem! Since then, while continuing to develop his career, Gao Zhihong has put his energy on helping the village to open up a lively life and put forward many good suggestions. Whenever the village studies major activities, he will come back to participate. A big boss has to worry about thousands of enterprises every day. No matter how big things are in the village, they are just small things. However,

Gao Zhihong's enthusiasm, courage and wisdom have won wide trust and praise from the villagers. On December 5, 2014, the village branch was changed. Gao Zhihong was elected branch secretary with a high vote of 98%. The moderator of the meeting was Fu Jiping, then vice mayor. The ardent expectation of the villagers made Gao Zhihong feel a great responsibility. In the past, when he was the deputy director of the village committee, the company ran at both ends of the village without delay. Since he is in charge, he has to think carefully. First of all, what should the village branch secretary do? Second, how is your own business?

I asked, did you hesitate?

Gao Zhihong said without hesitation. I immediately decided that for the 1074 villagers in the village, in order to devote myself to the cause of poverty alleviation and prosperity in Baijialiang Village, I did not do business, so I shut down the labor service company and dismissed all the staff!

Oh, my God! I exclaimed, this is a hard battle! Does your mother-in-law agree? Where is she from? How did you two know each other?

Gao Zhihong said, you ask my pain! My mother-in-law and aunt came from another village and were introduced by others. She suffers as much as I do. When she heard that I was going back to the village, she was very unhappy. She said you finally pulled your feet out of the mud pit and wanted to sink again? After that, she didn't even wash my clothes. She said you should ask the villagers to wash it for you. But I'm determined to go back. I can't forget my miserable days. I quarreled with the captain for three cents. Since I have experience and can do something, I should go back and help the villagers.

I became a boss and left the village for many years. There are some situations I'm not familiar with. After taking office, Gao Zhihong visited some veteran party members and cadres and traveled all over the village. When he was a child, he walked through these places countless times just to find food. Now, he is the head of the village Party Secretary and entrepreneur, he is seriously thinking about how to get rid of poverty and lead all the villagers to get rich. This is one of the driving forces for the birth of the contemporary 'Chinese miracle': let the vitality burst out and the wisdom flow like a spring, even if it is just a small village Party Secretary!

Rectifying order and village style is the basic construction that must be done well. When he was the boss, he made a small mistake at the beginning of taking office: an idle young man threw cigarette butts in the square in front of the village department in violation of the regulations and was arrested by Gao Zhihong on the spot. He angrily taught a few words, but the young man refused and said only a few words. Gao Zhihong hit him with his fist angrily, and the young man fell to the ground. The villagers in the square were stunned. How can cadres beat people? It's too awesome!

Afterwards, Gao Zhihong made a review at the village committee.

Accompanied by Liu Lihong, who had been working in the countryside for 8 years, she said with a smile. The villagers were used to being casual. If you work in the village, you can't work hard. Sometimes you have to work hard, or you can't stop the unhealthy tendency.

What she said was reasonable. Gao Zhihong's fists can shake up the village. Since then, everyone in the village knew that Mr. Gao was a successful person, and he could not be messed with.

The next day, a middle-aged woman named Xi Suixi ran to the village. Gao Zhihong said, your name means happy, how can you cry like this?

The voice of Xi Suixi is getting louder and louder. She said the men in the family couldn't move because of a cerebral infarction. They asked me to feed them food and water every day. After his daughter got married, his son felt that his family was very poor and hopeless. He has no face when he goes out and does nothing at home every day. I asked him to go shopping. He went back by motorcycle. After dinner, he slept and ate again. There was no social contact or meeting anyone. The family is raised by a woman. I really can't carry it. I don't want to live anymore

Xi Suixi cried more.

This is the first thing Gao Zhihong encountered after taking office. This incident suddenly aroused his painful memories: when he was a child, his family was also the most despised poor household in BaiGailiang Village. He didn't want to see anyone, so he stayed in the kiln after school. He thinks saving a family is like saving himself. Only by pulling this young man out of despair and integrating him into society bravely can he support his family. He is mother's only hope.

Gao Zhihong told Xi Suixi that now the party has formulated a very good poverty alleviation policy. General Secretary Xi said that there are no backward families on the road to a well-off society. You must believe that the village committee will let you wait for the news.

Xi Suixi wiped his tears and walked away dubiously.

It happened that a deputy secretary of Yulin Municipal Party committee was responsible for helping Baigailiang Village. When the deputy secretary came to the village, Gao Zhihong made a special report to him. Soon, the deputy secretary personally arranged for the young man to enter the city and work as a security guard in a security company – Gao Zhihong personally drove him that day. Four years later, the young man is now very strong, earning four or five thousand a month and living with a girlfriend in the city. When he visited his parents in the village a few days ago, he happily discussed with Gao Zhihong what kind of car and house to buy. He has planned to get married!

The young man talked about his plans and dreams excitedly, and Gao Zhihong listened with satisfaction. Yes, to catch up with the good times and the party's good poverty alleviation policy, everything can be changed and any difficulties can be solved! Later, when he saw Xi Suixi, Gao Zhihong joked, 'isn't your name good?' Xi Suixi said shyly, this is not my name; this is the party's policy!

The people are rational and grateful.

3. Grandma asked, 'when did you grow up?'

Gao Zhihong was moved and educated by the responsibility of the Deputy Secretary of the municipal Party committee, and the senior leaders went to the grass-roots level one by one. There's nothing else he can say!

People who have been bosses in this city have a wide range of ideas and good skills. Under the impact of the tide of the times, the 'hollowing out' of rural economy and rural 'hollowing out' are becoming more and more intense. It is obviously impossible to get rid of poverty, get rich and revitalize rural areas by relying on the strength of each family, and it is difficult to narrow the gap between the rich and the poor. Gao Zhihong believes that we should unite all villagers and concentrate on running cooperatives and green industries so that everyone can make money.

—*The first big move.* The village cooperative was established, and Gao Zhihong was the president. He mobilized two old party members. In addition, he also invested 450,000 yuan to build 107 heat preservation greenhouses in the village. Poor households can plant for 10 years free of charge, and the village cooperative is responsible for sales. Gao Zhihong and other three investors recovered their costs year by year through sales. Poor families earn income through labor services. They can also take shares and pay dividends like other villagers. The women joined in a charitable shed free of charge, with an annual income of tens of thousands of yuan. When the security guard's son has hope, the husband who has been bedridden for many years is in a good mood. He even got up and could walk slowly and do some easy work in the shed. The villagers were surprised to find that Gao Zhishu's poverty alleviation project made the disabled stand up. What a miracle! I said maybe the man with cerebral infarction could walk because he had no hope of breaking up his family and didn't want to do anything. He lay on the Kang and died. In recent years, seeing that the party's poverty alleviation policy has fallen down and there is hope in life, we naturally stand up.

Gao Zhihong suddenly realized this and said with a smile. Unexpectedly, it was possible.

I said, I'm so cunning!

—*The second big move.* With the support of the government's poverty alleviation funds, a large farm with blue cover, gray wall and hard land has been built, and hundreds of black pigs and Huzhou sheep have been introduced. The mode of operation is still villagers' investment and dividend.

—*The third big move.* With the help of Gao Zhihong, the water supply project leading to the cultivated land, facilities and parks of the whole village is under construction. After household division in the field, a large number of fish fry were thrown into the reservoir that had been forgotten for many years. When visiting, Gao Zhihong said with great interest that several cruise ships would be built in the future, and then a cliff Hotel and several rows of cave style husband and wife rooms and restaurants would be built on the high slope on the shore. He goes fishing, boating, playing and eating. Looking at the rippling water and rolling mountains in the autumn sun, I was fascinated by his words.

—*The fourth big move.* With the deepening and innovation of reform, after years of cultivated land transfer and large-scale land leveling, the whole village has formed a pattern of cooperative continuous operation and orderly production. Looking up, the 1,160 Mu dam field is located in the mountains, vast. Red Sorghum fluttered in the wind, making a sound like the sea. Gao told me that it was planted according to the order of the cooperative unit Wuliangye distillery, and the villagers can ensure considerable income.

—*The fifth big move.* According to the new rural construction plan, 111 two-story villas were built on the slope and rose from the ground. Chrome plated iron fence, red tile and white wall, 197 square metres per building. The villagers can move in for 120,000 yuan. I exclaimed that in Beijing, only ministerial cadres can enjoy such a large housing area! Into the first house in the second row, there were only two old people. My son is out to work. Looking around, the windows are bright and spotless, and the terrazzo floor is bright enough to see people. The living room is covered with red carpet, sofa, refrigerator and color TV.

The decoration level is no different from that of the city. Where are the dark and thin youth who wear 'open crotch pants', the villagers who wear rag shoes without high heels, and the members who quarrel for a few cents and a half? They are still there, their memories are still there, but today they enjoy a better life than they ever dreamed of.

I asked the old man, how's the new life?

Mr. Gao, 72, showed his white and neat teeth (the dentures his son bought) and said with a smile: OK! How could I have thought of it before!

In 2018, Baigailiang village took the lead in poverty alleviation in the county.

Gao Zhihong was naughty and wild when he was a child. As a secretary of the village Party branch, the cause of the village has always been so wonderful. The villagers often praise Zhihong's grandmother and say that her grandson is a great man and a good man. Thank you for your wishes! Grandma couldn't shut her mouth with a smile. She felt that her grandson had changed a lot. One day, grandma asked, you were so naughty when you were a child. I don't understand. When did you grow up?

Gao Zhilong thought and said seriously: 'December 5, 2015, my first day on the job as a village.'

4. The mystery of 'love supermarket'

When I first came to the door of Baigailiang Village committee, I saw a notice board on the wall, which was divided into red list and blacklist. The red list says:

Liu Dianxi, Gao Dagang and other 8 people helped to put out the fire, and each person got 20 points

Volunteer Xi Suilan and other 6 families will be rewarded with 30 points for maintaining good hygiene.

Gao Lanlan, Gao Yuyan and other 14 students performed well in class, with 20 points for each

Gao Mengfan, Gao Mengyuan and other four college students voluntarily signed up to participate in the counseling for left behind children, with 20 points for each

The blacklist says:

The villager Gao littered on the road and deducted 20 points
50 points deducted from villager Liu for smoking on the mountain and lighting the forest land

Volunteer Liu ×× For poor hygiene, 10 points will be deducted this month and replaced next month if this behavior doesn't improve

I don't understand what this is. After talking with Gao Zhihong and senior director Gao Yuepeng, I walked into the 'love supermarket' in the yard and understood what this meant.

There are all kinds of goods in the supermarket. Some are purchased by the village committee, and some villagers accept gifts from relatives and friends or discount the necessities of life that cannot be eaten or used up. The 'love supermarket' goods sold to the supermarket will not receive cash. Villagers can exchange reward points for the goods they want. That is to say, as long as you have high moral quality, positive labor performance, due diligence, helping others, integrity and good family health, in short, as long as you seriously practice the requirements of the socialist core values, you can exchange points and save a lot of money.

Excellent quality is better than money and goods. This is really a novel creation! It is in line with the traditional saying and expectation of 'good people have good returns'. It plays a long-term and effective role in improving people's ideological consciousness and moral quality and guiding the transformation of local spiritual outlook. I appreciate this innovation. Gao Zhihong said that he learned this from Lankao. I checked the Internet. I didn't see any reports from Lankao. I think if love supermarket can be more popular, it will give full play to its positive energy.

Poverty alleviation contributes to wisdom, innovation, temperature, justice and socialist core values!

Since then, Gao Zhihong drew inferences from one instance and established a special 'love consulting school'. He knew that the cost of making up classes for children during the holidays was very high, and parents complained endlessly, but they could do nothing. The main task of the 'love school' in Baigailiang Village is to call on local college students and cultural and educational personnel to return home voluntarily and provide free consultation for children and left behind children in the village during student holidays.

The poverty alleviation for this child reflects Gao Zhihong's delicate love for the people and deep humanistic feelings.

In 2018, Gao Zhihong has been the Secretary of the village Party Committee for three years. It's time to change the village. He believes that the task of leading the whole village out of poverty has been basically completed. Now, he can leave, play drums again, start another company, start his own company again, or go home and enjoy happiness. However, in the election of the Party Congress, he was reelected as the Secretary of the village Party committee by one vote – the vote he lost was his own.

The villagers said, we will go with you wherever you go!!

People's expectations are as heavy as a mountain. They have no choice. Gao Zhihong decided to take them for another three years.

It's really not easy to make this decision. In the past, when I was the boss, my monthly income was tens of thousands, hundreds of thousands, hundreds of thousands of yuan. As a village party secretary, he gets a state subsidy of 2000 yuan a month, which looks like a poor family.

I asked, how's your mother-in-law's attitude?

Gao Zhihong said that after I became a Secretary for one year, the situation has improved. Instead of falling into the mud, I pulled out all the poor families. She's happy, too. She thinks her face is bright and doesn't use cosmetics. I smiled.

Nowadays, various honors from provinces and cities are pouring in. Gao Zhihong is a well-known person who is often invited by other units and localities to give lectures on the party and the 'Rural Revitalization Strategy'. Gao Zhihong was flattered. He said, 'even if I'm a billionaire, who can know me? It's a great honor to go out and talk about the party and make a report!'

5. Growth means going out of your comfort zone

In another place, another hero, Gao Pengcheng, Secretary of Gaojiagou Village branch, went up the mountain with me. He is not as dignified as Gao Zhihong, especially like a simple farmer with a sense of happiness. Although they are not poor, they laugh happily.

Gao Pengcheng was born in Gaojiagou Village, Shilipu Town, Suide County in 1975. It is located at the junction of Mizhi County, Zizhou County and Suide County. Large mountains, deep ditches, vertical and horizontal ditches and less cultivated land. Many surrounding villages are very poor, and Gaojiagou Village is the poorest. People go up and down the mountain to the county hospital for 27 kilometres. In the past, there were no cars and roads. I had to listen to fate. When I was seriously ill, I had to wait for death. During the Yan'an period, Xi Zhongxun served as secretary of the Suide prefectural Party committee and deeply sympathized with the people here. He often rolled up his trouser legs, went up and down the mountain to engage in production and chatted with farmers. I wrote this paragraph in the long documentary red Holmes (published by Shanghai Xuelin Publishing House). The title of the book personally inscribed by Comrade Xi Zhongxun is on display.

That generation of old revolutionaries left, but their desire to stay here is still strong.

When Gao Pengcheng was in high school, the spring breeze of reform and opening up moistened the gullies here, and his life was improved. Xiao Gao can ride a broken bike, go home on Saturday and go to school in the county on Sunday. But it's still hard. Every week he brought enough food – two Wotou and a little kimchi every day, because he couldn't afford the canteen. If he can be admitted to county No. 1 middle school, it can be imagined that his academic performance is good. But after graduating from senior three, he decided to give up the college entrance examination to reduce the burden on his parents and let his sister continue to go to school. Many days, Gao Pengcheng took his high school diploma and hid outside the earth kiln to cry secretly. His tears could not stop. He knew that this decision would affect his life and his future would become at a loss. The name 'Pengcheng' is futile. But he must do it for his family. In the interview, Gao Pengcheng mentioned this topic many times, 'I decided not to take the college entrance examination' 'in fact, I thought when I was a sophomore in high school' 'I hesitated, but what's the use of hesitation...' this shows his long-term pain in his heart.

I listened quietly to his conversation. I can feel the pain in his heart, which is still incurable. I know it affected his life. I can also guess the helplessness and sadness of his parents in those days. However, history and reality determine that in a poor and backward country, the place of birth is often doomed to be unfair.

After that, Gao Pengcheng dried his tears and, like all migrant workers, picked up his luggage roll and embarked on the road of working in the city in fear. This is the way of reform in China's rural areas and the way of life for poor farmers.

He has a high school culture and is very popular among migrant workers. Gao Pengcheng visited Yulin counties. The high-rise buildings in all counties are condensed with the sweat of him and his brothers. Like Gao Zhihong, after years of hard work, he has become a well-known boss in the construction industry in Yulin. He has a strong engineering team and more than a dozen large machinery. During this period, he did many good things for his hometown and became a member of the Standing Committee of the county people's Congress and a deputy to the Municipal People's Congress. The name 'Pengcheng' still seems to be valid.

In 2015, the village committee of Gaojiagou Village was changed. The villagers knew that Gao Pengcheng was a good boy and urged him to return to the village to participate in the election. He was moved by the feelings and wishes of the villagers. The heart always goes to a warm place. Gao Pengcheng, 40, listened to the phone without hesitation and was elected by a high vote.

Since then, Gaojiagou Village has started an unprecedented large-scale transformation. In order to change the appearance of the village, Gao Pengcheng often pays out of his own pocket. Their own large machinery is used free of charge in the village. His own company has never participated in project bidding. So far, he hasn't repaid a penny to the village. Like his unique personality of love and hate, everything is clearly separated. 'Everything is worth it for his hometown and villagers!' This is his spell. His parents have never seen big money, so they don't care about money. They particularly supported him in seeking welfare and dedication for the people.

With such a good people and countless selfless soldiers, what else can China do?

Gaojiagou Village has successively established three farmers' cooperatives, with large-scale land transfer, integrated more than 4,000 mu of land, and prepared to go up the mountain to plant apples, grapes, medicinal materials, greenhouses, etc. in addition to the strong support of the government, Gao Pengcheng's personal investment reached more than 8 million yuan. Some villagers who rely on ancient agricultural traditions do not understand and retain corn and millet. Gao Pengcheng rented several buses at his own expense and took the villagers to visit and study in the agricultural development park in the surrounding counties. The villagers were persuaded. In 2018, the per capita annual income of farmers in cooperatives reached more than 5,760 yuan. The square in front of the village is brightly lit, the cement mountain road is like a ribbon, and the happy nursing home is also very happy. The old revolutionary village finally realized the wish of the old revolutionary: 'upstairs and downstairs, electric lights and telephones'.

Gao Pengcheng and I drove to the top of a high mountain. The top of the mountain has been razed to the ground, and several surrounding mountains have been razed to the ground, forming layers of terraces, most of which are planted with apple trees. Gao Pengcheng proudly told me that in two or three years, it will become the largest apple orchard in Yulin and Gaojiagou Village will become a beautiful garden. Then you can have another look!

From Beijing, this is 'poetry and distance.'

Liu Lihong told me that there are many good secretaries like Yulin. How many people do you want to interview? I provide a list. She meant there was no need to go somewhere else. Yulin is enough to buy a book.

IV Internal power: the dream of standing

Historical activities are always vibrant and colorful. In the final analysis, they are the activities of the people. The people are the fundamental driving force for historical progress.

At the 2015 central poverty alleviation and development work conference, General Secretary Xi stressed that 'poverty alleviation and prosperity ultimately depend on the hard work of the poor.' No mountain is higher than people, and no road is longer than feet. We should attach importance to giving play to the enthusiasm of the broad masses of grass-roots cadres, warm their hearts, take action and strive to change the face of poverty and backwardness. '

1. The story of an ancient village

On the way to Jiaxian County, I passed Nihegou Village on the Bank of the Yellow River. There is no hope of hearing the name. Comrades in the county said that there are several millennium jujube trees here, which are worth seeing. Sure enough, walking into the village, there stood several tall, strong and fierce jujube trees in the orchard, which needed two people to support. Two of them have withered in half, but the thick trunk and branches protruding from the oblique thorns have opened a canopy like a dense canopy in the sky, with dense red dates hanging on it, glittering like stars in the autumn sun. In contrast, the jujube trees under the modern race look thin and weak, just like children who lack nutrition and ambition. It was late autumn. The grass on the ground is withered and yellow, and the leaves are half green and half yellow. Many ripe red dates fell on the grass and no one picked them up. I said, I'm sorry. It costs tens of yuan a kilogram to Beijing! The villagers smiled and said nothing.

I walked around the Millennium jujube tree. Outside the village, the Yellow River rippled, and the autumn wind brushed the leaves of the orchard, making my nostalgia leisurely. The village head told me that all the people in this village are surnamed Wu. According to our ancestors, we are all descendants of the Wu Zetian family in the Tang Dynasty. Because Wu Zetian loves red dates, but most of the red dates she worships don't like them, so she sent a tribe to bring a bag of the best and best quality red date stones to look for a geomantic treasure land with fertile soil and suitable climate along the Yellow River to plant red dates for her. He has read books and is naturally cheerful and elegant. He especially loves the great rivers and mountains of the motherland. He knew that there was no shortage of water for planting jujube trees, so he took a boat down the river, watching the mountains and water, and looking for a place to plant jujube trees. That day, when the boat floated here, there happened to be a young woman in a red skirt and green shirt washing clothes by the river. Where the boat didn't want to pass, a huge wave rolled one of her clothes into the river. The little woman jumped up and shouted, 'please get my clothes back, or I'll be beaten by my mother!' The official looked at the little woman with willow eyebrows, apricot eyes, cherry lips and thin waist. This is a rare natural beauty. The official was suddenly moved and ordered someone to pick up the girl's clothes, then stopped the boat, bowed deeply to the little woman and said, 'beauty has orders, how dare Xiaosheng not listen!' He looked around again. It is backed by green mountains and faces the Yellow River. There is a high incense temple on a mountain not far away. This is really an auspicious and convenient place. He shouted, 'young man, get off the boat. Let's open up wasteland and plant dates here!' Later, he married a little woman, carefully selected every year, wrapped red dates in yellow silk and transported them to Chang'an. Since then, the Wu family has multiplied here. After the village director finished, I asked, did you make it up based on Xi Shi's story?

The village head handed over the date several times and said with a smile that eight, nine and ten are inseparable anyway. If you don't believe it, try it.

Sure enough, the meat is thick, the core is small, tender and delicate, the sweetness is rich, and the aftertaste is long.

I said that jujube trees in your village should be vigorously developed to the best. I suggest naming this date 'the Queen's Royal date' and attaching a manual stating that it was specially provided by Wu Zetian. It has the effects of Nourishing Yin, strengthening yang and prolonging life. Wu Zetian can live to 82 years old. This date is very valuable! However, due to good quality and enough nutrition, you can't eat more. You can eat 8 capsules a day. If you eat more, your mouth and nose will be congested. Packaging and publicity are in place. The Wu aristocratic family are waiting to make a lot of money!

The surrounding villagers applauded one after another. Comrades in the county said that we should follow this golden rule in the future!

This is a gimmick, worth mentioning. Facts have proved that poverty alleviation and development begin with daring to think, and an idea can open a new world.

2. Live or die?

Under the setting sun, the Loess Plateau in late autumn is like the billowing waves of the Yellow River. Everything is bronze, just like our eternal ancestors.

At the poverty alleviation commendation conference held in Yulin, Liu Jiangui, a thin young farmer, came backstage with a crutch. I noticed that it was too difficult and laborious for him to move. He trembled violently at every step.

Yes, once he lay on the kiln Kang and looked at the kiln door a few steps and thousands of miles away. He burst into tears.

Yes, once, countless days and nights, like Hamlet, he asked himself countless times, is it life or death?

For the past, no – he has no past and no future.

I decided to go to Jiaxian to talk to him. In the evening, I drove to Jiaxian County by the Yellow River, on the top of the mountain. Standing on the edge of the cliff, overlooking the majestic Yellow River, the waves of history beat my heart again and again. Hehe, I've heard about the county for a long time! Here, the people of the whole county did their best to support Mao Zedong and the Northwest Field Army in moving to northern Shaanxi; Here, shepherd Li Youyuan spoke out for the first time the great choice of the Chinese people: 'the East is red, the sun rises, China has a Mao Zedong...'

Unexpectedly, the county on the hillside is very small but very lively. At night, the lights are bright, full of modern color and noise, and pedestrians and private cars are crowded like beehives. What makes me more shocked is that compared with many high-rise buildings, the county Party committee and the county government is still located in a courtyard on the top of the mountain. From county leaders to departments, they all worked in caves with white curtains, just like old Yan'an in those days. The gate was unguarded and people were free to go in and out. It may be the only county in the country.

The next morning, we drove dozens of kilometres to Yukou town. Then climb the high slope to the earth kiln of Liu Jiangui's house in Tanjiaping Village. Jiangui and his parents are already waiting at the door. He specially wore a dark suit, leaned on two crutches, smiled and said hello to me. I hurried up and said, come on, come in and talk.

In 1989, Liu Jiangui was born. He could climb mountains at the age of one, walk at the age of two and run at the age of three. After school, they are very lively and add a lot of joy to their parents. The children of the poor are in charge early. After graduating from high school, Liu Jiangui became an automobile repairman in the countryside. He was happy all day and covered in oil. He is deeply loved by his boss and colleagues. In early 2010, Jiangui had an acne and a little inflammation on her shoulder. He doesn't care. He took some medicine casually and went out to work. I didn't expect that a few days later, the back pain was unbearable, and the pain of walking could reach the heel. Jiangui rushed to the local hospital for examination and was diagnosed as 'epidural abscess'. The doctor said it was a rare disease with serious consequences. He was transferred to the Second Affiliated Hospital of Xi'an Jiaotong University for surgery. But he still can't run faster than his condition worsens. He lost consciousness after the operation. When he woke up the next day, his head was numb and a catheter was inserted into his lower body, but he completely lost his feeling – paralyzed.

God, how can small acne cause such serious consequences!

If you have been paralyzed since childhood and don't know the fun of walking and running, you will accept your life. I tasted the sweat of climbing and walking, understood 'poetry and distance', and enjoyed the fun of running like the wind. At the age of 21, it was the season of youth. Jiangui fell down with a bang and couldn't stand up anymore. What a cruel blow! Several times, he took the doctor's hand and cried, 'doctor, will you please let me stand up? Otherwise, let me die!' The mother hugged him and cried, 'son, you can't do this. If you go, we must go with you.'

After the operation, it cost more than 100,000 yuan. This is too much for an ordinary peasant family. Next to the hospital bed, my parents talked about selling caves at home, continuing to treat my son and trying to restore the function of my legs. Jiangui strongly objected and asked to be discharged immediately. He said, you sold the cave. If I can't cure it, where do you live? You raised me, I not only can't be filial, but also let the second old man owe a lot of debt, and even have no place to live. What's the use of raising my son? Why don't you let me die!

The parents had to agree to take him out of the hospital.

Parents have the hardest jobs in the world. When a lively son became a paralyzed man overnight. In any case, the old man can't accept this reality. Without hesitation, he borrowed usury and carried his son to Xi'an Medical College, Peking Union Medical University Hospital, Capital Medical University and PLA Hospital again and again. After running for several years, Jiangui's stump still hasn't changed at all. An old professor in his 70s said that spinal cord injury is a worldwide problem, known as 'immortal cancer'. The young man could only lie in bed and sit in a wheelchair all his life. An old Chinese doctor concluded that he would not live for half a year. Mother didn't give up. She went to Baiyun Mountain Taoist temple and painted a lot of paintings. The last two sentences are: 'disaster comes to the West. The Taoist explained that the child could not have survived, but your ancestors did a lot of good deeds and accumulated a lot of Yin virtue, so the child can still survive. Mother came back happily and sadly.

Lying in the cave, watching the short day and long night, Liu Jiangui was in great pain. Recalling that it was difficult for his parents to support themselves and looking at the old man's sad and haggard face, he thought he would become a burden on his family in the future. When his parents went out to work several times, he wanted to settle down. But his parents knew his despair and thoughts and always hid all the sharp tools in the family. Then he jumped off the cliff and committed suicide. Within ten steps outside the door is a high cliff. But Jiangui doesn't even have the ability to jump.

After receiving the news, the town government issued 500-yuan relief to the Liu family and 300-yuan consolation to the director of the disabled persons' Federation. Care is especially warm in times of crisis. Jiangui shed tears. He thought that my parents did not give up themselves, nor did the party and government give up themselves. Why should I give up myself! He is determined to take the road of rehabilitation and make himself stand up again through exercise! Parents are very happy and help him together. In the later days, his mother carried him on his shoulders every day, and his father put his knees on his head and pulled his legs with his hands again and again, trying to make his contracted leg muscles stronger. But in order to survive and pay off his debts, his parents had to work in the fields. Jiangui asks his parents to tie him to the trunk with a rope and practice standing. Later, when they learned to walk with crutches, they would fall a few steps. Whenever their parents saw him falling, they would lie on the ground and let their son fall on them.

How great is the love of his parents.

Unconscious numb legs are as soft as noodles. It's too difficult to learn to walk again. Jiangui wanted to give up countless times, but with the encouragement and help of his parents again and again, courage finally defeated cowardice and confidence finally defeated despair. Slowly, he was able to walk on crutches, and later learned to drive cars for the disabled.

After the 18th National Congress of the Communist Party of China, the Liu family was recognized as a poor family and received help and relief from the government every year. Some villagers can sit down and pick up the 'big pie' falling from the sky and strive to be poor people. However, the strong Liu Jiangui always felt that it was not a glorious thing to be a poor family. On TV, he saw many successful examples of disabled people starting businesses. He thought, why can't I do what others can do? If he finds a good livelihood project, he can become the backbone of the family, help old and sick parents, and take on the responsibilities men should take. But he's not like the disabled in the city. He is in a remote village. What can he do? Later, seeing the increasingly active network economic activities, his idea suddenly came out: it's inconvenient for me to move and communicate with others. I can become a 'small and micro enterprise' and promote local characteristics in the WeChat circle of friends! Before the Spring Festival in 2017, Jiaxian County Party Secretary Liu went to the countryside to visit poor households and came to Liu's house. After listening to Liu Jiangui's opinions, secretary Liu appreciated and encouraged him to start a business boldly and strive to get rid of poverty through his own labor. A few days later, the village team sent him a sealing machine and a vacuum packaging machine. Since then, Jiang GUI and his parents have collected local specialties such as red dates, millet and self-made handmade vermicelli planted by the villagers. After screening, grading and packaging, they have promoted sales in the circle of friends, and created characteristic products such as 'walnut red dates'. In 2019, with the help of the poverty alleviation task force, he began to produce pure green handmade noodles. Slowly, Liu Jiangui won many customers. After eating the millet, he sent, an aunt in Beijing replied that I hadn't eaten such delicious millet for many years. She asked Jiangui to send it to her regularly and warmly introduce it to relatives and friends. More and more customers follow. In 2017, Liu Jiangui stayed at home and his net income from online sales exceeded 6000 yuan; In 2018, it reached more than 20000 yuan. This year, Liu Jiangui took the initiative to take off his hat for poor households. He felt relaxed, proud and glorious.

In early 2019, Liu Jiangui created the first disabled rural electric service station in Jia County and the WeChat official account of the disabled alliance, providing a platform for learning and communication among the disabled in the county. He also became a county volunteer, followed the volunteer team to visit left behind children and empty nesters in rural areas, and attended more than 50 times lecture in poor villages. He said, 'as the saying goes, relief can't save lives. People can't rely on strength. General Secretary Xi said that a good life depends on struggle. We can't use poverty as an excuse, but we should find a way to get rich. Targeted poverty alleviation provides us with a once-in-a-lifetime opportunity. Why don't we work hard?'

When he left, Liu Jiangui and his parents took him to the door. We went downhill for a long time. Looking back on the past, Liu Jiangui, who was on crutches, smiled and waved to us? Honest parents stood beside him

In my opinion, this is the most typical simple appearance of the Chinese working people.

3. Fractured life

Fold (Pronouced Zhé) bright round face sunshine big boy. Looking at his lovely smile, you can't believe that his life suddenly broke down at the age of 6.

Zhe Mingming's home is in Shandaping Village, Shijiawan Town, Suide County. In front of the door is national highway 307. Coal trucks roar past day and night, raising smoke and dust all over the sky. One day in the spring of 2002, his parents were very busy. When he was six years old, he ran across the road. A motor tricycle knocked him down. His life was saved and his legs lost consciousness.

Now his shelves are full of colorful bead fabrics loved by girls and children. There are small decorative boxes, toy boxes, small picture frames and shadow picture frames, which are colorful and dazzling. Zhe Mingming carefully weaves and weaves children's colorful childhood. His childhood and youth used to be gray.

At his home, Zhe Mingming recalled the car accident to me. In fact, he doesn't remember anything. I don't remember which month or day it was. For a moment, I only felt a dark shadow like a mountain rushing towards him. He felt no pain as if he had just fallen asleep. When I woke up, I found myself lying in the hospital with uncomfortable legs. Since then, Mingming can't leave the ground, climb the Kang or go to school. He can't reach anything higher or farther. He can only call his parents.

Little life is still in that dark moment. He didn't understand when he was a child. A toy can make him forget everything and play for a long time. 'In the yard, I was in a wheelchair. A group of children are playing hide and seek and throwing sandbags. I'm also very happy to watch them play.' Growing up, gradually, a destructive pain and despair followed.

Zhe Mingming's home is close to the school, but his disability makes the classroom far away from him. The sound of reading from school and the sound of teenagers running and playing on the playground made him deeply mysterious and yearning. One day when he was 12 years old, he couldn't write or read after school. He entered the campus in a wheelchair. He is the only one in the empty campus. He recalled that he was alone in the middle of the spacious campus. He was excited and sad and felt very uncomfortable here. Since then, he has never entered the campus and rarely went out. He closed himself deeply with endless sadness and inferiority. He lay in bed all day, didn't go out, didn't talk, and endured the cruel fate alone. When he was bored, he began to read and write, and learned to do some manual work from his mother, but he just tasted it and felt there was no way out. But he still cherishes the fruits of his labor. There are two picture frames and colored beads on the wall. One is cross stitch, the other is paper cutting. Both were his first attempts. He is carefully exploring the way to the outside world.

In 2015, mother was seriously ill. Mingming was very sad, which made him suddenly realize that he had lost a lot and could no longer lose his maternal love. He can no longer rely on his mother to do everything as before, and let his mother worry about his pain. He wants to find a way to live independently. He searches and thinks on the computer, but he can't think clearly.

In June 2017, the first secretary Liu Xinguo came to Shatanping Village. Liu Xinguo is the deputy director of Suide County medical insurance center. He has gray hair and a quiet disposition. When I came to the interview, he sat with me, didn't talk much, and never said himself. In 2015, he volunteered to go to the countryside to help the poor. He has successively served as the first Secretary of Dongjiazhuang, Xujiaping, Shatanping, Shijiawan and other villages, with a good reputation. He was rated as the excellent first Secretary of Suide County twice.

Liu Xinguo told Mingming how steel was made and encouraged him to work hard.

Mingming said, 'Can I do this?'

Liu Xinguo was concise and comprehensive: 'You can do anything you want!'

One sentence ignited Mingming's passion.

After that, Liu Xinguo went shopping for several days. Instead of going shopping, he was thinking about what he could do?

In this way, the colored bead cloth entered the bright field of vision. The next day, he bought the first batch of raw materials online and made the first Beaded pendant and a red lantern. Since then, Mingming has connected his life hope with beads and thread, opening a glorious road of life. The price of a small lamp is 12 yuan. After several hours of weaving, it cost 15 yuan. 3 yuan, which was the first money he made for his family, but it gave him a sense of achievement he had never experienced.

'Three yuan is the first pot of gold in my life,' Zhe Mingming said proudly.

The people in the village obviously have good skills and business. Many boys and girls want to learn from him. He became a master. In a room less than 20 square metres, there are often more than a dozen disciples crowded in it. Obviously, he never thought that he was also a valuable person who could help others. In April 2018, with the help of secretary Liu Xinguo, Zhe Mingming established the 'Suide County Chenxing folk craft farmers' professional cooperative', with more than 10 participants. In August, she won the first prize in the Story Telling Contest of 'happy poverty alleviation · glorious poverty alleviation' in Yulin city. This is the first time he went to Yulin in a wheelchair. In October, it won the title of 'advanced individual in poverty alleviation and prosperity in Shaanxi Province'. In June 2019, as a national model for the disabled to get rid of poverty, he made several tour reports. In October 2019, he reported his deeds at the provincial poverty alleviation award and recognition conference held at the Great Hall of the people of Shaanxi Province.

In the wheelchair, the new era and new life gave him the dream of standing high.

4. Meaning of 'falling to earth'

Beautiful hair on her ears, a red sweater, a half long silver-grey skirt and white high heels – Gao Qiong, Party Secretary of a 'post-80s' village in the mountains of Shaanxi, China.

She sat quietly on the sofa, with fair skin and beautiful eyes. She spoke softly and smiled softly. Everything in life is gentle to her.

This is an easy time. All human products become lighter because of the addition of scientific and technological elements; Due to the rapid changes of the times, all dreams, pursuits, choices and meanings have become easier; all the feelings and feelings, including love, friendship, joy, misfortune, pain and parting, become relaxed, because maybe tomorrow will change and start again. On WeChat, I saw Gao Qiong give herself a net name called 'falling to the earth' – she can float in the bright sky and finally fall to the earth. You can imagine how easy her life is. But 'falling from the earth' seems to have another meaning. I smiled and asked, 'girl, look at this net name. Are you the nine immortals who fell from the world?'

Gao Qiong smiled and said nothing, indicating acquiescence.

The country girl who grew up in the mountains is so confident. Now Chinese people are generally so confident.

In 1986, Gao Qiong was born in a cadre family (named after revolutionary martyr Li Zizhou) in Zhoujiajian Town, Zizhou County. When it comes to cadres, almost all his father deals with are farmers; It is said that in the town, you can see the quiet villages on the high loess slope without going out. She has been with the villagers since she was a child. Cried her grandparents, uncles and aunts affectionately. After graduating from college, Gao Qiong returned to her hometown. The place is small and there are few occupations to choose from. As the 'daughter' of the family, parents don't want birds to fly away. Only when they see them every day will they feel happy. The delicate Gao Qiong also loves her parents and family. She doesn't want to go to Beijing, Shanghai, Shenzhen and Guangzhou to test her achievement ability. 'I always like to stay quietly, or sit on the windowsill to see the scenery, watch people coming and going, and guess their fate; Or take a book and look back from page 29 or page 58,' maybe all the idle petty bourgeoisie in the world are like this. Soon, Gao Qiong worked as a teacher in a local school for two years, teaching Chinese and English, and then served as a head teacher. A big boy and a group of children get together. It is said that teachers are 'the most sacred work in the sun', but one day she suddenly thought that when she was young, with the love of her parents, she had always been like a child – was her life shaped like this? Three feet podium, youth and white hair, constant teaching materials, this is too simple and peaceful. After three minutes of thinking, she decided to apply for a college student village official because it was a new thing. The father smiled and said that his daughter 'bled for three minutes', but he was very supportive. Help villagers exercise. It's good not to leave his sight. On September 1, 2010, Gao Qiong, 24, went to Chejiagou Village as Deputy Secretary of the branch, just like the beginning of school and freshmen. It's three kilometres from home and five minutes' drive. A familiar and strange world unfolded before her eyes. Familiar because she saw all the villages when she was a child, strange because she never had a deep understanding of these villages. The next day, she began to visit caves, intersections and courtyards door to door. She sat down to talk with the villagers and asked about their life, production, family members and income. She also took a small notebook with her. The villagers saw such a beautiful girl talking to them in the sun and asked if you were not afraid of tanning? Gao Qiong said that blacks are healthy. The villagers laughed and regarded her as their baby girl.

Three months later, the village branch was officially renamed, and Gao Qiong was elected Deputy Secretary by unanimous vote. Her main job is to manage family planning. God, this was the 'first difficult' job in China at that time. It is even more difficult for a girl who is not married to take care of it. After visiting, Chejiagou village is not a 'super life guerrilla', but a 'super life base camp'. There are no boys in the villagers' home, only a group of boys. A born child cannot be stuffed back into her mother's stomach. Gao Qiong had to 'give priority to persuasion, supplemented by ventilation'. In other words, once someone from the higher authorities came to inspect, she immediately informed the villagers to take their children up the mountain and hide – a 'way' that cannot avoid punishing the villagers.

All extra children are 'black children'. They don't have Hukou or ID cards. When they grow up, they can't work elsewhere 'To tell you the truth, I sympathized with the villagers.' 'Every family has a litter of children,' Gao Qiong said. Their income is very low and their life is very difficult. They depend on planting some land and raising several sheep. I have no enthusiasm for my work, just to cope with the inspection of my superiors.

After the 18th CPC National Congress, a national census was conducted in 2015. The central government requires that 'one cannot be less' must be verified door by door. Gao Qiong was very happy and every family reported it. 'General Secretary Xi Jinping has solved this historical problem once and for all,' she said. Yes, if a country cannot accurately grasp the national economy and people's livelihood issues such as population, economic development, social distribution and infrastructure construction, there is no way to talk about Scientificity and Rationality – this is too dangerous!

As far as I know, China's first census was presided over and organized by the then great Sima Wang Mang in the late Eastern Han Dynasty. After verification, the population exceeds 40 million. How many households and people are there in cities and counties such as Chang'an and Luoyang (see the Han Dynasty for detailed records). Therefore, I don't believe historians' views on Wang Mang. This is a digression.

In 2016, Gao Qiong officially became a formal cadre and a cadre within the establishment through organizational assessment. Before that, she was not a formal cadre. She gets a little allowance every month. She can do whatever she wants and leave whatever she wants. When she became a regular guest, Gao Qiong, who was originally relaxed, suddenly realized the responsibility on her shoulder. Inspired by the census and out of the need of poverty alleviation, she believes that some long-term basic work should be done. She decided to register the car village from door to door: population, age, land mu, cultivation, migrant workers, working hours, income, etc., from grandpa to grandson, are all registered, much more detailed than registered residence. She has the most real situation. This is the first-hand information she got when she came into the house to chat in recent years. At that time, she spoke very kindly, and the villagers were not prepared for her. Gao Qiong also innovatively designed various forms and introduced the villagers' living and production data in detail. When the poverty alleviation investigation was officially launched, it was difficult for some villagers to tell the truth and disclose their real income in order to win the benefits of the poverty alleviation policy.

Ding Feng, then Secretary of the town Party committee, praised Gao Qiong at the cadre meeting and said that no one could hide Gao Qiong from the economic situation of the villagers in Chejiagou Village.

Chejiagou Village is a famous weak and lax village. The Secretary of the old Party branch has worked for decades, and his energy, ability and level cannot keep up with the needs of the development of the times. The village head has business outside and seldom goes back to the village. Gao Qiong can only see him two or three times a year. Therefore, the actual situation of Chejiagou Village is upside down. For a whole year, with the efforts of Gao Qiong, the true face of Chejiagou Village was finally 'shown to the world'. All the most complete and detailed farmer files in history were sorted into a book, and the village was filled with half a house. I don't know the situation all over the country, but in Yulin City and Zizhou County, Gao Qiong is a pioneer of 'one file for one household'. Chejiagou Village has become a typical demonstration village for targeted poverty alleviation in the county!

In late July 2017, Zizhou County experienced heavy rain for several consecutive days. The County launched an emergency plan to arrange for all residents in low-lying areas to quickly move to high places. Sure enough, on the 26th, the upstream reservoir suddenly burst and a 10 feet high mountain torrent rushed down. The buildings in the county were flooded to the first and second floors, and the whole county was cut off, causing unprecedented disasters to the people. Over the past few days, Gao Qiong has been assisting the town leaders in implementing the emergency plan. On the 26th, she saw that the rain was getting heavier and heavier, and the Dali River beside the town was surging and the water level soared. She thinks there is a big fishpond at the entrance of the highest village. Gao Qiong is very nervous. She called the village Party Secretary again and again, told the villagers to withdraw to the mountain, told each party member to take charge of a block, and asked the villagers to withdraw together. After going up the mountain, she should pay special attention to loosening the soil to prevent landslides. Report anything to her immediately.

After listening to this tone, a usually quiet and delicate girl seemed to become firm and decisive immediately. Around 7 p.m., Hongfeng rushed into Zhoujiajian Town, and many houses in various villages collapsed like playing cards. Fortunately, Ding Feng, Secretary of the municipal Party committee, has ordered the evacuation without serious consequences. Gao Qiong said that the superior leaders were very anxious at that time. They called one after another and asked the people in the town to do this and that. Secretary Dante basically didn't listen. Because he knows the actual situation of towns and villages best, he firmly follows the emergency plan and his own ideas. It turned out that he commanded and handled properly. Facing the unprecedented flood attack in a century, there were no casualties in the whole town.

At about 10 p.m., the Secretary of the old village committee called and said that many people had taken refuge in his house. It's crowded there. What should we do? Gao Qiong is on fire. It was the first fire in her life. She shouted on the phone: 'as the Secretary of the village Party committee, saving people is your bounden responsibility!' I left my phone over there. Call again. The line is broken. Gao Qiong's heart soared. She told Secretary Ding that the phone in the village was dead. I was worried about the fishpond at the entrance of the village, so I had to go and have a look.

Ding Feng resolutely stopped her: 'Can you be a little girl with so much water? I'll go!' With that, he opened the door and rushed into the pouring rain and dark night. A driver followed him.

More than half an hour later, Gao Qiong called the driver and asked how the situation was?

The driver said the water in the fishpond overflowed the dam, but fortunately, the dam didn't collapse.

Gao Qiong said, let Secretary Ding come back quickly. It's too dangerous!

The driver said, I can't move. Now he stood alone by the fishpond and said he would continue to observe for a while.

On the phone, Gao Qiong began to cry.

The night was picturesque, the rain was heavy and the waves were rough. Ding Feng stood at the entrance of the village for a long time.

An hour later, he came back wet.

At midnight, the turbulent Dali river overflowed the bank and merged into the fishpond at the entrance of the village. The dam collapsed and the flood flowed down the ditch. 30,000 krills put in the previous two years were destroyed.

The next day the rain stopped. Ding Feng took Gao Qiong and several Town cadres to Chejiagou Village to check the disaster. All the roads leading to the village were destroyed, and the broken cement boards were staggered. It was terrible. When you get to the village entrance with high terrain, the village entrance still stands, and there are many refuge villagers inside and outside. Gao Qiong wants to go and see the villagers' files stored in the house. Ding Feng caught her. Afraid that she could not stand the tragedy inside, he sent two cadres to have a look. In a little while, two cadres are back. Gao Qiong hurriedly asked, how about the file? The two cadres were silent. At that moment, Gao Qiong couldn't help crying! This is her hard work all year. She works overtime every night!

Ding Feng thought for a moment and said, 'go and have a look yourself.' You'll see it sooner or later.

Gao Qiong wiped her tears and ran over. The doors and windows of the village are missing. The ground is muddy and the high walls are muddy. All the papers piled on the ground were dumped in the mud and destroyed. There are piles of things on the table. Because they are heavy after soaking in water, they can still watch. Gao Qiong tried not to make herself cry. She knew that when she cried, the villagers' hearts were confused.

Overnight, the girl grew up. Since then, Gao Qiong has been living in this village, busy distributing disaster relief materials from the county and guiding the villagers to rebuild their homes. All 30,000 anchovy in the fishpond died on the ditch beach under the village. It was a hot summer and smelled bad. In order to prevent the epidemic, Gao Qiong took the lead in cleaning up the dead fish. In those days, she was covered with mud and water, and her face was drenched by the sun. She really fell into the world.

Subsequently, Zhoujiajian Town was praised by the county headquarters for its thoughtful and safe emergency command and treatment in major disasters, and there were no casualties in the town. Gao Qiong was awarded the title of 'advanced individual in flood fighting and disaster relief'. Soon, her face suddenly became swollen and painful – she was obviously poisoned when cleaning up dead fish, so she was urgently transferred to Xi'an hospital for treatment and recovered decades later.

Two months later, the old village Party Secretary of Chejiagou Village submitted his resignation, and Gao Qiong was appointed secretary of the village Party committee, leading the whole village on a new journey of poverty alleviation.

When I went to Chejiagou Village, I saw new caves and new farmhouses lined up on the sunny slope. The roads have hardened again, the streetlamps have been installed, the cultural square has been completed, new industries have developed, the mountains are full of walnut trees, the imported white cashmere goats are fat and strong, and the family drinking water project is under way... In 2017, Chejiagou Village was rated as 'county-level industrial leading demonstration village.'

This is what a quiet female college student does.

I seem to understand the deep meaning of Gao Qiong's net name 'falling to the earth'. Only when a young man and a cadre really enter the 'world' and the people can the people's dreams and their own dreams bloom.

5. 'Commander rabbit' uprising

Back in Zizhou County, I saw Ding Feng. Tall, black and thin, thick voice, fast step and decisive behavior. He comes from an ordinary cadre family. After leaving the army, he worked in Zhoujiajian Town. Because he can bear hardships, has courage and insight, a year later, he was abnormally promoted to vice mayor. He later served as the Secretary of the town Party committee and is now the director of Poverty Alleviation Office of Zizhou County. I wanted to talk to him, but he brought a 'rabbit commander' – He Hanxiong, a villager of Niuquanwan. Strangely, the name of this village is so local, but people's names are so powerful!

The young man is very handsome and takes going out to work as his main source of livelihood. After he got married in 2000, he had a daughter and lived a happy life. In 2003, bad luck suddenly came and lingered like a shadow. The second daughter died 27 days after birth; The third daughter was born with congenital heart disease and died more than two months later; The only child also suffers from congenital heart disease after birth. He had a major operation, which cost 120,000 yuan; Once, He Hanxiong fell off the roof of the shed while working on the construction site. He was unconscious. People saved him, but he found that he also had congenital heart disease. Before and after, He Hanxiong lost his property and owed more than 400000 yuan of foreign debt in order to cure his illness and save his life. A young farmer's home collapsed due to illness.

When you encounter a major disaster, the temperature of the country and society will be higher and deeper. Li Xiaoying, executive vice president of Zizhou Family Planning Association, came to criticize He Hanxiong. After hearing this pain, she appealed everywhere, mobilized donations, and gave him a lot of help in the snow. Qiao Yang, a poverty alleviation cadre, came to provide him with many subsidies according to the national poverty alleviation policy. Zhang Shenggang, executive vice minister of the Publicity Department of Zizhou County Party committee, came and gave him a computer. He Han Xiong said with emotion: 'after the 18th National Congress of the Communist Party of China, I enjoyed Xi Jinping most comprehensive preferential policies, including poverty alleviation funds, interest free loans, serious illness compensation, education poverty alleviation, as well as condolences and necessities issued by governments at all levels during the Spring Festival... I can't tell myself!'

He Hanxiong's enthusiasm rekindled his hope and determination: I can't lie in the countryside waiting for help like this. I should save myself with a good policy of poverty alleviation! But congenital heart disease makes him unable to engage in heavy physical labor, so what should he do? He Hanxiong searched everywhere on the Internet, and suddenly a big white rabbit jumped into his mind! Yes, rabbits are full of wealth, fast reproduction and low feeding conditions! The county poverty alleviation office gave strong support and provided an interest free loan of 50,000 yuan. In the winter of 2015, He Hanxiong's rabbit farm was built, and 120 Belgian long-haired rabbits jumped into the 'new home' like snow-white cotton balls. He Hanxiong took care of his sick daughter day and night in terms of seed selection, breeding and epidemic prevention. He said, 'I can't afford to lose!'

Today, there are more than 6,000 rabbits in the rabbit farm, and more than 1000 rabbits are sold every month. It has exported to many provinces and regions, with a net income of more than 10,000 yuan and an annual income of more than 100,000 yuan. In order to promote villagers to get rich together, He Hanxiong established villagers' breeding cooperatives. Not only the villagers in the village have joined, but also many villagers around have raised their own funds or invested in shares. Every day, a steady stream of people came to visit and learn He Hanxiong's technology. The name of 'rabbit commander' spread all over Yulin.

After four years of struggle, the foreign debt of more than 400,000 yuan was paid off, and the whole family was very happy. Han Xiong, 42, said proudly, 'my eldest daughter understands the difficulties at home, is very independent and has strong learning ability. Now she is a college student. She is the first college student in our family!'

I smiled and said to Ding Feng sitting next to him, 'He Hanxiong is great! Facing the heavy siege of suffering and pressure,' rabbit commander' led 6,000 rabbit soldiers to rise up and successfully break through the siege.

Ding Feng said, 'this is the ancient tradition of the people in Northern Shaanxi.'

6. 'Fitness ball' cadres

During the interview in Yulin, I had many contacts with Wang Zhiqiang, director of the municipal Poverty Alleviation Office. He is a 'self-contradictory person'. He is dark, strong and simple, with the demeanor and temperament of rural cadres. In fact, he grew up in this city. He also has a pair of cultural myopia glasses on the bridge of his nose, which is particularly uncoordinated; In his work, he has a rigorous attitude, does not smile and speaks sharply. Sometimes he roared like thunder. When he is angry, he wants to throw you out of the window. But occasionally a humorous remark made his subordinates laugh, but he said seriously, 'what are you laughing at? Work!'

In the early 1990s, Wang Zhiqiang, who graduated from University, entered the Ministry of foreign trade. His dream when he was young prompted him to go to work early, clean up every day and perform well. But unexpectedly, under the impact of the wave of reform and opening up, the national foreign trade system gradually disintegrated. There is nothing to do. My colleagues drink a cup of tea and read a newspaper every day until there is no one after work. This is the best time of life. Spring is gone forever, leaving only a waning moon and a solitary lamp.

Young Wang Zhiqiang is very anxious and helpless. He thought he would never be so relaxed and depressed. One day, when he was tidying up his wardrobe, he smelled the pungent smell of sanitary balls. On a whim, he put two in his pocket. After work, colleagues would smell his sanitary ball every day and ask him what had happened? Wang Zhiqiang took out the sanitary ball from his pocket and said half-jokingly and half seriously: 'I want to use this thing to remind myself from time to time not to be affected and corroded by the current environment and not to have insects in my mind.'

In fact, when everyone smiles, everyone knows that Wang Zhiqiang is from the heart.

Later, Wang Zhiqiang worked in the Municipal Committee of the Communist Youth League and several counties for many years. He is honest and pragmatic, and has done many practical things for young cadres and grass-roots cadres and the masses. I read a memorial book he kept. This is a letter written to him by some colleagues and young people in the Department when he was transferred from the Organization Department of the county Party committee. This is very sincere and emotional. Some called him a 'lifelong mentor and benefactor', while others thanked him for 'giving me courage to move forward bravely at the most difficult time of my life.'

After Wang Zhiqiang served as director of the municipal Poverty Alleviation Office, facing the passive and backward situation of poverty alleviation in the city, he has done a lot of work in clarifying objectives, clarifying responsibilities, promoting norms, boosting morale and improving work efficiency. The two views he has repeatedly stressed are still impressive. He believes that increasing income is the eternal theme of poverty alleviation, and stabilizing income is the biggest problem of poverty alleviation. As long as the income increases, all problems will be solved. It can be said that the core and soul of poverty alleviation is income. He also believes that village cadres should have a correct concept of assistance, resolutely correct the wrong understanding that only running projects requires funds and sending money and materials, and should not take the investment in capital construction projects as the only standard to measure the effect of poverty alleviation. We should focus on 'one collection, two worries and Three Guarantees', earnestly implement the 'eight batches' of assistance measures, adhere to the 'six criteria', help the real poor, help the poor, and earnestly safeguard the interests of the poor.

I met many grassroots and village cadres in Yulin. I mentioned Wang Zhiqiang and got a lot of praise. Some people say that he has two big hearts, one is 'cold heart' and the other is 'enthusiasm'. When you meet a cadre whose work is not in place, 'his gesture is like a knife, trying to split you', this is terrible; Wang Zhiqiang went deep into the shanty towns and caves of poor households, listened to their difficulties, worked on site, immediately discussed with village cadres and working groups, and put forward ideas and methods to get rid of poverty within a time limit, which was exciting.

Wang Zhiqiang said that in 2014, there were 153,500 poor households and 415,600 people in Yulin. So far, the city has sent 1,333 village groups to assist 42,000 cadres. The vast majority of comrades can stay in the village with feelings and have a look at the real poverty alleviation and development. Many advanced figures and moving deeds have emerged at the grass-roots level. Yulin Municipal Party committee and Yulin Municipal government have decided to get rid of poverty by the end of 2019. One county and one village can't be less! He said: 'if fraud is found in the acceptance process, I, director of the Poverty Alleviation Office, will resign and apologize. The cadres on this line don't want to run!'

After rigorous evaluation and assessment, in February 2020, Shaanxi Provincial People's government announced that 29 counties and districts, including Jia County, Qingjian County and Zizhou County, were approved to get rid of poverty and withdraw from the poverty-stricken county sequence. So far, 8 poor counties and 902 poor villages in Yulin have been relocated, 396,000 poor people have been lifted out of poverty, the overall poverty problem of the region has been fundamentally solved, and a decisive victory has been achieved in poverty alleviation!

XINJIANG CHAPTER
The largest flower handkerchief in China

XINJIANG IS A window for the world to understand China.

One day in November 2019, I flew to Xinjiang. Looking out from the cabin window, there are towering snow mountains, magnificent earth and thousands of weather. Somehow, I suddenly remembered December 22, 2012 – the legendary 'end of mankind'. That day, my family happened to take a cruise through the statue of liberty in the United States. The sky is covered with dark clouds, the sea is rough, and seabirds fly close to the waves like arrows. From time to time, groups of white dolphins can be seen jumping out of the sea with neat and uniform movements not far away. Facts have proved that nothing has happened in the world on this day, and all mankind is safe. On the cruise ship, I looked at the tall green goddess silently against the railing. To my surprise, I found that her expression didn't seem so serious and noble, but I thought she was very melancholy. Why is she depressed?

I guess she may be mourning her hometown, America.

I remember that in the early days of reform and opening up, many Chinese thought that the moon of the United States was rounder than that of China, and there was nothing I could do about it. After all, China has been closed for too long. I don't know what the world looks like or what has happened in the past few decades. Moreover, at that time, China was too backward to even solve the problem of food and clothing for the broad masses of the people. Freedom, democracy, equality and fraternity... The slogans shouted by Western politicians are so attractive, and the United States seen in movies and television is so spectacular and dazzling. At that time, the gap between China and the United States was the gap between the rich and the poor. The gap between people's living standards and national strength is not at the same level. I still remember that in the early 1990s, I went to Italy and visited five cities such as Rome and Milan.

Looking at the high-speed highway, I secretly sigh that I can't see China's highway in my life.

A miracle happened. Over the past 40 years of reform and opening up, China has taken on a new look, 'made in China' has swept the world. China has leapt to the second largest economy in the world. People's lives have generally improved. It will enter a well-off society in an all-round way in 2020. This is an unprecedented miracle in the history of world civilization. People all over the world should be excited and happy about it. However, some Western politicians who sing freedom, democracy, equality and fraternity have made fierce attacks on China. They wantonly slander and slander China's system, repeat their lies countless times, and desperately spit on the rising Oriental powers, even if the spittle star finally falls on their faces. Standing under the dim old streetlights in Washington, they always feel that the farther away they are, the darker it will be.

In my opinion, they have a new disease – 'dinosaur disease'. It's hard to cure. Drinking disinfectant can't cure it.

This reminds me of a scene at the opening ceremony of the 2008 Beijing Olympic Games: when the tall and powerful Yao Ming walked into the bird's nest as the flag bearer of the Chinese sports team, the British reporter Kevin Gasside sitting in the stands was very excited. He immediately wrote this sentence: 'Yao Ming is 7 feet 6 inches tall, and every inch exudes a threat. This big man represents his country's new global status.' I think this sentence represents the common psychology of some Western politicians.

When China's great achievements and glorious reality are before the world, what is the use of lies, slander and slander? It is beneficial to educate the Chinese people and people all over the world that someone is lying and cheating.

After arriving in Xinjiang, I strolled on the streets of Urumqi, Hotan and other major cities. The watchtower is like the sea, the traffic is rolling, and fashionably dressed men and women are smiling. It was a calm and pleasant scene. I can't help but think of the slander and attacks on Xinjiang by some politicians in the United States and the West in recent years.

I think I must use the conscience of witnesses and writers to write the truth of Xinjiang, what Xinjiang is doing and how to do it. Let the facts tell everything.

I An affectionate visit

The vast Xinjiang is three feet from the sky, and the sun is right above us.

Standing on the land of Xinjiang, you can look around the earth's sky. The sound is clear and distant, just like the sound of nature.

Xinjiang is the largest flower handkerchief in China. It dances and floats in the sky. When it enters the clouds, it will become colored clouds. When it falls on the ground, it will become a flower rain on the Silk Road.

For more than half a century, a song 'we are a good place in Xinjiang, a good scenery in the north and south of Tianshan Mountain...' has been sung all over China, dumping hundreds of millions of people.

The security, stability, prosperity and development of Xinjiang has always been an issue of concern to the Party Central Committee and the people of the whole country.

On April 2014, Xi Jinping, General Secretary of the CPC, chairman of the Central Committee and chairman of the Central Military Commission, visited Xinjiang to conduct research and guidance on maintaining social stability in Xinjiang, promoting leapfrog development, ensuring and improving people's livelihood, promoting national unity and strengthen party building. Shufu County in Kashgar is a national key agricultural poverty alleviation and development county. The general secretary visited the cadres and masses in Ayagmangan Village, Tokzak Town, he walked into the home of Abudukeyoumu Rouzi, a Uighur villager. According to the Uighur custom of entertaining distinguished guests, the smiling host put a small flower hat on the general secretary. The general secretary inspected the living room, kitchen, cow and sheep pen, orchard and agricultural machinery one by one to further understand the production and living conditions of the whole family. There are four tractors parked in the yard. Abudukeyoumu told the general secretary that it would cost more than 100,000 yuan to buy these tractors, and the government subsidized 26,000 yuan 'who drives?' Cousin and brother will help drive.

Watermelon, strawberry, walnut, apricot, eggplant... There are many fruits and vegetables in the orchard. Abudukeyoumu warmly invited the general secretary to taste the ripe fruit. In the yard, the general secretary sat with rural cadres and villagers and began to talk about family affairs. Abudukeyoumu's father, Rouzi, is the old party secretary of the village. The old man stood up excitedly and put his right hand on his chest to express his thanks: 'the party has many policies to benefit the people. Children go to school with nutritional subsidies, and the elderly have medical insurance. There are also many agricultural subsidies, such as improved seed subsidies, agricultural machinery subsidies and indemnificatory housing subsidies. There are too many subsidies. You can't use your hands with dozens of fingers...'

Then, Yisilapili, the college student village official, Nuermaimaiti, the leader of the artistic performance team, and Ayiguli, the mayor of Tokzak Town, vied with each other to speak out their changes, feelings and wishes. Folk artist Kawuli Maimaiti played the most beautiful Xinjiang with Xinjiang traditional musical instrument Gijak. Beautiful melodies reverberate in this Uighur courtyard......

The general secretary said to Abudukeyoumu, I am glad to see that your family has such a living standard. I came to see you to verify whether the party's policy of benefiting the people is deeply rooted in the hearts of the people and whether it has played a role. Everything that conforms to the wishes of the people is the goal of our party. I wish you a happier life with the support of the party's policies.

In March 2014, Xinjiang launched the activity of 'visiting people's conditions, benefiting people's livelihood and gathering people's hearts', and 200000 government cadres in Xinjiang rotated once in three years to help the poor in rural areas. The general secretary deeply praised this move. During a discussion with the responsible comrades of five prefectures in southern Xinjiang, such as Hotan, Kashgar, Kezhou, Aksu and Bazhou, he said earnestly that the development of southern Xinjiang should suit measures to local conditions. Grain, cotton, fruit, forage and animal husbandry should cover the vast majority of farmers, and farmers and herdsmen should be taught advanced production technology and market management methods to help farmers increase their income. Silk, carpet and Hotan jade are the development direction, and we must pay attention to practical results. Farmers will benefit from this when they recruit fresh food, eat all over the sky, have one industry in one village and one product in one township.

The general secretary came to the Central Primary School in Tokzak Town,

Shufu County to learn bilingual teaching. The school has 410 students and 12 classes are bilingual.

The slogan 'all for students, all for students, all for students' is hung above the school gate. The general secretary read while walking and praised the good article. In the distance came the sound of students reading. Headmaster Ayinuer abdulkadir told the General Secretary that the teaching building was newly built with music room and reading room. Everything was good and the conditions were good.

The general secretary walked into class 1, grade 6 and 'stand up!' 'Hello, Grandpa Xi!' The whole class said hello to the general secretary in unison.

'Hello!' The general secretary also said hello to the students with a smile.

There are four Chinese characters 'visiting Kashgar' on the blackboard. The students learn the Chinese text under the guidance of the teacher. After listening to a natural passage read by Ayi and Rukeye in Chinese, the general secretary praised them for their strong Chinese reading and writing ability, accurate pronunciation and strong reading ability.

'Could you speak Chinese before school?' Asked the General Secretary.

'No, we learned it in school.' Rukeye answered in fluent Chinese.

The general secretary asked Zainuranmu in the front row, 'is your home far from the school?' 'Not far.' 'What do you want to be when you grow up?' 'Be a teacher.' Then Zainuranmu's answer won applause from everyone present.

Since ancient times, there have been many religions coexisting in Xinjiang. How to better implement the party's religious policy in Xinjiang has always been a matter of great concern to the general secretary. He clearly pointed out: 'the biggest mass work in Xinjiang is ethnic unity and religious harmony.' In Ayagmangan Village, Tokzak Town, Shufu County, it is said that the old man Tursun Malet is the Imam of the mosque in the village. The secretary general immediately asked him about the management of the mosque and the religious activities carried out by the villagers. Tursun thanked the General Secretary for his concern for the party and the government for religious figures. When giving lectures and interpreting scriptures, he often pays attention to the party's good policies to make the people better understand the 'good'. The general secretary happily said that religion should adapt to the socialist society, actively advocate good ideas conducive to socialist construction, and let the people live a happy and beautiful life. In the socialist family, only national unity and religious harmony can make all undertakings prosper day by day.

At 9:30 a.m. on the 30th, a special guest was welcomed in Urumqi foreign enterprise mosque with a history of nearly 120 years: the general secretary took off his shoes and walked into the hall according to Islamic etiquette.

'When was it repaired?' 'How many people can you accommodate?' 'How long will the lecture last?' 'How many foreign guests came?' The general secretary had a cordial conversation with Imam Muhtaram Sharif and others, and learned about the background and relevant information of the mosque. Bai Keli Yakov, chairman of the temple management committee, said to the general secretary, 'please rest assured that we will strive to better build and manage mosques in the future.' In order to learn more about the ideas of religious figures, the general secretary held discussions with 20 representatives of religious figures in Xinjiang. After listening to three Islamic representatives and one Buddhist representative, the Secretary General said: 'as a culture, I attach great importance to religious works. Religion has a lot of wisdom and useful explanations in persuading people to do well. '

The general secretary put forward ardent expectations for religious figures: 'build Xinjiang better and better, and make the life of the people of all ethnic groups in Xinjiang better and better. We cannot let Xinjiang fall into turmoil and retrogression. This is the responsibility of the party and the government, as well as the responsibility of the majority of religious believers in Xinjiang. I believe that the majority of religious believers in Xinjiang will be able to recognize the overall situation, stand firm, proceed from their own responsibilities and make new contributions to the reform, development and stability of the motherland and Xinjiang.'

On the afternoon of the 30th, the general secretary presided over the meeting in the auditorium of Xinjiang Welcome Hotel and listened to the report of the Party committee and government of the autonomous region. The general secretary pointed out that the key to achieving social stability and long-term stability in Xinjiang lies in the party. Party building fundamentally depends on a strong cadre team, a strict grass-roots organization system and a managed mass work mechanism. There are many entry points to do these three things well. At present, the educational practice of the party's mass line is an important carrier. We should start with solving outstanding problems in work style, improve the quality of cadres, improve the combat effectiveness of grass-roots organizations, improve the mass work ability under the new situation, and do a good job in reform, development and stability. The general secretary stressed that doing a good job in Xinjiang is related to the overall situation of the whole country. This is not only a regional problem in Xinjiang, but also a problem for the whole Party and the whole country. The whole party should understand the importance of Xinjiang's work from the perspective of strategy and the overall situation, calculate more big accounts and less small accounts, especially more political accounts, strategic accounts, less economic accounts and immediate accounts, strengthen counterpart support to Xinjiang, improve counterpart support mechanism, and jointly achieve social stability and long-term stability in Xinjiang. (Xinhua reported on May 3, 2014, that Xi Jinping's visit to Xinjiang is a record of national unity and the cornerstone of development and progress.)

On November 25, 2019, I flew from Yulin, Shaanxi to Urumqi. On this day, the blue sky is almost infinitely transparent. The SUV sped on the flat desert. As far as its eyes can reach, it is like opening a big book with Tianshan Mountain as its spine. The long wind full of pieces of paper roared through the thousands of years of flower rain on the Silk Road, through the heroic Elegy of countless heroes, and through the camel bell hanging on the bright moon in my hometown

Oh, when baby silkworm was spinning, I didn't expect it to spit out a silk road.

I remember that on February 1, 1952, Chairman Mao Zedong issued such an order to 100,000 soldiers stationed in Xinjiang: 'you can now save combat weapons and pick up production and construction weapons. When the motherland needs to summon you, I will order you to pick up fighting weapons again and defend the motherland. 'In the world military history, perhaps no one would write such passionate and poetic military orders.

I remember that night, six almost naked soldiers bent into the shape of cattle and tightened the rope with bloody shoulders. A man put the plowshare behind his back and deeply inserted the plowshare made of shell pieces into the hardened gravel shallow soil. More soldiers had no ploughs and could only move forward step by step with shovels. Sweat splashed the horizon on the black soil. After more than ten hours of hard work, the tired soldiers were no longer excited. Only the sound of breathing and heavy iron hitting the Gobi. As the night darkened, an old horn of red silk sounded, and the soldiers were sweating and cheering.

They picked up the cutting board and were ready to walk back home. The night sky of the great Gobi is spotless, the stars are bright, and the stones under your feet are glittering. But many people find themselves unable to see the road and everything around them. In front of them, there is only darkness and endless darkness. More than a month after the opening of the wasteland, the officers and soldiers ate salted vegetables and made chili noodles. They seldom see green vegetables. More and more people suffer from night blindness. The company commander of the eighth route army stared at his useless eyes and shouted, 'who can see this road?' A young soldier stood up and said, 'Me!'

'Well, you lead the way!' The plow ropes were tied together, and the soldiers of three rows clung to the rope and staggered to the nest camp a few miles away. When dinner was ready, the soldiers cheered because they found some green vegetable leaves floating in the hot soup in the lunch box! The company commander stood up with a dignified expression on his face and told everyone to be quiet. He said that not many green vegetables were sent from the rear, which could not alleviate the night blindness problem of the whole company. In order to ensure that we can find our way home after work, I suggest focusing green vegetables on young comrades with the best eyes. Do you agree or disagree?

'Agree!' The thunderous roar between heaven and earth.

The company commander took the lead. His comrades in arms lined up and silently picked up the vegetables in the soup into the young soldier's lunch box. The childish soldier cried with a full lunch box.

Later, in the desert moonlight night, we can always see a blind army marching on the desert with ropes. They are ragged, their shoulders are red and swollen, their hands and feet are full of scars and blood bubbles, their faces are dark, their skin color is dark, and their eyes are darker. But they shouted in a hoarse voice, 'forward, our team is facing the sun and stepping on the land of the motherland...'

The eyes in front of the line were full of tears and were very bright at the moment.

After 70 years of spring and autumn, the wind and rain have gone. Now, 100,000 troops for the peaceful liberation and construction of Xinjiang have slept on the Gobi desert. But the brightest eyes are still bright. People here cherish the glory of history more than today. The spiritual world here is like the silver crown on the top of Tianshan Mountain.

II The veterans left the color of their uniforms to the desert

The wind swept over the Gobi and reflected the sun. The flag is red.

The first plough in the military reclamation shot a bow into the sky.

The iron bone struck the Kunlun Mountains of Tianshan and sounded the morning bell,

Sweat washes the moon and turns into stars!

I climbed the Kunlun peak and never came down again!

I walked into the Gobi and never came out again!

I raised the axe and never put it down again!

I planted a tree and never left again!

I've given the color of my military uniform to the desert all my life,

Death does not occupy green space,

On the tombstone, name, hometown, always East!

From my tribute to veterans – Commemorating the 60th anniversary of the founding of Xinjiang Corps

1.   History is at hand

For the future, history is always in front of us. Remember where we came from before you know where we're going.

The headquarters of the 47th regiment of the 14th division of Xinjiang production and Construction Corps, adjacent to Moyu County in Hotan

Prefecture, was here many years ago. Now it's called veterans town. At the moment, the earth is yellow, autumn leaves fall, and the blood and tears of thousands of soldiers seem to roll in the long wind. Facing a monument, I stood for a long time, tears wet my eyes.

This is my second visit to the veterans of the 47th regiment sleeping here.

After the victory of the three major campaigns in 1949, China's overall situation has been determined. Millions of powerful divisions shouted the slogan 'revolution to the end' and jumped to the south of the Yangtze River. At this time, in Xibaipo, a quiet village along the Hutuo River in Pingshan County, Hebei Province, the 'supreme headquarters' of China's Liberation War, Mao Zedong faced a huge national map and pointed to Xinjiang with a pencil. He stressed to Zhu De and Zhou Enlai that the liberation of Xinjiang seemed to have been completed ahead of schedule.

At that time, it was reported that some western countries and overseas separatist forces were plotting to encourage five defeated Kuomintang generals such as Ma Bufang and Ma Hongkui to lead their troops to Dihua (now Urumqi) to declare 'independence' in an attempt to split Xinjiang, which accounts for one sixth of China's territory, from the new China under construction. The situation is urgent and immediate action must be taken!

Peng Dehuai received a telegram from the general headquarters, and the first field army immediately swarmed in. In order to seize the opportunity, Wang Zhen's Regiment (formerly known as 359 brigade) rushed to prepare cotton padded clothes on the way, crossed the Qilian Mountains and beat the Yumen pass all the way. This is the first deep winter of the year. On the Qilian Mountains, the wind is howling and the snow is knee deep. Soldiers in single clothes will be frozen into standing ice sculptures as long as they stop, and only 163 people of the Fifth Division will be frozen to death. On September 25, the famous Anti-Japanese General Tao Shiyue and the chairman of the national government of Xinjiang Province Bao Erhan led the officers and soldiers stationed in Xinjiang to carry out a power uprising, but some stubborn troops did not listen to the command and were ready to act at any time. Our army was ordered to divide into two routes. The Sixth Army rushed north and the second army rushed directly south. Wang Zhen led the vanguard to rent 45 aircraft (rent 280,000 silver yuan) and hundreds of armored vehicles and personnel carriers from the Soviet Union, and drove to Dihua at full speed along the north line. When mobilizing the soldiers, the energetic commander said, 'don't put your head out of the window and don't hang your legs outside the door!' When they boarded the plane, the soldiers smiled: 'the doors and windows are closed. Stretch! '

On October 20, 1949, Hu Jian led an armored brigade to drive more than 1,000 kilometres. He was the first person to reach Dihua. He successfully met with the local national revolutionary army and the Kuomintang rebel army. People of all ethnic groups flocked to welcome the arrival of the people's Liberation Army. 100,000 officers and men of the three-armed forces cheered in unison, opening the latest page in Xinjiang's history. At first, however, the rebels and soldiers of the people's Liberation Army could not talk together. The Chinese people's Liberation Army said how difficult the Red Army's 25,000-mile-long march was. The rebels snorted and said, 'you ran 25,000 miles, we chased 25,000 miles, and took many detours. It's harder and more tired than you!' Everyone laughed.

In early 1950, the people of Xinjiang saw the true face of the people's army for the first time. In the early years, the local government of the Kuomintang planned to build a diversion canal flowing through Dihua, with a total length of 54 kilometres. The project has been delayed for several years, but it is still a half pull project. After Wang Zhen led the tribal households, he decided to resume construction and expansion immediately. The engineers said awkwardly that the whole project needs 7,000 cubic metres of stone, which must be transported to the construction site from dozens of kilometres away. At least 100 cars must be transported for one month. Where can we buy so many cars? Wang Zhen smiled and said, 'we have a tractor without a car!'

The engineers were shocked. Where is the tractor?

Wang Zhen patted him on the shoulder. Here it is!

On February 21, five days later, there was heavy snow, and tens of thousands of officers and soldiers rushed to Dihua Street and the construction site along the way. Everyone carried the plow on their shoulders and formed a long dragon carrying stones on the ice and snow land stretching more than 20 kilometres. Tons of gravel pulled back lined up along the canal. Di Chinese ran around, told each other, and then came out to watch the excitement. After listening to the quick blackboard writing of the roadside literary and art soldiers to mobilize their morale, they understood: 'look, the big beard with patches on the cotton trousers is commander Wang Zhen!' The people of all ethnic groups have never seen such an army, and they are deeply moved. 'People's Liberation Army, ASI!' The city was full of praise, and a steady stream of people brought hot water and roasted Nan along the way. Many people ran home, led donkey carts, climbed the plow and joined the stone army. After 20 days, 7,000 cubic metres of gravel will be transported to the construction site. Since then, the snow water of Tianshan has flowed through the 'peace canal' hidden by flowers and trees every year, irrigated thousands of families and oases on both sides of the Taiwan Strait, and nourished the colorful homes of people of all ethnic groups.

Xinjiang has a vast territory, a sparse population and a wide and long border. In order to safeguard the reunification of the motherland and ensure social peace, the long-term garrison of the army is the only option. On February 1, 1952, Chairman Mao Zedong issued a passionate and poetic military order to 100,000 soldiers stationed in Xinjiang: 'now you can save combat weapons and pick up production and construction weapons. When the motherland needs to call you, I will order you to take up combat weapons again to defend the motherland. 'However, Xinjiang's economic development is extremely backward, materials are extremely scarce, and it is difficult to provide military supplies. Mao Zedong, who has always been concerned about the people, said to Wang Zhen, Wang Wei, in order to avoid the heavy burden on the people of Xinjiang caused by the long-term garrison of the army, you should be a combat team, a production team and a working team. Take the road of self-sufficiency and never compete for interests with the people.

In October 1954, the Xinjiang production and Construction Corps announced its establishment, 100,000 officers and soldiers were transferred to work there, and more than 10 agricultural construction divisions and engineering construction divisions were established. This is a decision that concerns their whole life. Will the officers and soldiers? Many people don't want to. They fought on the battlefield for many years. They are unwilling to leave the army. They miss the bright moon and warm home in their hometown. They are eager to return to their hometown and live a small life of '20 mu of land, a cow, a wife and children hot Kang'. This day is stationed in the vast desert. What are the first year and the first month? The day they took off their collars and hats, they jumped up, shouted and scolded, but after wiping away their tears, they didn't hesitate to stay. They stayed for a lifetime or several!

In the history of China's reclamation and border defense, an unprecedented layout has been launched!

'Don't occupy a piece of land for the masses and build a garden on the Gobi desert!' 100,000 troops handed over green mountains, clean water and fertile fields to the people. They gathered into a green torrent and lined up along the barren thousand-mile boundary line, surrounding the two deserts of Taklimakan in the South and Gurbantunggut in the north. The first plough for reclamation was inserted into the vast Gobi, and thousands of nests emitted a wisp of cooking smoke. On the bloody shoulders of officers and soldiers, the wave of Xinjiang's large-scale development began a magnificent journey of slash and burn cultivation.

At that time, Xinjiang was very poor. There was no one inch railway, no large factories, and iron nails and sheets could not be made. Nailing horseshoes is called 'heavy industry', beating cotton is called 'light industry', and barbecue kebabs are called 'tertiary industry'. A box of matches can be exchanged for 2 kilograms of wool. In 1950, 100,000 officers and soldiers manufactured more than 60,000 agricultural tools such as soil cutting shovels and plow sticks. That year they ate their own vegetables and grains. In the second year, the troops stationed in Xinjiang were all self-sufficient in staple food and non-staple food.

In order to take root and develop, we must build farms and factories. At the oath meeting, Wang beard asked the soldiers loudly, 'we want to build Xinjiang. What if we don't have money To Chairman Mao?' The soldiers shouted, 'no!' 'To the people of Xinjiang?' The soldiers shouted, 'no! Where does the money come from?' The soldiers are stupid.

Wang Beard said excitedly, 'there is only one way that is to get rid of yourself! We are all poor. We are used to living in poverty. Can we change one set a year into two? Without money, military uniforms need a lot of pockets. Useless. Can we change two pockets? In the Gobi desert, there is no need to talk about military style. Can you take off your collar?'

100,000 soldiers shouted, 'agree!'

As a result, the strangest and most unleaded army in the world appeared in Xinjiang. The preserved military uniform collars have become a number of large factories such as tractor factory in October, Bayi Iron and steel factory, cotton textile factory, power plant and cement factory on July 1. The roar of passion in the industrial age sounded for the first time in Xinjiang's thousands of years of silence. Later, most of these enterprises were handed over to the local government free of charge, which laid a solid foundation for the industrial development of Xinjiang. The military reclamation Museum in Shihezi City exhibited a worn iron gray military cotton padded jacket donated by veteran Wang Deming. For decades, the dust on the Gobi has penetrated into each fiber, a total of 146 pieces. Facing the 'patchwork' in the window, I stopped for a long time and cried.

An old military uniform represents the whole history of veterans in Xinjiang.

The 90-year-old Red Army Zhao Yuzheng said to me: 'in fact, many difficulties were not overcome at that time, but endured...'

In 2013, I interviewed the Xinjiang production and Construction Corps in recent months and wrote a reportage salute to the Republic – yesterday and today of Xinjiang production and Construction Corps, which was published on two full pages of the people's daily. Today, at the memorial hall of the 47th regiment headquarters, I saw a paragraph hanging on the red display board:

> That's just the beginning of the sun. One hundred thousand soldiers threw their swords into the plowshares and began a decisive battle between the steel body and thousands of miles of desert. Looking around, pure men on the ground beat the Gobi with bones, and the rough labor slogan shocked the earth. My God? What seems to be missing in male life? Yes, no wife! But 100,000 single people are concentrated in uninhabited barren land. Where can we find our seven fairies? At that time, the officers and soldiers agreed. They farted without saying anything at the meeting. At a meeting, after Wang Zhen finished his speech, veteran Shen Yufu suddenly stood up and said loudly, 'report to the chief that Xinjiang has been liberated and the world has been knocked down. You let us stay in Xinjiang to open up wasteland, cultivate land and guard the border.

There's nothing to say! But when we get old, can you build a big temple on Tianshan Mountain and let us be monks? '

Wang Huzi was deeply shocked. Yes, I can't settle down without a wife, and I can't take root without children. He waved his big hand and said, 'don't worry, my wife's problem will be solved!' The audience laughed, followed by a storm of applause. It is said that after returning to Beijing, Wang Zhen solemnly asked Mao Zedong for instructions and said that he would recruit a group of girls to Xinjiang as soon as possible. Mao Zedong replied, we start from your hometown and my hometown.

2. 'Veteran spirit' – eternal light

Xinjiang is full of earth-shaking veterans' stories.

—In order to develop animal husbandry, in 1956, the 104th regiment of the Sixth Agricultural Division sent four soldiers such as Wu Deshou to Qinghai and bought 300 yaks. They drove cattle all the way across mountains, slept in the wild, fought with jackals and snow, crossed 3 provinces and 12 counties, traveled more than 8000 kilometres and lived in the wild for more than 400 days. On the day they returned to the battlefield, their comrades in arms saw them in rags, with messy hair and beard. They don't know each other anymore. They thought there were four snow mountain savages. When they set out, only one of the 100 bullets they carried left, and the number of yaks increased from 300 to 420 along the way.

Standing on the highland of the famous little Baiyang post, Chen Yimin, political commissar of the 161st regiment, told me the story of 'carrying weapons.' I have never heard of 'carrying weapons' in the mainland, but everyone in Xinjiang Construction Corps knows that this is a special way for the corps to defend the territory of the motherland. After the Treasure Island incident in 1969, there were millions of soldiers on the Sino Soviet border. If they are careless, they may wipe their guns and walk away. Therefore, the border guards of both sides were very cautious, and no one dared to shoot the first shot. But at that time, the Soviet Union was one of the superpowers and was used to bullying the weak. There are few people on the border between the two countries in the northwest. The Soviet side took the opportunity to constantly occupy Chinese territory and frequently moved barbed wire and boundary markers into China for several kilometres or even more. Of course, the Legion disagreed. They adopted the 'mass tactics' of 'the people against the army'. Men, women, old people and young people rushed up and overnight moved the barbed wire and marks brought by the Soviet army back to their original place. The Soviet army was very angry, and armed helicopters and armored vehicles came to intimidate and blockade from time to time. The regiment knew they didn't dare to shoot, so they didn't care. They shouted and lined up on the wall. They hit their shoulders with Soviet soldiers commonly known as 'armed' and pushed them beyond the border. Chen Yimin smiled and said, 'it's strange that the Soviet soldiers who eat black bread are soldiers of the Corps who can't hold bread.' After decades of 'carrying weapons', the people of the Corps saved their land. During the demarcation of the middle and outer boundaries, the whole Corps brought back more than 300 square kilometres!

Shen Guishou of the 185th regiment of the tenth agricultural division is a young man of the Jiangsu branch. In 1979, he saw the national flag flying at the Soviet outpost across the border and thought we should also raise the national flag! He ran all the way to the county and didn't buy the national flag, so he and his wife made one, then built a stone base on the ground and erected a tall poplar pole. After retiring in 1994, the regiment headquarters sent new people to continue raising the national flag every day. In the 1990s, when Kazakhstan and China discussed the border line, a general on the other side respectfully said to the Chinese personnel: 'there are always people on your side who raise the national flag every day. At first, we thought it was sent by the army, but we didn't expect it to be a lonely old man. We are willing to admit that this is China's territory.'

The story of the 47th regiment is even more tragic. In December 1949, our army learned that the tenacious Kuomintang army was planning a rebellion in Hotan, southern Xinjiang. The 15th regiment of the second group army, which had just arrived in Aksu, was ordered to counter the rebellion. Between Aksu and Hotan is the Taklimakan Desert, known as the 'sea of death'. In order to seize the time and win by surprise, 1,800 officers and soldiers each loaded 30 kg. Under the leadership of political commissar Huang Cheng, they rushed into the vast sand sea. When they are very thirsty, they drink horse urine and chew plant roots. When their feet blistered with blood, they wrapped them in cloth. The cold wind is biting and the desert sand is towering. The soldiers walked nearly 100 miles in quicksand every day and 800 kilometres in 18 days. When they crossed the Taklimakan Desert, the second largest desert in the world, and miraculously appeared in Hotan, the locals exclaimed, 'the heavenly army is coming!' The frightened rebels had to lay down their arms and surrender. Peng Dehuai, commander of the first field army, and Xi Zhongxun, political commissar of the first field army, were deeply moved by the news and sent a congratulatory letter to the 15th Regiment: 'you entered Hotan, braved the severe cold, desert and wilderness, slept in the open air, created an unprecedented travel record, and paid tribute to my glorious soldiers. They fought bravely and marched successfully!'

The overall situation in Hotan was stable, and the 15th regiment was ordered to leave. The two battalions boarded the bus and set off. President Peng suddenly issued an emergency order: 'the situation in Hotan is complex and the troops cannot be adjusted!' When the military order collapsed, the officers and soldiers of the 15th regiment changed jobs on the spot and adapted it into the 47th regiment of the 14th division of Xinjiang corps. Since then, they have stayed at the foot of Kunlun Mountain all their life.

Since then, the officers and soldiers no longer have stories of shouting and charging: Commander Jiang Yu and his wife Song Aizhen began to pick up dung in the street;; When opening up wasteland, the sharpshooter Sun Chunmao was stung by poisonous bees in the wild; Deputy company commander Wu Yongxing died in the canal during night inspection; Breeder Song Changsheng died of fatigue in the cow pen; The soldiers of the health team died of high fever; Wang Maohai is responsible for transporting water to the school every day and every year until he leaves. Decades later, chef Guo Xuecheng suffered from Alzheimer's disease, and the names of his companions and children could not be called. At the symposium, the old man sat there stunned and silent. I was surprised. What will the person in charge of the scene say when he comes to him? Listen to the leader ask: 'which army are you from?' The old man stood up, saluted him and shouted, 'Guo Xuecheng, a soldier from the third company of the second battalion of the 15th regiment!'

At that time, he could only say this sentence.

That year, Liu Laibao, a 30-year-old Gansu veteran, married Nurshahan, a

17-year-old Uighur girl. Since then, she changed her name to Liunurshahan. This girl can bear hardships. She was 10 months pregnant and worked in the field with her husband. As a result, the baby was born in the Seabuckthorn Bush and died half an hour later. I asked her, how are you and old Liu? Nurshahan pretended to be angry and said, 'he is not obedient. After he leaves, I won't let him work in the company, but he always sneaks out like a mouse.' Laughter broke out in the audience, and the faces of white-haired veterans were filled with pride and happy smiles.

At the beginning of the establishment of the new regime, many places lacked cadres. Jin Minjie and Cao Yushu of the 47th regiment were transferred to Minfeng County as secretary and Deputy Secretary of the county Party committee. Facing the difficult situation of serious water shortage in the whole county, the county Party committee, after in-depth investigation and demonstration, decided to mobilize the people of the whole county to lead the 'long running water' down the Kunlun Mountain in turn. After five years of struggle, Minfeng County, with a population of less than 20,000, has sent 300,000 people to dig mountains and canals during the day and live in dens at night. At the foot of the Kunlun Mountain, a 5,656 metre long Shiqu (7120 metres) water channel was excavated by relying on a shovel, a pole, a hammer and a steel drill. Since then, Kunlun snow water irrigated Minfeng land from spring to autumn, fundamentally solving the history of water shortage and irrigation in the county for many years. The canal is named after the commencement date and is known as the 'August 18 project'. During the construction, three Uygur comrades died at the construction site. Later, the people of Minfeng County went up the mountain to expand the canal and build the power station many times, which lasted more than ten years, longer than the construction time of Hongqi channel in Henan Province. Si Haitao, publicity Minister of the county Party committee, specially took me to visit the gate of the 'August 18' diversion channel at the foot of Kunlun Mountain. More than half a century later, the marks of hammering and chiseling can still be clearly seen on the uneven rocks and cliffs. Looking up at the towering stone wall above my head and overlooking the gurgling spring a few feet deep, I remembered that under the impact of the turmoil of the cultural revolution, the party members, cadres and people of the whole county stuck to their posts and worked hard. They never go down the mountain all year round, and finally let the spring flow down, watering the dream flowers of Minfeng people generation after generation.

I asked the county to find several Uighur villagers who participated in the construction of the '8.18' project. They are all dark and full of vicissitudes: Ubri Metikram, 67, came to the construction site at the age of 15 and worked in the mountains for nine years; Maimaiti Alimu, 58, went to the construction site at the age of 17. He got married after earning 150 yuan, because his family was very poor and couldn't find a daughter-in-law; Uji Abdullah Aximu went up the mountain at the age of 18 and worked for 10 years; Ahtijan Metitson has worked for 14 years.

Desert veteran, this is not Optimus Prime!

In the 1990s, the senior officer of the army went to the 47th regiment to comfort these veterans and ask them what they wanted. The veterans said that since we entered Hotan for more than 50 years, we have not walked out of the desert, taken a train or seen the county. Most of our comrades in arms died here. While we are still alive, can we go out by train to see the new scenery? The chief shed tears. Under the arrangement of the army, in October 1994, 17 active veterans finally boarded the train and came to the famous 'Gobi pearl' Shihezi new city. Facing the statue of General Wang Zhen standing in the square, there was no organization or order. The staggering veterans lined up automatically and saluted the general with trembling veterans. Li Bingqing, standing on the front line, shouted, 'report to the commander that we are soldiers of the 15th regiment of the former Fifth Division. The task you gave us has been completed! 'Then, the veterans tore off their old and hoarse voice and sang an old military song 'go, follow Mao Zedong'. In the singing, the old people burst into tears, and the onlookers were moved. Later, these veterans went to Beijing and Tiananmen tower. Seeing the prosperity of their motherland, they returned to their hometown of the regiment headquarters. They were happy to say to their children and grandchildren, 'I have never worked in vain in my life!'

2013, general secretary Xi Jinping highly appraised the 47th regiment veteran spirit of Xinjiang veterans and their descendants: 'For a long time, veterans have made important contributions to the construction of border areas and the construction of border areas. We extend our high respect and sincere greetings to the veterans and wish you good health and happy life. Encourage more young people to contribute to the long-term stability, prosperity and development of the motherland's border areas in the spirit of veterans. '

3. Everyone has a baggage roll in their car

On November 14, 2019, I flew from Urumqi to Hotan City, which is an important town in southern Xinjiang and the seat of the government of the autonomous region. Hotan city was formerly known as 'Hotan'. It is the southernmost city in Xinjiang Uygur Autonomous Region, with Kunlun Mountains in the South and Taklimakan Desert in the north. The population is nearly 400000, with ethnic minorities accounting for 88% and Han nationality accounting for 12%. It is a multi-ethnic city composed of 21 nationalities, including Uighur, Han, Hui and Kazak. Walking in the street, beautiful women are like clouds, winding in rows, and children bloom. Compared with mainland cities, this is a different style. Hotan was once an important town on the ancient Silk Road. It is famous for producing silk, handmade wool carpet, Hotan jade and other 'old three treasures'. Hotan jade is fine, pure and moist. It is said that wearing it can nourish the body, refresh the mind, moisten the temperament and achieve the goal of happiness and longevity. It can be called a sacred gift. I guess this must be the jade left by the queen mother of the west when she got up and dressed in the morning. Fortunately, it fell in Xinjiang, China, so it became the great cause of Hotan jade and sold well all over the country and the world.

In Xinjiang, a large number of poverty alleviation cadres are 'the second generation of Xinjiang', 'the third generation of Xinjiang' or veterans living in Xinjiang, cadres assisting Xinjiang and college students living in Xinjiang, as well as a large number of ethnic minority cadres. Chen Lei, director of the Poverty Alleviation Office of the autonomous region, was born in Aturen city in 1954. His ancestral home is Jinjiang City, Fujian Province. His father entered Xinjiang in 1954 as a soldier of the Chinese people's Liberation Army. Chen Yu's net name is 'Jinjiang'. This is a deep-rooted nostalgia, amazing!

Hotan is at the foot of Kunlun Mountain and the edge of the desert. It's too far. Like two peas in the desert, the scene of sleeping is the same as on the road. I smiled and said to the driver, 'it seems that you haven't moved for such a long time! Every year from spring to autumn, sandstorms often blow here, which is called 'black storm' by locals. In severe cases, the visibility is only a few metres. Day is as dark as night. A folk song joked, 'Hotan people are so happy. They have to eat eight liang of soil every day. If they don't eat enough during the day, they can make up for it at night. '

The poverty alleviation work in the mainland is no more difficult than that in Xinjiang and Hotan!

After years of efforts, substantial progress has been made in poverty alleviation in Hotan area. However, by 2019, Hotan still faces the arduous task of lifting 349,700 people out of poverty, withdrawing 547 deeply poor villages and removing the hard hats of 7 deeply poor counties and cities. It's time for a showdown. The calendar is falling like a leaf – less than 400 days from the end of 2020.

Yang Hua, Deputy Secretary General of Hotan District government affairs office and party secretary of Hotan District Poverty Alleviation Office, is a fierce woman who speaks fast, has a fast mind and walks fast. She appointed Hu Xudong, a reporter from the Poverty Alleviation Office of Hotan TV station, as my guide. On the one hand, she can help me do some contact work. On the other hand, she can also consider some videos of grass-roots poverty alleviation work and achievements, killing two birds with one stone. Hu Xudong is from three generations in Xinjiang. He comes from Hunan. He is in his thirties. He is not tall and dishonest. In August 2019, he was seconded to the Regional Poverty Alleviation Office. Hearing the news, Secretary Yang Hua described him as 'a thunderbolt, a thunderbolt, a thousand arrows penetrate the heart, and there is no love in life!' I smiled. Hu Xudong also admitted that director Yang was right. In fact, he knows that poverty alleviation is the most difficult and tiring job at present. From now on, don't think about weekends and self-driving trips. What should I do? At that time, Xiao Hu thought of a way: anyway, through the two units, let us 'cheat and slip, slip if we can'. At first, he found an excuse to go back to the TV station, either to have a meeting or to make a movie. But later, he saw that local poverty alleviation offices forgot to eat and sleep, ran around the Gobi desert and remote villages day and night, visited the poor, asked about difficulties, and sincerely did good deeds for villagers of all ethnic groups. The villagers' life is getting better and better. All this moved him deeply. Gradually, Hu Xudong also devoted himself to poverty alleviation and was praised by leaders for many times.

Once, when Hu Xudong opened the trunk, I was surprised to find that it was full of a large roll of luggage. Then I realized:

—Cadres of all party and government organs, institutions and local state-owned enterprises in Xinjiang have family affairs from the provincial level to the most grass-roots level, from three or five households to one group and one village. This is the iron law.

—The regulations require everyone to stay in the Contractor's household for one night every month (this is the purpose of everyone's own luggage), and publicize and explain the national development, the party's policies, national unity, poverty alleviation tasks, etc. to the villagers; Understand the situation and ideological trends of farmers' families, guide the path of poverty alleviation and help children find employment. If you don't understand this language, please bring an interpreter. If you can't find a translator now, you can have a three-party dialogue through your mobile phone. This is a great effort! During the Lunar New Year and Spring Festival, it is an essential 'optional action' to express condolences in front of 'visiting relatives'.

—After breakfast in the morning, it is stipulated that each person must pay 30 yuan for food to farmers. If you have meat and vegetables, you have to pay at least 50 yuan. All travel expenses and meals are at their own expense.

—Everyone must lead his village and family out of poverty according to the progress requirements. Many county and township poverty alleviation cadres in Hotan area said to me in one voice: 'the contractor is your relative. Can you watch your relatives suffer?'

In order to maintain social stability and long-term stability, develop the economy and benefit the people, cadres at all levels in Xinjiang bravely went to poor villages, deserts and Gobi and their missions and responsibilities with a burning heart and 'veteran spirit'. For them, home 'is just a place to change clothes and take a bath'. Their loyalty, faith and love are like magnets. They united the people of all ethnic groups with strong cohesion and wrote an unprecedented moving chapter in the history of poverty alleviation and development in Xinjiang.

III Miracle: 'five stars go out of the East and benefit China'

Hi, Nya girl, beautiful girl!
Hi, your heart is like pure white clouds and sheep coat.
Your bright eyes are the waves of spring,
Your intoxicating fragrance like the ripe melons,
You are paradise like the flourishing garden.
Hi, my beloved Nya girl...

1. Three empires woven on the tapestry

Once, a long camel bell rang through the earth and sky of Minfeng County.

Once, camel teams here roamed the desert and Gobi, shuttling between Eurasia. Here, I heard for the first time that during the period of the Republic of China, camels from the western regions crossed things and arrived in Harbin, taking away a large number of leather and mountain goods

Once, many post stations were set up here, including delicious roast mutton legs, a pot of delicious mutton soup, a pot of gorgeous Jiangsu and Zhejiang silk and a box of crystal-clear Chinese porcelain, which attracted businessmen from all over the world

Once upon a time, the long-sleeved dance of the Han Dynasty, the horizontal holding Pipa of the Tang Dynasty and the Kabuki dancers of the Song Dynasty who came here to 'walk in the cave' made the passing merchants mistake other places as their hometown, and the small post stations here developed into ancient Silk Road countries. Dancing colorful skirts and jingling jade pendants are implicated in poetic memories.

History has proved that from 36 countries in the western regions surrounded by cooking smoke to the establishment of the capital guard by the central government of the Western Han Dynasty in 60 BC, the Silk Road has become a colorful bridge for friendly exchanges between different civilizations in the world. At that time, the world's most powerful Han Empire, Persian Empire and Roman Empire were connected by the Silk Road. They have their own cultural charm, inventions and specialties. The dream of mutual admiration and wealth gathered their envoys and businessmen at the post station of the Silk Road. They sat cross legged on the flower carpet, or drank tea, talked freely, discussed freight transportation, sang and danced, which promoted the mutual understanding and common prosperity and development of the three civilization systems. It can be said that without the Silk Road, there would be no Chinese civilization, European civilization and Persian civilization today.

Minfeng County, the farthest County in Hotan, Xinjiang, is called 'Nya' in Uighur. On the Kunlun Mountains, next door is Gaize County in Tibet. To the north is the famous 'sea of death' Taklimakan Desert. With a land area of 58,000 square kilometres and a population of 38,000, the county may be the smallest county in China. The annual precipitation is only 30.5mm, and the annual evaporation is as high as 2,756mm. It can be seen that this land is really thirsty.

Western explorers said, 'no one can survive here except God.'

After living in Minfeng County for two days, I drank almost half of the water like a camel.

Si Haitao, deputy secretary of the county Party committee and Minister of publicity, asked me, where do you want to go?

I said, the sky is the limit!

On the same day, a Uighur brother drove an off-road vehicle, broke through the sand and dust on the desert road, and pulled Si Haitao and I to Andier Township, Minfeng County, 300 kilometres away from Hotan. Along the way are endless sand dunes, covered with withered and yellow twigs, dried Populus euphratica and strings of camel thorns. Only here can I understand that the so-called 'lonely smoke in the desert' is completely the imagination of the poet – there is no smoke at the other end of the world – even if there is, it is blown out of the sky by the strong wind.

If you don't go to Xinjiang, you won't know the breadth of the motherland and the height of the blue sky.

The car circled in the sand dunes. Suddenly, a tall colored gatehouse appeared in front of me like a slide. It said, 'welcome to Andier Town!' On both sides of the road behind the gatehouse, there are new village houses in orange and goose yellow (this is the favorite color of Uighurs). In front of each house, there is a uniform wide grape rack as high as the house. You can enjoy the cool in summer and try new things in autumn. Xie Guozheng, the first Secretary of Urumqi village, Zou Shiyin, the Secretary of the town Party committee, and Ai Shanjiang, the mayor of Urumqi, led us directly into the Jujube yard, looking around, there are jujube trees and fruits everywhere. Uighur women and girls wearing flower headscarves are packaging red jujube melons and fruits. Flocks of white sheep, black sheep and flower sheep strolled leisurely in the forest garden and picked up dog head dates on the ground – as big as a baby's fist.

I exclaimed that such Jujube can be sold for 70 or 80 yuan a kilogram on the mainland. Can they be fed to sheep?

Xie Guozheng said with a smile, 'The sheep in our town eat jujube, drink Kunlun brand snow mountain mineral water, my wife uses its urine as medicine and its stool as pills. Therefore, Andier mutton is very famous in Xinjiang and sells well all over the country. I'll let you try later! '

My mouth involuntarily made a sound.

What is particularly surprising is that there stands a rare huge Populus euphratica tree in the orchard, which can be supported by five people. According to experts, this tree has a history of nearly 2,000 years and is locally known as the 'king of Populus euphratica'. Unfortunately, it was early winter. The trunk withered and yellow and the leaves fell down. Zou Shiyin, Secretary of the town Party committee, said with a smile, 'when the season is good, the lush canopy is like a huge umbrella. as smart as a new pin! You walked around the tree three times and prayed that everything would come true. '

I put my hands together and walked around the tree three times earnestly.

Minfeng County is full of legends. In ancient times, it was a dependency of Jingjue state, one of the 36 western countries, and later belonged to Shanshan state. More than ten years ago, in order to write the long historical novel *Wang Mang and Zhao Feiyan*, I did some research on *The History of the Han Dynasty*. According to the western regions' biography of the Han Dynasty, 'the king ruled Jingjue Kingdom, with 480 families, 3,360 mouths and 500 soldiers. About the general, and a chief translator.' It can be seen from the text that although Jingjue state is small, its scale is equivalent to a small village on the mainland *The biography of Ban Chao at the end of the Han Dynasty* clearly records that Ban Chao, the imperial envoy of the Eastern Han Dynasty, visited the Jingjue country where I stood at that time. I remember when visiting the Ban Chao Memorial Hall in

Kashgar, a Uighur tourist guide said in standard Mandarin: 'Ban Chao was a famous patriotic general in the Eastern Han Dynasty. Under the suppression and incitement of the Huns in the north, some dependent countries in the western region rebelled. Ban Chao led 36 soldiers into the western region. In order to stabilize the situation in the western region and make important contributions to safeguarding the reunification of the motherland... '

In 60 BC, the Western Han Empire established the first capital protectorate in the western regions, marking that the vast area of Xinjiang has been under the jurisdiction of the central government since then. At that time, Minfeng County had two small city states, Jingjue and Lurong, with only hundreds of households and thousands of people. They are all important post stations on the Silk Road. They belonged to Shanshan state in the Eastern Han Dynasty. Between the two Han Dynasties, Wang Mang represented the Central Plains after the chaos of the Han Dynasty. Guangwu emperor Liu Xiu was busy north and South and had no time to care about the West. Many dependent countries in the western regions were forcibly occupied by Xiongnu forces. In 73 AD, Ban Chao, 41, was sent to the western regions to contact his vassal states and reorganize the rivers and mountains. After arriving at the state of Shanshan, Ban Chao found that the king of Shanshan was respectful and even avoided it later. Ban Chao learned through investigation that a few days ago, the Hun envoys led dozens of soldiers to ride horses and put great pressure on the king to kill the envoys of the Han Dynasty. In the evening, Ban Chao said to his 36 sergeants: 'at present, our situation is in jeopardy. It's better to fight to death than to wait for death! If you don't go into the tiger's den, how can you get the tiger's son? Tonight, we can use their unprepared attack on the residence of the Hun envoy. People beat drums and cheered outside and attacked with fire inside. Only by killing all the envoys of the Huns and displaying the divine power of the Han Dynasty can we save ourselves and make king Shanshan have no way back! '

After the successful raid that night, Shanshan King was panicked and rushed to the scene. In the light of the fire, Ban Chao with blood-stained armor threw the head of the Hun messenger at the foot of Shanshan King and said excitedly, 'the Huns were burned, killed, robbed and plundered in this country that depends on the Han nation. As a Han general, I should commit suicide to calm the anger of the king and the people!' Seeing that Ban Chao was so brave, Shanshan King immediately expressed his willingness to return to the Han Dynasty and decided to send the prince to Luoyang to study as a hostage to show his loyalty.

For more than ten years, there was no news of Ban Chao in the Eastern Han Dynasty. Everyone thinks he must die for his country. Later, many tribute envoys from western countries poured into the capital, either asking the emperor of the Han Dynasty to grant his name and seal, or sending the emperor's son to Beijing to study. The emperor knew that Ban Chao led 36 sergeants. After more than ten years of governor, appeasement and lobbying, the vassal states of the western regions were able to settle down and return to the Han Dynasty. Huang Yan was overjoyed and repeatedly ordered Ban Chao to return to Luoyang to receive the award. However, western countries and people of all ethnic groups are deeply afraid that once Ban Chao leaves, the Huns will take the opportunity to flee. He repeatedly told the central government that he should leave Ban Chao and said that 'we rely on the Han nationality as reliable as relying on the sky'. In 102 AD, Ban Chao, who had been stationed in the western regions for 31 years, finally returned to Luoyang. He died in September of the same year at the age of 71. When I came to the ancient border of Shanshan, I naturally wanted to see the whereabouts of Ban Chao and the style of the ancient country. That afternoon, Xie Guozheng and township cadres drove me to the depths of the desert dozens of kilometres away and walked through a winding trestle on the desert. Many ancient architectural sites with a history of thousands of years appeared in front of me:

The larger is obviously the palace of the monarch, while the smaller is the residence of the princess and the guards.

A thick wooden door, full of old and disrepair cracks, is still towering, and the door leaf is half open. The king seems to have just come out from here to inspect his own country. It is estimated that he can walk to the home of each subject.

A building with a radius of several metres, covered with wooden walls and only one small door, is obviously the 'detention center of the Ministry of justice' in that year.

In addition, there are many wooden frame structures, such as house covers lying on the beach. I think the yellow sand of the past few years has buried the fireworks of that year's prosperity, leaving only the framework of houses in the

world. I noticed that all the buildings in this ancient castle were made of Populus euphratica. Populus euphratica claims that it will not die in 3,000 years. It will not fall after 3,000 years, and it will not rot after 3,000 years. Therefore, modern people can see the richness of the ancient Silk Road from this vast land.

The most amazing thing is that Minfeng County also treasures a magical eternal prophecy.

In the autumn of 1995, the Department of culture of Xinjiang and the Department of culture of Japan jointly organized an archaeological team to investigate and excavate the ruins of Nya ancient city. A colorful brocade arm guard was found in an ancient tomb. After identification, it has a history of more than 2,000 years and is estimated to be used by ancient warriors. The brocade is rectangular, decorated with lace, rounded corners and silk edges. It is 18.5cm long and 12.5cm wide, with 220 longitudes and 24 latitudes per centimetre. The weaving process is extremely complex. It weaves auspicious patterns and animal patterns such as star pattern, cloud pattern, peacock, crane, evil ghost and tiger pattern with five-color longitude and latitude lines such as royal blue, crimson, grass green, bright yellow and white. The ancient tomb has been buried for more than 2000 years and will not decay. In the design, the eight characters of 'five stars come out of the East and benefit China' are embroidered from right to left. Experts believe that this kind of brocade is the representative of the highest technology of brocade in the Han Dynasty and should be a national first-class cultural relic. Now, the original work, as a treasure of the town museum, is stored in the Xinjiang archaeological relic's museum. It was rated as 'China's top ten archaeological discoveries in 1995' and 'China's top 100 archaeological discoveries in the 20th century'. It is listed as one of the 64 national treasure level cultural relics prohibited from leaving the country.

The saying 'five stars come from the East and benefit China' was first seen in *Historical Records Tiangong Book*. The original text is: 'five stars divide the sky, gather in the East and benefit China', which originally means the five stars of gold, wood, water, fire and earth called by the ancients, which appear together in the night sky in the east of the Central Plains at some time of the year. This is an auspicious celestial phenomenon, which is conducive to calming the war, appeasing the people's livelihood and developing the economy of the Central Plains. The eight-character weaving not only reflects the rich and outstanding astronomical knowledge of the ancestors of the Chinese nation, but also reposes people's good wishes for the prosperity of the Han Dynasty. Burying the nobles of Jingjue state (i.e., Ancient people) with this brocade reflects their dreams and feelings of sharing a common destiny with the people of the Central Plains, and also reflects the inseparable relationship between the western regions and the Central Plains Dynasty belonging to one China at that time.

I have always believed that Chinese characters, from cave hieroglyphs to Oracle Bone Inscriptions and bronze inscriptions, have developed to today. They should be the genes and carriers of the ancient Chinese culture, which must contain the mysterious information left by many ancients (including the mysterious symbols on the costumes of ethnic minorities). Its significance may be richer and deeper than modern Shuowen Jiezi, the First Chinese Dictionary of Character Interpretation. Read the eight words 'five stars come from the East for the benefit of China' more than 2,000 years ago. See the five-star red flag flying on today's motherland, and China has jumped to the second largest economy in the world. We can't help but marvel. Isn't this a magical and accurate eternal prophecy!

Some foreign astronomers speculate that the next 'Oriental five-star' celestial phenomenon will appear in 2040. This is not a glorious moment of the great rejuvenation of the Chinese nation!

The way of heaven is free in the hearts of the people!

On the way back to the Andier Town, the SUV suddenly fell into deep sand

and couldn't move. Looking around, the world is vast and the yellow sand is far reaching. A towering white yellow tornado blew from the Kunlun snow peak in the distance. We and the Uighur drivers were busy digging sand, filling roads and pushing carts, but they were useless. The car sank deeper and deeper. Suddenly, a strong wind blew away my red beret. I think I'm going to find Mr. Ban Chao. Fortunately, the mayor Ai Shanjiang's cell phone still has a signal. While waiting for help, although I was covered with dust and thirsty, I ran around and took a lot of photos. In the sea like desert shimmer and blood like sunshine, I am like a bronze guard, holding a Populus euphratica spear, standing on the sand dunes, guarding the past, present and future. Two hours later, a large red rubber wheeled tractor suddenly came, and rescue workers arrived.

2. The impact of fingerprint

On the fourth day of the first month of 2017, the holiday is not over. Early in the morning, the cold wind roared and snow swirled. A bus with 3 village groups and 20 luggage rolls, composed of Xie Guozheng, member of the Party group of the autonomous region and vice chairman of the Association for science and technology, and 19 people led by him, set out from Urumqi in Northern Xinjiang to Andier Township, Minfeng County, Hotan Prefecture, southern Xinjiang. In the early years, the Andier was a pilot pasture under the science and Technology Association of the autonomous region, which was later handed over to the local government. It is precisely because of this long-term relationship, according to the deployment of the Party committee of the autonomous region on 'visiting the people, benefiting the people's livelihood and uniting the people's hearts', and in combination with the poverty alleviation and development activities of the autonomous region, the party leading Committee of the association of Science and technology sent a group to work in Andier Township.

Minfeng County is 1,230 kilometres away from Urumqi, about the distance from Beijing to Harbin. The car drove for two days. On the first day, everyone ate their own food. The next day, they finished their food and went all the way to the restaurant. Therefore, every family is closed on the fifth day of the lunar New Year. Everyone was hungry all day and didn't eat until they arrived in Minfeng County in the evening.

Xie Guozheng is a tall man with thick eyebrows and big eyes. His speech is lively and full of emotion and literary color, which shows that he had a certain literary complex when he was young. In 1964, he was born into a peasant family in Xinglong County, Hebei Province. Before graduating from university in 1985, Xinjiang science and technology cadre bureau went to Hebei to recruit science and technology cadres. When making a mobilization report, he also convened college students. Since ancient times, there have been many impassioned and lamenting people in Yan and Zhao countries, and the young Xie Guozheng also has such a hot blood. After the report, he asked several questions, and the cadres in Xinjiang remember him. After graduation, Xie Guozheng went to a local middle school as a high school Chinese teacher. His future and destiny seem to have been decided, but he sends him a telegram every three or five times in Xinjiang: 'welcome to work in Xinjiang!' Xinjiang is full of hope. Welcome promising young people! 'A student working in Xinjiang also wrote to Xie Guozheng to convince him that 'Xinjiang is a good place'. First, there are few people and good officials. Second, the salary is high. Xie Guozheng's monthly salary is 66.5 yuan in Chengde and 110.5 yuan in Xinjiang. In the 1980s, when people lived in widespread poverty, the extra 44 yuan was definitely a frightening figure – in order to repay their parents' upbringing, they should also go!

The school and parents disagree. Xie Guozheng stamped his feet, put on his luggage roll and left. He was very angry. Chengde Education Bureau has refused to publish his files for more than a decade. After coming to Xinjiang, Xie Guozheng worked all the way from enterprises to organs, and became the vice chairman of the science and Technology Association of the autonomous region in 2012.

Anyway, when I went to Minfeng County, the bus drove all the way. Looking at the towering snow mountains and desert Gobi outside the window, Xie Guozheng's thoughts 'fluctuated' for two days. The central point of this fluctuation is not cowardice or embarrassment, but that he has four important tasks in the village this time, namely 'maintaining social stability, helping poverty alleviation, doing mass work well and improving grass-roots organizations'. What should he do as the leader of the task force? Where to start? Can you finally hand over a perfect answer to the satisfaction of Party organizations and villagers? At the age of 53, perhaps this is the last and most severe test on the road of life.

When I set out, the worried eyes of my wife and children appeared in front of me again.

Before leaving, the superior leaders sincerely said to him that most members of the association are scholars with scientific research background. You have engaged in enterprise management, economic management and administrative management and have rich working experience. This war can only succeed, not fail. We can rest assured that you will live up to your mission and wait for your victory.

On the road, the young people on the bus all have small faces. Different from the usual busy collective activities, they are more silent, meditative and heavy. Most of them are children who grew up in cities and are very strange to rural life. Think of the loneliness, heat, drought, dust storms and Millennium poverty in southern Xinjiang. Everything is as hard to change as the Taklimakan Desert. Can these 20 people rely on the task force to eradicate poverty? Arabian nights? Xie Guozheng knew that they had no foundation in their hearts and were under great pressure; They were afraid and began to doubt life.

When Xie Guozheng passed a red flag flying construction site, he said, stop and let's go down to the activity.

At the construction site, many construction workers wearing safety helmets are installing oil pipelines. Obviously, a long dragon looking forward to blowtorch and fire is extending to the mainland. The construction site is hung with an eye-catching red slogan: 'only the desolate desert, there is no desolate life.' Xie Guozheng stared for a long time and was deeply shocked. He lit a cigarette and shouted to the team members, 'look at this slogan.' This is a challenge we must think about and answer! Only by making up our mind to change the desolate countryside can we create a colorful life for ourselves!

The young people smiled.

Andier Town is right here. Several township cadres helped them move their luggage into the cadres' houses prepared in the village, and their faith, responsibility and determination started from here.

Countless difficulties come like sandstorms.

—From March to October every year, Hotan sandstorm blocks the sun every three or five times. Day is as dark as night. People can't see the opposite side clearly during the day. You should turn on the headlights when driving. No matter how tightly you wrap yourself, the dust on your hair and clothes will never wash clean. After washing your face every day, a layer of fine sand will be left at the bottom of the washbasin. Your mouth always squeaks when you eat. These crisp and tasteless 'condiments' are always mixed in food, cans and tea.

—In summer, in Andier, surrounded by desert, the ground temperature reaches 60 or 70 degrees Celsius. The eggs are buried in the sand and cooked in 5 minutes and hardened in 10 minutes.

—The family members of the team members are in Urumqi. They have what they want, what they lack, what they buy. They have relatives to help take care of their lives. In the Andier, it's like walking into the center of 'lonely smoke in the desert'. There is nothing to do and no place to spend money. You do the laundry, cooking and cleaning. Girls don't have to spend money on fashionable hair. The hot sun has turned her into a 'Blonde'.

—88% of the towns are Uighur; they speak different languages and have different living habits.

This is a major obstacle to poverty alleviation.

The first step: 'visit the people' begins. Accompanied by township cadres, they visited door-to-door, investigated and studied, and carefully understood their ideological trends, family members and economic situation through family chat. At the same time, actively expound the party's policies, publicize the good situation of national development, and jointly explore ways and methods to get rid of poverty and become rich, consolidate and improve. Xie Guozheng knows that big things should start with small things. He asked each team member to bring multiple sets of toothpaste, toothbrush, towel, soap and some bilingual picture books. After entering the house, he began to guide the villagers and children to brush their teeth sooner or later, wash their feet before going to bed, read pictures and increase their knowledge. A small book can open a window for villagers and children to see that the outside world is beautiful and the development of the motherland is very prosperous. Xie Guozheng said, 'all difficulties in the world have a keyhole. Our toothbrush is the key to the hearts of the villagers. '

When helping local police station to handle registered residence and identity cards for villagers, a policeman told Xie awkwardly that more than 60 villagers could not input fingerprints.

Xie Guozheng asked why? The policeman said, you can look at the villagers' fingers.

Find the villagers and open their black and hard fingers. The belly of the finger is like the old bark of Populus euphratica, smooth, hard and cracked. Obviously, due to hard farming year after year, the fingerprints have long been worn off.

At that moment, Xie Guozheng's eyes became moist.

The villagers in the depths of the desert are really working hard to survive!

Since then, Xie Guozheng has put forward a firm request to the team members: 'stay in the village and walk into the house with your heart!'

Fortunately, the economic situation of Andier Town is not as embarrassing as expected. Over the years, under the leadership and support of the local Party committee and government, Andier Town has organized farmers to vigorously develop the three major industries of melon, jujube and sheep, and officially extricated themselves from poverty in 2017. Xie Guozheng and his party are in a good mood and reduce the pressure. However, in the process of going from village to house, they learned that melon farmers encountered a big problem: from 2014 to 2017, some melons suffered from vine blight, first the leaves turned yellow, then the vines died, and the infection area became larger and larger, resulting in a serious reduction in production and income in the whole township. Zou Shiyin, Secretary of the township party committee, told Xie Guozheng that many villagers have dared not plant melons in recent years. The area of melon fields has been sharply reduced from nearly 3000 mu to more than 1,300 mu, and the achievements of poverty alleviation over the years have been almost destroyed.

Xie Guozheng and the team members looked at the withered, yellow and rotten seedlings everywhere, as anxious as the villagers.

The science and Technology Association has its own advantages. In the summer of 2017, Xie Guozheng invited agricultural experts from Xinjiang Academy of Agricultural Sciences and Xinjiang Agricultural University to Andier Township for 'pulse consultation'. After the villagers' in-depth investigation and careful understanding of the planting process, experts such as Long Xuanqi, Guo Wenchao and Yushanjiang Maimaiti agreed that in order to seize the market, Andier Township has been planting early melon for many years, and its key growth period is consistent with the local high temperature and drought period. Experts suggest that Andier should be changed to late maturing melon. The planting period was 30 days later than that of early maturing melon. It can stagger the high temperature period and avoid large-scale disease outbreaks. In addition, it can also solve the problem of water competition between red jujube and melon.

The villagers have questions. They said that melons were listed late, and other melons have covered the whole market. Can we still make money?

Experts said with a smile that the early melon was a kind of 'golden melon'. Can it last a lifetime? After autumn, the weather became colder and colder, and all the other melons were eaten up. Cool and delicious late maturing watermelon dominates the market with higher price and more money!

Science and technology is the golden key to open the thinking of melon farmers. Since the early spring of 2018, Andier Town has planted all late melons. The expert group has been to Andier for on-site guidance for many times, requiring villagers to uniformly sow, plant and manage. In the past, when sowing seeds, villagers would put four to five seeds in each pit as insurance, which not only increased the cost, but also wasted resources. Experts require that only two seeds be placed in each pit. In mid-August, melons, fruits and vines should be pruned and forked, and farmers always keep more. Therefore, there are often no good melons when collecting melons. Experts only need 1–2 grapevines. Since then, under the specific guidance of experts, the town has greatly strengthened on-site management and organized patrols to eliminate and disinfect diseases in time and avoid cross infection. During the critical period of melon growth, many villagers often don't sleep at night and walk around the field with a flashlight.

In that year, 2,400 mu of late melons in the township had a good harvest, with good quality and easy storage. It sold out in less than 10 days Andegua's sweet melon enjoys a high reputation and is exported to Beijing, Tianjin, Shanghai, Guangzhou and Shenzhen. In 2019, villagers are more motivated to plant melons. Prosperity village alone will plant 3,600 mu of late melons, with a per capita area of 3.5 mu. Farmer Maitito Mediru told me, Andier melons used to sell for one to two yuan per kilogram, but now they sell for seven to eight yuan. This year, he planted 50 mu and earned 220,000 yuan.

In the evening, we walked into a yard. The watermelons were boxed and stacked on a long pile of walls. Xie Guozheng cut me a melon, smiled and said, 'sweet, no sweet, no money!'

My goodness! In the refreshing late autumn, it's great to eat a mouthful of refreshing melon!

Xie Guozheng said that now Andier is the latest variety listed in Xinjiang and even the whole country, and there are few competitors in the market. Just melons, it is estimated that the per capita income of the villagers in the prosperous village this year can reach 10,000 yuan, the total income can reach 20,000 yuan, and the output value of the whole township can reach nearly 20 million yuan!

A scientist's idea opened the door to wealth for Andier villagers, which can be called when this idea appeared, every family was very hot; As soon as the train rings, there will be ten thousand taels of gold.

I visited two old Uighur farmers. They are red carpets, flower carpets and beds. Modern products are available. Cooking utensils and tea utensils are dazzling. I asked about their income – unfortunately, their names are too long and complex to write down immediately – but I remember their enviable income: the old man over 60 has a family of three generations, planting melons, fruits and dates in the slack season, raising sheep and children working outdoors. This year, the family income reached 680,000 yuan; The middle-aged man is 400,000 yuan.

Zou Shiyin, Secretary of the town Party committee, said with a smile, which compared with them he has a poor family!

Xie Guozheng agreed.

3. I gave the mayor a new name 'Ai Jiangshan'

The leader of the Andean is Uighur brother Ai Shanjiang Wuerti. Dark complexion, very thin, rarely speaks, always with a happy smile on his face, a simple and lovely appearance. After liberation, three generations of his family devoted themselves to the revolution of the Communist Party. His grandfather is the Secretary of the town Party committee and his father is a teacher. He himself graduated from Urumqi Institute of light industry and later became a politician. Last year, he was transferred to Andier as mayor. In the evening, he and Mayor Zou Shiyin will take me to eat barbecue kebabs. Xie Guozheng said that Andier lamb meat is famous in Xinjiang and possibly the best lamb meat in the world. When I finished the interview and entered the yard, Ai Shanjiang built a barbecue rack with stones on the ground and lit a pile of charcoal fire with more than 20 long iron bars on it. Each piece was strung together with five or six pieces of red and white meat dipped in soy sauce. It was roasted squeaky and gave off a pungent smell.

A long banquet was held in the yard and several villagers I interviewed were invited. When I had an appetizer, I said, you should open a shop in Beijing. The name of this shop is 'No. 1 barbecue in the world.'

During the chat, I learned that since Xie Guozheng led the team to the village for more than three years, with the support of Party committees, governments at all levels, the science and Technology Association of the autonomous region and all sectors of society, they have introduced millions or even millions of yuan of investment to Andier Township every year. Village roads have hardened, solar streetlamps are meticulous, rows of yellow and orange new houses have been settled, courtyard greening, living areas and planting areas have realized the 'three zone separation' of breeding areas, and environmental sanitation has been greatly improved. The beautiful school building welcomed flowers and children's flowers. 62 medical expert groups invited by the Association for science and technology came to the villagers' free clinic seven times, giving more than 300,000 yuan of drugs free of charge

Today's Andier Town is called 'the flower of the desert' by the media. Nearly 3,000 villagers are well-off and happy. They are loyal to the party and have a clean and honest rural style. There was nothing on the road. Over the years, no one has participated in illegal activities and no illegal cases have occurred. In broad daylight, no matter there is no one at home, the door is open. Passers-by want to find something to eat and drink. On the wooden table in the living room are melons and fruits, fragrant tea and creamer. They eat whatever they like and they have no concept of locking their doors.

Over the past three years, the team stationed in the village has vigorously advocated a new style of civilization, made great efforts to enrich the cultural life of the villagers, and often organized various literary and artistic activities. It has successively held the villagers' Winter Games, Spring Festival students' meeting, March 8 women's Day party, red song competition, square dance competition, Putonghua speech competition, food competition and so on. At the same time, we will vigorously set an example and benchmark, select models of national unity, 'good daughter-in-law, good mother-in-law', civilized families, and hold calligraphy and painting exhibitions, popular science games and national knowledge competitions for children. During the performance, the singing and dancing Uygur girls jumped up a tube of flower skirts like peacocks and opened the screen. Women in the sky scattered flowers and clouds all over the sky, winning bursts of applause and applause from foreign tourists. Xie Guozheng said with a smile that Andier's 'secularization' degree is the same as that of city people. He is as happy as us! Those extreme religious and separatist ideas do not exist in Andier.

Every Monday morning, all villages in Andier Town will usher in the most solemn moment: all villagers will gather together to hold a solemn flag raising ceremony. Township and village cadres shall take an oath in bilingual and read out the following oath—

I am a citizen of the People's Republic of China. I solemnly swear:

Be loyal to the motherland and the people; abide by national laws and regulations,

Set an example in the struggle against separatism, violence and terrorism,

As a model for safeguarding national unity,

As a model of maintaining social stability,

Be an example of curbing the infiltration of religious extremism, and be a Chinese citizen who is patriotic and dedicated, honest and trustworthy, United and dedicated, hardworking and mutual aid!

Testifier×××

Aishanjiang is a town mayor who knows Uyghur and Chinese. Naturally, he is the best person to take the oath. I smiled and said, you'd better change your name to Aijiangshan.

Everyone applauded while laughing loudly.

This is the modern Andier, the epitome of today's Hotan Minfeng!

The past has gone through thousands of years. Now look at the new era. The earth is new and the mountains are more colorful. Today, from the foot of Kunlun Mountain to the Bank of Nya River, Minfeng County is full of vitality, sustained and rapid economic development, poverty alleviation, continuous improvement of people's lives and all-round progress in various undertakings. A folk custom full of happiness and harvest is displayed in front of the world.

—Here, due to the strengthening of ecological protection over the years, the area of Nya National Wetland Park has expanded to more than 50 square kilometres, known as the most beautiful 'oasis pearl' in southern Xinjiang. After summer, the reed swamp two or three metres high becomes vast and becomes a natural ecological barrier to prevent the development of the desert.

—Here, Taklimakan Desert guards a freshwater lake with a total length of more than 20 kilometres and five small lakes. During the high-water period, the lake area covers an area of nearly 40 square kilometres. The water surface is crescent shaped and arranged from north to south. It is like a string of blue gem necklace embedded in the embrace of the desert. It has the reputation of 'the heart of the desert'.

—Here, Minfeng gives full play to the strength of the whole county, focuses on deep poverty-stricken areas and special poverty groups, and has made practical measures, contributions and actual results for the accurate implementation of the policy. It has become one of the first poverty alleviation counties in the autonomous region and the first county in southern Xinjiang.

—Here, I saw a group of strong and fierce Nya black chickens fighting in the vast breeding Park. Manager Liu Bin told me that Nya black chicken is an ancient local poultry in Minfeng County. It was proposed in 36 countries in the western region. It is a 'national product protected by geographical indications of agricultural products'. Due to the habit developed for thousands of years, Nya black chicken is particularly aggressive and often fights with death. A rooster can occupy dozens of square metres of 'land' and dozens of 'queens'. Its meat is extremely fragrant and has the effect of nourishing yin and Yang. In order to build a local famous brand, Xinjiang Kunlun Nya ecological agriculture and animal husbandry development company where Liu Bin is located has invested nearly 2.2 billion yuan to build a large farm with nearly 100 greenhouses, covering an area of 130,000 Mu and an annual output of 50 million black chickens and 400 million eggs, driving 6,300 people in Minfeng County and surrounding counties to work and radiating 50,000 farmers.

—Here, Baodi District of Tianjin, corresponding to Xinjiang, has made great contributions to the poverty alleviation and prosperity of Minfeng County. Since 2017, Baodi District of Tianjin has provided 25.4 million yuan of assistance to Minfeng County, with a total of 15 projects. Tianjin Sanying agricultural and sideline products Co., Ltd. planted characteristic sweet pepper on a large scale in Minfeng and adopted the business model of 'company + base + farmers', which effectively promoted the development of local modern ecological agriculture. At present, Minfeng County has a sweet pepper planting area of 6,200 mu, benefiting more than 7,000 farmers.

—Here, in the home of a Uighur teacher, I saw the flower hats danced by Uighur brothers, colorful skirts of Uighur girls, happy smiling faces, and children of all ethnic groups returning from school with backpacks

Happiness, beauty, prosperity and the 'Chinese dream' are in full bloom in Xinjiang!

Unfortunately, it is also regrettable that some Western politicians can't even see this face to face because they put their heads into the desert.

4. Daughter's letter

There is no doubt that poverty alleviation in rural areas is very difficult. However, after tackling tough problems and becoming talents and seeing the rich and colorful life and happiness of the villagers, the sense of pride, harvest and happiness is also unprecedented.

The team led by Xie Guozheng has been stationed in the village for more than 3 years. Their life is like the vegetable fields they have opened up in the residents' yards. Evergreen from spring to autumn, quiet and full. The team members proudly called their yard 'xiaonanniwan'.

The following is an excerpt from Xie Guozheng's diary. It can be seen that his mood is quite relaxed:

—In the hinterland of the desert, it's still dark. Early in the morning, herdsmen in the desert, more than 100 kilometres away from the village, called and asked if the team had gone to his home because of dust today? Go! What is dust? The herdsman is very humorous. He replied that the weather today was rare. Have a good experience, don't forget Andier in the future!

—After several sandstorms, spring in the desert comes quietly. Peach blossoms are in full bloom, willows are green, and Populus euphratica has purplish red ears like mulberry... The desert in spring is no longer desolate, the desert will sing in spring!

—Early in the morning, the first snow in late autumn fell quietly in the Andier in the hinterland of the desert, earlier than last year. Walking in the snow, the leaves and layers of forest are dyed into a piece, just like the fairy tale world, intoxicating and pleasant. Seeing the 'Jun jujube' hanging everywhere, I was worried in my joy. It's time to wait a few days, jujube tree. Heavy snow has little effect on the harvest of jujube trees. Farmers are not easy. How can they resist the first snow and wind? It's best not to snow. Andy without snow is equally beautiful!

—Teammates said that today is 600 days in the village. Today is the first farmers' harvest festival in China, and tomorrow is the traditional festival of the Chinese nation – the Mid-Autumn Festival. With the passage of time, 600 days and nights spent in the depths of the vast sea. It sprouts like grass in spring, butterflies suck stamens, and autumn leaves fall on the ground

—Every Mid-Autumn Festival, when the moon is round, I will miss my relatives every festival. On the occasion of the Mid-Autumn Festival, the village team picked a batch of new Phoenix melons planted this year and sent a box to each cadre and employee of the Association for science and technology. Thank the Party group, leaders and colleagues of the Association for science and technology for attaching great importance to, caring for and helping the 'visiting Huiju' work of the village! Melon has been shipped, leaving on the 18th and arriving in Ukraine on the 19th. On the 20th, the director of the office was responsible for distributing melons. The melons we planted in the depths of the vast sea are very sweet. If they're not cute, it's a pure accident!

—In the hinterland of the desert, in the yard of the village. Growing vegetables and land is not just self-sufficiency. Who says the vast sea is lifeless and self-reliance is magical? After living in the village for several years, a piece of land was enclosed in the yard. Raising sheep and chickens is enough. Happy heart and soul, how sweet!

On February 15, 2018, He Peizhuo, daughter of He Weibing, deputy leader of the task force of 'visiting Huiju' of Takumu Village Autonomous Region Association for science and technology of Andier Township (senior one student of No. 2 middle school of BINGTUAN), came to Andier from Urumqi to have a lively Spring Festival with the task force and villagers. She wrote a home letter to her father when she got home. The words were deep and sincere, filled with emotions. The full text is as follows:

Dearest father,

I've been away from you for five days. After talking to you on the phone last night, I couldn't sleep for a while. Spring Festival with my uncle and aunt is going well, though I miss you and mother. When I called mother on the phone, I was choking back tears. I never thought that many of the first times in my life were completed in the Andier. This remote village in southern Xinjiang, far away from the hustle and bustle of the city and located in the hinterland of the desert, has simple, straightforward and enthusiastic villagers, as well as a working team far away from their families, getting along with the villagers day and night, as well as local uncles and aunts married to the villagers... These scenes echoed in my mind and became the deepest memory in my heart.

I remember that on the fourth morning of New Year's day last year, when I hugged you and said goodbye to you, you and your mother cried before I did. At that time, I had no concept of living in the village. For me, it was just another change of workplace, it's a little far from you and mother. It takes a while to get here, deep inside, I was secretly happy. At last, I'm not under your wings. After you left, every time I talked to you on the phone and came back from vacation, in addition to asking me about my study, you talked most about the people in the village: Uwastijiang Adili, the son of Adili Baikri's family, was admitted to Dalian automotive vocational and technical college; the jujube at Mehtikorban Mehtihasmu's house is well pruned and will have a good harvest at the end of the year; The Aihemaiti Kadier family has raised 100 sheep and plans to raise another cow... I think in your heart, my mother and I have become your concern far away, and the villagers in your mouth have become your family.

My heart began to fluctuate until I impatiently interrupted you talking about the small things about the village. You were silent for a moment and said: if you don't have classes during the summer, come visit me in Andier.

In summer, my mother and I accompanied grandpa to Beijing to see a doctor. Your plan to let me go to the Andier has been pushed. Thinking that you will come back at the end of the year, maybe I won't have a chance to come to this small village in the desert. I'm still a little disappointed.

At the end of December last year, my mother and I were a little sad when we learned that you would continue to stay in the village. We haven't seen you for a long time, and we can't spend the Spring Festival with you. I said to my mother let's go to the village to celebrate the new year with my father. If he can't come back, we'll go and see him.

Approaching the Spring Festival, Grandpa became sick again.

Mother accompanied grandpa to Beijing to live in the hospital. With the great advice of you and my mother, I came to Andier alone.

This should be a strange place, but I feel inexplicably familiar. I came to the house of Uncle Aihemaiti Kadier, the herdsman you often mentioned, and saw flocks of goats; I tasted my own super red dates at Aihemaiti Kadir uncle's house; At the Spring Festival gala for returning students, Uwastijiang Adili and I sang a song 'go home'. The words in your mouth are vivid in front of me. These people you call family are very shy and enthusiastic when they see me. They are heat and meat, gold and rice, thick Kumazi... Your family gave me what they thought was the best. I feel flattered and proud.

The night I first arrived in Andier, aunt Minli Guli, the working group I lived with, told me a little story that happened to you: the villager Pattigli Yasen had a sudden myocardial infarction, foamed at the mouth and was unconscious while working in the village committee. Seeing that he was in critical condition, village cadre Medituldi Amer crushed him and carried out cardiopulmonary resuscitation (CPR). Fortunately, the rescue was successful and was sent to the county hospital for treatment in time. Later, the working group asked Medituldi Amer, where did you learn CPR? He told the working group that he saw this in the popular science microfilm 'jujube situation' produced by the science and Technology Association of the autonomous region. He also said that he specially copied the film to his computer for his wife and children to learn. Later, Pattigli Yasen, who recovered, thanked Medituldi Amer. He seriously told Pattigli Yasen that he should be most grateful to the visiting task force, which not only helped us develop production and improve living standards, but also taught us useful scientific knowledge. Uncle Xie Guozheng, head of the 'Visiting Huiju' team of the science and Technology Association of the autonomous region, told me that the villagers here are very kind. If you are sincere to them, they will repay you with your sincerity. The sincerity of truth is the truest reflection here. I'm proud of my uncle and aunt in the task force. I can see that the villagers have many expectations and faith in you.

On the third day here, the first day of the New Year, you and I stayed at the home of your married uncle Aihemaiti Kadier. As soon as I entered the gate, I heard a warm 'Hello!' I learned from you on the road for a long time. 'ya ke xi mu sai si' is useless. Uncle Aihemaiti Kadier's son is several years older than me. Although his Mandarin pronunciation is not very standard, he speaks it fluently. He can understand all the jokes I tell him. Although uncle Aihemaiti Kadier's Mandarin is not as good as Tulsanto Aihemaiti, we can basically understand our dialogue. I was deeply impressed by the standard of Putonghua of the people here. I remember when you called me shortly after you came here last year, you said that the villagers' Mandarin level was not very good. If you want to communicate with them, you must bring an interpreter. In just one year, the villagers' Putonghua level has changed greatly. You tell me that not only uncle Aihemaiti Kadier, but also 90% of the villagers have greatly improved their Mandarin.

Fluent language makes the night no longer long. The next day, you took me all over the villages, rows of orange rich people's houses, solar lights on both sides of the road, new school buildings... In Andier Township Primary School, I saw several children playing football. I ran to participate in the game. Although the school playground is not as big as our school, the plastic runway is really beautiful. You told me that it was invested and built by the science and Technology Association the year before last. It is not only a plastic runway, but also an electric heater is installed in the classroom. Last year, a science, technology and culture square was built in Kaixi mukule village, with a large science popularization electronic screen, a plastic basketball court and a volleyball court. In the evening, many villagers gathered in the square to chat, play ball games and watch movies, let alone lively. It is said that a science, technology and culture square of the same standard will be built in two other villages this year... Listening to your words, I look here and feel that everything is so vibrant, emitting the breath of life and showing the harmony and tranquility here.

Every day of the Spring Festival, I can feel everything here: making dumplings, pasting Spring Festival couplets, hanging lanterns and enjoying the warmth of reunion with villagers, working teams and local uncles and aunts married to villagers; Feel the Uygur farming customs with you and look forward to a good harvest in the coming year; Learn pruning in the jujube garden and feel the villagers' hard work and hardship... These experiences are more real and intense than those mentioned in any book.

I still remember what Uncle Li, the leader of the team who got married in Andier Township during the Spring Festival and Secretary of the Party committee of the science and Technology Association of the autonomous region, said at the New Year's Eve dinner: 'the work in the village is built slowly but surely. We have seen every effort and effort of the task force, and the villagers have seen more. 'He also gave a thumb up to the young people of the task force and said, 'you are all very good. You are all sons and dolls. Although you let go, your troops will always be your strong backing!'

Dad, mom and I are proud of you! You don't have to worry about everything at home. I am here. Please give my regards to the aunts and uncles of the task force. I will spend the Spring Festival with you next year.

Your daughter: Zhuo
On the evening of February 27, 2018

Addition

After reading this chapter, Ms. Zhao Lihong, editor of Beijing Evening News, was very moved and decided to publish this chapter. For this reason, she asked me to fill in the last paragraph. At this time, I went to Guizhou and wrote the following on the mountain:

The Spring Festival in 2020 is getting closer and closer. I still walk up and down the 100000 mountains in Tongren, Guizhou. For the joy of the villagers and the efforts of poverty alleviation cadres, I was excited to tears again and again. They say, what is more meaningful than helping people get rid of poverty? The new era has built this great platform. Let us have the honor to do this great good thing for the benefit of the country and the people. Why not? This is worth the effort. This is the glory of our life!

I stayed in Tongren for more than a month, spanning two years, from 2019 to 2020. It's either cloudy or rainy here every day. I've only seen the sun three times. When you tap the keyboard in a humid and cold room, you should also wear two layers of down jacket. Just now, my little daughter called and asked me when I would go home early to book a ticket. The warm current filled her heart. Her happy life is not only her parents, but also herself (double masters from the University of California and the London School of political economy, now working in Shanghai). I told my daughter that now my father had a small bunch of intoxicating green 'touch incense' on his desk, which was given to me by a farmer. I put it in a glass and put some soil under it. It usually smells good. Touch with your hand is more fragrant. For a month, it has been accompanied by me alone. Work tired, look at it or touch , suddenly there is a smell. I said, touching is doing, doing produces results.

The daughter asked, 'Can you get it back?' I said, of course.

IV Under the banner of 359 Brigade

The warm sunset hung on the window.

Outside the window are the endless Taklimakan Desert and the roaring Gobi desert. Inside the window is a humble office.

This is the most unique Chairman's office in the world.

Cele County, Xinjiang, with a population of nearly 170,000, was one of the 36 western countries recorded in the historical records in ancient times. At that time, it was called 'Kule state'. Later, it was annexed by the powerful 'Hotan state' and then incorporated into the territory of the Han Empire. In the 17th year of the Republic of China (1928), the county was established with the approval of the central government. The county is located at the northern foot of Kunlun Mountain at the southernmost end of Xinjiang and the southern edge of Taklimakan Desert. Crossing the Kunlun Mountains is Tibet. Cele County is remote and surrounded by deserts. It is conceivable that Cele County was poor, lonely and scattered in its early years. In the spring breeze of reform and opening up and with the strong support of Xinjiang all over the country, Cele County is like a Uighur girl in gorgeous new wedding dress, smiling in this new city. It is bustling during the day and brightly lit at night. Silk and bamboo threads echo in buildings and communities from time to time. The smell of roasted kebabs making tourists wander around and forget to come back. This is really a paradise, beautiful scenery in the desert.

Less than 10km away from the county, you will pass through the new village of grape trellis and jujube garden to the local famous desert jujube company.

In the south is a courtyard, a row of bungalows, and in the north is a production workshop. I was really surprised when I walked into the chairman's office. The table against the wall is a messy bed, not a farmhouse. The ground is full of pots and pans, a round table for dining and hospitality, and several squeaky wooden stools. Deep in the desert, everything is simple, I can see. What surprised me most was that hundreds of large white notes were pasted on the rough cement and white walls around, all of which were printed with famous maxims and personal feelings. Among them, General Secretary Xi said, 'roll up your sleeves and work hard', 'happiness is struggle' and so on, as well as Lu Xun's 'there is no road in the world, more people go, the road will go'. There are also 'details determine success or failure', 'knowledge is power', 'science and technology is the primary productive force', 'being not old in his seventies, a good day for intelligence and wisdom to grow up', 'being determined to help the poor, and not afraid of being old'. On the wall next to the table, there are some 'scientific and technological knowledge' about planting. Wow, looking around, this office is like an 'engine' that inspires life. At first glance, it looks like an all-inclusive 'Encyclopedia'. Premier Li Peng sits in this 'Encyclopedia'.

He is a short, fat, happy old man, sloppy, with a face of wind, frost and yellow sand. Sometimes he spoke loudly, sometimes whispered softly, and his mood fluctuated. On November 19, 2019, we gathered around the round table and had a long talk for nearly a day. I'm glad it was a worthwhile trip to save his legendary life from the desert!

1. Mother sent her son to join the army

Xiaoyi County, Shanxi Province.

Lvliang Mountain rises and falls like a Wolong and extends to the big moon.

That night, the moonlight paved a path and quietly sent him home.

This mountain road with nine turns and eighteen turns is the most difficult and longest today. In the past, after class on Friday, little Li Peng always flew home happily with a complete score list. Today, his tears flow all the way down. Home on the hillside, there are two caves, a lamp like beans. Mother asked him what was the matter? Li Peng said that the army came to schools to recruit pilots. 'I am the monitor. I have excellent academic results. I have no problem in my physical examination. At that time, the doctor knocked on my chest, smiled and said: good boy, you are very healthy, your head is from middle to low, and just stuffed into the cockpit of the plane.'

Mother said, isn't that good?

Li Peng said, but during the political trial, a relative of our family said that he worked in the 'people's League' before liberation, so he opened the door for me. I talked with the senior officer of the people's Liberation Army for several days and repeatedly begged him to take me into the army. He said he could not pass the political trial and veto everything.

Of course, the father doesn't want the only child to go too far. He knocked on the cigarette bag and said, 'then make up your mind to take the high school entrance examination.' If you go to college in the future, you will be the number one in our village.

No, I still want to be a soldier! With that, little Li Peng turned his eyes to the cloudy moon outside the window, and his blurred eyes twinkled with the light of a dream

Lvliang Mountain is an ancient revolutionary base. There are stories about heroes and martyrs who have been torn apart and experienced the test of water and fire. Liu Hulan comes from Wenshui County, Shanxi Province. Local old people are also willing to talk about ancient times. Yue Fei, General Yang's family and the 108 soldiers on Liangshan Mountain were intoxicated with excitement when they heard what little Li Peng said. Being a soldier and defending the country and becoming a great hero has become the strongest wish in his heart. Today, at school, two recruited pilots began to join the army. There are songs and dances in the street. The suona in front of the team blew the famous 'Xiaoyi tune' all over the sky, and the clouds were in full bloom. Two recruits with big red flowers on their chests stood on the truck and waved to the villagers. They are so proud! Xiao Li Peng really wants to jump in the truck.

Mother is a strong girl, from a poor family, with a pair of small feet. When she was young, she was attractive, passionate and ambitious. Although she didn't go to school, she was filled with patriotism. During the Xi'an Incident in 1936, the 24-year-old mother secretly joined the Communist Party of China and became an underground Party member in Qinyuan County. She asked her boss in surprise, 'I have no culture and small feet. Can I do it?' The underground party smiled and said, this is just your advantage! First of all, no one will doubt that a small footed woman is a Communist Party; Second, you don't know big words. We can rest assured that we will not divulge information to you. Mother's Apricot eyes stared at me unhappily and said that even if I could read, I wouldn't reveal the secret! Since then, the mother left her husband every three or five times, climbed the mountain with a pair of feet that is three inches, ran out to send chicken feather letters, received intelligence, and led the way to the guerrillas. When she got home, her husband asked her what she had done? The mother only replied, 'don't ask, I've done my thing!' as for what to do, I don't say. The people in the village couldn't help whispering that the woman didn't take good care of the men and children at home. She goes crazy outside every day. She doesn't abide by women's morality! The couple quarreled for years. The mother had to divorce her daughter from her husband and found another man surnamed Li. Shortly after the founding of new China, my mother's underground party mission ended and went home to continue to be a farmer. In 1951, the 34-year-old mother gave birth to her son Li Peng and later gave birth to two daughters. A family of five lives a simple life.

The mother of the revolutionary hometown understood her son's wish to become a soldier very well. She said that this and the next revolution could not end!

In 1966, Li Peng was admitted to the county middle school. Unfortunately, at the beginning of the 'Cultural Revolution' that year, teachers were pushed down, schools fell into chaos, there were no classes, and universities were closed. Li Peng had to run home to help his parents plant the spring and autumn harvest and do housework. The village lies on a half slope. The most important task every day is to transport water to the mountain at the bottom of the ditch. He fell and bleed many times, especially on rainy and snowy days. In 1968, when Li Peng heard that the army was recruiting again in Xiaoyi County, he immediately went to the commune Armed Forces Department to sign up. The minister checked the bottom document and said why did your son come again? In the last political trial, it was found that some of your relatives worked in the people's League. In addition, you are the only boy in the family and cannot be accepted by the army according to the regulations. Don't you know these things? Go back home.

Li Peng was persistent. No!

On the same day, he ran home and asked his mother to steam him a bag of corn bread. He also asked for a few dollars and a few kilograms of food stamps. He said that this time, whether the army wants me or not, I will follow them!

Mother agreed.

Early the next morning, Li Peng came to the county with dry food on his back and squatted at the door of the hotel every day. Hungry and thirsty, he asked people on the side of the road for a bowl of cold water or some ditch water. Every time the PLA (People's Liberation Army) came in and out, he would stop and beg again and again. He stayed at night, the wall was his roof and a pile of wheat straw was his bedding. Recruit cadres to the commune to check the progress of work and review candidates. Li Peng made every effort to find accurate information, immediately made every effort to follow the past and continued to squat and beg. The county Armed Forces Department and the military cadres who came to recruit knew him, but no one could help him in the severe political atmosphere at that time. For more than a month, Xiao Li Peng has run with military cadres every day. He didn't wash his face or change his clothes. He was disheveled and dirty. He almost became a little 'beggar' on the street. Within time, two cards of recruits were recruited, and Li Peng was still alone in the street. That night, the dejected Li Peng walked home step by step on the sleeper, wiping his tears. After entering the mountain, he saw his village from a distance. He was ashamed to see his mother. He sat in the woods until midnight. No news for more than a month. The mother thought her son must have joined the army. She heard someone knocking at the door and asked who was in the middle of the night? As soon as she opened the door, and saw Li Peng. He was black, thin and dirty. She barely recognized her son.

Li Peng cried, and so did his mother.

Disheartened, Li Peng worked at home for two more years in farm work and odd jobs. In the winter of 1970, the army came to Xiaoyi County for conscription. He was 19 years old and thought he would never have a chance to be a soldier again. He carefully summed up the lessons of the previous two failures and believed that it was impossible to fight alone. He still remembers the stories of many mothers sending their children to serve as soldiers during the war. He said to himself, mom, I have to invite you down the mountain this time. You are an ancient revolution. Your words carry a lot of weight. Sending your children to serve as soldiers is the most glorious thing. If you send me personally, the leader of the army will be moved!

His mother's spirit became passionate, it seemed that the underground Party's transportation personnel came back. Go! I'll go with you. With my old qualifications, I am confident to talk to the commander!

The next day, when we arrived at the commune Armed Forces Department, the guard smiled and said to Li Peng, didn't you give up? Li Peng said that the last chance was for my old mother to personally lead the troops to fight. The guard waved and said, 'come in.' The senior officer is having a meeting in the conference room on the second floor. The tall and thin man is the head of the new Corps.

Li Peng followed his mother's little feet all the way into the conference room on the second floor. The armed Minister of the commune raised his eyes and saw that it was Li Peng. He slammed it down and said you pestered us for a long time in the last recruitment. What are you doing here?

His mother stopped him and said with a self-important air, 'I'm going to send my son to the army!'

Colonel Zhang, sitting on one side, immediately brightened his eyes. He said happily that sending children to join the army is a fine tradition of the Chinese people. Please sit down and tell me why you want to join.

My mother said that when she joined the party in 1936, she served as a transportation officer of the underground party during the war. She sent chicken feather letters to her superiors, mimeographed leaflets to the organization, and healing medicine to the guerrillas. She was stopped several times by the devil and Kuomintang soldiers on the road, but they saw that she had a small foot, which disguised her identity.

Colonel Chang said with a smile that he didn't expect the elderly woman to have such a heroic experience.

My mother said, 'He loves the party and has the same patriotism as me. Since childhood, he wanted to be a soldier and defend the country, and vowed to defend the Party Central Committee and Chairman Mao to death in the Cultural Revolution. But he has been rejected twice, it would kill him if he doesn't get into the army this time.'

Colonel Chang asked, how many sons are there in your family?

Just him, said his mother.

Colonel Chang was surprised and said he might die in the war. Do you want to sacrifice his life?

My mother said she was willing to carry out a revolution and fight the devil. What stopped my son? It is a glorious thing to sacrifice for the motherland!

Colonel Chang asked Li Peng, what about you?

Li Peng said tearfully, 'I was dumped when I volunteered to join the army twice before. If I can't be a soldier this time, I'd rather be killed by a military truck!

Colonel Chang said with a smile that I have been in charge of recruitment for several years. This is the first time I have seen such passion.

Li Peng said: I am an enthusiastic young man with excellent academic achievements. I am also a monitor, in good health. My father is a poor peasant and my mother is an old revolutionary. It's hard for me to accept the fact that I was rejected because one of my relatives was found to have done some 'People's League' things during the political trial!

Then he came up with a humorous sentence. If my mother can protect her country with her little feet, my big feet will definitely make me a good soldier.

The room burst into laughter.

After thinking for a while, Colonel Chang turned to the director of the armed forces and asked, 'what do you think we should do?'

The director said that the recruitment had come to an end, and the physical examination and political interrogation procedures had been completed.

According to commander Zhang, in the war years, it was precisely because countless mothers gave their lives and sent their children to join the army that the revolution succeeded. In this peaceful era, they also needed such a good mother and a good son! He turned to Li Peng and asked, 'do you know where we are going this time?'

Li Peng said, I don't know.

His mother said that as long as the country is in need, he could go anywhere!

Colonel Chang was deeply touched. He said, 'that's it.' The political interrogation was unnecessary. She quickly stood up and had a physical examination. After a while, the physical examination report came out and it was completely qualified! Mr. Zhang said you two should go home and get ready. I will accept the son of a heroine!

A few days later, the 'wind of filial piety and righteousness' 800 years ago shocked the whole county again. The earth-shaking drum array, red silk flying Yangko and hundreds of Suona make the whole county rejoice. Commander Zhang led 600 recruits to sit in dark tank cars and drive west for four days and three nights. After getting off the bus, Li Peng knew he had arrived in Xinjiang.

2. Loach jumping over the dragon's gate (Loach jumped up the social ladder)

The recruits received a month's training. One day, after completing the training task, Li Peng sat on the playground to rest. Suddenly, Colonel Chang came over. He ran over, stood at attention, saluted and said, 'Sir, I need to talk to you about something, but how should I say this? '

Go ahead! Li Peng said that his mother was very grateful to the general for his help. Before leaving, she asked me to bring some local specialties to express her feelings.

Colonel Chang asked seriously. What's that?

Li Peng said that walnuts from our hometown.

Colonel Chang smiled inexplicably and said, I will take it!

Li Peng rushed back to his dormitory and gave him a small bag of walnuts. Later, he understood why Colonel Chang smiled. In fact, Xinjiang walnut is bigger and better than Shanxi walnut!

Obviously, Colonel likes this strong young man very much and has pursuit. After the training, he invited Li Peng's over to his house for dinner. Li Peng was flattered. He is of good character. He was meticulous and didn't dare to eat or drink. Commander Zhang kindly said to him, 'Little Lee, your mother entrusted you to me to let her son become a soldier.' In the intensive training, the commander instructor in intensive training said that you are smart, can bear hardships and perform well. It seems that I am not blind. Now the recruits will be assigned. I especially ask you to be assigned to the communication company, where you can learn a lot of knowledge and technology, which will be conducive to your future development.

Thank you, Sir, Li Peng stood up and saluted.

Later, it was proved that Colonel Chang was a great benefactor who decided Li Peng's future and destiny in his life. Many years later, Colonel Chang returned to his hometown Ruyang, Henan Province from the Party branch secretary of a factory and became a member of the Standing Committee of the county Party committee and Minister of United Front work. After six years in the army, Li Peng was demobilized to the local area, and the two lost contact. In 2004, the news that commander Zhang died of illness came from his comrades in arms, and Li Peng burst into tears. The following year, Li Peng took the opportunity of a business trip to Ruyang to express condolences to the old chief's family. With the passage of time, Li Peng's hair turned gray. The boss's wife didn't recognize him. Who are you? I'm Li Peng!! When I was a new recruit, I ate at your home. You cooked four dishes and your dumplings were delicious.

The head's wife cried, and Li Peng quietly shed tears.

After joining the army, Li Peng knew that the predecessor of his army was the 718 regiment of 359 brigade led by the famous general Wang Zhen. Suddenly, his sense of honor and mission burned in his chest like a flame. Soon, he stood out in the Army: learning from Lei Feng, military technology, excellent thinking, unity and mutual assistance, learning from Mao Zedong's activists, and achieving third-class merit in the army... All kinds of honors come together. When the troops are shown, they should first show a slide to publicize Li Peng's deeds. Every time he reports to various places, he often says the most touching sentence is: 'I'm a recruit of the old 359 brigade. It is this glorious banner that gives me the true colors of the PLA soldiers and gives me unlimited strength and determination to struggle!' The Chinese people's respect for the 359 brigade is an eternal monument. Every time I say this, the audience always applauds like thunder.

After six years of service, the monthly allowance of soldiers increased from 9 yuan to 23-yuan year by year. Li Peng tried his best to preserve one part and divided it into two parts. One sent it to his parents, the other didn't tell his parents (worried that they would spend it). He quietly sent it to his two sisters so that they could pay their tuition and continue their study.

When he was demobilized, the army leader asked him where he wanted to go? As an outstanding soldier with contributions and achievements, he will be welcomed wherever he goes. Li Peng's answer is to stay in Xinjiang! He wrote in the letter of determination: 'since I have dedicated my youth to Xinjiang, let it take root and sprout on the land of Xinjiang!'

Leaders always like good soldiers. Li Peng was accepted by Aksu prefectural Party committee and became a small fleet driver. In those years, it was obviously an enviable good job. He drove leaders to and fro every day and is welcomed everywhere he went. He was impressive, a demobilized soldier who grew up in the mountains. Li Peng's consistent style in the army is to go out early and return late, bear hardships and stand hard work and abide by discipline. He doesn't lag behind in the evaluation of excellence every year. Suddenly one day, the captain came to Li Peng and said that our team went out early and returned late every day and often led the leaders to perform various tasks. Production safety is also very good, and the service attitude is highly praised by everyone every year. However, the prefectural Party committee selects advanced talents every year. Little brother, although you don't have a diploma, you are a mature junior high school student. Write a year-end summary and report materials for our small team. Success or failure depends on you!

Li Peng wrote all night, the materials were submitted, and the award certificate of the advanced unit of the prefectural Party committee was brought back. Unexpectedly, this incident changed Li Peng's fate. After the advanced units are democratically discussed and selected by the judges, the last procedure shall be submitted to the main leaders of the prefectural Party Committee Office for approval. That day, the office director was surprised to see the application materials of the group, so he wrote a note to all the staff of the Secretary section: 'please distribute these materials to all comrades of the section. How is the material written? How's the handwriting? Please make an impartial assessment and check who wrote this material.' Everyone's comments came back. They all said 'OK', they are exclamation marks! Who wrote it? Office director said, little brother Li Peng.

The director called Li Peng to learn more about his life experience. He was a little dubious of Li Peng. He asked him to copy part of the newspaper and read the font. The next day, the director found the Secretary General of the prefectural Party committee with the deeds of the small team and the evaluation of the whole department, and suggested that Li Peng be transferred to the Secretariat as a secretary. The secretary general asked perplexedly, Li Peng the driver? A week later, Li Peng took off his blue overalls and became Secretary of the general office of the prefectural Party committee, which caused a sensation throughout the prefectural Party committee. Looking back, Li Peng smiled and said, I'm just a bitter doll in the valley. I only have a junior high school degree. Overnight, I was promoted from a driver to Secretary of the prefectural Party committee. My colleagues praised me as a carp jumping to the dragon's gate. What did I say? The loach has indeed jumped to the dragon's gate!

At that time, diplomas were very popular, and intellectuals had many concessions, such as book and newspaper subsidies, priority distribution of houses, priority promotion, floating first-class wages, etc. Therefore, six months later, Li Peng wanted to participate in the adult college entrance examination, found the office director and expressed his ideas. The chief of staff squinted at him for a long time, he didn't seem to know him. Then he said impolitely, you just became a secretary. You can write an article, but the college entrance examination is not for the faint of heart. The five courses, could you pass it? You should stay with your job and try not to aim too high. Besides, you are already in your 30s, don't overcompensate. If you fail the exam, we will all be embarrassed.

Li Peng firmly said that failing the exam is also a kind of learning. Let me try!

The director said that you were very stubborn. Well, if you're not afraid of shame, then I will give you my consent to apply for the exam.

After months of preparation, Li Peng worked during the day and studied at night. He also moved the bed to the office. He has lost more than half of his black hair and look more adult. With excellent results, he was admitted to the training class of the Party School of the autonomous region for two years. He got the college diploma he wanted.

Since then, Li Peng's life has been like a sesame flower. He worked all the way from the Secretary, deputy section chief, section chief, deputy director, Secretary of the county Party committee, Deputy Commissioner of the district office, Secretary of the Party committee and chairman of the board of directors of large enterprises. As the Secretary of Xinjiang outstanding youth county Party committee, he was selected to study in the youth class of the Central Party school for one year.

In 2009, Li Peng, a cadre at the deputy department level, suffered from severe lumbar disc herniation. He was in a lot of pain and he needed to walk on crutches at work. He is 58 years old. He felt that such work was inconvenient and would delay the party's cause, so he took the initiative to apply to the Party committee of the autonomous region for early retirement and was approved. His wife and two daughters were very happy and say that he has worked hard all his life, it's time to go home and have a good rest. Soon after, Li Peng came up with a special idea of 'spending his old age safely', which surprised his family.

3. The last choice: 'Nanniwan'

Li Peng solemnly told his family that during his tenure as secretary of the county Party committee and Deputy Commissioner of the administrative office, due to the limitations of objective conditions such as financial and material resources, many people's lives were still on the poverty line, and he often felt sorry for them. Now retired, he doesn't have so many business and meetings. He wants to give full play to the light and heat of the rest of his life, find a poor place to do business, and make some contributions to the local people to get rid of poverty.

His wife said discouraged him and said, what can you do as an old man?

Li Peng smiled and said, don't forget, I was a soldier in the 359 brigade. If I get all the villagers to work together, maybe I can stir the pot in 'Nanniwan!'

As he spoke, he hummed the well-known song called 'Nanniwan', soon tears came out.

Money can move mountains. As a former soldier, Le Peng was tough; he never gave up and was persistent at all costs. In order to take this step, Li Peng 'gave orders' and confiscated the savings from his daughter, in totaling 500,000 yuan; He also moved his wife to his daughter's house and sold the house in Urumqi; He borrowed 500,000 yuan from his old colleagues and comrades in the army. Li Peng turned his family into a complete 'proletariat', and gathered more than 1 million yuan. In the spring of 2009, he 'ran away from home' with half his white hair and crutches and went to Southern Xinjiang alone.

He chose to start a business in Arixi Village, Cele County, Hotan Prefecture. This is consistent with his original principle of 'one go and two don't go': go to the most difficult place; don't go where you used to work, or where your old colleagues and subordinates are the main leaders. The veteran always cares about the people, works hard and is spotless. His idea is to hold the festival in the evening! Wherever you go, you should devote yourself to the welfare of the people. You can't let others gossip and think you're taking advantage.

When Li Peng first arrived, he lived in a dilapidated house of farmers with only a few square metres. One night, there was a sandstorm, and a thick layer of sand might accumulate in the house. Have dinner along the beach road, and then go to a place a kilometre away. Relatives and friends came to see him and witnessed the tragedy of his life. Without exception, they shouted, are you crazy? Li Peng said with a smile, if you want to realize your dream in a difficult place, you need to be a little crazy!!

Arixi Village is an extremely poor Uighur village. The whole village is surrounded by desert and the ecological environment is poor. It can only barely survive on one-third of an acre of land per capita. In addition, many young men and women do not speak Mandarin. It's inconvenient to go out to work. They can only walk around at home and do other things, which are not conducive to local poverty alleviation and development, or to social stability. When he arrived in the village, Li Peng smiled bravely against the occasional dust storm. Sometimes he had to walk around the village with crutches every day to mobilize the villagers to develop the jujube industry with him. Male workers receive monthly wages and female workers receive daily wages. The villagers said suspiciously that we had lived here for generations. Watering in the desert can't grow crops. Do you think old Li wants to run a jujube garden?

Old Li smiled and said: We shall see!

Li Peng spared no effort to prevent wind, fix sand and cultivate land. He spent three years building power lines, drilling wells, leveling sand dunes, building roads and bridges, planting windbreaks and wheat to improve the soil. We don't have enough money, so we have to apply to the bank for a loan. The bank sent people to investigate for many times, then said 'go back and report to the superior', said 'ask experts to demonstrate', and said 'wait for the approval of the leadership'. At the end, there was no letter. Li Peng asked why the bank didn't give him a loan. The bank was very frank with him, 'your intention is very good, and even spent your life savings, but the bank doesn't want to participate in this dying project.'

I have no choice but to borrow it from my friends. I have borrowed a total of 5 million pounds in the past 10 years, and now I still owe 2 million pounds. Li Peng smiled and said, 'in recent years, I can repay 3 million yuan, which proves that my entrepreneurship is profitable!'

Three years later, when the road was smooth, the land was fertile and the river flowed out of the canal, the jujube seedlings finally spit out bright green. Seeing hope, the villagers called him 'Team leader' according to the old habit of the production team.

Sowing, watering, farming, fertilization, spraying and pruning. Technicians and translators are invited to teach Uighur brothers and sisters various technologies and tell everyone to remember the management points of each planting link. The captain did the same and took a notebook. After early spring, there was a sandstorm. Like the villagers, Lao Li put on his hat and worked in the field. He got along with the villagers day and night and found that Uighurs did not have the habit of washing and brushing their teeth, and their teeth broke when they were very young. Therefore, he asked the company to give each poor family in the village a set of laundry products, and asked them to improve their hygiene awareness and brush their teeth every morning and evening.

Li Peng is a retired veteran cadre arranged by the Party committee of the autonomous region. His living standard is equivalent to that of local poor households. In addition, he generously extended his hands to help the local people. An employee's son suffered from severe renal failure just after graduating from college, it cost hundreds of thousands of dollars to treat the disease. Li Peng found two friends to donate 150,000 yuan and set up a minimum living guarantee for his family. Another employee died of a heart attack; his youngest daughter is only 14 years old and goes to junior high school in Karamay. Li Peng took the initiative to bear the living and learning expenses of the girl until she graduated and found a job. The third is an old low-income family in their 70s. They picked up an abandoned Han girl 19 years ago. The old couple named her Baireku Kurbaniyazi. They have been raising her as their own child and admitted to university in 2019. But at the beginning of this year, his blind wife died, and the old man's health was much worse than before. The old man thought, I don't know when he left. I'm really worried about leaving this Han daughter. So, everyone said they wanted to give the girl to a reliable and trustworthy person who would not leave here. Hearing the news, Li Peng went to the door and took the initiative to accept the great trust of the elderly and subsidize girls to go to college. In the speech of college students, white hot pants tearfully told the story of 'I have two Uygur and Han grandfathers', and the audience cried

—For 11 years, Li Peng has spent the Spring Festival in Arixi Village every year. He said his wife and daughter can only come to Southern Xinjiangto see Old Lee like 'relatives.'

After his old mother died, Li Peng took his father in his 90s to Arixi Village. After work, I won't forget to give the old man a bath, wash clothes and cook his favorite home cooking. The old man especially supported Li Peng's action. Before his death at the age of 97, the only will left was: 'bury me here with you.'

—Over the past 11 years, Li Peng's Jujube Company has employed 140,000 people locally, paid labor fees of more than 16 million yuan and donated more than 300,000 yuan to the masses. In view of the epidemic situation in 2020, 150,000 yuan was donated to the front-line staff in Cele County. Li Peng said: 'although there is great pressure to repay the loan, I would rather smash the pot and sell iron than owe the masses a penny.'

—Over the past 11 years, Li Peng has finally built Arixi Village into a small 'Nanniwan' in Cele County, with spring flowers, green leaves and surging water waves; Autumn is the season of red dates and cucumbers. The per capita net income of the whole village increased from 2,173 yuan in 2009 to 10,425 yuan in 2019, an increase of 4.79 times, exceeding the per capita level of the whole county (9276 yuan) by 1,149 yuan. By the end of 2019, Arixi Village will be fully lifted out of poverty. At the same time, with the help of Xinjiang Zhongtai group, the company has built a 10,000-tonne red jujube processing plant, which can arrange the employment of more than 300 villagers and solve the primary processing of more than 50% of the red jujube in the county.

Li Peng doesn't need to say it, but looking around his company's office, we can see that he regards Arixi Village as his home. He won't go anywhere.

He said: 'in Arixi Village, I am a team leader who will never retire and a poverty alleviation team member who will never leave.'

In 2019, Li Peng, 68, won the honorary titles of 'national poverty alleviation dedication Award' and 'national model individual for unity and progress.'

Interestingly, in 2014, Li Peng's Jujube company suddenly became an uninvited guest: the tall and thin Zhu Taizeng. Zhu Taizeng was born in Nanjing, Jiangsu Province in 1946 and became a cadre after returning home. In the 1980s, he successively served as a member of the Standing Committee of Lianyungang Municipal Party committee and the head of Haizhou District of Guanyun County. In 1997, as the first batch of cadres in the country, he went to the Tacheng District of Xinjiang as Deputy Commissioner and worked with Deputy Commissioner Li Peng, who was transferred two years later. Three years later, Zhu Taizeng returned to Lianyungang as deputy director of the Standing Committee of the Municipal People's Congress. After retirement, enjoy flowers, children and grandchildren and a leisurely life. One day, he saw a report on TV that Li Peng, a veteran cadre in Xinjiang, did not forget his original intention after retirement. With his family's savings, he came to a Rixi village, Cele County, southern Xinjiang to plant and develops jujube poverty alleviation, which changed the appearance and customs of the village. Zhu Tai was deeply moved by Li Peng's deeds. Although he recovered early, he flew all the way to Hotan and rushed to Alixi Village, Cele County to see Li Peng. The two spent time together day and night, and Zhu Tai also resolutely changed his retirement life. He has always liked photography and played with photography, so he specially brought a camera from home and decided to record Li Peng's struggle in Alixi Village. Since then, the villagers can see almost every day that a 73-year-old, thin and tall 'old photographer' always takes photos with the 68-year-old short and fat 'Captain', sometimes sideways, sometimes upside down and sometimes kneeling down.

Knowing that I was here to interview Li Peng, Zhu Taizeng immediately put down his work, turned on the TV and let me watch his three-episode documentary 'three years of aid to Xinjiang, life in Xinjiang'. I know that this is the common feeling and concern of the two veteran comrades at the deputy department level. They decided to devote themselves to the people of Xinjiang until they pass away.

V Xinjiang guy's lifecycle

1. From Xinjiang to Shanghai

In the evening, the wheat, 17-year-old wheat Maimaiti is like a Phoenix Tree falling in the autumn wind and falling quietly on the streets of Shanghai. He walked out of the railway station with some clothes on his back. His bright big eyes looked timidly at the big city with tall buildings and heavy traffic. He felt as humble as a drop of snow on the Kunlun Mountains. He was swept into this strange 'ocean' by the great times and couldn't find himself for a moment. His only contact with metropolis is a small note in his hand, which records the mobile phone number of a fellow countryman.

In 1982, Maimaitimin Abdulhalik was born in Kumuxikuole Village, Kaersai Township, Moyu County, Southern Xinjiang. Several acres of thin fields, two huts and a dozen thin goats maintain a trace of vitality in the life of the whole family. His first memory of his hometown and the world was carried on his back by his father or mother and moved in the corn field. His parents were too tired to hold on, so they had to put him on the ground weeding. He cried and shouted in fear, but his parents who disappeared in the corn field and the wind and sand ignored him completely. He never wears new clothes and shoes. They were handed down by his brothers and sisters. The wool on the sheepskin boots was polished

In 1996, the hard-working father died and the pillars of the family collapsed.

My brothers and sisters got married one after another. They didn't have the ability and time to take care of their sick mother. Just after the first day of junior high school, Maimaitimin realized that he must help his mother support his family like a man in the future. After seeing off her father, she wrapped some bread in her luggage bag, said goodbye to her mother, left her hometown and began to travel and work everywhere. He has been to several counties near his hometown, as well as Aksu and Korla. Because he is a semi laborer, he earns less than half of his money. Hunger is common. In a strong sandstorm, he can blow thin people all over the ground. Only by holding a pole or a room post can he fix himself. Every two or three months, tired, black and thin Maimaitimin would go home and give her mother a pile of hard-earned money.

In the 1990s, the wave of farmers working swept Xinjiang. Many young people in Xinjiang followed this trend and broke into big cities in the mainland. The delicious kebabs, sweet raisins, cantaloupes and Korla fragrant pears, coupled with the happy selling of Uygur boys, soon became a delicious scenic spot for mainland snacks and became popular all over the country. Before the Spring Festival in 1999, a villager of Kumuxikuole Village came back from Shanghai, wearing a suit and shoes, ruddy face and looking like a successful person. He knew that Maimaitimin was a clever and diligent child. He said he would go to Shanghai to do business with me in autumn. Money will be much faster than his hometown! In the autumn of 1999, Maimaitimin, 17, set out with more than a dozen village boys and bosses. He brought more than 300 yuan along the way, and only 100 yuan remained from Southern Xinjiang to Urumqi. The boss doesn't want to pay for him. He said my business was urgent. When you get to Shanghai, take your time to find me. Since then, Maimaitimin traveled to four cities on the way, earned travel expenses through work, and arrived in Shanghai more than 20 days later. The boss arranged for him to go to the basement near Cao'an market in Putuo District. 8 square metres of space, 10 boys, 7 yuan a person per day.

The boss reached a gentleman's agreement with Maimaitimin: he took a 15-yuan commission for 100 yuan. Since then, he has pushed a small scooter along the street to sell melons, fruits, red dates and raisins. In two or three years, Maimaitimin has traveled all over the cities of greater Shanghai to prepare for five pairs of shoes. Some of his friends couldn't stand the hard work and suggested that he go back to his hometown and find another job. Maimaitimin refused. He said, 'there is only one way in life, that is the way of struggle. If you don't struggle, you can't go anywhere!' in order to earn more money, Maimaitimin pushed a cart to sell melons and fruits during the day and found a job at night. There is a large wholesale morning market in the suburbs of Shanghai. At dusk, canteens, hotels, restaurants, butchers and vegetable vendors come here to buy the ingredients needed for the day. The market is located by the river and the terrain is low. The goods need to be transported to the side of the road on the slope before they are transported away. The clever Maimaitimin found this business opportunity. He gets up at midnight every night and squats down the slope waiting for work. Some shippers need help to transport baskets of meat and vegetables to the roadside for one yuan each time. By eight or nine o'clock in the morning, the morning market had dispersed and made forty or fifty yuan. After operating for a long time, Maimaitimin was tanned. Sitting in the night before dawn, only a pair of bright big eyes twinkle, which often surprises passers-by. A Han friend laughed at him and said, 'when others fall to the ground, they can't find it because it's as black as the ground; when you fall to the ground, you can find it because you're darker than the ground!'

Maimaitimin is kind, diligent and enthusiastic. He helped clean up the market, took the initiative to help others carry goods, and took the initiative to mediate with anyone in dispute. In short, when you see work and difficulties, you can help. Moreover, he always pays great attention to abiding by the market management system and never quarrels with anyone. Marketing managers, landlords and cohabiting partners all like him very much. Gradually, he learned to do business and accumulated some money. In 2003, he and his new wife came to Shanghai and decided to start their own business. Lao Wang, Deputy Marketing Manager of Cao'an, is an educated youth in Shanghai. He has lived in Xinjiang for 17 years and can speak fluent Uighur. With his help, Maimaitimin built an oven in Cao'an market. His wife also sells fresh and dried fruits, and then asks his hometown brothers to help organize the purchase. The young couple's business is booming. Later, they developed a wholesale store, a cold storage and three retail stores, employing more than a dozen employees from their hometown. Their business expanded to counties around Shanghai and even Jiaxing. Some media learned about Maimaitimin's struggle experience and good reputation in the local area, and specially produced a feature film in Shanghai about him, which was broadcast on the Internet, causing a great sensation.

Maimaitimin became a rich boss. It gradually spread among Uighurs in Moyu County and Shanghai. Some malicious people often invite him to drink and play cards. Within a few days, all the savings accumulated over the years disappeared, and even the purchase funds and employees' wages could not be taken out. Maimaitimin's friends saw that he had no more oil and water to squeeze, so they dispersed and disappeared. Then, Maimaitimin realized that he had fallen into the trap of his buddies.

After years of hard work and sweat, the business almost stopped except for the inventory in the warehouse. In those days, Maimaitimin thought he had acted recklessly and lost all her family's property. He really felt sorry for his mother, wife and children. He was very depressed. His gentle wife didn't say a word of blame, but she cried every day. At the critical moment, several of Han and Uygur's friends who knew about business came, as did Lao Wang, Cao An's Deputy Marketing Manager. Maimaitimin is sensitive to warmth. They asked seriously, 'can you make up your mind not to play cards in the future?' 'Yes!' 'Can you start from scratch?' 'Yes!'

His friends raised a sum of money to lend him, and Old Wang exempted some of his expenses within the scope of the policy. Maimaitimin is full of regret and frantically plunges into her new efforts. There are many roads in life, but only the road of struggle can lead to dreams and happiness. Sure enough, within a few years, Maimaitimin became a hero again, with an annual income of nearly one million yuan. By 2017, Maimaitimin, 35, had worked hard in Shanghai for 19 years and made himself a multimillionaire.

2. Return to Xinjiang from Shanghai

At the end of 2016, Maimaitimin returned to his hometown Moyu County with his wife and two children. He told his mother that he was going to buy a house in Shanghai and take his mother so that he could live a good life. The old mother shook her head and said that I was not going. Kumuxikuole Village is where I was born and raised. The whole village is my good friend day and night. I can't leave them. The old mother also said that you are rich now, but the villagers in the village still live in poverty. When our family suffered, the villagers did not reduce their help to us. Today's family will send rice bowls and tomorrow's family will send cloth. Don't you think about how to help the villagers? This is your mother's and your father's wish! With that, my mother shed tears.

Maimaitimin was stunned and cried.

In the next few days, Maimaitimin took gifts to many families in the village and visited the village, the county and the headquarters of the 47th regiment nearby. Seeing that some villagers were still destitute, he was deeply shocked and saddened, blaming himself for living in Shanghai for 19 years and almost forgetting the villagers; In the exhibition hall of the 47th regiment, he recalled that when he was at school, his teacher took the whole class to visit. When they heard the story of these veterans 'dedicating their youth, life and children', they burst into tears. Then he wrote a composition, its titled 'I love veterans'; In the county and township, some friends who had been cadres introduced him to the magnificent party. Since the eighteen Party leadership, under the leadership of General Secretary Xi Jinping, the whole country has launched a struggle against poverty. Although Maimaitimin, who lived in Shanghai, has heard of this great livelihood project, he has never cared. After listening to the introduction of his hometown friends, his heart was suddenly ignited. He asked, 'what can I do to help the poor?'

Friends said to him: 'There's more than enough for you to do!'

On the way home, the excited Maimaitimin made an important decision. He said to his mother and wife, 'I'm not going back to Shanghai. I want to do something big to help the villagers get rid of poverty!'

The wife asked, 'No plans to buy a house or start a business?'

'Yep!'

Mother laughed and cried, wrinkled and tearful.

Then, Maimaitimin handed over all the businesses and shops in Shanghai to his brother's children. He returned to the starting point of his life and returned to the villagers from his boss. Soon, a new enterprise, desert green orchard agricultural products cooperative of Moyu County, was established in Kumuxikuole Village. The government allocated 60 mu of land, invested 13.6 million yuan in supporting funds, and Maimaitimin raised 9 million yuan. The cooperative mainly produces the local characteristic product 'walnut jujube', and has 9 workshops, which are divided into screening, cleaning, drying, processing, refrigeration, grading, packaging and other workshops. There are also party branches, young workers, headquarters, canteens, kindergartens and other office and living areas. At present, the cooperative has more than 2000 employees, including 1200 poor villagers, with a monthly salary ranging from 1500 yuan to 4000 yuan, and an annual processing capacity of 4000 tons of red dates and 6000 tons of walnuts. During the interview, Mai Maimaitimin led me to visit various workshops and product exhibition halls. The working environment is spotless and the employees work orderly. Maimaitimin proudly introduced that today, the main product of the cooperative, 'red jujube walnut', sells well in Urumqi, Shanghai, Harbin, Hebei and other places, with an annual output value of nearly 10 million yuan and a net profit of more than 5 million yuan. The busiest time of every month is pay day. Uighur villagers received a lot of 100 yuan. Some people have never seen so much money in their life!

Walk into the 200 square metre product exhibition hall, spacious, bright and modern. There are dates, walnuts, apricots and raisins on the stall. There are several crystal raisins in the red 'walnut jujube', which makes people salivate. There are many awards, certificates and minority art works on the purple red wooden box, such as wood carving, root carving, embroidery, flower blanket and porcelain. It's really enjoyable and beautiful!

I asked Maimaitimin, do you still want to go back to Shanghai?

Maimaitimin smiled and said that he couldn't get away even if he wanted to.

In the evening, the colorful lights in Moyu County were bright, and the comrades of the Poverty Alleviation Office accompanied me to the night market. The whole night market was ablaze with lights. It crosses several streets from east to west and from north to south. Hundreds of snack stalls are steaming, with constant flow of people and booming business. Behind the tables and stools stood many passengers. There are families, couples, young parents with children, and tourists who speak Xinjiang Dialect. Of course, the loudest voice is the rude old man from his hometown Heilongjiang. My friends and I ate seven stalls and filled them with Xinjiang special food. Cattle, sheep, chickens, rabbits, fresh fruits and dried fruits were brushed with a mobile phone. Everything gathered together and disappeared in an instant.

A tall and fat Uygur cook, wearing a high white hat and a white apron on his shoulder, kept waving a spatula and turning over the hot and fragrant barbecue on an iron plate. I noticed a gold map of China embroidered on the upper left corner of his apron and five red stars embroidered on Xinjiang. I asked loudly, 'where did you get your apron?'

The cook raised his red face and said, 'my wife embroidered it!'

I gave him a thumb up, letting him know I like it.

Facing such a prosperous, harmonious and happy Xinjiang, I feel very excited and deeply happy.

Harmony is beautiful, peace is beautiful, happiness is beautiful, and the people living in it are more beautiful. Along the way, I saw the people of all ethnic groups in Xinjiang begin to move towards happiness. Where is happiness? Happiness at home. China is the common home of 1.4 billion people of all ethnic groups. A beautiful and quiet home is our common happiness!

VI Great love to aid Xinjiang, unprecedented

1. Children decide the future

When you raise a smiling child over your head, another sun is added to the world.

At that moment, in Hotan Moyu County, the earth, snow mountains, sunshine, flowers and plants suddenly became so beautiful, so brilliant and so intoxicating! Because in a spacious and beautiful kindergarten square, I saw a magnificent sea of flowers!

I shouted to the children playing games, 'children, come here!'

The flowers came to me bouncing. Bang! I pressed the shutter on my cell phone.

I believe that all kind and loving people will send out knowing and warm smiles when they see these children in full bloom.

I also believe that some malicious people in the West will be proven wrong when they see this picture. Because they have been slandering and slandering China's Xinjiang, describing the life of the people in Xinjiang as 'darkness'. This photo clearly tells them that children of all ethnic groups living in Xinjiang are deeply cared for and cherished by the great motherland and receive a good education. They will decide that Xinjiang has a bright future; Those Western politicians who are hostile to China will also be despised by history.

No one can stop this historical trend, and no one can change it. Just as no one can stop the sun from rising in the East, no one can change the direction of Greater China.

This large kindergarten is a 'turnkey project' funded by Beijing, with an investment of 20.7 million yuan, covering an area of nearly 10,000 square metres and a greening area of 2,700 square metres. It will open in September 2018. Ma Lingyu, President and Party branch secretary, is a beautiful and elegant Hotan girl. She was born in 1992. After graduating from college, she applied for kindergarten. There are 30 teachers and employees in the park, all of whom are young and energetic. They come from Beijing, Gansu, Shandong, Inner Mongolia and Yunnan. When the Education Department of Moyu County recruited locally, they went to register out of strong patriotic enthusiasm and young desire. After written examination and interview, more than one tenth of them were lucky to be selected, and many of them were only children. After receiving the admission notice, they resolutely bid farewell to their parents and flew to Xinjiang like a bird out of its nest, into their own dreams and into their children's dreams.

I asked why Moyu County built such a big kindergarten. Ling Yu said that in line with the strategic vision of 'focusing on the long term, cultivating new people, focusing on education and serving the people', the county Party committee and the county government took the initiative to put forward this proposal to the Beijing Construction assistance department, which has been strongly supported by Beijing.

Entering the park, there is a wide and flat orange plastic playground with various game equipment. Under the protection of teachers and nurses, hundreds of children shouted, laughed, ran and played games. The building has a unique modeling and artistic atmosphere. The front and rear walls are mainly glass, and the building is spacious and bright. From the corridor to the classroom, the walls are colorful, and there are many children's paintings especially suitable for children's psychology, which seem to pull me back to my distant childhood. There are piano, TV, computer, toys, small bed, cabinet and so on in the classroom. In the kitchen, there are noodle machines, large refrigerators, disinfection cabinets, steam cars, electric rice cookers, etc. they are polished spotlessly and glittering. In the classroom, some are teaching singing and dancing, some are teaching painting, some are taking bilingual classes or health care classes, and some are playing the game of 'beating drums and passing flowers'. The children's laughter reveals the warmth of the big family of the motherland and the gorgeous characteristics of Chinese culture. Oh, full of flowers, full of joy, full of happy childhood.

Ling Yu told me that when parents came to pick up their children, there is a large private car parked in front of the garden. From this scene, we can see that the residents and relocated farmers in Moyu County are getting richer and richer. Not long ago, the kindergarten sent a questionnaire to all parents, and everyone checked the 'satisfaction' box.

Many years ago, I came to southern Xinjiang many times and visited many places, counties and townships. The desolation of the desert Gobi, the intermittent roads, the silent and depressed towns, the dilapidated villages and low mud and grass houses along the way, and the sandstorms in the yellow sand made me feel desolate and sad. After all, the harsh natural environment and weak infrastructure, coupled with the vast territory, sparse population, lack of resources and remote transportation, have brought great difficulties to economic and social development. Since the reform and opening up, although great progress and changes have been made, the gap has widened significantly compared with the rapid development of the eastern coast and the mainland.

It is our party's solemn commitment to let poor areas enter a well-off society in an all-round way with the whole country.

When I came to Xinjiang this time, I was excited to see that the city has changed, with many buildings, unobstructed streets, tidal traffic and prosperous market; new houses with red roofs and yellow walls have been arranged in farmers' new villages. In front of their house, wide grape racks, hardened roads, streetlamps and plastic greenhouses stand side by side; With the vigorous development of modern enterprises, most farmers have become industrial workers and work hard on the production lines.

The solemn commitment of the Party is accelerating to become an exciting reality in Xinjiang!

2. Only China can do it.

This major change is the decisive decision and strategic deployment of the Party

Central Committee, the strong support of the people all over the country and the efforts of the people of all ethnic groups in Xinjiang.

In March 2010, the national counterpart support work conference for Xinjiang was held in Beijing. The current situation provided by the meeting is that in the past 10 years, the financial investment in people's livelihood in Xinjiang has increased 10 times, and the situation of people's livelihood has been greatly improved, but the problems are still prominent. There are 30 poverty-stricken counties in the autonomous region, including 27 national poverty-stricken counties with a poverty population of 2.53 million. The CPC Central Committee has decided that 19 provinces and cities including Beijing, Tianjin, Shanghai, Guangdong, Liaoning and Shenzhen will undertake the task of counterpart support to Xinjiang. Relevant provinces, autonomous regions and municipalities directly under the central government should establish regular mechanisms for all-round assistance to Xinjiang in terms of talents, technology, management and funds, give priority to ensuring and improving people's livelihood, strive to help people of all ethnic groups solve basic livelihood problems such as employment, and support the development of characteristic and advantageous industries in Xinjiang. China has set off an unprecedented tide of aid to Xinjiang!!

—Beijing Municipal supported the construction of the 14th agricultural division of Hotan City, Moyu County, Hotan County, Luopu County and the Corps.

—Tianjin assisted in the construction of Yutian County, Cele County and Minfeng County.

—Anhui Province has provided support for the construction of Pishan County.

—Jiangsu Province and Jiangxi Province assisted in the construction of Aktao County, Kizilsu Kirgiz Autonomous Prefecture.

—Guangdong Province and Shenzhen respectively provided support to Shufu County, Jiashi County, the third agricultural division of Land reclamation corps, Tumushuke City, Kashgar City and Tashkent County in Kashgar region.

—Zhejiang Province has provided counterpart support to Aksu region of the first agricultural division of Xinjiang production and Construction Corps and eight counties of Alar city.

—Shanghai has provided support to Kashgar.

——Henan Province assisted the construction of Hami City.

——Heilongjiang and Jilin provinces provided support to Altay region.

——Hunan Province supported Turpan City, and so on.

A large number of cadres of provinces, autonomous regions and municipalities directly under the central government who helped Xinjiang immediately bid farewell to their relatives, shoulder important tasks and rush to all parts of Xinjiang,; A large number of central enterprises, state-owned enterprises and private enterprises have sprung up; A large number of funds have been invested in social construction and livelihood projects. The relay race was in full swing one by one, with countless pairs of warm and powerful hands holding the hands of villagers of all nationalities. At the same time, the Party committee and government of the autonomous region have comprehensively strengthened social governance and border defense management, carried out in-depth and extensive patriotic education, resolutely cracked down on and resisted religious extremism and the criminal activities of the 'three forces', worked hard to promote education and established vocational training schools, so that the majority of rural teenagers can learn a skill well and get employed smoothly. I can't calculate all these data, nor can I fully describe all these stories. However, it is certain that since the launch of the national aid project to Xinjiang and the poverty alleviation and development in Xinjiang, Xinjiang has rapidly achieved great cohesion of the people, great ideological progress, great social progress and great economic development. Today's Xinjiang is unfolding in front of the world with a brand-new face, which has undergone earth shaking changes!

There is no doubt that looking at the world, only China can realize this great cause.

Social prosperity and progress, happiness and prosperity, 'two worries and Three Guarantees' are implemented village by village and household by household. The world is peaceful and the people are firm. Since 2017, there have been no violent terrorist incidents in Xinjiang. In Urumqi, a friend asked me to go to a luxury music restaurant transformed from a cinema. The stage there may rise and fall. Folk art troupes from Russia and Kazakhstan danced with young men and women from ethnic minorities, intoxicating the audience and the guests in the boxes on the upper two floors. In the bustling yard, a humorous advertisement is particularly eye-catching: 'the peach blossom pool is thousands of feet deep. It's better to drink to death tonight!' after midnight, the warm and colorful songs and dances continue.

History has proved and will continue to prove that small ponds can be changed, but the ocean cannot be changed by anyone or any force. China is an ocean. No one can change or stop the great pace of the all-round revitalization of the Chinese nation, the inviolability of the great cause of national reunification and the prosperity of Xinjiang.

Some Western politicians can only sigh. Their lies are just chicken feathers. After the chicken feather was pulled out, the image is ugly.

Tongren Chapter
'Sun wash basin'

Guizhou, straightforward.

At a glance, the clouds are infinite, the years are long, and the dreams are long

Suddenly, the red sunrise jumped out of the mountain. I don't know who waved 100,000 crazy flowers and sprinkled thousands of colors of red, orange, yellow, green, blue and purple, depicting a magnificent land and mountains. This place is called Guizhou.

Folk songs are more than words, dance sleeves are more than clouds, love is more than flowers, and dreams are more than mountain roads.

Tongren City is located in a basin surrounded by mountains in the northeast of Guizhou. Even the wind, cloud and rain are unwilling to leave after they pay a visit. I have been here for more than a month, the sun has only appeared for three days. I was a bit puzzled. Walking in the fresh drizzle, I romantically imagine that this must be the place where the sunbathes and dresses up before sunrise every day. The flying rain is her water spray, the fog is her scarf, and the gorgeous clouds are her dance clothes. So, it became a little poem: 'Green mountains embrace Longren, bamboo shoots spring up, sunrise dressing place, washbasin flowers are in disorder.'

'The sky is clear without three days, the earth is flat without three feet, and people have no three cents', people's description of Guizhou in history is reasonable. Why is Guizhou called Guizhou? Because there are many stones and mountains, the land is very expensive. Why is Guiyang called Guiyang? Because it's raining, foggy and rare to see the sun.

Beauty and suffering have created Guizhou. Guizhou was born with mountains. Living in Guizhou, life does not walk, only climb. Living in Guizhou, all roads are full of twists and turns, and all fates have experienced hardships. Living in Guizhou, people climb and go down the mountain all my life, and will never see the horizon. Living in Guizhou, you have only two choices: either rely on the mountain or get out of the mountain. To live in Guizhou, you must be cruel to yourself, 'Pull on the three-foot shame cloth, and the foot board should be a slate mill'. To live in Guizhou, you must guard your dream carefully, because there is a cliff on the left and an abyss on the right. To live in Guizhou, you must make yourself strong and have indomitable will and courage. When you come out of the womb, you will shout: 'Order the mountains to open the way, I'm coming!'

The following is a report by Xinhua News Agency on June 22, 2015:

Facing the poverty corner of China
—Poverty alleviation site investigation report

How do the poorest people in China live?

Today, when China has become the world's second largest economy, this problem seems to be beyond the vision of many people, especially urban residents.

According to the data of the National Bureau of statistics, there are still 70.17 million poor people in rural areas, accounting for about 7.2% of rural residents.

In the past six months, Xinhua has sent nine investigation teams to poor areas in central and Western China to observe the living conditions of fellow countrymen. On the one hand, since more than 30 years of poverty alleviation, the rural poor have been greatly reduced, and poverty has been pushed to the 'corner'. On the other hand, the future poverty alleviation will have to bite the hardest 'bones'. The poorest place is also a fortress of poverty, with the weakest foundation, the worst conditions and the most arduous projects.

'Utter destitution' is often used to describe poverty. But in Lan Jinhua's home in Baping village, Yaoshan Township, Libo County, Guizhou Province, there is not even a 'wall' in the strict sense.

The thatched house where he and his mother lived has a history of decades. It is made of branches and bamboo. There is some cow manure in the gap, and the cold wind and cold light pass-through countless holes.

Meng Ermei, a 66-year-old villager, stands in front of her house in Nonghong group, Baping village, Yaoshan Township, Libo County, Guizhou Province. The thatched cottage where she and her son LAN Jinhua live has a history of several decades, consisting of branches and bamboo (photographed by Tao Liang of Xinhua News Agency on March 22, 2015)

Under the dim light bulb, firewood, sundries and simple farm tools are piled together. Years of fireworks condensed into black wool from the roof and wooden frame. In the corner, two small nests surrounded by bamboo strips are the 'bedrooms' of mother and son.

Not long ago, the roof leaked, and Lan Jinhua had to go to his brother's house next door to make a floor shop. Her brother's house is a brick house built with a government subsidy of 20,000 yuan a few years ago, but so far there is no door panel, only a thin piece of bamboo.

In the concentrated poverty-stricken area, through the continuous efforts of the Party committee, the government and all sectors of society, the era of 'naked and hungry' has long passed. However, the reporter saw that some extremely poor families still have mixed feelings.

In Jiadui village, Zhansheng village, Jiamian Township, Congjiang County, Guizhou Province, the reporter came to the old owner of Long Laodong, a deputy to the town's people's Congress and a 51-year-old representative of the villagers' group. The white plastic bucket contains five or six kilograms of lard, which is a delicacy for the whole family to improve their life. When cooking, cut a small piece and wipe it in the pot, even if there is oil. Most of the time, they use water to cook wild vegetables.

When the reporter was interviewing, suddenly someone brought a big cock. It turned out that Long Laodong wanted to keep us for dinner. There was no chicken in his house, so he borrowed one from his neighbor and planned to kill it for us. His family can only eat meat once in two or three months, but he wants to kill chickens for us. When declined the interview, the reporter's mood was really indescribable.

His TV set is the only electrical appliance used by 67 people in 19 households in the village, It is not bought, but donated by the society. His bedroom had no door, only a piece of plastic cloth hung, and the bed was covered with a layer of scattered straw.

In some mountainous areas with severe rocky desertification in Southwest

China, there are still seasonal food shortages. The government gives each person 30 kilograms of relief food every month. Some villagers still don't have enough food. They can only borrow money from relatives and friends to pay back new grain next year.

Rocky desertification mountainous areas have more rocks and less soil, and the soil layer is barren. Under the soil is the 'funnel' of karst landform, which cannot hold rainwater. Chengdu's annual harvest is very meager. One side water and soil cannot raise its own residents.

In Siqu Town, Yanhe County, Wuling mountain area, Guizhou Province, there is a village called 'Yi koudao', which means 'built on the back of the knife'. There are 34 households in the village, with only 1.5 mu of paddy field. Every family must take turns farming, and those who cannot do so will plant some corn on barren dry land. In other words, a bowl of rice will take turns in the whole village for decades. When the reporter interviewed, there were more than ten families.

A folk house photographed in Mukeji village, Fugong County, Nujiang Prefecture, Yunnan Province (photographed by Xinhua News Agency reporter Hu Chao on March 28, 2015)

Xiaoqikong, the core area of Karst World Natural Heritage in southern China, is always overcrowded in the peak tourist season, and even often overcrowded. However, 5 kilometres away from the scenic spot is the extremely poor area of Yaoshan Township, Libo County, Guizhou Province.

Gu Lei Village, of 357 households in the whole village, almost no one gets rich by the scenic spot except one family opens a farmhouse. Yaoshan chicken is a local specialty. It tastes good and has not yet opened a closed market.

There are more than 1,200 people in the village, of which more than 1,100 are illiterate and semi-illiterate. Most villagers still can't find or dare not find the market. They can only rely on agriculture to maintain food and clothing.

Lack of education has become a deep obstacle for some difficult groups to get rid of poverty.

The nine-year compulsory education in China is relatively perfect, and measures such as free and nutritious lunch benefit countless children. However, in poor mountainous areas, it is not uncommon for children to drop out of junior middle school or even primary school. Some parents take their children out to work early. For the poorest families, schooling itself is an unbearable cost... 'No tuition fees, but also book fees, miscellaneous expenses and living expenses?'

In most rural areas, 'the best house is a school' has become a reality. However, backward educational facilities and lack of teachers are still common problems in poor areas.

On the day the report was published, I saved it on my computer. I hope that one day this situation can change, and I hope that one day I can make a contribution to change. The day finally came. On December 17, 2019, I flew to Tongren.

In Mukeji Village, Fugong County, Nujiang Prefecture, Yunnan Province, a child is doing her homework in bed. There is no table in her home (photographed by Hu Chao of Xinhua News Agency on March 28, 2015)

Tongren City is located within the poverty-stricken area in the hinterland of Wuling Mountain, one of the national key poverty alleviation and development zones. Truthfully recording the changes of Tongren has important empirical significance.

I Communist Party's 'big treat'

1. Why is Guizhou called Guizhou?

It was a long night. The torch lights up the Winding mountain road, and there is endless suffering at the end of the mountain road. Why is Guizhou called Guizhou? Because there are many stones and mountains, the land is very expensive. Why is Guiyang called Guiyang? Because it's raining, foggy and sunny. Therefore, here, life has a sonorous and powerful meaning. Living in Guizhou, all roads are full of twists and turns, and all fates have experienced hardships. Living in Guizhou, people have been climbing down the mountain all their lives and never see the horizon. Living in Guizhou, there are only two choices in life: either rely on the mountains or get out of the mountains. To live in Guizhou, you must guard your dream carefully, because there is a cliff on the left and an abyss on the right. Living in Guizhou, there is only one way: rock climbing!

So, people in Guizhou seldom speak because they want to stand on this mountain and shout that mountain.

Therefore, Guizhou people are very hardworking. They should plant several corn and wear a big straw hat on this land.

Therefore, Guizhou people are very patient, because if they can't climb the mountain, they can't find a way out.

Therefore, Guizhou people attach great importance to love. One mountain connects with another.

Therefore, Guizhou people are brave. When they came out of the womb, they shouted, 'Order three mountains and five mountains to open the way, I'm coming!'

Therefore, Guizhou people are tragically heoric. They live to be heroes!

Guizhou is the only province without flatland in China. Eight mountains of water a sub-fields of which more than 60% are karst landforms, with thousands of cracks and caves. Looking at the mountains and picturesque scenery, in fact, they are all stones. The soil layer is only more than ten centimetres, and tens of centimetres is a rare fertile soil. For hundreds of millions of years, although Guizhou has abundant rainfall, it is difficult to keep water on the ground. Water drips from the stone and flows like a knife. The rain washed away the overlapping karst rocks and flowed down the ground joints. The ground vegetation and crops are flooded in rain and dry in drought. In Haique Village, Hezhang County, I heard Miao girl Luo Qiaohua singing sadly:

Corns no longer than palms. Plant a basket and collect a basket.

Pull on a three-foot-thick rag and the baseboard should be ground into stone.

Guizhou is located in the hinterland of Southwest China, bordering Guangdong and Guangxi in the south, Yunnan in the west, two lakes in the East and Sichuan and Chongqing in the north. Strategic planning was important, Guizhou therefore falls under the Chinese territory. Guizhou has experienced a long process of cultural exchange and ethnic integration, but three 'interesting events' have become historical nodes:

First, a can of cinnabar. After the First Emperor of Qin of great talent and bold visions, he swept through the six countries, his reputation spread all over the world, and everyone on the land was afraid. During the Warring States period, a rare cinnabar mine (i.e., Mercury mine, now Wanshan town) was found in Tongren mountain area of Guizhou, and Taoists who went to refine Dan medicine flocked to it. In order to maintain Qin Shihuang's rule, local leaders bought Qin Shihuang a can of pills and said he could live forever. That day, the eunuch wiped the Royal table with a rag, took out the pottery pot and opened the lid. The first emperor excitedly called a prime minister standing next to him, but when he hurried forward, he accidentally tripped over the red carpet and spilled the pills. The first Emperor of Qin, was furious and said, 'Do you not want me to be immortal?' The emperor ordered his head cut off. Although the prime minister was very clever, he said we could wait because he had a suggestion.

What is the suggestion?

Li Si said, Dan medicine is so bright red, with the color of dawn and the power of blood, which is unforgettable. Your majesty is an eternal emperor who has made great contributions to heaven and earth. His works should be different from the themes around the world. I believe that the Royal approval can turn black ink into red ink in the future to show the power of the emperor's words. The first emperor was very happy to hear the speech, so he took up his pen rolling up his sleeve, dipped it in cinnabar water, and wrote four bright red words on a series of national strategy monuments presented by Li Sigang: 'do as you want.' After that, the enfeoffment system was abolished and the county system was implemented; characters, rail wheel distance and length, capacity and weight were unified. He had built post roads and the Great Wall, and resolutely implement the propositions of the six countries, old and young, such as 'burning books and advocating Confucianism'. Zhu Rongji's imperial edict with written instructions spread everywhere, and China's great empire was formed in this way. Since then, despite the split and war, the imperial customs remained basically unchanged.

Zhu Pi of the 422 emperors in previous dynasties, never changed until more than 2,000 years later, Puyi, the last emperor of the Qing Dynasty, stepped down. It is said that it took 39 years to build the mausoleum of Qin Shihuang, which has a 'Mercury sea'. A large part of it must be proposed by the chiefs of Tongren.

Second, idioms. At the end of the Western Han Dynasty, Liu Ao, Emperor of the Han Dynasty, married Zhao Feiyan, the 'first dancer of the Empire', as the queen. They lingered in bed day and night. Since then, he no longer asked political questions, and everything was handled by Wang Mang, the Minister of war. At that time, the Han Empire had Beihai county, Donghai County and Nanhai County. The ambitious Wang Mang felt it a pity, so they sent a large number of special envoys to Yunnan and Guizhou in the southwest, carrying gold and silver treasures, wine, beautiful women, silk and satin. Along the way, they wantonly publicized the great national strength, bribed local leaders with generous gifts, and asked them to press their fingerprints on paper, that is, they agreed to obey the great leader. In this way, without a soldier, Wang Mang drew a big circle on the imperial territory including Yunnan, Guizhou and Western Hunan, and marked 'Xihai County' on the circle. Wang Mang knows that place names alone are not enough to stabilize the land. Therefore, he specially formulated a law, such as stipulating that men and women must walk left and right respectively, dress neatly in the street, and do not litter or spit everywhere. Violators should be sent to Xihai County. It is said that millions of Han immigrants have entered the southwest. Since then, the idiom 'Home everywhere' has appeared in Chinese dictionaries.

Third, a banquet. In 1413, Ming Dynasty's emperor Yongle established the firs administrative commissioner's office (the capital in charge of military and political affairs) in Guizhou. After arriving at the presidential palace, leaders and heads from all over the country were specially summoned to Guiyang to attend the banquet. The decree was read out on the spot, and Guizhou was officially determined as the 13th province. All heads were asked to kneel down and receive the head appointment certificate and seal. These leaders were originally Mountain Kings. This time, they were officially appointed by the Ming Dynasty and received a large amount of jewelry, silk and satin from the emperor. They all laughed and knelt down to thank them. After several drinks, the overall situation of Guizhou has been determined. As soon as the cavalry arrived, although several leaders rebelled, all the Mountain Kings disappeared.

After the reunification of the country, people's life is still difficult. According to the statistics of the 1502 in Ming Dynasty, among the 13 envoys to China, Guizhou's annual tax accounts for only 0.7% of the national tax and autumn grain tax accounts for only 2.8%. The same is true in Wanli 70 years later, with little growth. During the Jiajing period, in Guizhou annual reports-wealth tax states: 'Guizhou's financial government cannot be equal to one of the big counties.' 71% of Guizhou's finance cannot be solved by itself. Therefore, most of the salaries of officials from other provinces who come to Guizhou need to be drawn from their original place of office. Those with low positions and wages are unwilling to come to Guizhou. 'Most people who obey orders without seeing officials are like this.' Officials are promoted here. They have no money to make new official clothes, so they have to buy old ones from their predecessors. It is not uncommon for them to have patches on their necklines and cuffs. In the Qing Dynasty, in order to solve the problem of financial expenditure and shortage of grain and cloth in Guizhou, the Qing government strictly stipulated that Huguang, Sichuan provided 50,000 stone grains, 60,000 cloth and 51,000 silver to Guizhou every year. As Guizhou is the gateway to Yunnan, it is stipulated that Yunnan will provide 1,500 liang of silver to Guizhou post office every year, and so on.

Years are long, suffering is long. In the Battle of Shanghai at the beginning of the Anti-Japanese War, the Guizhou army who came all the way to reinforce was called the 'straw sandal army', and there was far from enough guns and ammunition. Therefore, the war was very fierce. Most of them died and the pile of bodies became fortifications. Some Japanese reporters said that the position firmly defended by the Guizhou army was a 'flesh and blood factory.'

After the founding of The People's Republic of China, in the face of the economic foundation left by the old society and the cleaning up of the ruins of war, all walks of life in the country were prosperous and had limited financial resources. It was difficult to provide more support to the old, young, border and poor areas. At that time, there were seignorial economy in remote and backward minority areas of Guizhou. After the land reform, farmers' lives have improved slightly and poverty has eased slightly. However, due to the lack of cultivated land, low grain output and extremely backward productivity, tens of millions of farmers are still struggling on the hunger line. According to statistics, at the beginning of reform and opening up, Guizhou was still the most poverty-stricken and widely distributed area in China.

II The world's largest 'poached egg'

Tongren is located in a basin with mountains as a barrier.

There is a Wanshan Town on the mountain, which is the origin of Dansha mine.

After the founding of The People's Republic of China, Wanshan cinnabar mining company was established locally, becoming one of the proudest state-owned enterprises in Guizhou. The income of the workers there is many times higher than that of the local farmers. They are especially respected, especially by the local girls. In the 1960s, China and the Soviet Union had a bad relationship, and the Soviet side was very anxious to press for debt. China had to bear the pain and come up with many precious products to repay its debts. Tongren cinnabar mine is one of them. Therefore, Premier Zhou once called Tongren cinnabar mine 'patriotic mercury'. In the 1980s, mineral resources gradually dried up. By the end of the 20th century, the mountains had been hollowed out. On October 18, 2001, Wanshan mining company had to declare permanent closure. Within a few days after the announcement, these workers received compensation of nearly 10,000 yuan or tens of thousands of yuan according to their years of service, and have been unemployed since then. They left their beloved factory step by step, and then shed tears in the tavern in the town. The whole Wanshan town fell into unprecedented difficulties.

Resources are exhausted and people are empty handed. Since then, the ancient town of cinnabar, which has been vibrant and prosperous for more than 2,000 years, fell into silence, and the sound of machines and trains echoing for nearly a century suddenly disappeared. It seems that people woke up from a dream, when they wake up, they suddenly return to the almost semi primitive slash and burn farming and animal husbandry life. In 2015, Wanshan District introduced Jiangxi Shangrao Jiyang group to invest 2 billion yuan to develop and build the Golden

Triangle tourist area of 'Zhusha ancient town, Fanjing Mountain and phoenix ancient city'. In order to protect historical relics, Wanshan district has carefully developed labyrinth mine caves and connected underground karst caves into tourist attractions. The silent mountains have finally regained their vitality.

Along the winding plank road, they went deep into the mountain. They saw many gouges on the stone wall, indicative of a history of nearly 3,000 years from the Spring and Autumn period to the end of 2001. From stone tools to bronze weapons, steel tools to the last excavators, and the tools used by generations of miners represented the history of civilization and pioneering work of the Chinese people. For an instant, tears and blood and piles of white bones were laid bare, and bursts of sad wails were heard from the depths of the tunnel, 'The way stretches endless ahead, I shall search heaven and earth.' Thank the people of Wan Shan for making such a great sacrifice.

In the 1960s, the scenic spot of Wan Shan town and a small street leading to the gate of the plant were restored. During the walk, ancient black brick grain shops, shops, small restaurants, supply and marketing institutions, humble workers' dormitories and a workers' club with a row of benches were established. With slogans such as 'Learn from Daqing in industry, from Dazhai in agriculture', all the pictures of 'cultural reform' are still vivid, as if they were yesterday. Outside the door of an old office is a small blackboard with the notice of that year:

Please take the Supply Certificate to the logistics department to get the grain and oil ticket of the fourth quarter. Food coupon: 14 kg per person per month.

Cloth ticket: 6 feet 7 inches per person per season.

Cooking oil ticket: 50 grams per person monthly. Meat ticket: half a kilo per person per month. Tofu ticket: 1kg per person per month.

Coal ticket: 7.5 kg per person per month.

Logistics Department of the plant September 15, 1967

I stopped here for a long time and read it carefully. Recalling the pain, hunger, hardship and turbulence of those years, I can't help feeling sad. Even though the above treatment is very limited and can only barely survive, it is many times higher than the living standard of local farmers!

Later, I went to Dejiang County and climbed the cave again. This is a high and wide karst cave with far-reaching influence. The large cave is covered by small holes, which bend and overlap. There are strange stones and different scenes, flowing springs and running water, shining with dreamlike brilliance under the illumination of colored lights. Down to dozens of metres, I climbed over a stone wall. Suddenly, the best 'boiled egg' appeared in front of me! The translucent golden yolk is as white as jade. The protein is half cooked and the edge is slightly rolled up. It seems that it is lying in a steaming frying pan and will be fried soon. It's unimaginable that nature's magical craft can create such coveted wonders! I looked down for a long time and my mouth was full of admiration. It's so alike, said Yang Xu, a local writer!

I said, unfortunately, it will never be cooked. It will always be a cold stone.

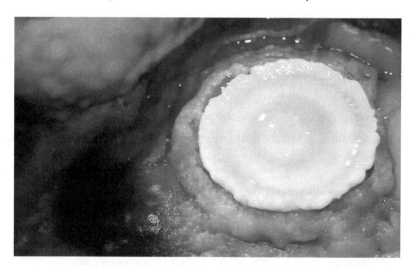

After my words fell, I suddenly realized that Guizhou has been poor for thousands of years. Surrounded by mountains, people yearn for a rich and beautiful life, just as they yearn for this 'boiled egg' to cook. Can their dreams be realized?

2. Wujiang, a rope intertwined with hot blood

That day, I climbed the mountain and looked up. Wujiang, Tongren's mother river. Winds through the mountains! Wujiang will always be a part of the Red Army story.

Under the cloudy sky, she is bright and plump, elegant and sharp, deep and quiet. I also saw the Red Army's bullet marks and red flags still flying. The bullet rain on the iron cable bridge splashed the blood of the soldiers. I can still hear the 'grass shoe army' in Guizhou shouting in the mountains, and the majestic horn echoed in the long march.

In Guizhou, there is too little valuable land for farmers to cultivate. Therefore, the flat dam at the foot of the mountain is called 'field' and the reclaimed land on the hillside is called 'land'. There is a separation between high and low. With the growth of population, in some deep poverty-stricken areas, 'The earth and water in one land cannot feed one people group.' This big problem is a big curse for the people of Guizhou.

In January 2008, when Tongren was suffering from the severe frozen snow disaster, Xi Jinping, the former member of the Standing Committee of the Political Bureau and the Secretary of the Secretary Department of the party, visited the poor and the suffering in the Wanshan district.

In March 2009, Wanshan district was listed as the second batch of national resource exhausted cities and enjoyed relevant national support policies.

In May 2013, general secretary Xi Jinping made important instructions to Wanshan district and asked Tongren city and Wanshan district to make full use of national policies to speed up transformation and sustainable development.

After the national poverty alleviation and development project was launched, due to the fact that the land in Guizhou was small and the population was small, in June 2015, general secretary Xi Jinping held a forum on poverty alleviation in Guiyang. 'One party, one person, water and soil' We should relocate these people to places with better conditions. Demolition should be easy and fundamentally solve their living problems.

The important instructions of the general secretary pointed out the direction for poverty alleviation and development in Guizhou. 2015 is the first year of The 13th Five-Year Plan. According to the detailed investigation of relevant provincial departments, by 2020, the total number of poor people in Guizhou who need to be relocated within five years will reach 1.88 million, which is the area with the largest number of poverty alleviation immigrants in China. Oh, remember the Three Gorges resettlement project? At that time, it was called 'unprecedented in the history of World Water Conservancy', that is, when the water level of the Three Gorges reaches 175 metres, the number of immigrants will reach 1.2 million. Since then, it has taken more than 10 years to complete all the resettlement tasks in the Three Gorges Reservoir area. In 2002, CCTV selected 'China's inspirational role models', and the 'million immigrants' of the Three Gorges won a special award.

In the battle of poverty alleviation in Guizhou, 1.88 million immigrants need to be relocated, which greatly exceeds the number of immigrants in Shaanxi and Shaanxi. It must be completed before 2020. This is an unprecedented task! Among them, Tongren City is the area with the heaviest resettlement task: as one of the 14 concentrated and contiguous poverty-stricken areas in China, Tongren City governs 10 districts and counties as poverty-stricken districts and counties, with a total of 1,565 poverty-stricken villages, including 1 deep poverty-stricken county (Yanhe County), 2 extremely poor towns and 319 extremely poor villages. In 2014, 927,000 poor people were registered. In addition, most of the poor live in deep mountain areas, rocky mountain areas and high mountain areas. They live in scattered areas, lack of cultivated land, difficulty in water use, and extremely backward infrastructure, culture and education. In short, living there means being trapped there and dying there. There is no other way out. The only way out of poverty is to move!

By the end of 2020, 293,300 people will need to be relocated, accounting for nearly one tenth of the city's population. Among them, 125,500 people need to move across districts and counties. The relocation population of prefecture level cities is large, which is unique in the country.

At the mobilization meeting, Chen Changxu, Secretary of the municipal Party committee, announced with emotion: 'We can't lag behind the whole province, but can only provide power for the whole province!' the cadres reflected that mobilizing the masses to go out of their hometown is like pulling out their roots. It's too hard! Chen Changxu, a cadre of the Communist Youth League, replied with a special enthusiasm and image: 'even if we twist the Wujiang into a rope, we should pull the people out!' he asked party committees and governments at all levels to show the spirit of 'true feelings, real gold and silver and true things', take positive action and start war as soon as possible. The municipal Party committee decided that the municipal leading cadres should contact the designated districts and counties to help the three extremely poor villages; Each county-level cadre has a village; Poverty relief cadres should sign military orders and move around frequently if poverty relieve is not achieved. In terms of promotion and use, recognition and reward, treatment guarantee, etc., a set of new regulations and new policies have been formulated to actively encourage outstanding poverty alleviation cadres. 91 people have been promoted in 2019 alone. At the same time, Party committees and governments at all levels should seriously investigate the responsibilities of cadres who are not taking their work seriously, do not act, act slowly and or behave disorderly. In 2019, 452 people were punished, 8 were transferred to the judiciary and 165 were held accountable.

After a period of practice, Tongren City has explored a unique new method of poverty alleviation, namely '76,554 working method'. There are two '5', the first is '5 look': that is, we can know whether the poor are worried about food and clothing by looking at their 'what is put at home, what is worn, what is spread on the bed, what is put in the cupboard and what is cooked in the pot'. The second is the 'five consistencies': that is, according to the standard of 'hanging on the wall, in the bag, what to say and what to record systematically and objectively', as the yardstick for accepting the results of poverty alleviation, effectively eliminate the phenomena of 'digital poverty alleviation' and 'false poverty alleviation'. This highly innovative '76,554 work method' was later listed as a typical poverty alleviation case specially reported by China Poverty Alleviation magazine by the Poverty Alleviation Office of the State Council. It is particularly noteworthy that many poverty alleviation cadres are urban people and are not familiar with rural life. It will take some time to find the way to the village. With this working method, they can enter the state faster. Tan Xiaohong is vice Chairman of Tongren Federation of literary and art circles and a female writer. She came downstairs to interview me and grew up in this city. She also has homework. At first, she was a little confused. She doesn't know where to start. She can't understand the local dialect. She doesn't know where to put my hands and feet opposite the villagers.

Later, she learned the '76554 working method' and soon entered this situation. 'Later, I had more time to walk around,' she said. 'I soon got close to the people and started my work. Don't say I often come and go, help me find ways to get rid of poverty as soon as possible. I must attend weddings and funerals during the new year.'

According to the requirements of the provincial Party committee and the decision of the municipal Party committee, Tongren City has carried out the 'four movements' at the same time and achieved fruitful results, which is exciting:

—Rural infrastructure has changed the world. By 2019, the previous 'four impasses' in water, electricity, roads and telecommunications will be fundamentally reversed. The city has completed 12103 kilometres of 'group access' roads, all 5,982 villagers' groups are unblocked, and the beneficiary population is 320,000 households and 124,300 people; meanwhile, the rural drinking water safety project was fully completed, 798 projects were completed, and the tap water penetration rate reached 95%. In the past, farmers carried water up the mountain every day, and every family had to pay for labor. The history of Tongren using a basin of water from morning to night and finally watering the land with pigs is gone forever. In addition, each administrative village has basically realized the full coverage of optical fiber broadband, 4G network and radio and television network.

The relocation and poverty alleviation work has made rapid progress. There were 125 poor townships and 1,565 poor villages in the city, 144 resettlement sites were planned and constructed, and 293,300 people were resettled. Among them, 126,000 people moved across regions to Tongren City, and 1,853 natural villages were relocated as a whole and completed by the end of 2020. At the same time, Tongren paid special attention to the 'second half of poverty alleviation and relocation, and has built schools, hospitals, supermarkets, factories, citizen activity centers, public service systems, etc. in the relocation and resettlement sites. At the same time, enterprises were strongly encouraged to set up 'poverty alleviation micro factories' in resettlement sites, so that farmers who used to work in other places can 'increase their income and support their families', and immigrants can 'have a good home step by step and slowly better their lives'.

—Industrial poverty alleviation is everywhere. Based on local realities and advantages, we focused on developing and supporting six leading industries such as ecological tea, traditional Chinese medicine, ecological animal husbandry, fruits and vegetables, oil tea and edible fungi, cultivated and organized 11,365 professional cooperatives, including more than 500 leading enterprises at or above the provincial and municipal level and 1,811 family farms, helping nearly 320,000 poor people. Once bare mountains have become tea gardens and flower and fruit mountains, and new villages have been transformed into tourist attractions and 'farmhouses' one by one. The small piece of cultivated land transferred intensively has been built into a greenhouse. Generations after generation of villagers who can only grow corn and potatoes have learned the new technology of getting rid of poverty and becoming rich.

—The 'Three Guarantees' for education, medical care and housing were fully launched. We will strictly implement various poverty alleviation and support policies to achieve full coverage of financial aid for poor families and hospitalization reimbursement for the poor. The city has completely put an end to the phenomenon of dropping out of school because of poverty. The reconstruction of dilapidated houses in rural areas was completed ahead of schedule. Through new rural construction and relocation, most of the nearly 300,000 poor people live in beautiful new houses.

Tongren had been working hard to get rid of poverty for 8 consecutive years and ranked the top in Guizhou. In 2017 and 2018, it ranked the first in the province in two consecutive years.

In the poverty alleviation and development project, the most arduous task is Cross-regional relocation. It is undoubtedly the most labor-intensive work with the most investment in people, money and materials. Where does the money come from for such a big investment?? When Yang Xingcai, director of Tongren Ecological Immigration Bureau, told me that Poverty alleviation was the country's first livelihood project. The CPC Central Committee has truly achieved 'the great strength of the country and the achievements of hundreds of years'. In Guizhou, after comprehensive and accurate investigation and statistics, the national finance will invest US $8,000 for each poor population and US $50,000 to support the municipal finance, Invest another $2,000 for each poor person. A total of $60,000 per person is enough to complete the construction of a new house. For example, a family of five or those who move to another new place will pay $10,000 and they will be able to get a house of 60,000 square metres. In addition, they will be able to move into a new five-bedroom house. The contracted land for a farmer's house and old house still belonged to them.

I shouted, 'This is a gift from heaven!'

Yang Xingcai said with a smile that the Communist Party has done good for the people. Don't think everyone is happy. In places where one side of the soil and water can't support one side of the people. The party and government provide policies, housing and welfare to make farmers urban citizens. This is an unexpected, good thing, but many poor families just don't want to move!

Why? I'm shocked.

Yang Xingcai said that first of all, it is difficult to leave home, especially the elderly. They are accustomed to poverty and are unwilling to leave the place where they have lived for generations; Secondly, poor families lack the ability to stand on their own. They are worried that they will spend a lot of money when they enter the city. They want money to buy lettuce and scallions. They worry that they can't afford it; Third, some farmers are afraid of cremation after death. In order to mobilize these people into the city, our poverty alleviation cadres come to the door every day to talk about policies and principles. Some are as difficult as forcing good people to do bad things. Many people have big bubbles in their mouths. They have made great efforts! For example, a peasant woman had no milk two months after giving birth to a child. She can't buy milk powder on the mountain now. A female cadre who took a half-year-old baby to participate in poverty alleviation did not say a word. She picked up the peasant woman's child and fed it. During the Spring Festival, in order to express his ideas, an old farmer had to send a piece of fresh pork to pairs of poverty alleviation cadres. The cadres repeatedly refused. The old man was very angry and said you wouldn't accept it. When the evaluation team comes, I will talk nonsense and say that your work is 'unqualified!' Cadres have to accept it. I couldn't help laughing.

In the past few months, I have visited villages all over the country. I followed grassroots cadres and poverty alleviation cadre's door to door, from Kang to ground, from door to intersection. Villagers and cadres greeted each other with a smile. Many poverty alleviation cadres can call out the names of villagers. This feeling of intimacy deeply moved me. The broad masses of poverty alleviation cadres have also been deeply baptized in their work. They discussed with their parents and villagers how to get rid of poverty and find a way to get rich. Tongren Yinjiang Tujia and Miao Autonomous County officially withdrew from the list of poor counties in April 2019. On New Year's Eve this year, a poverty alleviation cadre wrote a sentimental little Fu:

My brothers, comrades in arms, comrades–

Thoughts on New Year's Eve

The sound of firecrackers is fast. The year is like a fleeting show. Looking back, the poverty relief order was put forward, and the direction of the flag was like the direction of the arm. At the foot of Fanshan Mountain, on the Bank of water, on the Baisha slope, on the baomu beam, next to the mountain and under He Jialiang, 2,000 soldiers were stationed in the village and 6,000 athletes entered the house. One (the author's note to the book: i.e., 'one standard') as the standard, and two or three (i.e., 'two concerns' and 'Three Guarantees') as the standard, dominated by knowledge.

Where is the road? Is the water clean? Is the food clean? Is everything going well? These are the worries. So, when you meet in the village, hold your son's hand, release your confusion and push your heart. Meet a life, enter the people's home, bend down and put down your stomach. Replace those that are difficult to handle, repair those that are damaged, repair those that are leaking, repair those that are impassable, connect those with inconvenient traffic, and lead the way for those that are not clean. What you have is detailed. All callers will respond and all inquirers will do something. Gradually, it will eventually become people's direction; Fortunately, we have achieved the combination of cadres and the masses and achieved increasing results.

However, this is difficult to do and obtain. If you want to complain, it's hard to cry. The trip to the village and the road of assistance have gone through hardships. Body and skin, bitter and tired. However, it is difficult to be filial to the elderly, to educate a son and to comfort a wife. Every time there is a complaint, the gentle language is modest. Those who touch the inner pain will cover their tears where there is no one and cry on a silent night. The hardest thing is to feel embarrassed. If there is slight negligence, people will complain; I am occasionally responsible for some small mistakes. Although it is bent in the heart, there is no resentment. We should believe in the organization, the hope of the people, the desire to catch up and surpass, wipe away tears and lick blood. With all her strength to settle disputes and old grievances. Fighting with your bare hands to make up for your shortcomings. You were hurt, but you never retreat. Your time is short, painful yet happy.

Great responsibility comes from heaven. It makes the body and skin painful, exhausts the muscles and bones, and sharpens the mind. Along the way, despite the pain and resentment, and even ask all the questions, the responsibility is heavy. However, the ant helps you go and the mole helps me go. They will not shrink back or give up their responsibilities. Just as it has done, it has completed its thinking, overcome its difficulties, overcome its difficulties, and finally get the support of the people. It reproduces the overall situation of cadres and the masses. No matter bitter, tired or hate, there is no regret.

A hundred and a half, ninety miles 'The thicker the smoke, the louder the drum.' I hope that in the coming year, together with all people and then encourage you to fight again and succeed. When we get rid of poverty, we burn a big pot, tripod cattle and sheep, hold a big bowl, burn wine, drink up to the sky, howl and tell our hearts, beat drums and flags, and run a horse to embark on a new journey.

From November 13, 2018, to March 20, 2019, 'great change – a large exhibition celebrating the 40th anniversary of reform and opening up' was exhibited in the National Museum. What a grand national exhibition! People in Yinjiang never expected that a classical Chinese note written by Ran Wei, a 25-year-old local poverty alleviation cadre, was selected for exhibition, and the whole county was very excited. Ran Wei is the youngest resident cadre of the poverty alleviation team in Fengyi Village. He strictly abides by work discipline and never asks for leave. On August 1, 2018, Tongren's 'summer and autumn battles' was fully launched, which coincided with his sister's wedding day. On the one hand, people have launched a tense and fierce struggle to get rid of poverty. On the other hand, he was looking forward to marrying a little sister. After thinking and thinking, ran Wei wrote a leave note in classical Chinese and asked the organization for leave:

> I have been in the village for a long time. I deeply appreciate the care and love of leaders at all levels. Recently, my sister is getting married. I often laugh when I recall the interesting stories of my childhood. It's spring and autumn now. It is said that brotherhood is deep. As a brother, he should present blessings, express the feelings of siblings and comfort the pain of marrying a daughter. Two or three days is enough. However, I had no leisure time out of fight against poverty, and I couldn't get together as soon as possible. My parents and family complained a lot about this, and I felt deeply unfilial. Therefore, I want to take this opportunity to go home, reunite with my family and fulfil my filial duties. I hope all leaders will understand and complete the three-day holiday. She must hurry back when she gets married. We look forward to your approval!

Ran Wei's leave was approved. Interestingly, the leaders who signed the leave application form would write poems to answer, which may be a 'small emotion' in addition to the high tension and fatigue of poverty alleviation.

The captain of Fengyi Village rescue team replied: 'loyalty and filial piety have been hard to find since ancient times. We have rushed to the front line of poverty alleviation. Now my sister is married so you should go home in time.'

The Organization Department of Yinjiang County Party committee replied: 'Fighting poverty is for all the people. Both in public and private, people should care about everything. It can gather in front of the hall for three days and go to the front line after the candlelight blooms.'

Later, somehow, this classical Chinese note was distributed. Like a 'gimmick', it has been released on the official website 'Jiemian Global', 'Guizhou today',

'*Guizhou daily*', people.cn, China Economic Net and other media. Netizens from all walks of life praised it one after another, and its influence has been expanding. Subsequently, it was successfully selected as the 'great change – large exhibition celebrating the 40th anniversary of reform and opening up' in Beijing.

A small note stirred thousands of waves. We can see the prosperity of Yin Jiang's literary style; We can fully recognize the burden of poverty alleviation in the village. They use the simplest words to express their brave persistence and convey their love persistence and dedication. They travel in hot weather and in cold winter. They measure every inch of barren land with their feet and irrigate every dream of getting rid of poverty with sweat. They overcame many difficulties. With hard work, tenacity and perseverance, they performed moving stories one by one.

At the door of the village committee of poverty relief village deep in the mountains, I also saw such a couplet written by the Secretary of the village committee:

Crying, laughing and winning will be remembered by history.

Bitterness, fatigue and participation are heroes to get rid of poverty!

3. The mystery of the square in the moonlight

I came to Guanzhou Town, the resettlement site of Yanjiang Tujia Autonomous County. In a tall new building, Ran Yueguang and I met by chance.

Yanhe County, with a population of 680,000, is the largest and only deeply poor county in Tongren City. Ran Yueguang is the director of the county Immigration Bureau. It is conceivable that his task is heavy and so are his responsibilities.

Let's find a place to talk. I told him.

Ran Yueguang is 52. He is tall, elegant and well behaved. He looks very handsome. I wonder why he has such a gentle and ordinary name. He smiled and said, 'I am a descendant of Confucius seventy-two kind people surnamed Ran. I have a genealogy as evidence Confucius has 3000 disciples and he has six abilities. 'Among the 72 people, Ran's surname is 5. It may be because of the inheritance and influence of DNA. He is a literary heir from generation to generation. In his father's generation, he came from a rich family. He had 6 children, and Ran was the youngest one. According to his father, his grandfather was in charge of the land before it was liberated. His father taught in a private school in his hometown Quanba Town. There were many well-educated people there, most of whom are his students. Later, during the soil improvement movement, his father was mistaken for a 'landlord', and a well-educated teacher disappeared in Quanba Town. The local environment has been greatly affected. Although his fate has been destroyed many times, his father, who is full of poetry and books, turned a blind eye to it. He named his youngest son Ran Yueguang, which means he hopes his son will stick to his family style and study hard. Even if our family is unlucky and can't get the sun, we should stick to our way in the moonlight. Ran recalls that when he was a child, there was a film in the village. Every time they showed something, he went crazy with his friends, he would sit on his shoes. He couldn't see, so he tried to fight the crowd and lost a pair of shoes. During the cultural revolution, there were no new films, everything was about mine warfare, tunnel warfare and the northern expedition. After watching it again and again, he remembered all the lines. He still remembered that at the end of each film screening, the production team leader had to stand in front and say a few words, assign the labor tasks for the next day, then everybody left.

The night was dark. There are mountain roads along the way. Father was in poor health, so Ran accompanied him all the way in case of an accident. There are six main things in the house, including motor, projector, screen, speaker, film box and oil barrel. Father carried them back and forth six times. When they were brought back, it was dawn.

Ran Yueguang always kept in mind his father's teachings and his academic achievements have always been among the best. In the 1990s, he was admitted to the University and became the first college student in the village. After graduation, he developed smoothly in the county authorities and later became the head of the discipline inspection team of the Immigration Bureau. After the 18th CPC National Congress, poverty alleviation and development projects have been vigorously carried out throughout the country. Yanhe County, as the only poor county in the city, needs to understand the relocation work and the minimum number of people from village to household; Building houses requires land selection, land acquisition, survey and design. At the same time, we should find the supervision unit to raise funds. Through environmental protection, we should consider greening and improving living facilities, schools, hospitals and kindergartens. Due to heavy work and tight time, the cadres of the immigration bureau have difficulty breathing. The two old directors can't do anything. They would rather hang their seals and leave their posts. In 2017, the position of director was vacant for two months and no one answered. The Secretary of the county Party committee was very angry and shouted at the Standing Committee. Reducing poverty is war. After the death of the company commander, the deputy company commander was promoted! Find discipline inspection team leader Ran and catch him alive!

At that time, Ran was dealing with several major cases and couldn't get rid of them. A friend told him that you had sent six people to prison. It's all about 'dealing with people'. You'd better change your career and do something to 'save people'. Ran smiled and said that for the sake of the party and the country, he became the party secretary and director of the Immigration Bureau.

Ran Yueguang has experienced hardships since he was a child. As a child of the 'Five Black Categories', he has experienced many difficulties. All these have accumulated a profound positive energy in his heart, which is compassion and sense of responsibility. In our conversation, we mentioned the poverty of villagers in mountainous areas. He was often too excited to speak, and his face was full of tears because of heartache. When it comes to mobilizing villagers to move, he has a loud voice, full of passion and eyes. Speaking of those 'nail households' who died and did not move, he reluctantly said: 'it is much more difficult to let those old farmers who love their homes and soil move out than to repair their houses. I really want to tie people to new houses with ropes!'

Ran Yueguang is definitely a good man. He knows the data like the back of his hand and can even recite it. He said that a total of 51,089 people in the county need to be relocated, including 24,774 in the county and 26,315 in Tongren City. The basic principle of this work is 'provided by the government and voluntary by the masses', which is not difficult to achieve. In order to mobilize the relocation, the Immigration Bureau has rented buses for many times to take people to the city to visit houses and the environment. If a person pays 2,000 yuan, he will give

20 square metres. Isn't it made in vain? But some old farmers just don't nod! Ran and his subordinates came up with many ways: inviting relatives and friends of the villagers to persuade, inviting the relocated people to return to their hometown to talk about the benefits of a new home, and close school, medical treatment and employment. They have said good things thousands of times, but there are still a few 'nail households' who do not move. Later, they came up with a method called 'small hands hold big hands' to take students to the county and urban areas to see new houses. The children keep cheering. It works! When a child cries, his parents accept it. This is a common practice in China.

More than 50,000 people in the county were relocated in batches. Ran and his subordinates followed them again and again, often returning on the same day. Tens of kilometres away, you can imagine how busy and tired they are! Ran was too tired and fell ill several times, he had to go home and hang the needle in the middle of the night. But he was happy, too. Once, at the 'Wangjia Garden' settlement in Wanshan District, Tongren City, he met three kids from Yanhe County after school. He asked, how about going to school in the city? The kids said in unison: OK! Why? A 12-year-old girl said that in the primary school in the village, we only have two books, Chinese and arithmetic. We also have music and art. We can learn to sing and dance. We are very happy! The other little boy looks very strong. He speaks the local dialect very frankly. He said that the female teachers in this city are very beautiful. There are many 'rotten old men' in the village. It's ugly! Ran smiled at the little boy's words.

On another occasion, Ran sent a group of immigrants to Wanshan District. At more than 6 p.m., he and his colleagues were ready to go home. At this time, a middle-aged man hurried to the roadside and asked, 'how many people are there in your car?' Ran moonlight said, there were four drivers. What can I do for you? The middle-aged man said: wait, I'll come. He went back to the roadside supermarket, took out four cans of Red Bull drinks, and then said sincerely: 'I am an immigrant from Yikoudao Village. I have lived here for two months. You are too hard. I have nothing. I plan to buy a bottle of water for each of you. I can only do that.'

Ran Yueguang's eyes were moist. On the way back, he sent a WeChat message in his circle of friends: 'today, the four of us drank the drink sent by a guy in the four-tank car. I think it's happier than drinking Maotai in a big hotel!'

Ran and I and talked all afternoon. After dinner, we took a walk in Guangzhou new community. Ran said that an intelligent management center has been built here for all-round monitoring. The children won't get lost and the thieves won't run away. If residents have anything to do, they can call the center immediately. At this time, the dead of night. Looking around, there are many tall buildings and bright lights. Behind all kinds of curtains, there are quiet and happy homes. Although the autumn wind is cool, I can still feel the warmth in my heart. Walking, I found that every building here has a name, such as diligence and thrift building, self-improvement building, Thanksgiving building, Zhien building, Lianzheng (integrity) building, justice building and so on. I asked who initiated this. Ran said proudly, 'There are also some scholars. Have you seen? There is also a pair of gold-plated couplets under the name of the building.'

I saw it. In the name of thrift construction, it is 'getting rich through thrift and self-cultivation through thrift.'

Ran said, 'in order to give people some reminders and education, I've been thinking about it for three months.' I once asked a fellow, do you know what frugal architecture means? The villagers smiled and said, I know, just let us live less and work more. Ran asked another, do you know what self-improvement building means? Let's do one thing in local dialect (strong) things.

Did I say that the names of clean government construction and judicial construction are too politicized? Ran said, you see, below the integrity building is the community office, and below the justice building is the police station. This is the goal!

The moon on the mountain is bright. Walk through several restaurants, supermarkets, shoe stores and clothing stores – all run by young immigrants – to the community square. In front of it stands a magnificent huge stone carving, like an abstract bull. There is a circle of fixed round stone benches around the square. Ran said that when people came to see the house, they all complained that my square had expanded and wasted space. Now damas some out to dance in the square every day. They think the square is too small. It's hard for everyone to do good for the people! Then he asked me to take a closer look at each stone bench. Strangely, there is an idiom engraved on it, but each idiom has no last word. For example, there is no word 'city' in 'unified into one city', there is no word 'source' in 'source of drinking water', and so on. I see. This is what he used to test the children.

Hehe, I've seen meticulous work, but I've never seen such meticulous work. This moonlight night is really comfortable.

4. The most unique 'special training course'

The square was crowded with people, red flags fluttering and thundering with joy.

When firecrackers and smoke soared into the air, an exciting 'square feast' began.

There are nearly 100 tables in the third row, and nearly 1,000 people are dining. Food is not extravagant. It just collects ordinary boxed meals into plates and bowls, and then serves the public. Those who eat are immigrants who have just moved in, and those in charge of food are the Communist Party. In the morning, the immigrants set out from the deep mountains, dragging their families and children to the resettlement sites in Bijiang district and Wanshan District of Tongren. After noon, the party and government organized everyone to have a group meal before they had time to cook. This is also a celebration of the immigrants' housewarming. The waiters who deliver meals are cadres of Party and government organs, including directors, directors, section chiefs, poverty alleviation cadres, township heads, town heads, village heads, etc. However, the villagers did not sit down honestly. From time to time, they look around with their jobs to see the buildings, roads, green belts, property service centers, love restaurants, kindergartens, libraries, cultural entertainment rooms, supermarkets, etc. around the square. Of course, the happiest thing is the dolls in the village. Their little faces were hung with rice grains, circling in the crowd, and a scream rushed into the blue sky.

The excited and moving light flows in everyone's heart, face and eyes. Yes, it looks like an ordinary group dinner, but it has special holiday significance. For poverty alleviation cadres, this is a great achievement of their hard work, which is worth celebrating. For Tongren City and the poor, it has created many historic firsts: for the first time, ethnic minority villagers in mountainous areas no longer live with cattle and sheep, become citizens for the first time, live in high-rise buildings for the first time, and stand on the balcony of high-rise buildings to overlook the urban scenery. Countless firsts made the villagers span thousands of years overnight, from the era of agriculture and animal husbandry to modern cities. They're like crazy roller coasters. This is a colorful and strange new era.

What moved immigrants even more were that the party, the government and all poverty alleviation cadres were too cautious and considered too thoroughly. Relocated farmers are poor households. Many families have no money to buy furniture and household appliances for their new house. The Poverty Alleviation Office and the Immigration Bureau mobilize social forces and caring people to do their best to raise funds and send wooden beds, tables, closets, curtains, televisions, induction furnaces, water heaters, and even rice flour and meat to the new homes of immigrant families, so that they can start a new life and bring their bags into the house.

In the agricultural park in Wanshan District aided by Shandong Jiufeng group

Yanhe County has a famous poor village called Yikoudao. From the name of this village, we can imagine how dangerous and barren its terrain is: farmers are scattered on rocky peaks and valleys, the hillside is steep and long, looks like a knife, and the turbulent Wujiang is 800 metres below. Due to the large population, less land and steep mountain roads, the villagers live in extreme poverty. After the land was divided into different families, a hill with an area of 1.5mu was allocated to 34 families. After the harvest, each family could only harvest half a bag of rice. Later, they had to take turns and agree to plant a family for a year. However, it had become a big problem who sat in the front row. The villagers had to use the most ancient method of Chin−se – drawing lots. Before the migration, those families had not finished their rounds.

In Wanshan District, I casually walked into a villager's house in Yikoudao. Listen to the Henan accent of the housewife Yuan Xinzhi. I asked her why you went to Yikoudao? No matter how poor your hometown is, it's better than this town.

Yuan Xinzhi glanced at her husband Zhu Yongxi and said, 'he lied to me!' it turned out that they met when they were young working in a new enterprise in Guangdong. Xinzhi felt good when she saw Zhu Yongxi working hard and honest. Moving luggage together is even a marriage. It doesn't matter to talk about hometown. Zhu Yongxi said, Yikoudao is so beautiful. Fishing boats sing at the foot of the mountain. Flowers and fruits smell on the mountain. Every family lives in a beautiful stilt building. Yuan Xinzhi is ecstatic and urges Zhu Yongxi to take her home every New Year, but Yongxi just doesn't move. Until the first child was approaching school age, the three members of the family picked up and went to Yikoudao. Along the way, we took a bus, a boat, climbed a mountain, and made seven and eight turns. At a glance, I saw my husband's h–me – a half broken wooden house with no walls and nothing. There is also a semi paralyzed father lying inside. Yuan Xinzhi's tears fell down, cried in the middle of the night, but it was too late to regret.

A few months ago, the couple and their three children moved to Wangjia garden, a resettlement site in Wanshan District, and lived in a new house with 100 square metres, three bedrooms and a hall. Under the arrangement of the community, Zhu Yongxi became a security guard and Yuan Xinzhi became a cleaner. Yuan Xinzhi's family has stable income and comfortable life. Yuan Xinzhi bought a set of red silk clothes and trousers, joined the community dance team and went to the square to dance every night. It can be imagined that under the tall buildings, under the colorful lights and in the beautiful, warm and rhythmic dance music, she must have harvested the 'second youth' at the age of 50!

But the new life also has 'happy troubles'. When they first arrived, when villagers who had been in contact with hoes for a lifetime entered the supermarket, they could not press the elevator, lock the door, use the induction cooker, brush the mobile phone, and did not know how to withdraw money from the bank. Therefore, each new community in Tongren has established a unique 'special training course' in the world. The staff will gather the elderly immigrants and teach them the technical work needed for their new life one by one. If you study today and forget tomorrow, teach again. In order to solve the worries of immigrants, various districts and counties have formulated various preferential policies and made use of the advantages of 'demographic dividend' to increase investment attraction, such as the famous Nongfu Shanquan, Hubei Yuguo mushroom industry company, Shandong Jiufeng agricultural group, Guiyang haocaitou food company, processing industry, footwear industry, clothing industry and many other small and medium-sized enterprises. Many people have come to Tongren to build factories and settle down, A large number of immigrants can be employed nearby. Yuguo mushroom industry plans to build 3,000 greenhouses in Bijiang District, which can solve the living problems of 3,000 families. At present, the project is under construction.

In a supermarket, I met a short old lady named Lu Laochan (I didn't call her this name when I was a child), Tujia. She moved from Yinjiang Tujia and Miao Autonomous County. I asked, is it nice to live in a new building? She shook her head and couldn't say. Zhang Wenjuan, a cadre of the Publicity Department of the district Party committee who accompanied him, asked why? She said there were too many buildings. They all looked the same. I can't read. I can't find my home several times. The crowd nearby laughed. The old man is cheerful and straightforward. She's cute. I just want to buy something for Lu Laochan as a gift. Careful Wen Juan holds a bag of fruit in her hand.

The old lady followed the crowd to the door and suddenly turned to us and shouted, 'thank you, Communist Party!'

Once chatted with the leaders of the municipal Poverty Alleviation Office. She said that the summer and autumn of 2019 is the climax of immigration relocation, with thousands of immigrants moving into the urban area. It is understood that within a month, the high heels of several large shopping malls in Bijiang District have been sold out.

I smiled and said that when the girls in the village come to the city, they wanted to do the catwalk!

As the Yikoudao villager Yuan Xinzhi said, 'A happy life came so fast!'

III   The horn of l

1. The horn kept ringing

The sun jumped up from behind the mountain. Wang Mingli stood on the top of the mountain with his hands on his hips, overlooking the bright Wujiang winding through the mountains. The autumn wind roared and the yellow leaves rolled up all over the mountain. He stood motionless like a rock.

He is the 'old bugler' of Tongren Mount–in – a 55-year-old Miao veteran. After ninety-nine and eighty-one difficulties, he fell many times, resolutely stood up, died many times, and fortunately survived. The shrapnel reduced the height by 4 cm, and then miraculously increased by 5 cm. Now it is majestic. The people who walk around the green mountains are not old, and the inspiring 'horn' sounds from time to time.

In fact, the veteran standing on the top of the mountain has only half a leg.

At about 9 am, we drove to the village committee of Datoupo Village, Yingwuxi Town, Si'nan County, Tongren City. On the second floor of a small white building, a kindergarten teacher with ponytail in the courtyard was leading a group of children to play games. I was surprised. When I looked carefully, it turned out that the first floor was the kindergarten and the second floor was the office. This is obviously not the original design. This is obviously not the original design. I'm very moved that village cadres can give up their office space to the children. Now, several Town and village cadres came out to shake hands. When greeting, someone pointed to a short and strong man behind him and said that he was Wang Mingli. Wang Mingli, with an old black down jacket and a pair of muddy sneakers, walked over to shake hands with me. Big face, wide forehead, long eyes, loud voice, with an overwhelming sense of pride. During the conversation, I suddenly heard a loud noise. I looked around in surprise. The horn came from the village on the mountain? Wang Mingli took out his cell phone and went to the roadside to answer the phone – Oh, his cell phone rang! I was shocked. Worthy of the feelings of veterans!

I said, I carried a gun when I was young.

Wang Mingli asked, have you ever served in the army?

I smiled and said, it's just wood.

Wang Mingli smiled, then waved his cell phone and said: let's go up the mountain!

Halfway down the road, we climbed the high slope, and the road became more and more difficult. The soles of the shoes were covered with thick soil, which was as heavy as lead. Wang Mingli looked relaxed and introduced to me the new tea mountain of 1000 mu being planted. At the same time, his 'horn' has been ringing, which seems very busy and encouraging. Watching him stride forward, I was in a trance for a while. They all said that Wang Mingli was a retired soldier with a broken leg. Why does he walk and climb mountains so powerfully without any abnormality? Maybe I don't think disability is that serious. On the hillside, several excavators are leveling the land, and several groups of male and female villagers are taking care of the tea garden. Wang Mingli greeted them like an old friend and asked them questions. Later, he told me that these were poor households in the surrounding villages. After working in the tea mountain, they have a fixed salary and live a more comfortable life.

After seeing the new tea mountain, we drove to the Wanjiashan sightseeing tea garden developed and cultivated by him and his comrades in arms for 10 years. There is no need to climb here. A flat concrete road turned over more than ten times to the top of the mountain. There are office area, conference hall, tea tasting room, wooden plank road leading to various scenic spots, beautiful huge white canopy, viewing platform and pavilion. Overlooked from a high altitude, the mountains are undulating, surrounded by clouds, and the roads are winding like ribbons, connected with the white New Farmers' village, which looks quiet and warm. On the hillside far and near, rows of low and neat tea trees seem to be continuous layers of green waves, with spectacular scenery. It was the middle of winter and it was cold on the mountain. We walked into the room and sat around the 'electric heating table' (this is a 'specialty' of Guizhou: there is a cotton curtain around the table, in which there is an electric heater, and our feet can stretch in to keep warm). We talked from morning to night. His half-life experience made me angry and surprised me again and again. Finally, I said, let me see your injured leg. They all said you were badly hurt, but you walk like flying. Why can't you see at all?

Wang Mingli rolled his trouser legs onto his thighs. There is a belt buckle on the upper part of the left leg. After unlocking, pull out the thin half of the leg and stand on the ground with a prosthetic limb about 30 cm high! I was shocked. I looked at the prosthetic tube. There is gauze at the bottom, a little fish red. Obviously, this is because there is a river of blood when walking. Look at the right leg. The skin and muscles look normal, but uneven. There are some light black scars. Wang Mingli said that when he was injured, the bone of his right leg was cut off by the shell skin, and only part of the residual bone and a piece of meat were left under his knee. The military doctors performed more than 10 operations. Finally, they use a steel plate as a support to connect their knees and feet. Now they can walk, but they are completely unconscious. I felt my calf. The skin is cold, hard and straight. Pointing to the scar on his left thigh, Wang Mingli said that the skin covered with steel plate on his right leg was transplanted from here.

I was surprised, towered, and in awestruck. What a shock! On the bloody battlefield, he can survive and work until today, just as it is not easy for a camel to pass through a pinhole!

For nearly 8 hours, Wang Mingli solemnly recalled and told, during which the 'horn' kept ringing. Speaking of the blood, sweat and tears of these years, they seemed to blend in with his laughter and horn. They still swaggered, loud and broad, touching the hearts of everyone sitting in their seats. Yuan Ming, a young cadre of Tongren Poverty Alleviation Office, and Chen Weichun, a young girl of Si'nan Poverty Alleviation Office, listened carefully – suddenly, we were not ready – he suddenly took off his left leg prosthesis and moved very neatly. Bang, bang, he threw the prosthetic into the corner of the room and shouted, 'I can walk up and down. What's terrible!'

I've never seen such a humorous person. I couldn't help laughing. After laughing, I burst into tears!

2. Battle of naked cat's ears

Everybody, work hard!
There is a dangerous beach ahead. We should speed up the pace!
Let's work together,
The boat is about to dock, everybody step it up!

This is the song of Wujiang tracker sung by Wang Mingli to me.

He sang and I listened. In the roar of the tracker, there seemed to be bursts of cold waves flying in front of them

For a long time, Si'nan County in Tongren was once a prosperous water transport terminal along the Wujiang, with thousands of sails competing and merchants gathering. Wooden boats transporting salt, kerosene, cloth, grain and merchants, or flowing along the Jialing River from Si'nan Wujiang wharf to Fuling, Chongqing; Or about 300 miles from the upper reaches of Fuling to Si'nan. Most of the young villagers along the Wujiang in Si'nan County make a living by pulling fibers. A large wooden ship carrying people and goods can carry 50 tons and needs 30 trackers. It takes more than a month to rise and 15 days to fall. During the people's commune period, Wang Mingli's father was a famous local tracker and old captain. He is the helmsman in charge of turning the rudder when the ship passes through rapids and dangerous beaches. In case of danger, he handed the rudder to the vice rudder and supported the stone bank or reef by the river with a thick bamboo pole to prevent the wooden boat from hitting the boulder. The life and death of people and goods is often a matter of a minute. Wang Mingli was born in 1964. He was the late son of his family. His two brothers are more than ten years older than him. Unfortunately, his two sisters died of illness when they were young. Before the Spring Festival, his mother usually makes two pairs of cloth shoes for his two brothers until the fourth day of the New Year, so that they can go out to visit their parents and find their daughter-in-law. After the fourth day of the New Year, she will dress Xiao Ming with new clothes. In the cold winter, the two brothers were barefoot. Because the shoes are too big, Xiao Mingli can only drag them away with hemp rope, which makes the earth dusty and rattling, which makes him very proud. In order to help poor families, Wang Mingli followed his father and brother at the age of 12. Adults record 10 work points every day and children record 2 work points. In the wind and rain, choppy and often overloaded wooden boats are prone to accidents. People often roll off the cliff on the slippery cliff plank road, or die or get injured. When pulling the fiber, the skinny little Mingli and the adults were naked above the waist, wearing rag shorts, with a cloth pad with thick threads and dense needles on his shoulders. He bent deeply on the plank road barefoot, shouting the TrackMan's call, and struggling to pull a 100-metre-long fiber rope forward. At first, the shoulders and soles of the feet were bloody. Later, they formed thick callus as hard as slate. It's a long way to go. He pulls fibers during the day and sleeps on the boat board at night. Xiao Mingli is so tired that he cries with hunger. Later, he stopped crying. At a young age, he learned to bite his teeth, be patient and strong. My father didn't get off the ship until he was 70. It's good to get 10 yuan or 8 yuan from the production team at the end of each year. This is how the great Wujiang rolls forward under the pull of the rope.

In 1981, 17-year-old Wang Mingli graduated from high school and joined the army. The family is very supportive. My mother said, 'only when he becomes a soldier can he eat enough.' my father said, 'Only heroes can find a good wife.' What he said is true. The villagers scraped together 3 yuan and 80 cents as gifts for him. Three years later, Wang Mingli went to the battlefield with the army.

As we all know, China's self-defense counterattack against Vietnam occurred from February 17 to March 16, 1979. According to the order of the Central Military Commission, the Chinese people's liberation army attacked and occupied more than 20 important cities, counties and towns in northern Vietnam in a short time to counterattack the Vietnamese army that constantly violated Chinese territory. After its overwhelming victory, it quickly withdrew from Vietnam as a lesson. However, the war is not over. Since then, the two armies have continued to break out border conflicts in Luojiapingshan, Fakashan, Koulinshan, Laoshan, Zheyinshan and other places for more than 10 years.

For actual combat, the 'devil training' of recruits is extremely cruel: stand upright for 3 hours in the poisonous sun, stay still, and lift them down when they faint. They are not allowed to come back,; Through the tropical jungle for 10 days, each person carries 35-40 kg of weapons and equipment, and runs 5km every day without rest; Each person will send two kilograms of rice to eat raw rice, and then rely on wild fruits, grass roots and leaves to catch voles, rabbits and live snakes to fill their stomachs; A mobile flashlight with 100 small bulbs 100 metres away in the dark. They look like dark red cigarette butts. They finished early and returned to the dormitory early. If you can't finish the battle, you can't finish the task. You should resolutely abandon it and send it to the place where you grow vegetables, cook and raise pigs. When Wang Mingli was young, he climbed more than

100,000 mountains in strong winds and waves. He is brave and clever. He can live and do anything he eats. Shoot 5 guns and 50 rings; When the gun goes out, the small bulb goes out; The first recruit company dropped more than 50 metres. After the training, he was rated as 'special gunner' and 'five excellent soldiers', and became the monitor of the recruit class. Later, he was assigned to a field army in Yunnan as the squad leader of the fast knife squad, leading an infantry squad and two machine gun squads, with a total of 32 brothers, equivalent to the strength of a platoon.

The tiger came out of the mountain. On the early morning of April 28, 1984, Wang Mingli, 20, led his intensive class to follow the army and use the long night to force the army up the Yinshan Mountain. There are slippery trails and steep rocks all the way. Military regulations: in order to ensure the marching speed and concealed propulsion, no one shall shout when he falls, and no one shall save him. If he dies, he will die. If you can climb up, keep up with the follow-up troops. When we reached the secluded place of Zheyin Mountain, it was a hillside with weeds. The mountain 100 metres ahead is Chinese territory occupied by the Vietnamese army. Countless mines are buried on the hillside, with dense bamboo leaves. In order to prevent injury, our soldiers had to wear a special long iron boot with a steel plate and a thick water dragon cloth at the bottom. When they went to fight, the soldiers brought two cans of compressed biscuits and said they could last seven days, but the next day, some soldiers ate one. Wang Mingli was so angry that he ordered, 'Whoever dares to eat again will shoot on the spot!' then, under the cover of night, the soldiers quietly dug holes in the cat's ears with engineering shovels. Since then, they ate there for 10 months and slept there for 10 months! At the same time, small-scale contact wars have occurred. Our army often sends small teams to touch the mountains late at night to harass the Vietnamese army, paralyzing and weakening their vigilance and fighting spirit. Tropical mountainous areas are extremely hot during the day, and the ground temperature is as high as more than 40 degrees Celsius. I've been lurking in the cat's ear holes for a long time. I'm covered with sores, skin ulcers, thighs and crotches. No way. The soldiers must walk naked. At night, the temperature on the mountain suddenly dropped and people trembled with cold. Every time there is a rainstorm, the clothes and blankets in the cat's ear hole float. In order to prevent our attack, the Vietnamese army not only set up minefields in front of the position, but also sprayed a large amount of deadly poison. Water can't be drunk, grass can't be eaten, and the skin will be inflamed and purulent. Only when it rains can our officers and soldiers wear steel helmets and drink water from the 'tap water' in the sky. It was hidden near the enemy camp and supplies could not reach. The soldiers were very hungry. They waited for the rain and tried to taste the washed weeds. After finding a soldier poisoned, Wang Mingli ordered: 'whoever wants to eat grass, I'll try it first!' he was poisoned several times. His face was swollen like a big fat cake and his eyes were squeezed into a seam, but he couldn't stick to the line of fire. Once, a little wild boar fell into a cat's ear hole. The soldiers held it down and killed it. Each person has a small piece of raw meat. Everyone is as happy as the New Year. Do you eat it raw? Wang Mingli stood up on the spot and performed for us: his mouth was wide open, his palm wiped on his outstretched tongue, and the imaginary meat disappeared. He exaggerated the action five times in a row and really succeeded. His palm was full of bright saliva, as if he had really swallowed a piece of meat, which made us laugh. When the soldiers in the performance smoked at night, Wang Mingli stood up, grabbed a cigarette, covered his mouth with his hand, pretended to take a big sip, and then quickly poked the cigarette end down and stuffed it into the imaginary grass. He repeated this action seven or eight times, and the room was full of laughter, but his expression was serious and serious, and his eyes glittered. I deeply realize that these acts look like 'jokes' today, but they contain his unforgettable memories of wartime life and his eternal memories of his dead comrades in arms. My eyes are wet again.

Laughter is actually pain. Improvisation is actually a silent long song.

It rained heavily around 1 p.m. on May 10, 1984. A few days ago, our headquarters issued a mobilization order. Recently, we have chosen an opportunity to attack the enemy's position. Wang Mingli understood that this stormy night was the best time to launch an attack. Perhaps tonight, the Vietnamese army also had an ominous feeling and shot at our camp from time to time. As shells roared everywhere, explosions occurred from time to time, fires rushed into the sky, and stones and soil splashed. Not long ago, two soldiers more than ten metres away from Wang Mingli reported to him with a walkie talkie: 'we are injured, one arm is missing, and one leg is missing, requesting reinforcements.' Wang

Mingli immediately reported to the company commander: '001, 001, I am 007, the two soldiers in front are seriously injured, and I am ready to rescue!' with the consent of the company commander, Wang Mingli put on the first aid kit and quickly jumped out of the bomb shelter, He bent down and rushed forward. After urgently bandaging the two wounded, he quickly dragged them back to the position. Wang Mingli gasped and found that a platoon leader bent down and rushed to the bomb shelter. There was a hole in front of him. He obviously didn't notice that Wang Mingli saved two wounded soldiers. Wang Mingli shouted, 'platoon leader –' before his voice died, he heard a loud noise. In the light of the fire, the platoon leader flew up and landed on the ground again. In despair, Wang Mingli jumped out of the bomb shelter and rushed to the platoon leader again. On the flickering hillside, fire and darkness intertwined. He picked up the broken leg platoon leader and bent down all the way. Suddenly another shell came and detonated the mines around him. Wang Mingli fell with a bang. His left leg flew up and his right leg was bleeding. Fortunately, he is still awake. He immediately took off his shirt and tightly grabbed the broken leg (it was this action that saved his life), then dragged the platoon leader with one hand and struggled to support him to climb forward for more than ten metres for more than ten minutes. 'This is the longest road I have taken in my life,' he said

Finally, he dragged the platoon leader into the trench and Wang Mingli fainted. Later, he learned that there were no stretchers on the position because there were too many wounded soldiers. His comrades in arms dragged him and the platoon leader down the mountain with two rubber raincoats. He had bruises on his back and hips, and his muscles were blurred by rocks. Subconsciously, he vaguely heard one of his comrades in arms shouting, 'look up, don't knock on the door!' another said, 'well, you can't let the monitor sleep, you can't wake up!' later, he also heard that when he fainted in the trench, his comrades in arms thought he couldn't work. They found his application for joining the party written before the war in the left chest pocket of his bloody military uniform. The instructor cried and said, 'I agree with Wang Mingli's joining the party!'

A few days later, Wang Mingli woke up. He found himself lying in a field hospital. He inserted various tubes into his body, and more than a dozen wounds were wrapped with thick gauze. His left leg is missing and a muscle hangs on his right leg. He cried and wondered how to live in the future? How do you meet your parents? If he becomes a burden to your parents all your life, what is the meaning of life? The military doctor naturally understood his psychology and told him in his ear: 'you have been in a coma for 5 days and have been in shock twice. We have carried out many emergency rescue. Now your life is out of danger.'

Wang Mingli shed tears and said, 'I'm so disabled. What's the use of living?'

The military doctor said, 'young man, you are only 20 years old. Compared with those martyrs, living is happy!'

Later, the leader of the army came to see him and told him that he had joined the party and became a glorious Communist. Desperate Wang Mingli suddenly felt a torrent of new life, new strength and new hope injected into his body. After crying for a long time, Wang Mingli asked, 'did you tear down the Yinshan Mountain?'

The chief said, 'don't worry, Zheyin Mountain and Laoshan Mountain are firmly in our hands!'

Wang Mingli asked, 'how about the three wounded I saved?'

The doctor standing nearby said, 'they are still alive!'

A huge warm current poured into his heart like sunlight. Yes, the doctor is right. Life is happiness!

Wang Mingli was hospitalized for 11 months and his height was shortened by 4 cm. The first major operation lasted more than 20 hours, and the doctor took out more than 100 shrapnel from his whole body. Later amputation, plate implantation, knee repair, skin grafting, esophageal perforation repair... He doesn't remember how many times he did it altogether. So far, there are still more than a dozen small shrapnel that cannot be removed from his head, chest, armpits and legs.

Finally, relying on steel plates, prosthetics and crutches, Wang Mingli struggled to stand up and learned to walk again. Therefore, his height 'grows' by 5cm. During this period, he served as the monitor of the wounded team again. The main task of his 16 disabled soldiers is to educate everyone not to be sad, discouraged and discolored, maintain revolutionary will and optimism, and actively contribute to the construction of his hometown after retirement. During this period, because Wang Mingli's troops performed bravely on the battlefield, they won the reward of the general order of the Central Military Commission and were personally awarded second-class merit.

To my shock, Wang Mingli did another unexpected heroic act: Luo Jincheng, a little comrade in arms of his intensive class, will soon be demobilized to his hometown in rural Sichuan. Xiao Luo took part in the battle of Zheyin Mountain with everyone. He did well, but he was not injured or meritorious. Back home, as an ordinary veteran, according to relevant regulations, Xiao Luo certainly can't get special arrangements and can only go home to work in agriculture. Considering that Xiao Luo's family was extremely poor and needed a paid job, Wang Mingli made a decisive decision: he gave Luo Jincheng second-class merit and only got himself a third-class merit.

What a wonderful story! In order to defend the motherland and save his comrades in arms, Wang Mingli was fearless and selfless. He's so brave! Twenty years later, Luo Jincheng made a special trip from Sichuan to Si'nan County to visit Wang Mingli. They fought for friendship and cried for each other.

Later, general secretary Xi Jinping summed up the 'Laoshan spirit': 'no fear of hardship, no fear of death, no fear of loss.'

3. From 'postman' of double crutches to 8 villages

In November 1985, after four years in the army, Wang Mingli, 21, retired from the army with a grade IV disabled soldier certificate and a crutch and returned to Puguitang Village, Guanzhongba Township, Si'nan County. Hearing the name of the village, I knew it was a poor and miserable place. The mother saw her son. He was still alive when he left and is now disabled. She hugged him in tears. The father who has been a captain for decades is very strong. Why are you crying? It is glorious to sacrifice and get hurt in order to defend our country! The brothers and brother said excitedly that you should take good care of yourself. We will take care of everything at home!

Wang Mingli was assigned to Si'nan County Federation of trade unions. The leader saw that it was difficult for him to walk, so he took good care of him. He was specially assigned as an organ postman. He sits in the concierge every day to send and receive letters and newspapers. In this way, he can avoid walking a lot. But heroes have their own qualities. No matter how ordinary things are, they can be great. Over time, Wang Mingli found that most of the letters and documents sent by the trade union had been sent to the county Party and government organs, enterprises and institutions, and the road was not long. He believes that although the postage of a letter is only 8 cents, a little can make a lot of money. This is a big number over the years! In order to save some money for the union, he decided to send it himself. Si'nan is a mountain city, distributed on both sides of the Wujiang, with sloping roads everywhere. Since then, every afternoon, Wang Mingli has struggled to move his heavy body on the road with crutches and mail on his back. Whether it is windy and rainy, hot summer or cold winter, he goes up and down the mountain, takes a boat across the bridge, crosses the street, and sends each email to each unit. Everyone was shocked and moved to see his appearance. They said they had to send eight cents. Why do you eat so much! Wang Mingli wiped sweat and said that the road is not far, it's better to save money. Where does the recipient know that the visitor is not only on crutches, but also has two legs, one leg is a prosthetic and the other is a steel plate! He walked a lot. His prosthetic left leg was bleeding. When he came home in the evening, his mother helped him wash and bandage. He couldn't help crying and fell into the pool. Wang Mingli said, mom, don't cry! Many of my comrades died on the ancient mountain battlefield. I can breathe and stand in front of you alive. I'm so happy!

One winter, the ground was covered with ice and snow. Wang Mingli rolled down a steep slope, his forehead fell down, bleeding, and his two crutches were thrown far away. Not far down the slope is the undulating Wujiang. He lay there in pain and could not move for a long time. Suddenly, he laughed alone. He looked at the clouds and said to himself: Damn it! When I hit Yinshan and saved my comrades in arms, I didn't die. I posted letters back and forth on the mountain and fell several times. It seems that God must let me continue!

In this way, Wang Mingli, a 'volunteer postman', has worked for 10 years and sent more than 100,000 letters without mistakes. Needless to say, there is one advantage: after 10 years of 'Long March', his body is very strong and his two thighs are very strong. Wang Mingli threw away his crutches.

The reputation of a hero is always glorious and admirable. Two years later, a beautiful girl Xu Dahua fell in love with him. The girl's family firmly opposed it and had a big quarrel, but the girl's attitude was firm and unwavering. Unless he doesn't get married, his parents have to admit it. Every time he went to visit his future father-in-law and mother-in-law, Wang Mingli would hide his crutch in his hiding place, and then walk in with dignity, stride and smile to say hello. The old man asked how your injured leg was? Wang Mingli said softly, it doesn't matter, small problem!

Dahua married the girl and she gave birth to a son and a daughter. After graduating from college, my son was sent to the Laoshan army. He obtained the third-class merit and became an excellent soldier. He retired home five years later. Now he is the first Secretary of poverty alleviation in the village. My daughter became a soldier after graduating from university and was praised by the leaders many times. More than 40 of his family and villagers joined the army at the call of Liming. Now more than 20 people join the army. Spring Festival home reunion, big family strong patriotic complex, full of heroism, as long as the horn rings, stand up a majestic 'intensive class'!

In 1998, heroic stories came again. In the upsurge of 'new rural construction' in China, Wang Liming took the initiative to apply for work in the village. This once again surprised relatives, friends and colleagues. Can you, a disabled man with only two and a half legs, climb the mountain? Wang Mingli replied, 'I am still alive!'

The first stop is Shimenkan Village on the high mountain. The broken house is leaking. There is no road, no water and electricity. Wang Mingli went deep into all departments of the county, impassioned and reasonable. The leader was moved and gave him what he wanted. With this investment, he led all the villagers to be volunteers, chiseling stones, erecting power poles, digging ditches and erecting pipelines. After a year of hard work, all difficulties were easily solved. When there is water and electricity, the whole mountain village is as happy as thunder. Then, Wang Mingli turned to the second stop: Huaping Village on the hillside. This is also a problem of the water cycle and extreme poverty. After a year of fighting, the hero fell his head and blood on the construction site. The steel plate hit the mountain. The villagers were moved to tears. All the difficulties were kicked down the mountain by Wang Mingli. And Gongzhai Village, Zhushan Village and Guotian Village – you can imagine how tall this village is... Over the past nine years, with the support of steel plates and prosthetics, Wang Mingli has climbed mountains and mountains, fought against 8 national poverty-stricken villages, built 68 water kilns and built more than 60 kilometres of roads. In addition, he also promoted the diversified management of agricultural and sideline products and asked agricultural experts to guide villagers to improve planting technology, so that most people can get rid of poverty and achieve food and clothing. At the same time, the leaders of the County Federation of trade unions repeatedly advised him to come back and rest. Don't work too hard. But Wang Mingli repeatedly refused. He said: 'many of my comrades in arms grew up in the countryside. They said poverty made me cry many times. I was for them and helped their relatives. I can't go!'

In 2008, the construction of Silin Hydropower Station on the Wujiang started, requiring all villagers along the river to move. However, many villagers miss their hometown very much, and local cadres will not leave after repeated persuasion. Wang Mingli, who had just moved to Baiyang Village, came out. He came to visit with a bottle of wine or a piece of meat. He talked about the overall situation, hopes and benefits of the treatment of the elderly and the schooling of children. After drinking three rounds of wine, the vast majority of farmers soon agreed. Finally, there are only six 'nail households', of which villager Yang Chunmao is the most stubborn. One day in May, it rained cats and dogs. Mingli heard that Yang Chunmao was herding cattle on the other side of the mountain. He thought the weather was dangerous, so he put on his raincoat and hurried across the river to find him. On the bridge, I met Lao Yang leading a cow home. They talked as they crossed the bridge in the rain. The bridge is an old wooden bridge built in an early age, and its slab is worn-out. They are chatting. Suddenly, the big black cow stepped on the broken bridge board and fell into the river with a plop. Li Ming knows that cattle are the lifeblood of farmers! He completely forgot that he was a broken leg man. He immediately took off his raincoat and jumped into the river in the strong wind, huge waves and boundless rain and fog. When Ming Li was young, he followed his father to the river to pull fibers and formed a good water-based body. However, the prosthetics and steel plates on his body were too heavy at that time, which soon dragged him into the rapids and disappeared. Yang Chunmao ran to the bridge and shouted, 'no, someone was washed away by the water. Come and help!'

Soon more than ten people gathered on the shore. They swam down with Yang Chunmao and ran frantically to find someone. At a distance of more than 200 metres, we saw Wang Mingli wipe the river and rain on his face and lead the big black cow ashore step by step. The old man Yang came forward, clenched his hand, choked and said, 'Lao Wang, you are a man without legs. I won't say anything. I'll move tomorrow!'

Township leaders said that the last 'nail household' was bought by Lao Wang with his life!!

4. Always Kept The List of Comrades

The hearts of heroes always belong to the people.

Working in the village made Wang Mingli more deeply feel the poverty and hardships of villagers in mountainous areas, including many military families, martyr families and many veterans. During the interview, Wang Zhiqian, one of his comrades in arms, left a small shrapnel on his rib after being injured by a mine on the battlefield. Before leaving the army, Wang Zhiqian thought that his family was very poor and had no money to marry a daughter-in-law. He couldn't find his daughter-in-law with the disability certificate, so he gave up the disability certificate, pretended not to be injured and returned to Si'nan's hometown. Later, the daughter-in-law was 'cheated', but her ribs were inflamed every year and the pain was unbearable. She stays in the hospital several times a year. All the doctors and nurses in the hospital know him. When they met, they shouted 'President Wang' and then came again? It was not until 2018, more than 30 years later, that Wang Zhiqian made up his mind to take out the shrapnel.

Every time he hears similar words, Wang Mingli's heart hurts and he can't calm down for a long time. It has become Wang Mingli's strong desire to stop the demobilized soldiers and their relatives from bleeding and crying and help them live a better life. During his stay in the village, he noticed that most young people in rural areas went to work in cities. The elderly, the weak, the sick and the disabled at home cannot climb the hillside and do heavy work. Many slopes have been abandoned. Wang Mingli believes that if these barren mountains are used in the industrial economy and villagers are allowed to work, barren mountains can be realized and farmers can increase their income. Why not? In 2007, Wang

Mingli sold his house, raised funds with several comrades in arms and began to build Wanjiashan tea farm.

With high altitude, fertile land, sufficient sunshine, abundant rainfall and heavy fog in the morning and evening, Wanjia Mountain is a geomantic treasure land for the development of ecological tea industry. He went up the mountain with his comrades in arms. There was no way out. He picked up an iron hoe and a firewood knife and planed while cutting; If the funds are not enough, borrow a pen from relatives and friends; If there is no electricity in the tent, turn on the kerosene lamp; Without water, tea seedlings all over the mountain are planted like this. Day after day, Wang Mingli's leg bone stump was worn by a prosthetic limb for a long time, with continuous pus and blood. He clenched his teeth with anti-inflammatory and painkillers. After more than 200 days and nights of hard work, the barren mountain of more than 1,000 mu has finally become a green tea garden. But unexpectedly, a rare snow disaster occurred in Tongren area the next year, and a large number of tea seedlings froze to death on the ground. Wang Mingli, 44, sat on the top of the mountain and cried in the snow. Several comrades in arms desperately wanted to retreat. Wang Mingli roared, 'We are all soldiers. As soon as the charge horn rings, we have to rush up! What's the difficulty now?' then he solemnly said: 'If I have a gun in my hand, who will be a deserter and be shot on the spot!'

The comrades in arms immediately regained their amazing pride. Yang Xiuwen, who has been a soldier in Xinjiang for eight years, said with a smile: 'the monitor will put people under the gun! As long as you don't retreat, we will follow!'

It is common for God to change his face. 'The sun rises in the East and it rains in the West. The road is sunny.' after large-scale tree planting with bank loans, Wanjiashan returned to green the next year. Green waves connect the sky and flowers bloom like the sea. Wang Mingli and his comrades in arms have done more vividly. In order to achieve the original intention of getting rid of poverty and becoming rich and more extensive radiation, Dingsheng ecological agriculture development company, Chenxi ecological agriculture professional cooperative and veterans entrepreneurship training base have been established successively. Today, the tea garden area has expanded to more than 5,000 mu, the excellent fruit base has reached more than 300 mu, and more than 4,000 chickens, geese and sheep have been bred. Nearly 4000 people in the surrounding villages and towns have been lifted out of poverty, with an annual per capita income of nearly 10,000 yuan, and 80 poor households have received nearly one million yuan in dividends. By employing experts to create rich strontium 'Yan tea', Swire Group and Lipton company are attracted to settle in Si'nan County and invest in the construction of tea sales headquarters in China. In 2017, Wang Mingli and his comrades in arms developed a new tea mountain, opened up more than 2,000 mu of wasteland, planted tea, and led nearly 1,000 people in four poor villages to increase their income and get rid of poverty. In the past two years, they have paid a total of more than 2.2 million yuan to migrant workers. Business is booming, product sales are increasing year by year, and villagers' income is increasing. Wang Mingli didn't get a penny. He still gets his salary from the County Federation of trade unions.

Another heroic feat!

The years of war are getting farther and farther away, but in Wang Mingli's heart, his comrades in arms feel more and more strongly about life and death. Everywhere he went, he asked the relevant departments how many veterans and disabled soldiers there were, and carefully asked about their living conditions. Then visit those poor comrades in arms again and again and invite them to work in the tea garden or participate in entrepreneurship training. In this way, Yang Xiuwen's wife suffers from depression, Wang Zhiqian has shrapnel in her ribs, and Wu Jiaxiao works outside... Nearly 100 veterans across the country learned from the Internet that Si'nan County has a training base and signed up one after another, which was greatly encouraged. Now, Wang Mingli's 'horn' rings from time to time, and many of his comrades in arms from all over the country.

During the interview, Wang Mingli took out an old, edged list of comrades in arms from his faded backpack. The paper is light yellow. The handwriting looks like that old typewriter. Each page of paper is wrapped in a transparent plastic bag, which shows the owner's careful care. When I read page by page, the names of dozens of his comrades in arms from all over the world left a deep impression, and some of them briefly recorded their lives. Wang Mingli said that I have remembered this roster for decades and will not leave my body every day. Every time I look at them, their images, their past battles and current lives appear in front of me. Some of them have died and some have died of disease. Every time I see it, I am very excited. I think I have too many things to do for my comrades in arms and the common people. I will never stop.

He wept, and so did I.

There is such a great hero hidden in the mountains of Guizhou – an ordinary soldier!

At this time, I decided to change my cell phone ring tone into the bugle sound.

IV Write your life in green mountains and green waters

1. Martyr's entrusted love

Veteran An Jingxu, a strong man with dark skin. From his mouth, I know that in the battles of Laoshan and Zheyin Mountain after the self-defense counterattack against Vietnam, all front-line soldiers of our army carried a body bag with their names, ages and native places written on it. Many tombs were also excavated in advance in the rear Malipo Martyrs Cemetery. Those who died on the battlefield shall be immediately put into body bags and returned to the martyrs' cemetery. The youth's life came to an abrupt end, leaving eternal grief and memory to the motherland and the people.

After flying to Tongren, Guizhou, the next day I went to Wangjia garden, a resettlement site in Wanshan District, where I met An Jingxu, 56. Unexpectedly, more than ten days later, I went to Si'nan County to interview 'old military horn' Wang Mingli. I saw this name on the list of comrades in arms he kept: An Jingxu.

Another tragic veteran story.

In the early morning of April 30, 1984, the general offensive against Zheyin Mountain was about to begin. Machine gunners Yu Yong (also on Wang Mingli's list of comrades in arms) and An Jingxu are villagers in Si'nan County. When they were young, they studied in the same middle school and joined the army at the same time. They are as close as brothers. I just got up in the morning of the general attack. I don't know why Yu Yong suddenly had an ominous feeling. He smoked a cigarette and said to An Jingxu, 'I don't think I'll ever come back.' I have to ask you for help.

An Jingxu said, don't think about it, what's up!!

Yu Yong said, you know Su Derong and I are engaged

Su Derong is An Jingxu's classmate. Yu Yong is one year older than them. They know each other very well.

Yu Yong then said, if I can't come back from this battle, you can take Xiao Su back. I know you are a good brother and won't let Xiao Su be wronged. I love her so much that I can't give up... After that, his tears came out.

After the fierce battle, the Bayi military flag with bullet marks was inserted in Zheyin Mountain. Yu Yong was blown away by a shell. There were only a few pieces of flesh and blood in the body bag. In 1985, An Jingxu retired from the army and returned to Tianqiao Township, Si'nan County. She found Su Derong. The girl burst into tears when she saw him. An Jingxu also cried. After the girl calmed down, An Jingxu said that Yu Yong had a hunch before he died. That morning, he told me that if he died, he would entrust you to me because he loved you so much that he didn't want you to suffer. Although I am poor, I have strength after all. I'll take good care of you! If you like

The girl was silent for a while and said with tears, 'I will live up to Yu Yong's heart, and I do.'

However, An Jingxu's family is the poorest in the village. There was only a half-thatched house on the stone slope, and some crops were squeezed in the stone cracks. In the spring before joining the army, An Jingxu had not eaten for three days. He was so hungry that he sat on the side of the road and couldn't breathe. Fortunately, the neighbor's aunt gave him a white radish to keep him alive. Until now, during the New Year, Jingxu must bring gifts to visit the old woman and thank her for saving her life. After the news of the good relationship between An Jingxu and Su Derong came, the Su family's parents resolutely opposed it, as did the whole village. The family quarreled. But the girl clenched her teeth and remained firm. No matter who her parents and villagers introduced to her, she vowed to die. She said it was the last wish of the martyrs. Even if I have suffered all my life, I can't change!

In order to sacrifice the sacred heart of his comrades in arms and girls, An Jingxu decided to show it to the villagers. I almost died when I went to the coal mine to dig coal. Burning lime makes me sweat every day, but my income is still very low. There is almost nothing left except my parents. He had to borrow things from his colleagues, get close to the villagers and quietly stuffed them into Su Derong's house to protect her from the grievances of her family. Later, the village advocated planting flue-cured tobacco. An Jingxu was determined to turn the situation around and borrowed a lot of money to do it. I didn't expect to encounter mountain torrents in summer, and the smoke seedlings were washed away. Seeing that the situation was bad, the creditors rushed to his house to collect the debt. An Jingxu hid in the mountains and didn't even dare to go home.

Everything is hopeless. One night, he let Su Derong out of the house and said, 'I'm penniless and heavily in debt.' I can't do anything. I can only run away. I can find another place to play drums and start another company.

The girl said, you take me away, we live and die together!

An Jingxu said that this is impossible. Let's go together. People think I have no debt. I can't do that! If you stay at home, it's also a personal commitment. If someone has collected the debt, you can say Jingxu left a message. As long as you have one breath, you will pay off your debts, a lot! When I look like myself, I'll come back and marry you!

The girl cried, went home, stole some steamed bread and sent him to the pass. That night, the wind was strong and the moon was dark. An Jingxu is afraid of being met by the villagers. He went through the steep slope under the forest, and a soldier fled to the end of the world.

Guangdong is the forefront of reform and opening up and a place for all migrant workers. An Jingxu has traveled to many towns and done countless jobs. Transport bricks and soil in Guangzhou, dig pits and plant trees in Dongguan, and transport packaging ships at Humen Wharf. After making money, he ate frugally, sent the money back to his hometown and asked Su Derong to pay his debts for him. Creditors were calm when they saw the money returned. They even praised the quality and integrity of An Jingxu, who was born in the Chinese people's Liberation Army. 'In a word, the poles of the earth will remain unchanged!'

A man with pursuit, dream and determination can't resist the fate of difficulties and hardships. For a while, An Jingxu found a small restaurant as a cook. When he works, he stares at the cook to see how to cook, how to cook and how to look at calories. The cook is a young man with many friends. Seeing that An Jingxu is very attentive, he often asks An Jingxu to practice martial arts by the fire. When he took part in social activities, he secretly asked brother An to take the post. But six months later, Jingxu felt that he had learned enough to become a chef, so he found another restaurant and said to the boss, let me give you a spoon, as long as half of the chef's salary. The boss was overjoyed. As soon as he set out, diners swarmed in, very angry. Later, An Jingxu became the workshop director of a brick factory through enterprise bidding. He recruited more than 30 young people from his hometown. They work hard to earn money.

After wandering outside for four years, the debts of his hometown have been paid off, and I have a savings of six or seven hundred thousand Yuan. An Jingxu called Su Derong and said in a very brave voice, 'now your hostages can be released.' Come to Guangdong, let's get married!

A few days later, the girl flew in like a swallow in spring. The restaurant owner rented a pavilion for the couple. Su Derong found a job in a tissue factory and gave birth to a fat boy a year later. Since then, An Jingxu has employed several employees and opened two grocery stores and a fruit store. Killing three pigs a week is not enough. Once the money is thrown into the plastic bucket under your feet, when it rises, you press it hard, and you don't have time to count it until night. Because of his diligence and ability, integrity, no price increase, no adulteration and willingness to help others, he has won a good reputation in the local area. 'I drive around every day. I'm surrounded by acquaintances. I don't need a driver's license!' he said with a smile. The love of the martyrs finally led a happy life. Although Derong's choice was firmly opposed by the whole family, An Jingxu sent 500 yuan to his wife's parents every month after his marriage. Derong has a sister and a sister. Later, the old man praised everyone: 'my three son-in-law, the second son-in-law is the most filial!'

Everything looks good. I didn't expect that in the spring of 2016, Jingxu, 53, was overworked, seriously ill, half paralyzed and couldn't do anything. My family's savings were spent, and I sold all my property. I'm not getting better. There is no income to support the life of the city. The whole family had to move back to Dawuji Village, Tianqiao Township, Si'nan County. The hometown is still poor and closed, and family life seems to have returned to the era of extreme poverty. An Jingxu didn't give up. She limps to exercise every day. More than a year later, her body gradually recovered, but after all, she was old and it was still difficult to walk.

The battle of poverty alleviation kicked off, and the whole village was sunny after rain. In Dawuji village, An Jingxu's family was identified as a deeply poor household after accurate identification by the poverty alleviation group, election and voting of villagers' representatives and review by superior units at all levels. In April 2018, the whole family immigrated to 'Wangjia garden' in Wanshan District, Tongren City. An Jingxu is very grateful. He especially wrote a thank-you letter to the community party organization, hoping to run a small supermarket in the community to solve the problem of personal employment and serve the masses on the one hand.

Today, An Jingxu runs two stores in the new community, a supermarket and an electrical appliance seller. He was in a good mood and recovered strangely.

A few years ago, his eldest son worked outside and got a girlfriend from Guangxi. He has reached the point of marriage and has a child. They happily took their children back to Si'nan's hometown to visit their parents. They crossed the mountains to the terrible Dawuji Village. The girl's face immediately changed and was startled. A few days later, the girl left the child and ran away. When they moved to Wang's garden, their independent son also opened a shop and soon met a good girl. They made an appointment to travel and get married in the spring of 2020.

In order to express the gratitude of the whole family, An Jingxu gives a bucket of Nongfu Shanquan to community security and cleaners free of charge every week.

2. The bird that flew into the meeting

It's dark. As long as Li Zhengfen is idle and she stops, Wen Weihong will come back. The voice and appearance are very vivid, especially the bright smile, very loud but very quiet.

Li Zhengfen burst into tears. The mobile phone rang the prompt tone and sent WeChat to Weihong continuously.

—'I can't help thinking of you one day when I see that everyone is busy fighting poverty and running back and forth. I always hope that one day you can come back after you are busy fighting poverty. It's really lucky. I don't know if you are the same in heaven. You think about the people on earth, their poverty and fatigue, and unfinished work every day. Let's have a look today WeChat moments, it snows in some places. I really want to record a video with you and ask you if

Daping Village is snowing too? Is it cold? Will you walk back? Let me see your family scene from the window again and again... These memories are the pain you left me all my life, do you know.'

—'Once the smile was so happy and natural, but now we must try to learn what laughter is. The song of this song took away sadness and happiness, but for me, you quietly took away our common happiness...'

—'Missing you is a kind of infatuation that cannot be changed. Your good and bad fascinate me. Real feelings and deep-rooted tenderness linger in my mind for a long time and refuse to leave...'

—'You took me to change the way I didn't want to go before. Now, no matter how difficult the road is, I must move on. No matter how many tears I shed, I can't change anything...'

—'Your shadow is everywhere except at home. With you, we can cross ditches and ridges. Now, you throw me into the abyss alone. Without your company, I don't know how to get out of the abyss. I lose my direction and don't know where to go. I want to paralyze myself and don't want anything, but that's impossible. You know'

—'Today, you have been away from me for three months. Today, at the publicity meeting of the county Party committee, I saw a bird fly around so close and leave. Have you come back?'

—'At this moment, I really want to call you and send you a WeChat video, but I know you won't reply. I really have a lot to say to you in my heart. I cry again. When I get up in the morning, I will become a 'panda eye' Everyone advised me not to cry and be strong, but I wanted to do it, but I just couldn't. You told me I was good at everything, but I had a lot of tears I wasn't good at. You left me a lifetime of pain and memories. Do you think I won't get hurt? If a woman doesn't cry, is she still a woman? Everything in the past 20 years can't be put down. If you are very disabled to me Endure, maybe I won't be so sad today'

—'Honey, I controlled my emotions tonight, not you. Look! You should have received the award yourself, but I stood on the stage with tears...'

This is a WeChat sent by Li Zhengfen to her husband Wen Weihong. After July 22, 2019, Zhengfen is drowned in tears, one by one, endless and unstoppable; He was silent, like a bright star next to the moon, with only light and no sound, listening with deep attachment. Unfortunately, people who love each other in the world are always too busy, busy working and supporting their families. There are only simple 'work words' left in life. When life and death are boundless, one here and one there, I find that so much love can only be poured out in tears.

Villagers and poverty alleviation colleagues said that unfortunately, Wen Weihong should not have taken this step on that rainy night. He fell on the step.

No! Wen Weihong said thoughtfully on a rainy night with another world that someone must walk home. If I don't accept it, others will accept it. As Mr. Lu Xun said, 'there is no road in the world. When there are many people, it becomes a road.'

History tells us that the road to our hometown is the road carrying the original heart of Nanhu red boat.

I decided to see Li Zhengfen and talk about Wen Weihong. Driving into Yanhe County, an ancient tall building stands on a small street. There was no elevator. Li Zhengfen, wrapped in a dark gray down jacket, opened the door for us with a sad face. The room was simple, quiet and cold. Photos of Zhang Wenwei when he was young, a love photo of him and Zheng Fen, and a family photo of the couple and their son are quietly displayed in front of me. Zhengfen is beautiful, weak and gentle. It can be seen that she is a woman with birds. Because of sadness, she dared not touch her husband's books and notes for months, and did not want to wipe the dust off the table, because there were still high red temperatures and traces on the table.

The world outside the window starts from here

The two families are far apart. They are all Tu family tribe in the mountains. Just because of an accident, a beautiful spark suddenly lit up on the road of life of two young people. Both of them liked reading when they were young, but because their family could not afford tuition, Wen Weihong went to technical secondary school and Li Zhengfen went to junior middle school. Wei Hong later became a cadre of Yanhe County Economic Development Zone. Zheng Fen is the youngest daughter in the family. She was spoiled. Her parents won't let her go out to work. She lives with her brother and sister-in-law and helps take care of her children. One day, Wen Weihong went to a rural research and development project. At noon, he was taken by village cadres to Li's house for dinner. Seeing the beautiful Li Zhengfen for the first time, I think God gave him a 'seven fairies'. The two young people talked about the difficulties of their families when they were young and the pain of dropping out of school. They sympathized with each other. Although Wen Weihong is gentle, she is very decisive when she meets a beloved girl. The next day, he asked the village cadres to take a message to the Li family. On the third day, he asked Li Zhengfen out. They walked side by side in the moonlight. Wen Weihong said, 'if two people share a share of pain, only half of the pain; if two people share a share of happiness, there will be two happiness.' this sentence fascinated Li zhengfen and moved him. At that time, she was very happy that her family had no money and could not send her to high school and University; I'm especially glad my parents didn't let her go out to work. I'm also glad that my brother and sister-in-law have just given birth to a child and asked her to help at home. In short, all the twists and turns and suffering are lucky. She met Wen Weihong. There is a big mountain called Juchi Mountain in Yanhe County. You can imagine its majesty and precipitousness from its name. The Wen family lives at the foot of the mountain. After marriage, Wen Weihong told Zheng Fen an interesting story. When he was a child, he liked to listen to his father set up the Longmen array and told him the story of 'making red' and suppressing bandits in sawtooth mountain, which fascinated the young Wei Hong. Once, he stared into his small eyes and said: if I want to catch up with that good time, I must be the head of the children's regiment! My father was very happy. He said it was a 'good time' in the war years! It's hard for dead people to fight every day. Wei Hong said, fighting for the people, we are not afraid of death!

This has become the character Wen Weihong has been pursuing and shaping in her short life.

In 2013, after the 18th National Congress of the Communist Party of China, the nationwide anti-poverty struggle began. Wen Weihong was well aware of the hardships of his parents and villagers and took the initiative to write an invitation letter asking leaders to help the poor in the village. After approval, he said goodbye to his wife and children, picked up his luggage and went down the mountain. There is no need to elaborate on the hard work of visiting the poor and traveling around, because his work is very effective. Every time he went to a village, he soon realized that 'one standard, two standards, don't worry about three guarantees'.

The leaders specially sent him to gnaw hard bones and fight for many years:

First stop: Heping Village, Qitan Town, successfully lifted out of poverty.
The second stop: Penghua Village in the same town successfully got rid of poverty.
The third stop: Tuanjie Township and Shexiang Village have successfully lifted themselves out of poverty.

Work in the village usually lasts three years. Wen Weihong worked wholeheartedly and vigorously on the mountain for five years, and Li Zhengfen looked forward to five years at home. Every weekend, as long as Wei Hong says she wants to go home, after noon, Zhengfen looks on the balcony from time to time, hoping to see her husband hurry home. Wen Weihong usually dotes on her wife. I live on the ninth floor. There is no elevator. Slightly heavier rice and vegetables, as well as weak Zhengfen, can't move. Wen Weihong did it. Wei Hong is not at home these years. Zheng Fen can only walk one floor with heavy objects to rest. When they shoot videos, Wei Hong often jokes that I'm not at home. Don't be hungry!

After marriage, the whole family can only live on Wen Weihong's salary and can only feed their son who goes to school. Life is tense. Zhengfen has always wanted to go out to work to supplement her family. Wei Hong resolutely disagrees, fearing that Zhengfen will be tired. But after he entered the village, he could not manage, and there were not many things at home. Li Zhengfen worked as a home appliance salesman in a large shopping mall in the county. His monthly basic salary plus commission income exceeded 4000 yuan, and his living conditions were greatly improved.

In 2018, Wen Weihong, who won many red awards, volunteered to join the organization again and stayed in the village. He copied a paragraph in his application for Party membership: 'as a member of the Communist Party of China, I will always go to the front line of the construction of the motherland, never shrink back in any difficult crisis, and stand up for the prosperity and development of the motherland.'

Zhengfen is a little resentful. He said you had extended your service and continued to work?

Wei Hong said that anyone can do what the unit uploads and releases, while the earth is still rotating. I am a peasant child suffering from suffering and poverty. What I should do is to make the villagers live a good life.

He went up the mountain again and named Daping Village, an extremely poor village in Zhongzhai Town on the edge of Juchi Mountain, as the first Secretary of the village.

I don't know why. It may be the 'only village' in the world: farmers here are used to planting only one crop a year. The land was idle for a long time, but they had to go down the mountain to buy vegetables in a small town 20 kilometres away. Wen Weihong said to the village cadres, 'You bought a lot of land, but if you are lazy and don't plant vegetables, you will always poor.' It's difficult to change their habits. He said it many times, but there was still no movement in the village. So, Wen Weihong bought a bag of vegetables from her pocket and distributed them to the villagers door to door. In order to mobilize, he said to the villagers when he entered the door, you help me plant it first, and then I have no food to eat. Go to your house and get it. Later, the villagers 'colluded' and found that Secretary Wen said this to everyone. Everyone smiled and said that Secretary Wen's heart can adapt to Juchi Mountain!! Soon, everyone moved away. That year, the whole village ate their own dishes, which were cheap and fresh. When Wei Hong returned home, she happily told Zheng Fen that the poverty alleviation work was not as difficult as expected. Sometimes a good idea can solve a problem.

—Daping village has a bad habit handed down from generation to generation. The funeral lasted ten and a half days. They cry, worship and observe filial piety. No one was planting or earning, but it cost a lot to treat and entertain people. The cost is very huge, which has brought a heavy burden to the villagers. But no matter who doesn't do so, he will feel shameless and afraid of being said unfilial. Wen Weihong advocated a new trend of civilization and the truth of thick support and thin burial through cadre meetings, Party member meetings and villagers' representative meetings. After Yang Hua's father died, the villagers listened to Secretary Wen's suggestions and saved more than 40,000 yuan at the frugal funeral. For poor villagers, this is astronomical!

—In Daping Village for more than a year, Wen Weihong led the villagers to build 18.7 kilometres of hardened Tongzu Road, seven 230 cubic metres of drinking water pools and 24.5 kilometres of water pipes. He received 300,000 yuan of support fund for the development of flue-cured tobacco and beekeeping industry and helped 368 people from 80 poor households move to the new community in Bijiang District, Tongren City.

Work in the electrical department means having to move up to the mountains. First, as a 'flue-cured tobacco planting demonstration household', Li Zhengfen works carefully and works hard to become successful; Second, she is gentle and warm-hearted. She helped him do the ideological work of the villagers and it was easy to communicate. In the past five years, the couple, one working in the mountains, the other working in the city. They didn't meet much until their son went to Guizhou University. They became empty nesters, which means they don't have much to do. Zhengfen agreed to join her husband up in the mountain to help the poor. This may be the first case in the whole county and even the whole city. Soon, they became the couple on the mountain. He is a Dongyong and she is a fairy, 'you weave my farm, you carry water, and I water the garden', indeed an idyllic scene. Li Zhengfen is kind and gentle. She was good at chatting with the villagers and soon won the support of the masses. She was asked to go to every family to eat any delicious food. Planting flue-cured tobacco can't be ignored, Wen Weihong mobilized Gao Tengke, the village party secretary, to lead 40 mu. Li Zhengfen mobilized the villagers Tian Maosuo to take 20 mu, and the whole village spread out rapidly to work. Since then, the whole village has expanded rapidly. The villagers joked that Li Zhengfen was 'the first deputy secretary of the village.'

'Secretary Wen's work in the village is the most devoted and touching. We are even more moved that he invited his wife up the mountain. In just over a year, the economic situation of Daping Village has improved greatly, and the appearance of the village has also changed greatly.' Tan Pengfei, Secretary of Zhongzhai Town, commented.

On the evening of July 22, 2019, it rained slightly. Wen Weihong, who was busy in the village, received a call saying that a poor family had an idea of entrepreneurship and wanted to discuss it with him. He hopes he can go as soon as possible. Wen Weihong put down what he was doing and rushed to the villagers' house. Unfortunately, on a dark rainy night, he stepped on a leaking wire and was electrocuted. He immediately fell to the ground. He died unexpectedly, because no one found him for a long time, so he died at work. When it was found more than two hours later, Wen Weihong, 45, had stopped breathing.

Someone told Li Zhengfen and she ran frantically from her temporary 'home' to the scene, and Wei Hong's body had been removed – kind people didn't want her to see him. Zhengfen ran to the muddy hillside and cried in the rain at night, 'Wei Hong! Where is my Wei Hong? Give him to me!' She had a lot of uncertainties for the future.

The heaven shed tears.

An ordinary poverty relief cadre quietly left his post, he left so suddenly and calmly that he was not as strong as people thought or expected. However, the road he paved, the water fountain he built, and the love and warmth he left to the villagers are still there. Wen Weihong will always be there.

When he was sent off, many villagers, old and young, came to the scene. They came back from working in other counties and provinces, and many immigrants from Tongren City came back. That day, the mountain roads were crying and the mountains were crying. Cui Suying, a 76-year-old farmer, pulled the car and cried, 'good boy, Ni Lang Kai (Tujia dialect: why!) left like this. God, it's terrible...'

When Li Zhengfen spoke in tears in the county, a bird flew into the meeting. As she said on WeChat, it must be Wen Weihong. With his warm heart and deep attachment.

3. School for one

Big eyes, bright smile. Memory is like an old primary school textbook. Her story came to me from the mountain road.

Early in the morning, Cui Song, deputy director of the Publicity Department of Dejiang County Party committee, Yang Xu, a local writer, and Xiao Yuan of the municipal Poverty Alleviation Office set out from the county seat, drove for countless turns in the clouds and fog on Winding mountain road, crossed the Wujiang by boat, and then we climbed mountains and mountains before we arrived at Du Dian'e's home and school. Signs along the road indicate: Tongjing Township, Xiaping Village, Dawuji formation – Ancient Villages in the mountains. On the hillside stands an old and simple wooden brick small two-story building. Is this school? Doesn't look like one!

For decades, the classes here have been irregular and there are no fixed number of students. Three levels are concentrated in one house. She is the only teacher responsible for the principal, head teacher, Chinese, arithmetic, painting and other disciplines. The children leave after finishing the third grade. The handyman, cook and security guard is her husband Jian Guangxuan. When the children gathered, Du Dian'e's knocked on the iron plate hanging on the door frame, which had rusted into a cultural relic (now an electric bell). There is a small blackboard hanging in the classroom. Some children's pictures were pasted on the wall. Small colored plastic tables and stools are placed one by one. The children crowded around the table. Some people are writing new words, some are drawing, some are doing arithmetic problems. Next door is the kitchen, the main room and the office. There is a small slide for playing games in the yard. Everything is informal. It was not until the flag raising ceremony in the front yard on Monday that the atmosphere became particularly serious. Du Dian'e's put the national anthem on her mobile phone, and her husband pulled the raised five-star red flag with a rope. She and her students stood upright and sang the national anthem to the music. There is a steep slope in front of the yard fence, shaded by trees and dotted with civilian houses. Looking around, the misty mountains and the unknown world behind the mountains.

Several generations of mud dolls in the nearby mountains waved goodbye through Du Dian'e's tearful eyes. However, do not underestimate this informal school. Now it is a 'famous school' officially registered by the County Education Commission.

Du Dian'e was born in 1967 and is the only child in her family. In difficult times, girls in rural Guizhou are rarely sent to school. First, because they are poor, they can't afford 80 cents of tuition; Secondly, this is because of the old idea that boys take precedence over girls: the girls will eventually become other peoples' water – why spend money to raise children for other people's families. Dian'e's parents are illiterate, but her mother is an old Party member and a representative of county women in the 1950s. She has a high degree of consciousness and insight. When she went to a meeting in the county, she couldn't write her name, couldn't understand the report, and didn't dare to go out because she didn't know the road sign. After suffering from blindness, she decided to sell the iron in the pot and send her daughter to school – this is the first example of Dawuji Village, which can be said to be a new generation. Every day before dawn, her mother urged little Dian'e to get up and take some potatoes to school. On the way to school, Dian'e has to cross a big mountain, it's still dark in the morning. Little Dian'e was so scared that she had to wait for her friends. When winter comes, the children shiver with cold. Some people carry a small drying cage and put their hands on it when it is cold (I saw an exhibit in the local 'homesickness Museum': a small bamboo cage with a small rough porcelain bowl or iron plate inside, which can be lit for heating when they go out in winter). In rural primary schools, from class to lunch break, the children build a small stove with three stones, cook a bowl of porridge with the brought rice or potatoes, and then go to class in the afternoon. Because Dian'e's family only has her father, she can't get much work in the production team and lives in extreme poverty. Digging wild vegetables and grass roots is the main work of the shop. Because she couldn't afford the tuition, she dropped out several times and repeated it several times. She didn't graduate from junior high school until 1987, when she was 20. At this age, most farm girls are already mothers.

Du Dian'e is a filial child. She had thought about taking exams in high school or technical secondary school, but she couldn't bear to increase the burden on her family. If she wants to work elsewhere, she must leave her lonely and old parents. She still can't stand it. Has been hesitating and tangled. In those days, I went up the mountain to raise pigs and had more contact with many farm girls around me. Everyone envies her for reading and writing. They usually don't write their names. Selling rice and vegetables is not money. They turned black when they entered the city. Some people went out to work. When the employer heard that they were illiterate, he spoke a difficult dialect and waved away. They had to go back to the lonely mountain village and wait for marriage and children. Generation after generation, they repeated the poverty and sadness of the older generation. Several times, a young girl who had never been to school ran to Du's house, asked Dian'e to teach her to write her name, and then ran away excitedly with a note. They said that if they went out to work, they could sign and get paid. Looking at their distant backs, Du Dian'e was full of sympathy and deep pain – what's the use of writing only her own name? Without education, they are destined to work and it is difficult to create a new life. Seeing so many young people go out to work, my mother asked, 'why don't you go yet?' Dianer said, I don't want to leave you both! In fact, she has a lot in her heart.

One day, the village head came to visit her parents and talked about the poverty and backwardness of Dawuji Village, too many bachelors and illiterates, too far and too tired, and the children couldn't go to school. Du Dian'e suddenly asked, can I run a primary school in the village?

The head of the village was surprised to say that school is not blowing bubbles. How can we do it without money, room and teacher?

Du Dian'e said, I will be the teacher and the classes can be held in my house. How difficult would it be to find children to teach them to read? However, I only have a junior high school degree and can't teach senior grades. I believe I can teach anything under grade three.

In a word, just like the sunshine through the window, it lit up the Du family's shed and the thought of the village director.

The village director and his parents shouted excitedly, 'yes!'

Once everything got started, Du Dian'e found that her small place could not run a school at all, and the children even had no place for activities. Under the chairmanship of the old Party member's mother, a family of three decided to replace their neighbors' land with their own land, freeing up a small playground of more than 20 square metres. Then, in order to expand the house and pave the road, my father borrowed some folk usury and took people up the mountain to blast stones. The workers paid 3 yuan to the workers. The workers carried 50 kg of stones and they had to walk 2 kilometres. The village committee is very poor and has no money or things. It just sent a few boards to help make some small tables and stools. During this period, Du Dian'e ran around in the surrounding mountain villages, door-to-door, mobilized all school-age children to go to school, and said that they no longer need to cross the mountain in a small oven in the dark.

The villagers asked, where is the money coming from?

Du Dian'e said she only puts up 3 kg of rice a year. If she can't hand it in, she could keep an account and give it when she has it.

What about textbooks? Mother said solemnly, 'we will sell our cattle!'

On September 1, 1987, the 'private' mountain village primary school with no name, no photo and only one undocumented teacher opened. More than 30 children from all over the country came happily carrying empty schoolbags. The oldest three girls were 17 years old, two of them had fiances, and the little boy was 6 years old. The room was full. At nine o'clock sharp, my mother rang the 'iron clock' hanging on the door frame. My father arranged the table and stool. Du Dian'e walked into the 'classroom' with her teaching notes and announced the beginning of the class. Because some students dropped out of school after a year or two, Dian'e divided the students into three grades and began to take turns in a room: giving lessons to little kids in the first grade, assigning homework in the second grade and playing games in the third grade. In this way, Dawuji Village, which has been silent for hundreds of years, sounded the sound of children's reading for the first time. Du Dian'e doesn't understand 'business' at all, nor does she understand primary school textbooks. The first word she taught was 'man', and the first noun was 'China'.

On the student roster, more than one-third of the students did not have a checkmark, which means that the 'Tuition' of 3KG rice for these children has not been paid.

It is difficult for Du Dian'e to buy textbooks for two semesters a year – only in Wenping Town on the other side of the Wujiang. Every time, Du Dian'e got up early, climbed the mountain, and then crossed the river by boat. That night, she had to pay for a place to spend the night. The next day, she went to town and bought two bags of textbooks. She had to spend most of the day and stay another night. On the third day, she crossed the river by boat, climbed mountains and ditches, and returned to Dawuji Village in the evening. However, she also had an unexpected 'harvest'. A student's parent said that a relative named Jian welcomed Dian'e to live in his house for free. She was able to live in his house and saved some accommodation fees. Du Dian'e was very happy and went as promised. The head of household, Old Jian, was a soldier for 7 years in his early years, straightforward and enthusiastic. After listening to Dianer's school running experience, old Jian was deeply moved. The next day, he ordered his eldest son Jian Guangxuan to help Dianer cross the river and send her to the village. Jian Guangxuan is black skinned but very honest. He seldom speaks, only laughs. Since then, whenever

Dian'e crossed the river to do business, she lived in his house. As time went on, the two young people got closer and closer. The next year, Dian'e went to buy textbooks. On the way, Jian Guangxuan said to her, I think your family lacks a person to support you. Let me wrap it up. Du Dian'e blushed and hit him with a bang. The blow knocked the young man into the house and became a door-to-door son-in-law. Until now, the 'occupation' is still the bell ringer and handyman in the school.

Du Dian'e can only teach until the third grade. In the fourth grade, when the children grow up, they can continue to study in primary school in the town across the river.

Year after year, groups of children come and go. Du Dian'e's contribution is that under the very difficult conditions of farmers in mountainous areas, when the 9-year compulsory education was not implemented, all school-age children in nearby mountain villages, especially girls, were 'nudged' to go to school. What a warm and respected little business it is!

This matter moved the leaders of Dejiang County.

—7 years later (1994), the relevant departments gave Du Dian'e a subsidy of 60 yuan per month in the name of 'substitute teachers.'

—21 years later (2008), Du Dian'e opened a kindergarten with more than 100 children. Unable to adapt to family life, the Du family had to hire people and horses at their own expense. They brought back the cement bricks from the brick factory 10 miles away and built a small second floor. The price of each brick at home is 5 yuan.

—22 years later (2009), Du Dian'e was officially admitted as a teacher with a monthly salary of more than 3,000 yuan. She can breathe a sigh of relief.

—32 years later (2019), Du Dian'e's black hair has turned grey, but her smile was still bright. When it comes to her students, Du Dian'e is full of pride and happiness. In the past 32 years, she has taught more than 1,500 children. After graduating from the third grade, more than 20 people went to college and became cadres.

During lunch at Ms. Du's house, she brought me a black old book. This is the account book for registering the tuition of '3 kg rice' over the years. The part inspected after paying the name, and the part not inspected is still in arrears. Du

Dian'e smiled and said, 'I have taught three generations. Some people ask their descendants to help them pay their tuition fees. I still keep this account book. In fact, it is not for bookkeeping. It is the record and memory of my life.'

At present, the 'one person school' has 14 students, one in grade one, four in grade two, nine classes in kindergarten, and a girl from the city – volunteer Chen Hualing. Mr. Du said that in recent years, there are not many children in school here, because through the poverty alleviation projects in recent years, many villagers have become rich and sent their children to the city to study. The conditions there are very good. The teacher teaches better than me. Of course, I'm happy for them.

Thank you, Ms. Du! In the great historical process of hundreds of millions of people getting rid of poverty and becoming rich, you have silently opened up a dream road for the children in the mountains. Without your efforts, maybe many people's dreams have long been lost in practice. Maybe they couldn't even dream of their futures.

4. (Garlic) You win

Is this a mountain garden? The two sculptures are magnificent. The Dragon flies in front and the Golden Phoenix spreads its wings behind. Ancient trees, flowing water, green and quiet, pavilions.

Is this a deep mountain villa? On both sides of the flat road, rows of two-story white attics with different shapes stand side by side, steel windows and glass doors spell out various patterns, and the curtains on the windows are colorful. Majestically climb the broad steps and face the majestic orange concave wooden building 'Farmhouse Hotel'. At noon, hundreds of tourists, young and old, sat around the table singing and drinking. Oh, it's a wedding. The bride in white wedding dress and the groom in suit toast at the table

Tangtou Town, Si'nan County, Tongren, at the end of the Winding mountain road and surrounded by mountains, how can there be such a beautiful and quiet place?

Looking at the old photos on the wall, yesterday seems to be eternal, just like all ancient villages in Guizhou: Dead vines, old trees and crows; Rubble, barren mountains and poor families; Barefoot, rotten shirt, lantern flower.

The new story begins with a head of garlic.

Leng Chaogang, Miao nationality, Party branch secretary of Qinggangba Village, Tangtou Town. He is not tall, dark, thin and firm. He sounds as if he has some political theories. He often 'debate' with me in conversation. Grandpa joined the party on the line of fire and lived a passionate life. In those years, he joined the mountain guerrillas, carried artillery, attacked the 'militia' and suppressed bandits. After liberation, he became a secretary of the village Party committee, from the land reform movement to the cooperative movement, and then to the household production contract movement. On New Year's Eve during the 'Cultural Revolution', the whole family ate half corn and half bran. A group of rebels (I was surprised that there were rebels in such a remote mountain village) suddenly rushed in, raised the table and smashed the rough porcelain bowl. Then he pressed his grandfather's head and forced him to kneel on the bowl to let him admit that he was a 'traitor' and a 'capitalist'. Grandpa's knee is dripping blood. The rebels fought and scolded a thousand times. Grandpa answered a thousand times: I'm a Communist! I'm a Communist! I'm a Communist! Leng Chaogang, who was only 4 years old at that time, was afraid to cry, but he remembered the bloody scene and grandpa's courage. My father later became a village cadre. I asked Leng Chaogang, how are your three generations of village cadres?? Leng Chaogang said, no, it's more difficult than ordinary villagers. In that year, as a cadre, we should take the lead in suffering and providing public food. The government should provide relief to the masses, my family lives in the most dilapidated thatched house. I remember when I was a child, when I drank potherb porridge, a big bug with a long palm suddenly fell out of the shed and into the bowl. I cried with fear. Grandpa sighed and said, 'Oh, he's hungry, too.'

After graduating from junior high school, under the pressure of life, Leng Chaogang followed the adults in the village to dig coal in the nearby coal mine. For illumination, he carried a small lamp, planed on his knees and crawled on his back. Floods, explosions and collapses occur from time to time. There are many casualties among migrant workers. They are called 'two stones and one meat' and 'eat sunny food and do cool work'. Leng Chaogang has been digging for nearly 20 years. Fortunately, he came out alive, but he suffered from severe pneumoconiosis. I have difficulty breathing. I was out of breath after a few steps. I can't sleep at night. I coughed up all black sputum. Go to the hospital and the doctor will wash his lungs. I asked how to wash it? Leng Chaogang said, where is the laundry? This is a difficult attempt! The doctor took out two straight steel pipes and inserted them into his lungs from his mouth. There are some soft wires at the end. The doctor kept stirring his lungs with this thing, which stimulated him to cough violently and spit out black sputum. He even vomited and vomited. Life is better than death. He tossed and turned for seven or eight hours.

The doctor wiped the sweat and said, you are very strong and the effect is good, but we need to do it again.

Leng Chaogang wiped his tears and said, I'm never coming back.

The coal mine is too dangerous, so he had to go back to the village to cultivate his farm. People who have died have great courage. He always finds the villagers around him strange. They seem to know only 'three big things' all their lives, wives, land and corn, which can only be planted once a year. As for what is in the sky, what is in the world and what is on the earth, the world is so huge and wonderful. They didn't seem to know and didn't respond. They would rather scratch their bodies against the wall in order to stop itching, and their eyes are empty. Leng Chaogang believes that planting food is neither enough to eat, nor enough to make money, nor enough to pay for public food. It's like money. He chose two: garlic and watermelon. This man is very deep. He doesn't say what he does. The villagers laughed at him and asked, can you fill your stomach with that? Leng Chaogang still doesn't speak and works hard. Seeing that his family's days were getting wetter and wetter, the villagers still had empty eyes and did not respond. Privately, they also said that his farming was 'immoral'. It is estimated that the rumor has spread. In the summer of 1999, the Secretary of Tangtou town went to the village to 'inspect'. He saw Leng Chaogang, barefoot, watering the watermelon field with a truck of dung water. He asked, 'have you joined the party?' Leng Chaogang said, no, I have written five applications, but the branch did not reply. The Secretary said, I'll arrange for you to join the party right away. You should be the village leader first.

As for the then village party secretary, the village leader was shocked. The town secretary personally arranged for Leng Chaogang to join the party. It seems that he has a good background. Maybe his own chair can't be guaranteed. Since then, he has been 'busy' with his work. He didn't have time to deal with it. Once, he even broke the town secretary phone.

The leaders of the village became leaders, but it took more than four years to join the party. It seems that 'I can't choose someone better than me because they may replace me.' for most places, talents are difficult to stand out, which means that many talents will suffer for a long time.

In 2004, Leng Chaogang joined the party. He began to vigorously advocate 'industrial adjustment' in his village group and called on villagers to grow garlic and watermelon. The villagers rolled their eyes and said, can that thing top hunger? Leng Chaogang said with a smile, is food worth money or money? Money is not everything, but you can't do without money. With money, what can't you buy? At the group meeting, he invited an accountant and a businessman who often came to buy his garlic and watermelon to calculate an account for the villagers on the spot: one mu of land can sell about 400 yuan for a season of corn; If I plant watermelon in summer and garlic in autumn, I can earn a total of more than 2,000 yuan, that is, I work for one year and you work for five years. The villagers suddenly realized that many of them did not go to school or learn arithmetic. Of course, they did not understand this truth.

But the villagers are still a little worried. Our village is high in mountains and far away from here. If we plant too much, can we sell it out? Many of them have never been to the county. They can't imagine how many people outside the world and the big country have, how vast the market is, and how much garlic and watermelon can be consumed every day.

Poverty limited the imagination of villagers.

Leng Chaogang made a statement on the spot: 'I'll pay for it!'

Another person said that he didn't have money to buy seeds.

Leng Chaogang said, I'll buy it for everyone, just pay it back after autumn. He also stressed that to tell everyone the truth, I can afford to give this money, but I hope everyone will give it back to me so that everyone can improve their market awareness.

That year, garlic and watermelon enveloped this small village group. A few years later, Leng Chaogang became the village party secretary, and garlic and watermelon captured the whole qinggangba Village. What surprised the villagers even more was that the 'garlic and melon' were making a lot of noise. Leng Chaogang established the garlic deep-processing industry in the village. The villagers' income soared. They can no longer hide their money under bamboo mats or in their pockets, so they have to deposit their money in the bank. Now the villagers are walking taller with their straight backs. They even stopped scratching under the wall.

Earth shaking changes followed, and many things are ahead of the whole province and the whole country.

—As early as 2006, the whole village became self-reliant and wealthy.

—In 2005, the cesspit of every household was cancelled, and the public toilet was rebuilt. Besides, they hired special personnel to clean up the whole village, which was earlier than most of the countryside in the country.

—In 2013, all the farmers scattered in the wild forest on Shipo went down the mountain for centralized resettlement, more than 100 mu of homestead or restored green mountains and rivers, or reclaimed farmland, and established greening companies and labor companies.

—As previously written, the new house is like a villa, the village looks like a park, and the four seasons are invincible. This was done many years ago. The village once carried out the layer industry of centralized feeding, with a high income, but it found that the smell in the air was bad and hurt the elegance, so it decided to dismount. The villagers laughed and said that Secretary Leng 'changed the sky, the ground and the air in the middle.'

—Qinggangba Village has strength. Leng Chaogang transferred the land of some neighboring villages, built a vegetable base, and implemented labor wages and profit dividends, which made

On one occasion, Zhao Kezhi, then Secretary of the provincial Party committee, led a group of provincial Party committee cadres to Qinggangba Village for investigation. Leng Chaogang reported that in the past, the village buried the dead, went up the mountain to find a place with good feng shui, built large and small tombs, and the rich built higher and more expensive tombs, which seriously affected the ecological environment. Therefore, the village built a cemetery in a gully to pay for burial. A department level cadre present said that this was not good. Zhao Kezhi has the final say to stop him. 'Don't listen to him.

I have the final say. We should respect the enthusiasm of the masses, help protect the beautiful country scene and help the masses behave according to the rules.' This is very good.

Garlic prices have soared in recent years, and netizens have changed his name to 'Garlic is the best', which also means you're the best. The young people in the village changed Leng Chaogang's surname to 'Garlic', and his formal name was called 'garlic, the best Secretary'.

Leng Chaogang said with a smile, call me whatever you want!

'You win' has a certain specialty, could make a living everywhere.

5. He left for love, came back for poverty relief

In Yuzhu Mountain, Dejiang County, I met a dark skinned 'Mountain King' by chance. I came up for tea on the way. Starting from the county town in the early morning, I crossed the Wujiang, climbed mountains and climbed high slopes. I went to Laowuji Village to interview Du Dian'e, the founder of 'one person school', and talked about it all the time at noon. On the way back, Cui song, deputy director of the Publicity Department of Dejiang County, who was the guide, asked me to have a rest in the villa teahouse on Yuzhu Mountain. The villa is very big and beautiful, with plank roads, pavilions, picking and sightseeing, children's amusement, tea and catering. After sitting down, the waiter brought me a cup of chrysanthemum tea, which brightened my eyes! In the past, chrysanthemum tea seen in other places was broken, small and withered, and this cup of chrysanthemum tea is really unusual! In the transparent glass, there is a big golden chrysanthemum in full bloom. The petals are slender, fresh, elegant and gentle, just like the slender jade finger of 'thousand hand Guanyin'. A few red Chinese wolfberry seeds and a few delicate and sweet green leaves float in the bright water, which is pleasing to the eye. I took a sip from my cup. Wow, what a masterpiece! It's like drinking a cup of brilliant autumn sunshine, sweeping away the fatigue of the whole body!

I asked, where did you come from? Who planted it?

Cui song pointed to a thin middle-aged man leaning against the counter in the distance and said, he is the villa owner Liu Jiquan.

The writer has a sharp eye. In fact, I noticed him as soon as I entered the house.

He was tall and expressionless, neither like a boss nor a worker, as if he had nothing to do with himself.

I said, come and have a seat. Let's have a talk.

This fellow strode over, his waist straight, his movements agile, and his face was still expressionless.

Why don't you smile? We have a large group of people here, and the leader of the county. What about your business?

A young woman behind the counter said that he didn't smile and was stubborn.

The room was filled with laughter; Liu Jiquan still sat there in a proper way without laughing.

I suddenly felt that he must have been a soldier before.

Then I asked like a judge sentence by sentence, and he answered like a telegram. It's entirely the habit of soldiers. After talking, I understand why he didn't smile.

Liu Jiquan had a miserable childhood. His father was the leader of the army of the production team. He was killed by others in a training. His mother couldn't bear the hard days, so she had to leave the little Jiquan spring and remarry in another place. So Liu had to live with his grandparents, he never saw his mother again, and he didn't enjoy much love. 'I grew up in a pile of rags. When I was in primary school, I didn't wear complete clothes or the first pair of shoes. There was a huge generation gap between my great parents. I didn't have brothers or sisters. Sometimes no one could talk all day long.' Loneliness and coldness nailed him into the miserable hut like a nail. After graduating from junior high school, Liu Jiquan took the initiative to sign up as a soldier and went to the battlefield of self-defense counterattack against Vietnam. Squatting in a cat's ear hole for several months, in addition to the sound of wind and rain, it is the roar of gunfire, which has trained a lonely soul as silent as steel. On another occasion, incendiary bombs from the Vietnamese army burned the battlefield into a sea of fire. Liu Jiquan's face was slightly burned. After being cured, his skin was hard, black and never white again, and it was difficult to laugh. Three years later, Liu Jiquan retired from the army and returned to his hometown. He was assigned to Dejiang County Materials Bureau as a clerk. His main task was to purchase materials for the project construction of the whole county. After war training, he was hurt and black faced. He was very determined and meticulous. When going out to purchase, the people in the bureau have negotiated the price with each other in advance. Once Liu Jiquan goes, a black face can be cut down by two or three percent, saving a lot of money for the county. The leader was very happy and praised him for many times and hinted that the young man would work hard and have a future!

The subsequent events almost shocked the county government. One day in 1993, Liu Jiquan suddenly disappeared. His desk was wiped clean and his papers were arranged neatly. No one seems to have used everything. He didn't say any reason or write a letter of resignation. Silence (there were few mobile phones in the county at that time) was like drilling into a crack in the ground. Ask the old people at home. They are also worried. They say they don't know where he had gone.

A civil servant suddenly disappeared. This is a big deal! And why didn't a soldier have an organized discipline? The leader was very angry. He sent people to visit everywhere, but there was no result. Later, it was rumored that Liu Jiquan had a girlfriend, which had reached the point of talking about marriage. But one day, Liu Jiquan suddenly found that his girlfriend secretly betrayed him. Just think, a lonely heart in childhood, a heart returning from war, how eager for love! Once his heart was broken and his temperament was strong, he didn't want to look at her again and disappeared the next day.

He had nowhere to hide but to leave. Someone guessed that he might have committed suicide in a secret place. His colleagues said that it was impossible!

Liu Jiquan went to Guangdong. Wandering around, working everywhere, transporting sand and bricks on the construction site, and working as a security guard and worker in the enterprise, but living in a shed and drinking a big pot of clear soup did not destroy his iron will. After saving a little money, he found a place to learn textile technology, mechanical repair, property management and so on, so as to expand his knowledge and skills as much as possible. Later, he became a foreman and led a group of migrant workers to build skyscrapers. He was sweating and filled with rubber boots. When you can't think of it, pour yourself down and get drunk. After 11 years of wandering and bloody war, the pain was completely erased, the living conditions were greatly improved, and a pair of iron bones and soft intestines were refined. Meanwhile, Liu Jiquan went home to visit his relatives many times and wandered around Guangdong. He was used to seeing the prosperity like brocade, the lights like a sea, and the traffic of men and women like a stream. But his hometown is still very poor, and the villagers are still counting food, which makes him feel very heavy. When he was young, he stamped my feet because of a heartbreak. Now he is middle-aged and has a little strength. He wanted to do something for his parents and villagers to get rid of poverty and become rich. In his opinion, except for a weak foundation, bad conditions, closed and backward hometown, the most important thing is: The villagers who had never walked out of the mountain lacked leaders who could and dared to do things. He decided to stretch out his hand and take the lead. In 2004, Liu Jiquan who was 39 years old, sold all the property of his family and returned to his hometown. He wanted to open up a way for the scattered small farm economy to survive, and the flame of collecting firewood was also very high. Only by developing the industrial economy can they strengthen themselves. His return completely changed the fate of the village.

The next year, in 2005, after extensive investigation, Liu Jiquan fell in love with Yuzhu Mountain in Tongjing Township. This mountain has beautiful scenery, neither high nor low, fertile soil and warm climate. It can be transformed into a 'flower and fruit mountain' that can be viewed, played and picked. After listening to his opinions, the county and township leaders were very happy and gave strong support. Liu Jiquan broke out and took out almost all his savings. He said, 'if you don't succeed, you will become kind. This is the temper of the soldiers!' coupled with loans and bank loans, he mobilized people around him to participate in yuzhushan orchard cooperative in the form of cash or labor. After three years of efforts, more than 2,000 mu and more than 100,000 fruit trees have been planted. But the fruit bearing rate of fruit trees is very slow, and the income will have to wait for several years. But fruit trees are slow to bear fruit, and the income will have to wait a few years. In order to pay the villagers on time, Liu Jiquan was already heavily in debt. He was so worried that his mouth blistered and his dark face became darker. One day he walked around the orchard alone and suddenly thought that the land under the fruit trees was idle. Why not introduce some fast-growing cash crops to increase income as soon as possible? He made a correct decision: to introduce 'golden silk chrysanthemum'- it was very noble to hear the name.

So far, the town has planted more than 1,000 mu of golden chrysanthemum from inside to outside the park, and established a processing plant at the foot of the mountain. After autumn, the mountains are covered with golden chrysanthemums. This is a beautiful scenery. Liu Jiquan said that this drink is pleasing to the eyes and has the functions of anti-inflammatory, dispelling fire and meditation. It is very expensive in the market, but it is very popular among white-collar workers and the rich. In fact, when we talked, we saw an endless stream of tourists buying boxes by Boxes – the villagers finally saw that green mountains and green waters had become golden mountains and silver mountains from labor income and shared dividends.

Later, I learned that the beautiful young woman in the counter was Liu Jiquan's 'village lady' – a hardworking village girl, not Xiaofang but Xiaoxia.

6. The Miao girl that walked out of the Cigarette box

In the depths of green, clouds and folk songs, this county is called Songtao Miao Autonomous County, this village is called Pipatang Village, and this Miao woman is called Long Jinzhen. Look at this place name, you can know that it nestles in the poetic distance; Looking at her name, she may have beautiful dreams, but her reality is harsh.

Short, fair skinned, smart left-handed (Like me!). Flexible, fluent, expressive, energetic, good dance moves. Now she's getting older, according to the Miao custom, her long black and grey hair should be rolled into a bun at the back of her head. It is inconceivable that a 63-year-old woman appeared in the TV series 'great turning point' broadcast by CCTV – although she only said one sentence. I was curious to know how the director found her and fished her out of the blue sea of Tongren. The real 'Deep Fishing'. (Name of a large franchise restaurant)

Long Jinzhen, who graduated from high school, is good at writing. In her early years, she opened a small shop in the village (it was called a consignment point at that time, but it is still open now). Because my family was poor and had no paper, after selling a few packs of cigarettes, there were still many white cartons left. She felt it a pity to throw it away, so she suddenly had an idea: when she had nothing to do, she continued to write down the first half of her life on it. So far, it has become more than 40 'memoirs'. She has a strong sense of history, especially at the beginning, she added a title 'mother's memory – for her daughter to keep'. This unique 'memoir of cigarette box' has been collected so far. The newspaper turned yellow, but there was an unexpected harvest, that is, it brought her daughter Long Fengbi to the road of literary creation. Now she is a member of the Chinese Writers Association and has published a book, which is very famous in the local area.

Long Jinzhen came to us from the cigarette box... With her first half of her life, with her sadness, joy, struggle and feelings.

Long Jinzhen was born in 1956. She is the daughter of the landlord – actually a granddaughter, which doomed her childhood and youth to be very unfortunate. One summer in the early 1950s, my grandparents fried a lot of wheat cakes and had a full meal. Little Jinzhen secretly hid one and left it to her mother, who was hungry and herding cattle on the slope. In the evening, her mother came back and took the wheat cake left by Little Jinzhen. She was very happy, but she didn't finish it. The rest was hidden in a basket and covered with cow grass. Unexpectedly, Grandpa found the wheat cake when he fed the cattle to eat night grass at night. The next morning, the angry grandpa beat Jin Zhen's mother hard, then took the piece of wheat cake and shouted all over the village, you all look, look, my cheating bad daughter-in-law will steal food! Little Jinzhen quickly explained to her grandfather that she stole it for her mother, but adults didn't believe it. At that time, her mother sat in the hall crying, and Little Jinzhen cried on her mother's back. Soon after it happened, my mother was kicked out. The seriously injured mother was full of hatred for the family and decided to leave. That day, when she left the village with her bag, Little Jinzhen cried and called her mother. Her mother strode without looking back. She must be in tears. She must be afraid. She was afraid that once she looked back, she couldn't walk. Since then, my mother never came to the door or came back to see her daughter.

The cigarette box also says the life of eating 'big pot rice' in the people's commune era, which is a very 'golden treasure' historical data – today's young people don't know at all.

'At that time, we had dinner together in the canteen of the team. The amount of food for each family was divided according to the population. The rice per day for adults was no more than 1 kilograms, and the small one was no more than 4 liang or two kilograms. The rice set was kept by the catering staff of the canteen. The whole white rice in the village was finished and cooked, and the manager asked everyone to eat it. Everyone took the rice back home, poured it into the pot, coupled with wild vegetables and water, and cooked it into vegetable porridge .Can't you eat the food? If you don't eat, you won't be able to fill your stomach. The whole family is waiting for the help of this pot of bitter rice. In the most difficult time, there is nothing in the dining hall, no wild vegetables and bark, and everyone only eats the sound and sound. A few people died, and your only aunt died in the past. '

Without her mother, the loneliness and desolation of little Jinzhen could be imagined. One day, her grandfather bought a pig, which soon became a toy she often played with. The pig also liked to be with her. No matter where little Jin went, the pig would follow her. Once he was put into the pig circle, he would scream out, eat nothing, and even sleep together. The pig would even sleep together. When little Jin went to school, she had to kick his leg but he couldn't catch up with her. It was impossible. She had to bring the pig into the classroom. This little guy even knew how to abide by the class discipline. In the class, he quietly lay under the chair; he performed better than the 'three good students'. Later, when the pig grew to 20 or 30 kilograms, the pig couldn't escape his fate. Little Jin was devastated.

After graduating from high school, Jin Zhen worked as a substitute teacher in the village primary school for five years. Later, due to simplification, she had to return to the land. Outside the house, she raises pigs. She was teaching and busy with the farm, she was a 'half the sky' woman. Her husband was an official teacher, he is very busy teaching every day. In a busy farming season, Jin Zhen shouted to drive cattle to plough – Miao women rarely do such heavy work – but she was out there working all day every day. In the evening, the old yellow cow plopped to the ground, foaming at the mouth and couldn't stand up anymore. The cow died from exhaustion.

In those years, Long Jinzhen's fiery enthusiasm and integrity were also revealed. She helped the villagers take care of things, when they are in trouble and most importantly, she was honest. Even village cadres respect her. The spring breeze of reform and opening up blew into the 1980s. Long Jinzhen saw that it was inconvenient for the villagers to buy daily necessities in the remote county, so she set up the first canteen in the village. The price is fair, and children and the elderly are not deceived. This not only facilitates villagers' shopping, but also makes some small money to subsidize their families. My husband specially wrote a pair of couplets for this store: 'Fuel, rice, oil and salt; The wind, frost, rain and snow will open at any time.' – this pair of couplets is neat, catchy, high-level, simple and friendly. Obviously, Mr. Zhang thought with his heart.

Jin Zhen went forward and did it.

When she was young, she received training from the health school, knew some simple pharmacology and some Miao medicine. At the same time, in order to facilitate the villagers, the store prepared some commonly used over-the-counter drugs. The people in the village have a minor illness. They became better after buying her medicine.

In addition, Long Jinzhen also did something major that caused a big significance for Pipatang Village. At that time, she was distressed that the villagers, especially women, were illiterate, lacked knowledge, could do nothing, and even couldn't make a phone call. Without education, poverty is difficult to change. Therefore, she volunteered to help everyone with literacy, and this activity flourished. Villagers could write their own names, learned about the calendar card, found ways to get rich. Long Jinzhen has done a major event of cultural poverty alleviation.

Honest and kind people always have luck. In 2005, Long Jinzhen, 49, appeared on the candidate list as a 'spare tyre' when the village committee was changed – in fact, she was ready to perform 'badly' in the differential election. Unexpectedly, the old saying 'full view of the public' worked. Long Jinzhen unexpectedly won the highest number of votes and was unexpectedly elected village head!

At that time, village cadres worked for free without any subsidies. But Jin Zhen left her family and canteen to her husband and devoted herself to her work. Looking back, the voluntary poverty alleviation activities in Longjin Town began. Lead the villagers to reclaim barren mountains, plant fruit forests and tea trees, and develop animal husbandry and aquaculture. It also called on all women in the village to 'break the old ideas, hold high half the sky,' plant green onions and cabbage, and raise pigs, chickens, ducks and geese. When you have money to live, you can put down your life. You can grow it and sell it. It's easy to earn seventy or eighty yuan a day. After years of efforts, the vast majority of villagers have solved the problem of food and clothing. In addition, no matter what disputes happened in the villagers' homes day and night, Jin Zhen would go to the door to persuade and educate them. She was busy. Her husband was unhappy to say that since Jin

Zhen became the head of the village, her heart has become 'wild'. People are like monkeys. After a while, they jump to the tree, and then jump to it again. Jin Zhen laughs away and says I am indeed a monkey. In recent years, although villagers live outside the food and clothing line and village-run industries have developed, there has not been a general atmosphere. Long Jinzhen felt lost and sad and resigned during the term.

At the villagers' meeting, she said emotionally that I have no ability to lead everyone out of poverty and become rich. I apologize to the villagers! She bowed to everyone with tears in her eyes. The audience applauded for more than a minute, and many villagers also shed tears.

Well, if you can't help the poor in public, let us restart cultural poverty relief – this is her nature and self-awareness. At that time, she had a lot of 'disharmonious' stories about the families in and out of the village. She suddenly had a sudden impulse. She wrote, directed and acted a piece of 'family and everything' with several old, middle and young friends in the village. The plot was vivid, interesting and touching. The performance in the village was performed in the town, causing a sensation. Later, he was invited to the county to participate in the holiday of 'January 14th' and 'April 8th.' These two holiday were the traditional holiday of the pine tree. All the villagers and even the parents and villagers of other counties, and even the Songtao Miao descendants who had emigrated to Guangxi more than 200 years ago, would participate. In this sketch, Jin Zhen plays a rural old woman who goes to the city to see his son. She worked hard to grow some food and vegetables, and sent her heart to the city to taste fresh for her son. It took a lot of effort to find her son's home, but her daughter-in-law in the city disliked her. On the stage, Jin Zhen performed vividly, falling twice and suffocating three times. The audience was moved to tears, and the applause lasted for a long time after the performance. This is the truth of 'literature and art originates from life.' Later, some netizens uploaded this sketch video to the Internet and named it 'the first Miao sketch in eastern Guizhou', which was highly praised by the Miao people. Gradually, Pipatang Village of Miaozhai formed a 'guerrilla' performance team. They got together as actors during rehearsal. After completing the task, they returned home, and the farmers were covered with soil and sweat. So, the farmers they play especially like it, more than the little red meat. Under the leadership of

Jin Zhen, the small team often produces some local programs, such as playing, singing, boasting, praising good things, criticizing laziness, encouraging and working, and calling for poverty alleviation and prosperity. In recent years, the CPC Central Committee has promoted the establishment of a 'new era practice center' in rural areas. With her direct experience and understanding of real life and a strong sense of responsibility, she has taken the lead in carrying out cultural poverty alleviation and building a strong cultural village.

The most 'professional' and effective stage performance 'dragon golden needle' has attracted the attention of the film and television industry to some extent. Soon, she received an invitation from the director to participate in the film 'the wind is singing', followed by the microfilm 'judge on Miaoling', 'Gaga and ferocity', and the online TV series 'women in Western Hunan'. Although they are all background actors, Jin Zhen is very happy and smiles like a flower. Her daughter Longfengbi asked her how she felt. Jin Zhen said that I like to play the Miao people, let everyone understand the life and changes of our Miao village, and encourage the audience to become a good and diligent person.

The daughter asked, 'now, the anti-poverty struggle across the country is in full swing.' You are an old village cadre. What do you think is the key to this big project?

Jin Zhen's answer is very pertinent and sharp: at least the farmers themselves should take the first step and work hard, while the state is only helping them. It's like sending charcoal in the snow. Charcoal has been sent to your house. You must make your own firewood before charcoal begins to work. You can't do anything for him, and you can't let him complain while baking. Looks like you owe him. In my opinion, almost all the promising rural people who are willing to bear hardships have gone to the city. In addition to seriously ill, disabled, illiterate and poor families, many lazy people remain in the countryside. These people should not only help, but also strengthen education. Some people in our village are too lazy to grow vegetables. They live on subsistence allowance. Anyway, they will get the money again in the past quarter.

Today, Long Jinzhen is still active on the rural stage.

As she got older, PiPatingg Village was also urbanized – renamed Pipa community.

SHANGHAI CHAPTER
The heart is close, the light is far away

I

SHANGHAI IS ONE of the most magnificent, magnificent, charming and dynamic metropolises in the world.

Shanghai is a luminous body, a dream intertwined with light and meteors. Shanghai has been a city full of dreams since its birth. Due to more and more dreams and more crowded, Shanghai must develop to a broader space and time. As a result, countless skyscrapers grew like forests, scrambling to surround the blue skylight to get more sunshine and rain, as if countless 'We' (Shanghai dialect) stretched out their steel arms to hold up the sky.

In Shanghai, every flower is open to dreams, every road is a T-shaped stage of dreams, and everyone is a model, chasing their dreams of becoming somebody.

In Shanghai, you can't live without dreams, so you must work hard for your dreams. After you succeed, you can stroll under the moonlight phoenix tree and enjoy your scenery on the balcony, because you have become part of the attraction.

II

Shanghai is a place with all kinds of lifestyles, but when all is said and done, there is a certain magic. Her style is an extension of history, full of progress and elegance.

Shanghai is a city with thousands of paths leading to a maze. Finally, whoever finds the exit of the maze has gone from the alley to the endless promise of urban skyscrapers.

Shanghai is like a magic box, when the lid is opened, a golden bird jumps out to proclaim and it warns you to get up and go on the road. It will remind you that the road is filled with sunshine and storms, joys and sorrows.

In Shanghai, this kind of magic makes people intoxicated. This magic is in the wind, flowers and snow, lost in poetry and distance. She is constantly looking for new dreams.

In Shanghai, there is a magic that is ever-changing but inseparable from its religion, that is, she inspires everyone with her beautiful appearance and variety, and turns the sea of life into a grain of salt.

Magic cube, magic capital, magic box, magic and magical nature constitute a kaleidoscope of prosperous and fuzzy 'Explorer paradise' – Shanghai.

III

Shanghai is fascinating. If Beijing is the flag of modern and contemporary China, then Shanghai is the totem of modern and contemporary China.

Shanghai is beautiful. Beauty lies not only in her beautiful and charming morning makeup every day, but also in her tenderness, kindness and temperament. Her light shines far away.

Shanghai is wealth. But her wealth comes from her 'caring' thinking and lifestyle. Every copper plate must be used where it should be used.

Shanghai is vast. She is a city without walls. Her growth comes from Shanghai will never be absent and will always exist. From the first wave of western industrial revolution into China to the establishment of the first party flag of the Communist Party of China; From the most important industrial production base in the period of socialist construction to the vanguard and pioneer in the great process of reform and opening up, innovation and development;; From the widely spread Shanghai style culture that embraces all rivers to the heat wave that supports the coastal areas of the central and western regions, Shanghai's great, firm, brave and calm image will always stand in the forefront of the trend of the times in the whole process of China's revolution, construction and reform.

Shanghai is trustworthy. For more than 100 years, as long as the 'made in China' made in Shanghai is high-end, it is guarantee, noble and brand. Like the big white rabbit milk candy, I ate when I was studying at Peking University. I will never forget it. In the barren and hard years of youth, it has been sweet in my heart until now. I was moved by it.

IV

Shanghai people are seldom excited. Their broad vision, profound knowledge and quiet life make them walk up and down the street. But when it comes to supporting all parts of the country, their eyes are bright and their blood is boiling. Although their expressions did not change, they were still calm.

In the 1990s, another great movement of strengthening the country and enriching the people was launched in China. In the counterpart support of poverty alleviation cooperation between the East and the West determined and deployed by the CPC Central Committee and the State Council, Shanghai is once again in the forefront of the country. So far, Shanghai has sent more than 50 batches of more than 2000 cadres and professionals to work in counterpart support areas, covering 7 provinces, 20 prefectures and cities, 101 counties and urban areas, including 98 poor counties, including Kashgar City in Xinjiang (4 counties) and Karamay City, Rikaze city in Tibet (5 counties), Golog Tibetan Autonomous Prefecture in Qinghai (6 counties) and 13 prefectures and cities in Yunnan (74 counties) Zunyi City, Guizhou (9 counties), the Three Gorges Reservoir Area (Wanzhou District, Chongqing, Yiling District, Yichang, Hubei) and Dalian carry out counterpart cooperation for the implementation of a new round of Northeast Revitalization Strategy. They carry forward the spirit of 'nailing nails', adhere to practical work and achievements, describe the dream blueprint of helping the region, pay attention to helping the current life and long-term development of local people, convey the temperature, strength and wisdom of Shanghai in targeted poverty alleviation, and emerge a large number of advanced models and touching deeds.

The guiding ideology of Shanghai's counterpart support and poverty alleviation work is wise, simple and realistic: 'central requirements, local needs and Shanghai can'. These three sentences are absolutely Shanghai Style: there is no noise of slogans, no loud oath, no brilliance of attitude, and only touching 'ability!'

Shanghai has turned its work guidelines into philosophy.

Over the past 20 years, Shanghai's actions have been fruitful: so far, 93 of the 98 poor counties they have helped have been lifted out of poverty. By the end of 2020, all the five counties and 400000 poor people that have not yet been lifted out of poverty will be lifted out of poverty. With the vigorous promotion of Shanghai and local efforts, the future is predictable.

In November 2019, general secretary Xi Jinping visited Shanghai during his visit to Shanghai, and highly praised the targeted aid and cooperation between Eastern Europe and Europe and the United States.

I No going back

To the Tune of Qin Yuan Chun
—March 8, 2020, made for the white coat soldiers on the front
line of anti-epidemic

The dark cloud enveloped the city, peach blossoms were cold, and the divine land was astonishing. The mountains and rivers were drunk and warm, and the spring breeze was blowing. The world had an appointment. However, a few days later, the plague broke out, and the director of the human world was different. Only obeying the orders, look at the angel in white, swear to God!

His courage was as strong as iron, burning the fingers of the common people for the long night. For the sake of the country, regardless of life or death; for the instructions of his relatives, he was speechless. But he looked forward to the day in the future, when the battlefield was green, he would not forget to share tears with the hero. He would cast an obelisk, cry for thousands of years of medical souls, and comfort me!

1. We have no other choice but to win

Passion is the torment in life, and responsibility is the steel in life. I flew from Guizhou Tongren to Shanghai, intending to continue the interview and writing of the book, but I didn't want everything to stop all of a sudden. Because of the sudden outbreak of the new crown pneumonia, I was trapped.

All of a sudden!

In 2020, the goal of building a well-off society in all aspects will be achieved, and it will be the year for the officials to get rid of poverty and overcome difficulties.

Just as the whole Party and the whole country are working hard to make the final spurt for the great victory, we have encountered the COVID pandemic, which has spread the fastest, spread the most widely and is the most difficult to control since the establishment of the new China.

The epidemic caused by a cough and a few stars of droplets instantly attacked the central area of China, suddenly cooled the happy atmosphere of the Chinese nation's Spring Festival reunion, and caught Hubei, Wuhan and even the whole country off guard!

This was an 'unusual war' and 'non-dual war' between humans and the virus: there was no early warning in the battle, no smoke, and it quietly went on in our indispensable air; there was no front or back in the 'war zone', which was boundless and omnipresent, and it was related to the life and death of all the 'soldiers' and 'civilians'. No one was an isolated island, and no one had anything to do with it. 'Enemy' He walked around in front of us all the time, but he was invisible and invisible. The threat of danger and death seemed to be far away but very close. The gentler the place was, the faster and more accurate the attack would be. In the confrontation, there were no blade and sword shadows, and blood and flesh were blurred. There were more family gathering, chatting and laughing. They didn't know that you were shot in an instant. When you fell down, you had no strength to fight back. You could only wait for the rescue that came

Similar battles had happened countless times in human history.

There was no prophet or angel in the world. Such a sudden disaster was like an earthquake. A moment of shock, fear, loss and confusion, and a moment of unprepared and lack of precaution were unavoidable. During this period, all the tears, pain, mistakes, and lessons that fell were the tools to push the wheel of human civilization forward. Only when one paid the price would they make progress. This was life and death. The fate of the human race is inevitable. When people need warmth, care and help most, the angry roars from their backs are like cold blades, which can only make people more panic and panic. The real sympathy, not only for the dead, but also for some knowledge about the beginning of the outbreak of the disease. They were inexperienced and unprepared. Looking back at the growth history and evolution history of the earth, disasters had always been the bridesmaid of humans. All lives, including humans, could live to today, just like a camel passing through the needle eye. Moreover, the process of life evolution and gene mutation was in essence to deal with disasters. Natural selection, the survival of the fittest, which means that our ancestors have been living from the plague till now. We are the descendants of the strong and the survivors of the disease!

Under the long-term lack of civilized knowledge and scientific methods to resist the pestilence, the helpless people could only escape or wait for death. The black death disease was in Europe (rabbit pestilence).Many riot occurred, making the corpses of the whole European continent rotten and stink. Because of the lack of soldiers, the war in the first world had to stop all of a sudden. With the development of civilization, the progress of thoughts, the prosperity of science and technology, the means of human resistance and victory greatly increased, and many pestilence had been completely eliminated. But who could say that this constantly changing and strange pestilence would be eliminated? What if it's over? Science tells us that the earth will be destroyed one day. If the earth can roam, the virus will also roam with us.

Look at human beings. Since the industrial revolution, we have sprayed a large number of chemicals and living garbage into the sky, buried them underground and thrown them into the sea. Therefore, the food, birds and beasts we eat may contain a small amount of toxins. Humans are not a kind of 'disease poison' on the earth, right? Fortunately, humans have awakened and begun to take action.

This is fate. All kinds of disasters have occurred again and again, and human's struggle has no end. For the pestilence, we have no choice but to fight; we have no other choice but to win.

On February 23, 2020, at the meeting on the overall planning for the promotion of the new crown pestilence prevention and control and the economic and social development, General secretary Xi Jinping firmly said: 'We must unswervingly complete the key task of poverty relief this year. We have to finish it in an all-round way and fight a lot of hard battles. Now we have to work hard to overcome the impact of the pestilence. We must work harder and focus on the key work.'

On March 6th, the general secretary personally presided over the biggest meeting of the eighteen major schools on how to get rid of poverty. He emphasized, 'To completely eliminate poverty by the present standard in rural areas by 2020 is a solemn commitment made by the Central Committee of the Party to the people of the whole country. It must be achieved as scheduled without any retreat or flexibility.'

On March 27, General secretary Xi Jinping presided over a meeting of the Central Political Bureau, listening to the results of the poverty relief and the special inspection, reviewing the examination results and the report. He gave full recognition to the previous work, asking for a clear understanding of the difficulties and challenges that he was facing, and to take hard measures to improve the problems, and to finish all the work in the end of the year.

In the face of the difficult situation and arduous task, the Chinese government took a strategic plan to confidently and resolutely fight for a decisive battle. The overall situation remained amazingly stable in the chaos of the world.

2. Love is rooted in our system

The vast sea shows his heroic temperament; On the one hand, difficulties show his national character; The disaster is coming, and the temperature is the highest in the country; The sudden onset of disease is lightning fast; The situation is as serious as a flood or beast; Every minute is the speed of life and death. Wuhan shudders! Beijing is shaking! The whole country is shaking! People are above all else, and life the most important thing. 'Plague is an order, and control is a responsibility'. Under the command of the Party Central Committee, the mountains and rivers roar surged in and out of the Great Wall. The Chinese people unanimously and quickly responded to the instructions and orders of the party leaders. On the first day of the new year, 9 million 600 thousand square kilometres of land is so solemn and quiet. The 1.4 billion people of all ethnic groups in the East are listening to Beijing's radio. The top leaders of the party and the state held a meeting and formulated a comprehensive plan. Xi Jinping, the general secretary personally led, personally directed, issued a strong mobilization order.

Immediately, the biggest ruling party in the world, the party with about 90,000,000 members, united all the members of the party to fight against the virus. Immediately, the biggest developing country in the world, with a population of more than 1.4 billion and a land of 9.6 million square kilometres, surrounded and blocked the virus from all directions!

This Chinese scientist announced the news of this gathering. Overnight, this unfamiliar and unexpected virus suddenly popped out of nowhere, is accurately identified. Seven days later, the main cause of the virus was separated. The 'big enemy' appeared, and the general attack began

The Chinese soldiers and the medical industry all over the country were talking about a great number of people. Even if the preparation of the control materials and medical devices was not complete at the moment, tens of thousands and 100 thousand soldiers in white rushed to the infected area and the battlefield with the heroic spirit of 'no matter life or death, no matter who I am'. Tens of thousands of experts and medical staff generously asked for a battle, rushing to Hubei province and Wuhan

In less than ten days, the two large-scale professional hospitals in Wuhan miraculously rose from the ground. More hospitals in the world were re equipped, and the ability to receive patients quickly increased by several levels. The broad masses of the people were gradually relieved, and the determination of the whole society to win the battle became more and more firm

Nearly 3 million Chinese policemen and their assistants whistled. They risked their lives to go through all the cities and towns, all roads, all streets and all communities to maintain order, safeguard peace, and strictly investigate all the cars passing by, in order to prevent any potential danger from hurting the people

Thousands of volunteers, donors and guardians in all towns and villages in the city sounded their horns. They guarded the roads, villages, houses, inspection, testing, registration, unprecedented strict and unprecedented extensive supervision and management, revealing the importance of the Great China to life, the people, the country and the world at this time:

> *All the steps are running;*
> *All the hot blood is boiling;*
> *All goals are frontlines;*
> *All journeys are retrograde!*
> *All life comes to a temporary halt;*
> *All laughter is left for tomorrow;*
> *All life enters the battlefield;*
> *All vows like a great bell!*

All the reactions, meetings and actions had witnessed the strong leadership, United mobilization and high discipline of the Chinese party and government, as well as the strong power and effect of the entire national system. A western scholar sighed, 'China is the most disciplined country in the world, no one else!' a European supermarket owner exclaimed, 'this country is intense!'

After all, China was too big, and the sudden attack of the pestilence was too serious. It could be imagined that if the action of the Chinese government was not effective, and if it was a little slower, it would be a disaster in the world. It was reasonable for Mr. Tan, the director general of the World Health Organization, to repeatedly show respect and gratitude to China. It was a pity that the country had reported the unprecedented risks, the fast and highly hidden infection of the new crown virus, and the serious consequences of the spread of the virus. Although the World Health Organization had also informed all the countries in the world at the first time, some western countries had regarded the virus and the pestilence as the notorious 'political weapons' without any precaution, his family began to slander and attack China for no reason and almost hysterically. Two months later, in China with such a vast territory and such a large population, the devastating epidemic has been effectively controlled and fundamentally reversed. In the peach blossom season, in Shanghai, where I live, and in Guiyang, where I have just been, although everyone wears masks, there are many people on the street, the hotel is overcrowded, and the night is full of lights. Great China reappears its great vitality, and China's economic engine roars again

I, as well as hundreds of millions of my compatriots, are very grateful to some Western politicians for their naked performance in this world pestilence. They took off their white gloves to cover people. They took away their so-called 'human rights', 'freedom', 'equality' The black flags were torn into pieces. At first, they took pleasure in the pestilence in Wuhan, but later they became the disaster-stricken area. Their racial ism was rampant on the street, and finally caused a large-scale street protest. The black people shouted, 'I can't breathe!' 'the life of the black people is also life!' After they lied once, they had to use one thousand times to cover up. They thought that if they repeated the lie one thousand times, it would become a 'fact'. They kicked the Great Wall again and again. Whoever gets hurt knows. I can't see anything else from their increasingly crazy attacks and slanders.

I only see their fear – the fear of a powerful China, which is a psychological disease called 'dinosaur disease' (Fear of China's rise). Some Western politicians' attacks and slanders against the eastern powers are like spittle in the sky, but now the spittle star has fallen on their faces. Nowadays, the epidemic situation in some western countries is becoming more and more serious, and the huge death toll is shocking. China, which has just emerged from the epidemic, has extended a helping hand to more than 100 countries in the world with a real humanitarian spirit and the great concept of 'a community with a shared future for mankind'

The facts proved and will continue to prove that the whole country's system is the love of the whole country. It loves its own people and the whole human race, because we are a team of fate.

History has proved that it is not fate but thought that imprisons mankind. Diversity is the essence of the world, and the coexistence of multiple civilizations is the glory of the world. If there is only one kind of flower on the earth, even roses, it is terrible. China has Chinese characteristics and Chinese thought. Great ideas must make great countries. China's strength, China's spirit, China's great changes and China's miracles have proved that China's ideological banner is great, outstanding, effective, full of vitality, keeping pace with the times, continuous innovation and development. Therefore, the Chinese people can fully control their own destiny.

3. Home, a topic related to the meaning of life

Countless people were fighting against the disease. They couldn't go home. Their relatives were looking forward to their victory day and night and coming back home as soon as possible.

In order to ensure the safety and health of the masses, the government asked the public to temporarily stop all social activities and stay at home, waiting for the pestilence to pass.

Ordinary home suddenly becomes a 'safe island' for everyone to protect themselves in special times; Home has become a social symbol of soldiers' victory. The significance of home suddenly becomes like a milestone, especially important, rich and profound. In fact, the meaning of home has existed from the moment it was born, because everyone comes from a home and everyone has a home, so we seldom think deeply about the meaning of home.

In my opinion, home is the greatest starting point in the history of mankind and civilization. With home, mankind ended the animal age of 'only knowing mother but not father'; With home, human beings have a sense of responsibility; With home, mankind has a dream of the future; With a home, wealth, knowledge and culture can be accumulated and inherited in an orderly and sustainable manner; With home, villages, cities, countries and all modern civilizations were born.

Xi Jinqing, the general secretary, said, 'it's our goal that people yearn for a good life.' where is the good life? Where will a better life be achieved at home in the end

Therefore, everyone's work and struggle, as well as their sacrifices and sacrifices, no matter how great and magnificent their dreams and pursuit were, in essence, for their family, everyone and their country. Their ultimate goal was to 'go home' – their family was the smallest country, and their country had tens of millions of families!

Yes, if the family didn't exist, how could it be possible? If the family didn't exist, where would the country be?

Yes, all great dreams and goals, all great struggles and parades, described in the warmest, kindest and most daily language, are for 'going home' and returning to a peaceful and beautiful home! In the final analysis, 'Chinese dream' is our 'home'. The hardworking, brave and wise Chinese people are working hard to create this great 'home'!

Yes, home is not only a small, limited material existence, but also a broad and rich spiritual home. In fact, it has no 'wall' It extends to the edge of the whole society, the whole country and the world – if the world has an edge. What is the 'era of globalization' Whether you agree or disagree, whether you welcome or disagree, this is a 'home' for all mankind to share happiness and difficulties! Just as all walls and borders can't block the air, everyone, every family, is closely related to others and the world.

On April 26, 2020, the Wuhan security and Construction Committee issued a notice, 'Ding, a 77-year-old patient with COVID-19 in Wuhan city's public hospital. The second nucleic acid testing result is negative. So far, there is no COVID-19 in Wuhan city.'

The 77-year-old man was the last one to go home safely after going through a lot of dangerous days and nights. He must have never thought that he would become a major stage or a decisive victory character in this 'big battle' of the whole country in the great, brave and solemn battle of fighting against the new crown pneumonia with all his strength.

The superiority of the socialist system with Chinese characteristics has once again been tested and proved by history! Under the direct leadership of general secretary Xi Jinping, the CPC Central Committee and the State Council decided to restore the work in an all-round way under the conditions of ensuring safety and order, start the economy, solve poverty, and reform and innovate. According to the plan, we should revitalize the momentum and vigorously promote it. 'There is no retreat and flexibility.'

I started working. How beautiful it is to work!

II Malipo, a place full of hot blood and tears

1. This was a sacred place

In Tongren City, Guizhou Province, there is a high 'horn sound throughout life' – Wang Mingli, a veteran fighting with Vietnam, with one and a half legs. From the postman to the volunteer postman, from being stationed in the village to helping the poor, to planting tea in the mountains, he left a long heroic footprint on everything. His comrade in arms An Jingxu dug a grave in advance and rushed to the battlefield with a body bag on his back. After returning home, he inherited the love given by the martyrs, fought with his wife all his life, succeeded with courage and diligence, and unfortunately failed due to serious illness. Now he has opened a small supermarket in the resettlement community of Wanshan District, Tongren City to make a living

Unexpectedly, with the extension of the interview journey, I broke into the battlefield where Wang Mingli and An Jingxu have gone through difficulties and dangers, risking life and death! Find the hot land soaked with blood and tears, and find the place where the famous Laoshan and Zheyin Mountain are located – Malipo County, Wenshan Prefecture, Yunnan Province.

Malipo County, with 5 words 'Frontier, minority, poverty, mountain, war', had forged her history and today. 'Border' had forged her national line of 277 kilometres; 'less': 40.6% of the minority's population; 'poverty': more than 30 thousand of the poor people who had built a file and registered a bank; 'mountain': 99.9% of the whole city's area was mountain areas, with more than 40.6% of the Karst topography; 'war': during the 14 years of self-defense, counterattack and defense against the Solamnia Kingdom, 2,122 young and middle-aged men were disabled because of the battle, and a direct economic loss of nearly 300 million dollars was caused. During the war, the front line was a sea of fire, and everything behind was in preparation for the battle. In order to prepare for the battle, they couldn't invest in this place, nor could they build houses, nor could they run schools. Moreover, there were mines everywhere in the mountains and at the foot of the mountains, which meant that the development of Malipo was better than that of the whole country, other regions were 14 years late.

Of course, it was a beautiful place with history and culture. There were the mysterious rock cliff painting of the king in the new stone age, the ancient tea horse road known as the South Silk Road, the camp and stone block left by the soldiers of previous generations, and the jungle path that the Chinese people selflessly supported the people of the Solamnia kingdom to resist the law and the war between the United States

In 1979, after our frontier troops launched a self-defense counterattack against the Solamnia Kingdom, the Solamnia Kingdom dispatched troops to occupy the high ground in Malipo City, such as the Koulin mountain, the Laoshan, the Zheyinshan and the Dongshan, Balihe. They built solid buildings, laid mines and set up iron wire net, in order to occupy our sacred territory for a long time. They also shot at our territory from time to time, beat our border citizens to death, and blew up many houses and roads. As a result, the good fields couldn't be cultivated normally, the villages were forced to move in, and some farm and enterprises couldn't be operated normally. On April 28, 1984, after retaking the forest mountain, our frontier troops won a series of battles. They recaptured the old mountain, the ghost mountain, the Eight Mile River East Mountain and other highlands that were occupied by the army of the Solamnia kingdom. After that, they had been through two mountain round battles for many years, which were named because we had dispatched 10 group armies to fight in turns in each military region. In the early 1990s, the relationship between the two countries gradually returned to normal, and the boundary of the land was finally decided.

Therefore, Malipo became a sacred place stained with the blood of the martyrs. The villagers here said, 'Malipo is the place that has suffered the longest time after the establishment of the new China, suffered the most damage, and sacrificed the most.' Every year on Tomb Sweeping Day, thousands of officers and soldiers, martyrs, survivors, government cadres and college students come from all over the country to hold a grand memorial ceremony for the martyrs who died here. In those days, hotels in the county could not find empty beds. Even residents lived in many guests. The streets were full of yellow military uniforms and rows of glittering meritorious medals hung on their chest. At the ceremony, the national flag was half hung, the sadness and music were low, the white flowers were like a sea, the name of the hero crossed the sky, the representatives of all parties burst into tears, and the venue was full of joy.

Martyrs who died for their country will always be the spiritual anchor of a nation and a country.

The Malipo Martyrs Cemetery was located 4 kilometres away from the Beijiao of the county, with its back against the green mountains and facing the green water. On the gate of the cemetery, there were 7 words, 'Malipo Martyrs Cemetery'. In the center of the cemetery stood a tower of raging martyrs, which was 15.32 metres high. On the front of the cemetery, there were 8 golden words, 'people's heroes will never die', and on the back, there were the hands of 7 people: 'The martyrs who have sacrificed themselves to defend the frontier of the motherland will never die.' in the cemetery, there were Beijing snow pine brought by the center of the people's alliance from the Zhongnanhai in Beijing, which was cultivated with water and soil, dragon cedar and gold cedar sent by the Ji'nan army, 2 sapling planted by the commander of the Kunming military region, and exotic flowers and herbs sent from all over the country. Initially, a total of 21 rows of 937 martyrs were placed from the foot of the mountain to the top of the mountain. Among them, the hero platform buried 15 heroes and was awarded the title of 'combat hero' by the Central Military Commission and the military region. Today, with the discovery and increasing year by year, 960 martyrs have been buried here, representing only 9.6 million square kilometres of Chinese territory and heroic martyrs from all over the country. The story of Shi Guangzhu, a national first-class combat hero and China's 'Paul Kochakin' takes place here. The story of Du Fuguo, a demining hero known as the 'model of the times', and the battle story of Wang Mingli, a sergeant of the Yunnan demining brigade of the southern theater army, are rated as the typical disabled veterans who are advanced in poverty alleviation in the country.

Today, China and Vietnam had returned to normal foreign relations and friendly contacts. The border trade was fully open, and the business of the people on the border was booming. The people of the two countries had experienced the hardships of war, and were full of expectations for maintaining a long-term peaceful and friendly relationship. However, no matter how the history changed, we will never forget the martyrs and heroes who have fought to the end for our country. They are the spirit of a country, and the torches of a race's soul.

The martyrs had been loyal to their souls for thousands of years, and heroes had existed for thousands of years. In Malipo, every mountain road, every forest, and every tombstone there was a touching story, and every story inspired thousands of young men.

2. 'Magic City' and The Border

Li Shenghui, a cadre of Shanghai's aid to Yunnan, was born in 1978. He is thin, pale and capable. After arriving at Malipo from Wenshan County, his mobile pedometer showed that he had walked more than 15,000 steps. In fact, after only a few dozen steps, he walked out of the door of a hotel in Wenshan County and boarded the car that took him to Malipo County. The car hit more than 15000 steps. After more than two hours, he sometimes bumped into the sky, stretched out his hand to touch the sun, and sometimes fell into a deep valley. When he looked up, he could only see a glimmer of the sky. On the Winding mountain road, there are pits in addition to stones. The car bumped all the way. It seems that at any time, all parts can fly out like shells and smash the mountains. In Li Shenghui's words, he must 'grasp his teeth with both hands and tighten his body.' Otherwise, life is as light as a feather. Unfortunately, people may fall apart and lose all their knowledge before they reach the front line of poverty alleviation. When he came to the door of Malipo County Party committee, the first thing he did was to spit out all the tension he experienced along the way.

Li Shenghui graduated from East China Normal University, passed the civil service examination and successfully entered the general office of Shanghai municipal government. The young man is smart, capable and brave. Many years later, he was sent to Caojiadu sub district office of Jing'an District as deputy director. In September 2017, Shanghai began to select and organize the tenth batch of foreign aid cadres. Since childhood, Li Shenghui considered himself a 'three door' child, that is, home, school and organ. He didn't know how beautiful and helpless the world outside was. He needs exercise, practice and real knowledge. He immediately sent an invitation to the leadership office. The leader smiled and said, 'to tell you the truth, I have to think twice when others sign up. I'm waiting for you to put your name in!'

The leader\s trust was encouragement. Three days later, Li Shenghui asked the leader, 'when do we leave? I have packed my luggage.'

Li Shenghui was appointed member of the Standing Committee of Malipo County Party committee and deputy county magistrate of Wenshan Prefecture, Yunnan Province. Previously, Shanghai's Yunnan aid cadres were subordinate to units above state organs. This time, as the tenth batch of Yunnan aid cadres, Li Shenghui sent additional troops to Zhili County, which is regarded as the first batch of Yunnan aid troops in Shanghai. This is the result of negotiations between Shanghai and Yunnan: Malipo County is a hot land soaked in the blood of martyrs. We should pay attention to arrangements and vigorously publicize, so that parents and villagers there can live a well-off life as soon as possible, and let the war-torn scenery draw a newer and more beautiful picture of a new era as soon as possible!

Li Shenghui/s heart was not calm. Why did you come here to participate in the local poverty relief struggle? What and what? He had been doing the research for three months. Did I say it was too long? He smiled and said, The point was that it was the first time for the leaders of the county to arrange temporary officials from Shanghai. They didn't know how to make use of me. More division of labor? I'm afraid I'm tired; is the division of labor too professional? I'm afraid I'm going to leave soon, leaving behind a mess that others can't take over. Many people think I'm young and think I'm just working for gold. Two or three years later, they can send me abroad and give me a good evaluation. In some people's eyes, temporary duty is a kind of virtual duty, without real power and without any need to do anything. As a result, in the first month, I mainly helped the county leaders to run meetings, participate in various training and learning, and temporarily acted as the post when the leaders were ill. Well, during this period, I went all over the villages and towns, giving me great spiritual incentives and knowing what I should do and how to do it.

In this land, he heard and saw many tearful stories:

Liu Guiyan, the only martyr from Shanghai—

960 martyrs were buried in the Maribo Martyrs Cemetery. Every year on Tomb Sweeping Day, martyr's birthday or war death day, relatives will come here to clean and sacrifice. However, one martyr's mausoleum is a little special: weeds grow in front of the tomb and a thick layer of dust accumulates on the tombstone. Obviously, relatives haven't been here for a long time. Li Shenghui learned that this is the only Shanghai martyr Liu Guiyan in the cemetery. Liu Guiyan lives in Yangpu District, Shanghai. His father was a veteran of the people's Liberation Army who participated in the river crossing campaign. His family cherished several medals of merit. After graduating from high school, Liu Guiyan joined Shanghai ocean shipping company. It must be the tragic experiences and heroic stories often told by his father during the war years that gave him great encouragement. Imagine how comfortable and quiet it is to live and work in Shanghai, but Liu Guiyan signed up for the army at the age of 19 and followed the army on the vast Yunnan Guizhou Plateau for seven years. In April 1984, Liu Guiyan's troops went to Malipo, the front line of Laoshan. He is the captain of the radar force. His main task is to find out the dynamics of the Vietnamese army in time so that our army can organize preparations and corresponding attacks as soon as possible. In other words, the radar he commands is the perspective eye and wind ear of our army. Of course, the enemy hates my radar. At about 2 a.m. on July 7, Liu Guiyan's radar troops were heavily bombed by enemy fire. The platoon leader and several soldiers died on the spot. The company commander lost too much blood due to back injury and was in a coma. Liu Guiyan was hit by shrapnel in as many as 32 places. He was badly wounded in the abdomen and his intestines flowed out. But he saw many of his comrades fall to the ground. Gritting his teeth, he climbed over and gave the last first aid kit to his comrades. Then he endured severe pain and sat on the ground directing the soldiers to carry the wounded.

After the withdrawal of the whole army, Liu Guiyan, only 26, fell to the ground and could no longer stand up.

A few months before his death, Liu Guiyan had asked for a leave to go home to celebrate his mother's 50-year-old birthday. The whole family had a family reunion dinner, which was the last time for his family to see him.

Later, because the martyr' parents were over 80 years old and in poor health, their meager pension was difficult to pay the transportation expenses to and from Shanghai and Yunnan, and the living conditions of other children were also very common. In the 24 years after Liu Guiyan's death, only his parents took his family once when he was buried. After that, he could no longer go to Maribo to sweep the floor for his son.

After listening to this story, Li Shenghui went to the martyrs' cemetery to worship martyr Liu Guiyan and carefully looked at the young and handsome remains of the martyrs on the tombstone. Li Shenghui burst into tears. Soon, when he returned to Shanghai on business, he accompanied the relevant leaders of Shanghai to Liu Guiyan's house to visit the old couple and other family members. Li Shenghui sighed: 'as a martyr of Shanghai nationality who died heroically in the counterattack war and border defense war, this old worker's home is really not easy, which has greatly stimulated my enthusiasm for poverty alleviation in Malipo.' at the martyr's home, Li Shenghui learned that Liu Guiyan had a girlfriend Zhang Yanping before his death. After his sacrifice, out of love and respect for the martyrs, Zhang Yanping came to comfort his old parents and help with the housework every day. She said she promised Guiyan that no matter how many years he served in the army, she would take good care of the second old man. Later, people all over the country knew that a fierce war had taken place on the border between China and Vietnam, and the fiancées of many officers and soldiers involved in the war were killed. A girl speciously said, 'you sacrificed a martyr, but you broke an arm or leg. How can I take care of you all your life?' but Zhang Yanping's love is iron. Her character is noble. Until she dies, she always takes good care of Guiyan's parents like her relatives. If the martyr had knowledge in the spring, he would be very happy.

On April 6, 2009, according to the decision of relevant parties in Shanghai, martyr Liu Guiyan's clothes tomb was buried in Binhai ancient garden. All sectors of society contributed one after another and built a bronze statue for the martyr.

3. 'Mom, I've been waiting for you for 20 years'

Zhao Zhanying, born in April 1963, is the child of a farmer in Haoming County, Kunming. He joined the army in 1982 and died in Laoshan on April 28, 1984. At the age of 21, he was buried in the Maribo Martyrs Cemetery. Because his family is very poor and can't afford to travel, his family can't come to Malipo to worship him for 20 years. The comrades in arms thought it was too tragic. The martyrs shed blood and devoted themselves to the holy land of the motherland. His relatives can't cry anymore. On the Tomb Sweeping Day in 2004, on the big day of victory on April 28, the comrades in arms raised funds, and the relevant departments in Malipo issued subsidies to all the martyrs' families. Zhan Ying's old mother, accompanied by her nephew and daughter-in-law, came from Haoming County to Malipo martyrs cemetery. The white-haired old man sat next to his son's tombstone, stroking his son's portrait and blood red name, crying, and his comrades in arms cried. After that, several comrades in arms wrote a poem for Zhao Zhanying, 'Mom, I've been waiting for you for 20 years', which was read out at the memorial service. The whole audience was stunned and began to cry.

Mom, I've been waiting for you for 20 years!
Mom! That must be you,
I heard that you made your own embroidered cloth shoes,
The sound of stepping on the ground.
I've been listening since I was a baby,
I've been hearing me wear a green military uniform.
When I woke up in the dream of the barracks,
As if I saw you walking gently to my bed,
Cover me with my army quilt.
When I endured days of hunger and thirst in my bomb shelter,
How I miss the bowl of sweet dumplings you made me when I was young.
Mom, 20 years ago,
When the evil bullet knocked me down in the front line,
At the last moment of my life, you are the only person I miss!
How I want to tell you face to face,
When I fell down,

My bloody spear still points to the highest peak!
How I want to prove to you,
Son, as a soldier, didn't humiliate you!
Mom, it's been 20 years,
My brothers have come to see me many times,
Shed endless tears on my grave.
But, but, but,
No one can replace my mother's touch,
No one can understand how much I miss my mother!
Mom, I haven't seen you for 20 years,
How I want to hear your call to me!
Mom, it's been 20 years. I know it's hard for you,
You can't cross mountains and rivers because you don't
     have enough money!
Mom, I've been waiting for you for 20 years,
When you say to me: you are my good son,
You are loyal to our country, your tears had dried up,
But you have a hero for a son, you have no regrets!
Mom, I've been waiting for you for 20 years,
Waiting for a great mother,
Come to your son!

Li Shenghui copied the poem into the work manual with tears. This poem and the stories of all the martyrs are his inexhaustible driving force to help poverty alleviation in Yunnan. When he walked into the mountains and villages, he felt that there were too many things to do for this hot red land, which was worth doing. What he did is a great responsibility and significance. What he did is necessary, necessary and necessary!

4. Behind him are thousands of hands from Shanghai

The first major event is not only poverty alleviation, but also salvation!

After years of 'War against Vietnam', Malipo is full of war wounds under the broad background of China's prosperous and towering buildings. They can't build houses, roads or even farms normally. The mountains are full of mines, some planted by the Vietnamese army and some by our army. Tens of thousands, 100,000 mines of various types, disguises and trigger methods have not been artificially buried like the old movie 'mine war'. Instead, they were transported up the mountain with forklifts and military vehicles. Once the car board is opened, all the mines will roll down the mountain. They are dense in the woods and grass. Wherever they roll, they are everywhere. There are dozens of anti-tank mines, anti infantry mines, loose mines, trip mines, jump mines, trick mines and so on. Due to the long ore distribution time and large topographic changes, it has become a rare mixed mining area with high ore density and difficult to identify in the world. Since 1979, nearly 10,000 people in Wenshan Prefecture have been injured and disabled by accidental lightning, ranging in age from 8 to 84. The casualties of animals and livestock cannot be counted. Among them, sharenzhai, Funing County, Wenshan Prefecture, 600 metres away from the border, is the most representative: 87 villagers have only 78 legs!

Villager Yang Zhuasao's hometown is Vietnam. In 1978, he met a girl from Shanjiao Village, Funing County in the border trade. They fell in love at first sight, soon got married and settled down in the village at the foot of the mountain. Later, he stepped on the thunder twice and lost his left leg. He said, 'my life is really big. It's not easy to walk in the thunder twice and still live!'

Villager Wang Milong joined the militia at the age of 16, actively supported the front line, helped the army transport materials and engaged in intelligence work. One day in February 1984, he and the boy scouts hurried back to the camp with the information they had collected. Unexpectedly, they stepped on a mine on the road and injured their left leg. He was 19 years old and his son was only five months old. Later, Wang Milong became a grandfather. He held his beloved grandson and said, 'fortunately, his daughter-in-law got married early, otherwise no one would want her!'

It is conceivable that so many parents and villagers are trapped in disability. It is necessary to rescue them from the suffering left by the war. Li Shenghui made a detailed report to the leaders of Jing'an District and the disabled persons' Federation. Talking about the heroic sacrifices of these martyrs and the great contributions made by the people in the border areas to defend the country, he and the leaders were relatively speechless and choked. Shanghai Municipal Civil Affairs, disabled persons' Federation and public welfare foundation responded positively through visits and contacts, and the charity actions jointly planned and organized by the two places were carried out rapidly. Paid in full by Shanghai, more than 1,300 war disabled people in Malipo County were included in the insurance coverage, which solved their concerns. Doctors from Shanghai made a special trip to Malipo to install prosthetics for the amputees free of charge and take out shrapnel hidden in their bodies for the villagers for 20 or 30 years. The disabled finally threw away their crutches and stood up happily. However, it is not over yet. After 'standing up', Li Shenghui had to 'work'. Shanghai Li Shenghui and relevant departments have extensive contact with caring enterprises, provide more than 50 public welfare jobs in Malipo every year (the annual average income is not less than 12,000 yuan), and gradually expand them, so that these disabled people who are difficult to go out to work can find employment locally and steadily get rid of poverty. Subsequently, Li Shenghui organized the county to carry out 'barrier free facilities transformation' to flatten the door, public toilets and all small steps. At the same time, starting from paying attention to the disabled, expand to the whole village and carry out the 'toilet revolution'. Prohibit and fill the once smelly private huts of each household, and establish a clean water toilet managed and cleaned by a specially assigned person. As soon as the toilet was changed, the appearance of the village changed greatly, and the environmental sanitation conditions of each family have been greatly improved. Asking villagers to say 'your house is not as clean as the toilet' will hurt their self-esteem. In order to solve the learning difficulties of children from poor families with disabilities, Shanghai Tobacco Group, non-governmental charitable organizations 'firefly' and 'love foundation' jointly carried out assistance to Yunnan, donating more than 1 million yuan to students every year. In this way, the whole 'rescue operation' formed by Malipo County to heal the wounds left by the war has become a set of systematic engineering, from the elderly to children, from peaceful life to happy work, from 'stand up' to 'work', and then to 'become stronger' and 'get rich'. The pace of poverty alleviation in the whole county has been greatly accelerated.

—After investigation, interview and in-depth thinking, Li Shenghui sorted the development and poverty alleviation projects he could think of into 'what Malipo needs and what Shanghai can do,' and then returned to Shanghai to carry out extensive lobbying, publicity and mobilization from the government to enterprises, from social organizations to lovers. Imagine that in the internationalized and high-end big Shanghai, hundreds of big projects and big projects cannot be completed. The deputy director of a small neighborhood office is one floor higher than the aunt of the neighborhood committee in the alley. Who will listen to him? Who cares about his sesame plan?' However, Li Shenghui has a thunderous 'steppingstone', that is, the photos of those broken leg villagers in Malipo! This is the picture of those tombstones with bright red names and relatives crying in Maribo Martyrs Cemetery! Everywhere Li Shenghui went, everyone was deafening, shocked and full of tears! The last sentence of all high-end people is: 'Xiao Li, come on, What should we do?'

This is the capital of Shanghai, this is the heartwarming Shanghai! In just two years, Shanghai has invested more than 50 aid funds to implement projects. Malipo soon formed a trinity pattern of special poverty alleviation, industrial poverty alleviation and social poverty alleviation, benefiting countless poor people. Four sub district offices and 28 enterprises in Jing'an District cooperate with 11 townships in Malipo (covering all villages in deep poverty) to help them enter the village; Malipo's cloud pure coffee, emerald, veal, tea and fruit have been placed in many supermarkets in Shanghai, and some have set up counters; The wartime 'tent primary school' was transformed, and Shanghai doctors with regular free clinics came; The cement road extended from village, group, home, and even to the mountain; 3,000 school uniforms, 5,000 school uniforms and 4,000 bedding donated by Shanghai have arrived. Before sending the bedding to poor families, Li Shenghui put forward a condition: before you get the quilt, you must clean the environment at home and abroad. When the village cadre reported to him, he smiled and said, 'your method is more effective than what I said a thousand times! As soon as bedding enters the village, every household is covered with dust and chickens fly and dogs jump. Aristocrats who never do housework clean the windows with rags!'

—Even his daughter and wife were moved and mobilized by Li Shenghui. When she learned that there was a serious debris flow disaster in Malipo, her daughter who went to school on the first day of junior middle school immediately reported to the teacher and asked all teachers and students to donate money to the disaster area. The school prepared a platform for her to preach Malibo to the whole school. Then the little girl burst into tears. The whole school moved and donated 34000 yuan to the disaster area. His wife is a doctor. She contacted a group of college students and formed a volunteer medical team. She went to Maribo many times to carry out oral health activities and donated a village drinking water project. Later, the whole family was rated as 'the most beautiful family in Shanghai.'

Over the past two years, Li Shenghui has done too much in Malipo and Shanghai. Many things are small and trivial, but they must be run many times and called countless times to achieve them. His arms seem to grow very long, becoming a warm bridge between Shanghai and Malipo, Yunnan. Li Shenghui was awarded 'Yunnan poverty alleviation advanced worker Award' and 'Yunling model' successively in 2018 and 2019. At the award ceremony, Li Shenghui sincerely said: 'it's not how well I did, but because there are thousands of enthusiastic hands behind me in Shanghai!'

After working for a long time, Malibo people almost forget that Li Shenghui is a temporary deputy county magistrate. They all think he is a real cadre and their family. On July 19, 2019, Li Shenghui was ordered to return to Shanghai to work. On the same day, he packed up and went out of the dormitory of the county organ. He was very surprised and moved that many local cadres and villagers came to see him off. Shaking hands, saying goodbye, thanking, hugging, taking photos, deep feelings and tears became the most moving scene in Malibo that day. On the highway, affectionate WeChat messages came one after another:

'Hello, county magistrate. I'm Li Pinjian's family. Thank you for giving us so much help. Our family will never forget it!'

'With a good leader like you and a poverty alleviation team like you, Malibo's development will be exceeded! Thank you on behalf of the Malibo people!'

'Your deep love for us makes it impossible for us to express and thank you in words. Xiaozhai people will always remember every great thing you have done for us, except thank you or thank you!'

'If you don't say thank you, I really can't think of any language to express our feelings. Remember to come home often!'

Brother Hui: thousands of words are not enough to express our gratitude to you. Over the past two years, you have paid too much for Malipo. All we can do is be grateful!! we can only do everything well and truly, which is the best return for all our efforts!

'I'm grateful to meet you. I'm grateful to have you!'

'I just came back from Maribo. My experiences in that red land, what I heard and what I saw on the farmland are still clearly visible in my mind. Excellent people are like a light ball. I have been with you and them for a long time, and I don't want to return to mediocrity. The power of my example has inspired more people to move forward. Congratulations to Shanghai Caring Man! '

5. Song 'well off', see off to station

The ethnic minority villagers in the deep mountains of Yunnan are very simple and hospitable, all of whom belong to the owner of 'Promises are as precious as gold. They are generous to their friends. If you want to drink, they can hold their liquor.' You must not be a guest during the poverty alleviation period. If you go, the host looks around the house carefully. The house is empty and the stove is empty. There is no delicious food to entertain distinguished guests, so he makes up his mind and kills the only pig in the house with tears. Please have a good drink and get drunk. When you wake up, you will find that the pig cub is the 'poverty alleviation leading pig' just given to him by the township government. After raising regenerated pigs and grandchildren, it will become rich after generation. I didn't expect that your luxurious meal blocked people's way to get rich again. But don't be afraid, the master won't blame you. You walked away. The host sat at the door, smoking a hookah bag, thinking that there was no food or meat here. What will you eat tomorrow? After making up his mind, he held his cigarette gun to his waist and went up the mountain to pick fruit. In any case, Yunnan is full of mountains and fields. The four seasons are like spring. There are delicious mountain fruits everywhere. The 'vitamin ABCDEFG' is enough to eat for 10,000 years. It is said that Yunnan did not starve to death during the 'three-year difficult period', so no matter how poor Yunnan people are, they can't come out to work. I have long found that it is rare for migrant workers from Yunnan to travel all over the country. They 'live and work in peace and contentment,' and they 'defend their homeland.'

It's really difficult to help the poor in the mountain areas of Yunnan. You have to change the two habits of the people in Yunnan.

On September 19, 2017, Song Jie and Li Shenghui flew to Kunming on the same plane. This is the tenth batch of cadres sent by Shanghai to Yunnan. Song Jie temporarily lives in Jingdong Yi Autonomous County, Pu'er City. He is a member of the Standing Committee of the county Party committee and deputy county magistrate for a term of two years. Jingdong County is located in the southwest of Yunnan Province, with a population of 370,000, fertile land and rich products. It is called the 'granary and meat warehouse' of Pu'er City. The famous Lancang River and red river flow through its territory and nourish the people of Jingdong.

Shanghai people are generally pale. Song Jie is the darkest one I have ever seen. In fact, he was tanned by the sun in Jingdong. In 1976, Song Jie was born into a cadre family in Shanghai. After graduating from University, he worked in Jinshan District. He served as secretary of the Youth League Committee for many years and established Jinshan 'digital city management' system. He served as Minister of the armed forces, but not as a soldier. He worked hard all the way. In 2017, Song Jie, 41, took the initiative to sign up for assistance to Yunnan and was finally selected to 'clear customs and kill generals' all the way. Why is he so eager? Song Jie said with a bitter smile that his family was really 'unstoppable!' His father was the first director of the Jinshan District Cooperation Office (now the cooperation and exchange office of the district government). Before retirement, he organized a large number of human, financial and material resources to assist Yunnan. His wife Chu Aiqun is a doctor. In 2016, as a medical expert volunteer, he went to Shanghai Pu'er City to assist Yunnan for half a year, and went to Pu'er City many times to support local medical undertakings. He also took the lead in helping Pu'er people's hospital to establish a general department. One morning, when she began to patrol the ward, a 13-year-old girl with big eyes timidly said to her in the corridor, 'aunt, can you arrange for my mother to have an early infusion?' Chu Aiqun asked why? The girl said, 'this is my mother's last infusion. After that, my mother and I will rush back to the county, go to the town, and then walk to my stockade. It will take more than ten hours. I'm afraid I can't go home before tonight. If I stay in hospital for another night, I will spend another day's hospitalization expenses.' the girl cried, and Chu Aiqun cried. She was wearing a white coat and had no money in her pocket, so she borrowed 50 yuan from her colleagues and stuffed it into the girl's pocket. Later, she arranged for the girl's mother to finish dripping water as soon as possible and watched her and her daughter went on the road.

When I came home to talk about it, my wife was still crying. My daughter goes to junior high school. She listened to her mother's introduction to the food and clothing in the poor mountainous areas of Pu'er, so she went to school to report to the teacher. Later, she mobilized students of all grades to donate hundreds of clothes and sent them to a middle school in the county where the local children lived. Chu Aiqun personally went to the school to distribute and change new clothes for the children. She squatted on the ground, smiled and said to a girl, 'this is a new dress my daughter bought for you.' a nearby colleague photographed the scene. Chu Aiqun took the photos home to her daughter and husband. Her daughter is very happy and proud. Song Jie said to me, 'that's the most beautiful picture of my wife. It's more beautiful than laughing at the wedding.'

The whole family has become a pioneer in poverty alleviation. Only Song Jie 'didn't do anything', so he couldn't wait to go to Jingdong. Before leaving, his father gave him eight words: 'heart, emotion, brain and strength.'

Compared with 2016, Shanghai's poverty alleviation funds for Jingdong County increased six times in 2020, which shows that with the launch of the poverty alleviation battle, Shanghai's poverty alleviation efforts have been greatly strengthened. Song Jie also began a comprehensive survey of the whole county: check the real estate resources of poor households, schools, roads, clinics and towns, and look for poverty alleviation support points. After the rain, the car encountered a mudslide on Winding mountain road. If the car leaves 10 minutes late, it may be hit by boulders and rolling stones and 'die for the country' (a local cadre died for this); Enter the place where the 'tribe' in the mountains goes for one day; Explore the road to groups and families and grind a layer of big blisters on the soles of your feet; Unable to return to the county at night, he had to live in a cold village and listen to the roar of the mountains... Seeing poverty, he was very sad and hoped that he would be happy to implement the project. The villagers' thanks moved him and made him excited, crying and crying. He connected Shanghai with one hand and Jingdong with the other, organized Shanghai doctors to

Jingdong free clinic and trained thousands of people; Organized Jingdong poor households to work in Shanghai for many times, and set up special 'service stations' to help them solve their daily life difficulties such as food and clothing, housing and their children's schooling in the local area; Introduce a number of Shanghai enterprises to build factories in Jingdong to develop the local industrial economy. After the completion of the mushroom planting base invested and constructed in Shanghai, it was originally planned to be exported to Shanghai for sales, but it was sold out in Kunming.

These villages have taken on a new look. The project has taken root and sprouted, and the road extends in all directions. The locals nicknamed Song Jie 'Song (send) well-off'.

According to the original plan of the provinces and cities, Jingdong County should get rid of poverty in 2018, and Song Jie's three-year poverty alleviation task will also expire. Yunnan Province sent an inspection team to Jingdong to inspect the work results, the number of people out of poverty and account registration. The survey found that some places did not fully meet the standards. The inspection team said angrily, 'you didn't pass the national examination here. Don't take the national examination again! Pick up the rest, fill in the gap and do it again!' after that, the county leaders made a major adjustment. Song Jie said with emotion: 'the provincial examination is stricter than the national examination. This rigorous attitude and working attitude of being responsible for the state and the people shocked and educated the cadres and the masses of the county.' as a member of the Standing Committee of the county Party committee and deputy county head, he felt a sense of responsibility and guilt. He resolutely reported to the Organization Department of the Shanghai municipal Party committee and asked Jingdong County to continue poverty alleviation for three years. He said: 'the locals call me 'Song (send) well-off'. I must take 'Well-off' to the station, otherwise I will have no face to see the old man!'

The father waiting for the operation in the hospital said, 'if you get 'well-off' to the station, don't come home!'

At the county cadres' meeting, Song Jie and the new team of the county Party committee and government publicly vowed: 'if we can't meet the standards in 2019, we are willing to take responsibility, resign and thank the world!'

At the beginning of 2020, after strict assessment, the whole county finally reached the standard and took off its hat.

'However, this has caused great difficulties for my assistance to Yunnan.' Song Xiaokang said with a smile. 'In the past, I took photos of dilapidated and poor shanzhais and dangerous houses of farmers in Jingdong County and mobilized assistance and donations in Shanghai. The effect is very good and successful. Unfortunately, I can't find any such houses now!'

III There is no place far in the world. Love is hometown

1. We are all children of a mother

Shanghai is actually the sea. She was built on the alluvial plain of the Yangtze River Estuary, with an average altitude of 2.19 metres. In other words, Shanghai people can swim in the East China Sea by jumping out of the first-floor window. At night, you can reach out from the window and catch a few small silverfish and a wet big moon. Maybe on a stormy night, the great white shark that rushed ashore will smash the glass window of whose house and open its bloody mouth to say hello to its owner. Therefore, Fu Xin, vice president of the middle school affiliated to Shanghai Normal University, who loves literature and the sea, has written a lot of feelings and poetic thoughts about the sea in his diary. He feels that he has been sleeping in Haitao's lullaby. He sleeps very steadily and peacefully, and can especially dream. His dream is full of waves and stars.

Life was peaceful, full and serene.

On May 23, 2016, Fu Xin's desk phone rang and he picked up the microphone. The other party is a familiar leader of the education committee, without greeting, in an eager tone: 'The first group of 40 members of Shanghai's group education and assistance to Tibet has been formed and will start soon. Unexpectedly, the captain who has been appointed can't go because of special circumstances at home. After research, we hope you will serve as the captain. The destination is the Shanghai Experimental School in Shigatse, Tibet, for a period of three years. The matter is very urgent. Think about it and call us back as soon as possible.'

Fu Xin was shocked because he was completely unprepared, because his work plan and life order were suddenly disrupted by the phone.

The first response was that it was really a long time to aid Tibet for three years! He is the leader of the post-80s generation. He was born in 1980 at the age of 36. He will be nearly 40 years old when he comes back three years later. The last green of youth will remain on the Qinghai Tibet Plateau. Anyway, this is also an unexpected accident and mutation. Also, at present, her daughter Niuniu is going to the first grade of primary school; His mother underwent lung cancer surgery last year and is recovering from the surgery; The mother-in-law had breast cancer surgery 3 months ago. The day before yesterday, eighth chemotherapy had just been carried out. The wife is also the backbone in the unit. She is very busy. It is really difficult for her to take care of her alone. In addition, the living environment in Tibet and Shanghai is so different that he doesn't know whether his body can adapt. At his home in Shanghai, he can sleep on the soft waves; In Tibet, he had to sleep on the snowy peak with strong wind – God! Can you sleep? I can't sleep. A colleague said that after entering Tibet, he took two sleeping pills every day and could only sleep for two hours. Dependence on sleeping pills for eight hours is almost equivalent to suicide. There are also low oxygen, high cold, poverty, open wilderness, the distance between people and villages, altitude reaction and so on. These unexpected difficulties – many unexpected difficulties – passed through Fu Xin's mind like a plateau wind. Have you ever hesitated? We can't refuse. After all, this difficult task came too suddenly. At this time, he can find a thousand reasons. Even if he found a reason, he could also say, 'thank you for your trust in this organization, but...' the man dodged and continued to dream at sea. However, this 'but' has a completely different meaning: This is not an ordinary job, this is a mission! This is the mission of contributing, contributing and working hard for the country! Just like soldiers who have served for three years, they are pure obligation and pure dedication. There is no price. When they rush into the battlefield, they must go to the front!

He was silent for three minutes and thought for three minutes. Fu Xin thought and decided. I'm used to spring and autumn in Shanghai. Going to the plateau for three years is also a new experience, a new realm and a new harvest! When a person makes up his mind to do something, all hesitation and burden will be suddenly released. Fu Xin called his wife. The wife was silent for 6 seconds, then said calmly, 'I support you, I can do well at home.' Fu Xin was moved and her eyes were moist. Shanghai women are very delicate, but in fact they are very strong. Such women are more lovely, and their wives are one of them. Subsequently, Fu Xin reported to the president and secretary. Then he called the head of the education committee, 'I agree. When do you start?' then he began to clean up the papers on the table... In this way, a total of 8 minutes will determine the direction of his last youth years, for the next three years – from Shanghai with an altitude of 2.19 metres to the 'roof of the world' with an average altitude of more than 4,000 metres, but you can't go, you can only fly. Flying is actually the most beautiful gesture of life and soul.

Fu Xin is a typical Shanghai intellectual with fair complexion, elegant conversation, clear thinking and calm. Of course, this decision is so decisive, first of all because of a Communist's consciousness and sense of responsibility, as well as the nature and quality of his family: His father is an old worker in Shanghai heavy machinery factory. In his life, his bones and steel collided with each other and sparks splashed everywhere. His wife's father is from Baosteel. He spoke and walked like an echo of steel. The red and hot iron flows into the blood of the family and casts a strong character and patriotism. Sitting opposite Fu Xin and listening to him, I don't think it's necessary to ask in detail. At first glance, I know he is a good student and never deviated when he was young. He has been studying for a doctorate in education at Shanghai Normal University and stayed at the school. Soon, I don't have to accept the 'test' to become the vice president of the middle school affiliated to normal university – unlike me, I have to pass the party's 'long-term test' to conclude that I am a good comrade. It's too late for me to be rated as 'the most beautiful volunteer in the country' until 2019.

The day I left was father's day. The night before yesterday, Fu Xin attended the kindergarten graduation ceremony of her daughter Niuniu. On the way, Niuniu took Fu Xin's hand and asked again and again, 'Dad, why did you leave me? Why did you go to Tibet?' Fu Xin picked up her daughter, kissed her little face and replied, 'in the highest place in the world, there are a group of brothers and sisters. They are eager to read, but they have no teachers. They need Dad's help more than you.'

On June 18th, the team leader Fu Xin, 36 years old, set off for the distant Shigatse. On the plane, the deputy leader Chen Qian showed him a WeChat message from his son, who was about to enter the third grade of senior high school, which was sent by him. 'When I was born, you were in the cotton field where you had helped grand councilor in the past 3 years; and now, when I was 18 years old, you were in the field where you had been helping him in the past 3 years. Father, take care of yourself!' After reading it, the two of them were speechless and their tears were wet.

Another team member Lu Lu wrote this diary:

Tonight, is the last night at home before leaving. Enter Sichuan tomorrow and Tibet the day after tomorrow to start a new year's journey. A few months ago, I had a vivid memory of receiving the notice of going to Tibet. Over the years, I have been used to roaming on the sea and traveling abroad. Now, entering Tibet is tomorrow. Not at all. Tossing and turning for a few nights is an example. I will remember my friends' suggestions: the first is to take good care of my body, and the second is to complete the task. One year, I looked at my parents' gray temples and lamented that I had no time to accompany them. Three days before I left, I finally cancelled all the invitations and had three meals a day with them. Don't forget to take care of them one by one, and don't forget to nag. I can feel their reluctance and worry. They also dyed their hair. I know they want their son to leave at his best... A year is short and will soon pass; But a year is also long. The pain of missing your family and friends is always with you. Return to Shanghai without any hindrance or regret – this is the oath I will remember.

Through the sea of clouds and snow peaks, the magnificent Tibet is at their feet.

This is the most mysterious plateau snow village in China. It is the highest place on earth. In Shanghai, you can reach out and take the moon out of the sea. In Tibet, you can reach out and touch the sun.

Fu Xin thought of the great Tibetan national heroes – Tibetan king Songzan Ganbu and beautiful Princess Wencheng. In the 7th century, the heroic Songzan Ganbu unified Tibet and established the Tubo Dynasty. Because he saw many beautiful porcelain, silk, clothes and weapons from the mainland, he admired the well-known prosperous Tang Dynasty at that time. In 634, the special envoy trekked to Chang'an to pay tribute and greet Li Yuan, Emperor Gaozu of the Tang Dynasty. Gaozu immediately sent a special mission to follow the special envoy back to Tibet and presented a large number of gifts. Friendly exchanges between Han and Tibetan people have entered official channels from the people. Songzan Ganbu knew that the economic and cultural development of Tibet was backward and hoped to greatly strengthen the emotional exchanges between the two sides for development, so he sent 'Da Lun' (equivalent to Prime Minister) Lu Dongzan to Chang'an to propose to Datang. After careful consideration, Li Shimin, the successor Emperor Taizong of the Tang Dynasty, selected the younger brother of the Li clan and the daughter of King Li Daozong of Jiangxia, and canonized him as Princess Wencheng. In 641, he formed a mighty escort team and 'relatives and friends group'. Li daozong himself led the team into Tibet and brought a large number of gold and silver treasures, silk and satin and production and living appliances in the mainland. Song Zan Ganbu was obviously shocked by Princess Wencheng's beautiful appearance and those brilliant gifts. At the welcoming ceremony, he said with passion: 'My grandfather and father have never had a precedent of intermarriage. Today, it is rare for the king to marry Princess Datang. I want to build the most gorgeous palace for the beautiful princess, so that the princess can live happily here and leave it to future generations. I hope to maintain close contact and friendly relations with Datang forever. Therefore, the king is willing to match my nephew and son-in-law to show that Datang is a beautiful princess A superior country.'

This magnificent palace is the Potala Palace. So far, the statues of Songzan Ganbu and Princess Wencheng are still enshrined in Jokhang Temple. The incense has been burning for thousands of years, and the butter lamp is on day and night. Princess Wencheng has been known as the 'Green Tara' by Tibetans for generations. She is the embodiment of Guanyin Bodhisattva and the goddess with the highest status in Tibetan Buddhism.

Princess Wen Cheng had lived in Tibet for 30 years, until her death in 680 years. She had devoted all her life to maintain the friendship between the two races, and had brought the advanced production technology and excellent culture of the central region into Tibet. The people of the Tibet race praised her outstanding contribution with many romantic and imaginative folk songs, and one of them was:

Princess Wencheng from Han nationality,

Brought 3800 kinds of grain,

Making the grain warehouse rich and sufficient;

Princess Wencheng from Han nationality,

Brought five thousand and five hundred magic craftsmen,

Open a glorious road for Tubo craft;

Princess Wencheng from Han nationality,

Bring all kinds of livestock 5500,

It made the cheese and crispy oil in Tibet taste sweet and delicious

After working in Tibet, when communicating with Tibetan students, Fu Xin often heard them sincerely say: 'we Tibetans and Han, and all nationalities in the motherland, are actually the children of one mother.'

Tibetan children can say this because they really feel the warmth from the motherland.

2. A battle without enough time to think

After the 18th CPC National Congress, the work of assisting Tibet has turned a new page and entered a new stage of being more solid, more extensive and closer to the people's livelihood. In 2015, the sixth Tibet work symposium of the CPC Central Committee stressed the need to adhere to the party's general plan for governing Tibet, unswervingly ensure and improve people's lives, unswervingly promote exchanges and integration among people of all ethnic groups, and ensure the sustained and healthy economic and social development of Tibet. The Shanghai 'group' education assistance team for Tibet maintains a scale of 40 people, 4 management cadres for three years and 36 full-time teachers for one year, and then rotates, which can effectively ensure the

Fu Xin led the eighth batch of cadres and the first batch of pioneering and innovative 'group' education and assistance teams in Shanghai since the reform and opening up. It can be said that the selected talents are talents and elites in Shanghai's educational circles. If you don't do well, you can't shoulder such a great responsibility. If you can't reach obvious results in a year, you might delaying yourself and eventually your children's future.

They reached the destination above 3800 metres above sea level: Shigatse Shanghai Experimental School.

Shigatse is a prefecture level city under the jurisdiction of the Tibet Autonomous Region. Located in the southwest of the Qinghai Tibet Plateau, it covers an area of 182,000 square kilometres and has a population of more than 870 thousand. It borders Nepal, Bhutan, India and other countries with a border of nearly 1800 kilometres. The world's highest peak, Mount Everest, is located in Dingri County, Shigatse.

Shigatse Shanghai experimental school is the only school in Tibet that has run schools for 12 consecutive years. Founded in 2004, it was personally planned by Yin Hong, then the leader of the Shanghai contact group of the third batch of cadres assisting Tibet, the current alternate member of the Central Committee, deputy secretary of Henan provincial Party committee and governor of Henan Province. On September 8, 2017, Yin Hong, then deputy secretary of Shanghai municipal Party committee, led a delegation to Tibet for exchange and visit, and specially came to the University for investigation and guidance. Fu Xin copied the design sketch of that year and handed it to Yin Hong. When Yin Hong saw the blueprint designed that year and the magnificent, spacious, bright and shining modern campus, he was very excited. Education is a great cause handed down from generation to generation, which determines the future and destiny of the country. Standing up is a dream, a mission and a future. Obviously, the development and outstanding contributions of this excellent school in the past ten years have moved all the cadres in Shanghai and Shigatse, and Yin Hong has also moved herself. He said with emotion that China's development from 'stand up' to 'get rich' and then to 'strong' was built brick by brick!!

The State implements the 'Three Guarantees' policy for all students' food, housing and school expenses, which are all inclusive and free. (just this time, how shameless and inhumane are some Western politicians' vicious attacks on Tibet's construction and development!)

Most of the team members have never entered Tibet. Their way of life, thinking and working are oriented by Shanghai.

It was a sudden challenge without time to think. Difficulties are unimaginable:

—Due to the special environment of the plateau, the damage rate of campus facilities is large, the facilities are old, the school gate is damaged, the library cannot be used, the playground is uneven, and the canteen is particularly crowded.

—Students' cultural achievements, large and small, are uneven. Many students can't speak Chinese and don't know Chinese characters. Shigatse welfare home has more than 100 students, many of whom are orphans after the Zhangmu earthquake. Since childhood, they lack the care of their parents and are lonely and arrogant. They are like little bison on the plateau. But once they enter the classroom, they immediately become very shy and timid. In the face of the teacher's questions, their answer was to stare at their shiny black eyes and scratch their heads.

—The local Han Tibetan teachers in our school have lived in a relatively closed environment for a long time, with different educational concepts and single teaching means. Their working mode has always been chalk, blackboard and cramming education.

—Due to low oxygen, high cold and strong altitude reaction, many teachers in Shanghai are shouting headaches according to their own minds every day. After taking sleeping pills, they vomited and diarrhea, fell down the stairs and couldn't sleep. The whole camp was full of wounded soldiers, including Fu Xin. Of course, the most difficult thing to suppress is homesickness. Fu Xin said to me, 'it's hard for you to imagine several men sitting together, talking about their families, talking about their children, crying in masks.'

—Shanghai experimental school is not only responsible for the education of students in the city, but also assists in the teaching guidance of 17 county teaching points in Shigatse city. From time to time, they have to bring audio-visual education equipment, take long-distance buses to counties to train teachers, give demonstration lectures, guide students, and sometimes go to villages and towns. When they reached Dingri County at the foot of Mount Everest, this was an exciting moment for them, as they look up at the sacred snow peak, they cheered, almost put felt hats on their heads and threw them on the top of Mount Everest.

In short, from eating to using the toilet, from walking to sleeping, from classroom to bilingual teaching materials, from local traditional teaching methods to modern upgrading, it is difficult for Shanghai 'We' (Shanghai dialect) to do everything every day and step after entering Tibet. All innovation and change cannot be carried out slowly. Everyone's time to help Tibet is limited. We must 'cherish time like gold'. When a scholar meets a soldier, whether he can do anything depends on his actions.

Youth means ambition. Fu Xin, a 36-year-old Doctor of Education, recalled Confucius' Teaching: 'if you want to do well, you must first sharpen your tools.' he quickly put forward the work objectives of 'seven glories', namely school running philosophy, guarantee conditions, curriculum system, management mechanism, teaching staff, cultural environment and teaching achievements.

Being outstanding was a very high indicator!

3. The podium stands at the door of the country, and the responsibility is higher than Mount Everest

Fu Xin first led the Tibetan aid teacher to launch a 'toilet revolution', dredging and painting all toilets, and providing toilet paper at each position to educate children's civilized habits. The old teachers and students in this school were moved. Subsequently, with the support of relevant departments in Shanghai, they transformed the canteen, playground, library and teachers' and student' dormitories, built a new solar student bathroom and magnificent gate, and installed solar streetlamps. The school environment has taken on a new look and become the most beautiful school in Shigatse.

We must introduce the most advanced teaching technology to make the concept and teaching more wonderful. Fu Xin made up his mind: 'Shigatse will have the same teaching equipment and resources as Shanghai!' So, he organized an information construction team among his team members and introduced a large number of modern teaching equipment from Shanghai. After two years of efforts, the past has passed and the future has come. The school has fully completed the construction of 'smart campus' platform. Through the school distance education center, the homework of school students and students from multiple teaching points in Shigatse County can be corrected and guided by famous teachers at key schools in Shanghai at the first time. No matter how high the altitude is and how far away it is, these Han and Tibetan children will be surprised to open their eyes and listen attentively in the face of remote 'video teaching', 'expert consultation' and 'resource sharing' from Shanghai.

Dr. Fu Xin still remembers Confucius' famous saying: 'education does not discriminate'. He knew that local children's academic performance generally fell behind, which was entirely due to remoteness, isolation, poverty and long-term nomadic life. Especially those orphans from welfare homes, who lack parental care and family warmth since childhood, should be given double care. In class, the teacher taught Tibetan children to write Chinese characters and draw one by one, and humbly learned Tibetan pronunciation and dialogue from them, which made the children very happy. In the evening, teachers often go to the dormitory or playground to chat and play games with students. On the rest day, they took a class of students to visit various scenic spots in the city. They told the children the history of revolution, the stories of patriotic heroes and the prosperity and development of the motherland. They hope that children will learn knowledge and skills well and participate in the construction of 'Beautiful Tibet' and 'beautiful motherland' when they grow up. On the afternoon of April 14, 2017, a special theme class meeting was held in class 6 of the first day of the new year. The school invited the elders and grandmother of the community to tell their classmates the miserable life of not having enough food before the release, not wearing warm, and working with shackles. They also told them the cruel and fierce life of the slave master who took off human skin as a drum and not allowed to leave but only to climb. At the party on festival 61, Fu Xin said to the children. 'Some of your classmates were born without knowing their parents, but since they entered this school, I and these teachers have been your fathers in Shanghai. Although we can't celebrate children's day in Shanghai with our children, we have more children in Shigatse. This is our glory and happiness!' The children clapped their hands, and the eldest children had tears in their eyes.

Fu Xin attached great importance to national unity. Due to historical reasons, the teaching level of local Han Tibetan teachers is relatively backward, which directly affects the students' academic performance. But he is not in a hurry to succeed. He hastily removed the local teacher and let the teacher in Shanghai take the post. After all, there is a time limit for aiding Tibet. Building an 'inalienable team of excellent teachers' is the fundamental plan to promote the development and progress of education in Tibet. Therefore, from the management to the director of the teaching and Research Office, and even to the subject teachers, he skillfully implemented the 'double post system' between Shanghai people and local people, paid attention to local teachers and supported Shanghai teachers. Through one-on-one cooperation and exchange, teachers in Shanghai have penetrated their advanced experience and methods into local teachers bit by bit. In just two or three years, the teaching level of local teachers has improved significantly.

Ge Liang, a Tibetan aid teacher at Shanghai Ganquan Foreign Language School, spends three classes a week tutoring welfare children of the relatively weak China foundation. He learned that children who had just started learning Chinese in the first grade of primary school read very fast, but their vocabulary accumulation slowed down a year later. After careful observation, he found that this was related to the teaching methods of local Chinese teachers. To this end, Ge Liang, based on his own teaching experience, specially compiled the book teaching suggestions for Tibetan Chinese teachers to help local Chinese teachers master more, richer and more effective teaching methods. This is a book that can be used for a long time.

After the expiration of the one-year assistance to Tibet, seven teachers offered to extend the assistance for one year. Among them, Zhong Yingjie, a Tibetan aid teacher of the second experimental middle school affiliated to Shanghai Normal University, compiled 'one class and one practice' for students in his spare time, hoping to be used as a reference textbook for the school. At the end of the year, he compiled two volumes in junior high school and four volumes in senior high school. He hopes to finish the work in the remaining year. Think about these new textbooks you wrote yourself. They are full of selfless dedication and love!

Yu Long, an information technology teacher in Putuo District, Shanghai, also proposed to stay in office for another year. He said: 'seeing the eyes of Tibetan children eager for knowledge, I have the responsibility to impart all my knowledge to them. Because knowledge and education are important ways to prevent the intergenerational transmission of poverty, I hope my assistance to Tibet goes beyond this place.'

In just three years, Shigatse Shanghai experimental school has been brilliant! Local people appreciate the magical power of 'Shanghai Education': the enrollment rate of college entrance examination has reached 100% for three consecutive years, the undergraduate rate has reached more than 94%, and the key undergraduate rate has exceeded 60%, ranking in the forefront of the autonomous region. The middle school entrance examination results rank first in the autonomous region; Six individual subjects have achieved the best results in history; The number of six-year students from two primary schools in the mainland entering Tibetan junior middle schools will nearly double on the basis of the highest record over the years.

Fu Xin's team learned to fight without enough time to think. With their sense of urgency of 'cherishing time like gold', their unremitting efforts of 'carving with gold and stone' and their working wisdom of 'turning stone into gold', the majority of Tibetan students have realized a leap in knowledge to change their destiny.

In 2018, at the national poverty alleviation award commendation conference, Fu Xin was awarded the 'Innovation Award' of the national poverty alleviation award by the poverty alleviation and development leading group of the State Council.

In 2019, among the 20 'most beautiful frontier figures' advanced individuals and one advanced collective announced by the Central Propaganda Department, Fu Xin is the only candidate in Shanghai.

On teacher's day in 2019, Fu Xin was rated as an advanced worker in the national education system.

'These honors actually belong to our whole team, and everyone is indispensable,' Fu Xin said

As he wrote in his diary, 'the podium is at the door of the country, and the responsibility is higher than Mount Everest.'

Just like the farewell speech of former Vice President Chen Qian: 'flowers bloom in spring and struggle is wonderful!'

Just as Jin Zhijun, the youngest post-90s teacher in the team, cried at the farewell party:

'We came! We conquered! We succeeded'

IV *Tending the roots of classics*: Cauliflower 'Great Leap'

Shanghai friend, do you know the origin of a cauliflower?

It took 300 years and three years to jump from the field to the table: 300 years ago, cauliflower followed the camel team of the Silk Road from the Mediterranean to 'A bite of China'. (Food Documentary) Then, from 2016 to 2019, cauliflower completed the 'great leap forward' from deep mountain canyon to greater Shanghai in Daozhen County, Zunyi. The author believes that this paper has important enlightenment significance for the construction of national poverty alleviation cadres and the realization of economic leapfrog development in Guizhou and other old, youth, border and poor areas. *Tending the roots of classics* is a collection of quotations about self-cultivation, life, life and fertility compiled by Taoist Hong Yingming in the early Ming Dynasty. Short sentences are as common as vegetable roots, but they are thought-provoking and memorable. This paper is a *Tending the roots of classics*.

1. The first battle of defeat

Shanghai is a gorgeous window of contemporary China. During the day, the traffic is rolling and colorful at night. Every workshop is full of wisdom, dreams and aspirations. It is their responsibility and obligation to support the whole country.

The poverty alleviation policy formulated by Shanghai is very simple: 'what the central government requires, what local needs, and what Shanghai can do'. Shanghai ranks in the forefront of the world. There are countless superpowers and abilities. Wherever you go, the sea will change with laughter, and a beautiful day is coming. But not all Shanghainese have the ability to call it wind and rain. On July 11, 2016, Zhou Ling, deputy director of Yangpu District Commission of Commerce, came to Gelao Miao Autonomous County, Dao Town, Zunyi city with her schoolbag and a family photo to serve as Deputy Secretary of the county Party Committee for poverty alleviation for three years. His boss chose him because his conditions are 'framework': male, university culture, associate department level, under the age of 45, excellent performance at ordinary times, serious, diligent, love the people and actively sign up. But what kind of high-end talent is he? Is he capable of asking questions to an outstanding university? I can't see. It is as simple and ordinary as his desk. In his early years, his only skill was to make the abacus smoke, but now the abacus is out of date. In 1975, Zhou Lingsheng was born in the home of an ordinary teacher in Jiangxi Province. He entered Shandong Institute of Finance in the college entrance examination. After graduation, he became a teacher at Jiangxi University of Finance and economics. In 2002,

Shanghai, eager for talents, recruited talents from all over the country. In fact, this is to recruit college students. Zhou Ling looked gentle and honest and passed the exam successfully. He said, 'I'm very lucky. Now it's difficult for returnees to squeeze into Shanghai.' Zhou Ling was sent to a small town in Yangpu District of Shanghai as the chief of the economic section, mainly responsible for attracting investment. Therefore, in the final analysis, he is an excellent 'accountant'. Due to his serious work, professionalism and achievements, later, he was promoted to deputy director of Yangpu District Commission of Commerce.

When he came to the town and county of Zunyi, Zhou Ling was at a loss when he saw the village full of clouds and smoke. He knows nothing about agriculture. 'He was absent-minded and did not divide food.' But he came with a cavity of blood. Poverty alleviation is a national activity and a great cause for thousands of years. He must make some contribution when he comes. If he can't come, he is 'passing by'. He believes that Dao Town, as a key county of national poverty alleviation and development, must be poor and dilapidated: tottering stilts and thatched houses in the cottage, old farmers with hoes and bamboo baskets walking on the mountain road, and small dolls with mud heads and flower faces running wildly on the mountain... But the reality far exceeded his expectations. From the city to the county, all the way is unimpeded; Entering the county, the buildings are towering, the streets are spacious, the traffic is rolling, the shops are connected, and the windows are bright. Everyone obeys the traffic lights very much when crossing the road, which is more regular than some places in Shanghai. Zhou Ling is more confused. This place is developing very well. What can we do to help the poor? His ambition was almost halved. Then he went to the deep mountain valley, during which there were two traffic accidents. He only heard a 'bang', his eyes blackened, and his life almost fell into the abyss with the front cover of the car. When we came to those villages in remote mountainous areas, we saw the photos of thousands of years ago: Grass houses, huts, earth houses and stone houses look very desolate; There is no road in the world, because there are not many people walking here, so there is still no road; Old wells and thin fields are short of water, the land is barren, and corncobs are only as long as the palm of the hand; The young man went out to work. The remaining '606138 troops' live a semi natural economic life. They grow and collect everything for their own use. The upsurge of market economy outside the mountain has nothing to do with them. Their days are like cooking smoke, slow and thin, lonely and long, but their vision is not as high as cooking smoke. Zhou Ling's eyes are not so confused. He finally found a 'battlefield' and poverty alleviation work he could do – mobilize and contact all contacts in Shanghai to fully support Daozhen to get rid of poverty as soon as possible through assistance and donations. Over the past few days, Zhou Ling opened her mobile phone contact information, checked and checked each friend again and again, accurately estimated their 'memory resources', and carefully considered how much 'oil and water' she squeezed from that person. Colleagues, relatives and friends far away in Shanghai miss him very much, but they don't know that Zhou Ling, hiding in the mountainous area of Guizhou, is preparing to 'attack' them.

The phone rang. Many friends said with emotion, 'Secretary Zhou, if you have any requirements, say, I will do my best to help you!' Zhou Ling was very happy. He is glad that he is sincerely welcome at ordinary times.

Generally speaking, local leaders respect outside temporary cadres very much. They do not divide or reduce the division of labor, and they do not give people pressure. You can do whatever you can and give a good comment when the deadline expires. Zhou Ling's heart is very relaxed. He began to conduct extensive research on fund projects, required funds and resettlement sites, such as left behind children, serious illness relief, housing reconstruction, road and bridge construction, etc. At that time, he seems more like a social philanthropist, not the Deputy Secretary of the county Party committee.

One autumn day, the Secretary of the county Party committee suddenly called him and said that a village had planted more than 200 mu of cauliflower (commonly known as cauliflower), and the middleman signed his name. Farmers get 70 cents per kilogram. They can sell it for about 1.8 yuan. But there are too many cauliflower on the market this year, and the price has fallen sharply. Middlemen can't make money, so they stop selling for various so-called 'quality' reasons. Seeing the vegetables rotting on the ground, the vegetable farmers cried for no reason. They couldn't bear to beat their hearts down the cliff. The Secretary asked Zhou Lingneng if he could find a way to sell these cauliflowers in Shanghai and help the people. Zhou Ling agreed. He thought, can't you digest this dish in the vast sea of Shanghai? Who is also a cadre of the District Business Committee? When I called, my friend said: 'Secretary Zhou, I won't help you. Haven't you explained clearly? I collected 70 cents per kilogram from the farmers and now sell 70 cents per kilogram in Shanghai. Who pays the labor cost of loading and unloading? Who pays the mobilization fee, parking fee and handling fee? Who will pay the freight of more than 10,000 yuan per vehicle on the road of more than 1700km? In addition, who will pay at least three yuan when vegetables are transported to Shanghai One third of the cost? So, this is a loss making business and can't be done!' Several people were contacted and they all answered the same question. Zhou Ling was shocked. Finally, one tenth of the cauliflower on more than 200 mu of land fed people, two tenths of the cauliflower fed pigs, and seven tenths of the cauliflower rotted in the ground as fertilizer. The whole village worked in vain for a year, empty handed and unhappy. Dozens of poor families lost their jobs and took off their hats and put them up.

The first anti-poverty campaign failed. The member of the Standing Committee of the county Party committee mentioned this matter. Zhou Ling was pale and embarrassed. He felt ashamed and lost his face.

2. The quilt was tossed

Depressed Zhou Ling came to the cauliflower planting village. The Deputy Secretary of the county Party committee came, and so did the township cadres. They say that in the past, farmers grew vegetables for their families, so they never used chemical fertilizers or pesticides. At most, they wait until the market day to sell some baskets with their baggage and earn some pocket money. Because cauliflower leaves a lot of stubbles a year and the price is good, the middleman saw that cauliflower is of good quality and pure green, so he signed an agreement with each family in one village and one village, claiming that it was 'purchased'. Unexpectedly, as soon as the market fell this year, the vegetable merchants changed their face and the farmers suffered heavy losses

Zhou Ling's heartbeat. His thoughts splashed like fireworks on New Year's Eve! First of all, Daozhen has beautiful mountains and rivers, good water and soil quality, and has no habit of applying chemical fertilizers and pesticides. This is the favorite dish of city people. The influx of vegetable traders proves that it must have a market; Second, some vegetable traders are dishonest and unreliable. If it is managed and organized by the government, and the three parties of production, supply and sales sincerely cooperate and trust each other, everyone will be happy; Third, if every household in Dao town is 'connected' and green vegetable planting is 'industrialized', and the whole planting and sales process is 'marketized' through land transfer or land rights and interests, Dao town will rely on its own advantages to develop a large-scale vegetable industry. The continuous increase and sustainable development of output value can greatly improve the 'blood production' function of the whole county, and a large number of poor households can get rid of poverty Self-improvement and prosperity. Zhou Ling was very excited to think of this. Sure enough, 'failure is the mother of success'. 200 mu cauliflower can't be sold, but it gives him a lot of enlightenment! The poverty alleviation methods he initially envisaged, such as using Shanghai's advantages to strive for more aid funds, such as using his contacts to donate more funds to Lila County, are just a kind of 'blood transfusion' assistance. Although it is very necessary, it is difficult to fundamentally solve the major problems of self-reliance, stable development and sustainable development of the whole county.

Zhou Ling understands that to run this event well, we must first learn from the market and practice. He wanted to witness with his own eyes how a cauliflower, a radish and a box of tomatoes from all over the world entered Shanghai. He made a special trip back to Shanghai. He got up in the middle of the night and changed into a blue suit with a small notebook in his pocket. He came to a large wholesale market in Pudong at 1 a.m. because it was stipulated that transport vehicles were not allowed to enter Shanghai before midnight and had to evacuate before 6 a.m. After becoming a Shanghai resident for more than ten years, this is the first time that Zhou Ling saw how the vegetables on his table came from. Around 2 a.m., on a dark night, large transport vehicles covered with rainproof cloth roared from nearby provinces and even Yunnan, Jiangxi, Henan, Shandong and other places, and boxes of sealed vegetables were unloaded by trucks. With the quotation of the seller and the buyer, the mountain of vegetable boxes were quickly washed away, the site was very clean, and the wholesaler happily went home to sleep. Zhou Ling wrote all the details one by one in a small book, which is the subtlety of Shanghai People's works.

If you understand this road, you must find a large dealer with consistent system. Those vegetable merchants who wander the Jianghu can only buy one hammer and sell one hammer. Zhou Ling asked about China's top ten chain dealers online. Among them, Fujian Yonghui company is one of the best and most powerful companies in China. Zhou Ling found the headquarters through his friends. The headquarters said that Zunyi is very close to Guiyang and Chongqing branches. Please contact them. But this enterprise is too busy, business is piled up, and logistics is like a long river. The branches in Guiyang and Chongqing felt that Zunyi had more mountains and less land and could not become a large base and industry, so they politely pushed around. Zhou Ling had to go to Guiyang to 'take care of the thatched cottage three times' and then Chongqing to 'take care of the thatched cottage five times'. Finally, the young boss in Chongqing was moved. He explained very seriously to the Deputy Secretary of the county Party committee: 'if you want to build a vegetable base, you must supply it on a large scale according to the standard for a long time. We will follow your wishes so that I can set a quota for you. If you don't have it today or tomorrow, it will destroy us.'

Zhou Ling nodded repeatedly and said sincerely, 'we already have a base.'

The young boss said suspiciously, 'I have to see it to believe.'

Zhou Ling was startled. This is also the 'truth blueprint' he imagined and planned. Where can he find the base camp?

He hurried back to do it. However, Guizhou is 'not three feet flat', while Tao is actually 'two feet and a half'. Debris everywhere. It's too late to organize, spread and splice now! Zhou Ling hurried everywhere to find a place. One day, he came to a town and climbed the mountain. He found that more than 2000 mu of slope land had been connected and neatly covered with white and bright plastic film. When asked in time, the town cadre said that we are the key town for the development of flue-cured tobacco and are ready to transplant tobacco seedlings with plastic film. Zhou Ling was overjoyed. What did he say? Temporarily take over the vegetable base. Later, he invited the young boss of Chongqing Yonghui company to come and proudly pointed out to him at the top of the mountain. The young boss looked at the snow-white film excitedly, like waves in the sun, and said, 'Secretary Zhou, if you have the courage to work so fast, I'll give you a sales quota of 20 million yuan a year!'

Ha! A brave beginning is half success!

With the help of Yonghui supermarket, Daozhen started the 'trial operation' of transporting cauliflower to Shanghai and Chongqing. We should train cadres, be familiar with business and explore experience. Although township leaders and village cadres are models and have a great atmosphere of conversation, in fact, most of them are black footed farmers. Large transport vehicles roared, cadres led the villagers to rub their hands, and bursts of laughter broke out in the silent cottage. But soon, they stopped laughing and blushing because they ran modern industry with thousands of years of old ideas, traditions and habits. They made mistakes again and again, full of loopholes.

The first car of cauliflower was transported to Chongqing and there was no movement for several days. Zhou Ling asked the town cadres, 'what will happen after transportation?'

The town cadre was confused: 'according to your instructions, we loaded the car and took it away. What should we do?'

Zhou Ling asked, 'what's the thermal insulation effect of this car? What's the loss on the road? What's the selling price? How long has it been sold out?'

The town cadre was stunned and gave a 'not know anything' look: 'I thought you would help us sell vegetables and drive. Why do you ask?'

Zhou Ling is angry and anxious, but cadres in Shanghai are generally gentle and won't complain. 'Industrial distribution has a set of strict rules and standards, so that we can exchange the minimum loss for the maximum profit. We don't know how much we lost and how much we sold. Even the pigs don't eat this stuff. Who will you sell them to?'

Later, he summoned Township and village cadres, took out his small book written in the Shanghai wholesale market, and taught them one by one:

First of all, it is necessary to ensure low-temperature refrigeration: when picking cauliflower, it should be quickly put into the refrigerator to reduce the heart temperature to about 3°C. On the road, we need to keep warm. There are more than 1,700 kilometres from Dao town to Shanghai to minimize the loss of long-distance transportation. 'Do you understand?' 'Yes!'

It turned out to be wrong. The mud footed men were sweating. They moved the collected cauliflower baskets into the cold storage, poured it on the ground, and then locked the door. Everything was fine. Two days later, when the temperature was measured, a pile of cauliflower was cold outside and hot inside, not to mention that the heart of cabbage was 'as tender as water'. Zhou Ling told them that the plates should be handled carefully and not damaged. They shall be arranged in order with a certain gap. Only in this way can they be refrigerated and heated equally. Zhou Ling also specially sent someone to buy them a batch of vegetable thermometers, which can be inserted into the heart of vegetables to test the temperature. 'Do you understand?' 'Yes!' everyone answered confidently.

Second, dishes should be standardized. Now people's quality of life has generally improved. They pay attention to quality and not too much. Zhou Ling asked that a standard plastic packing box can only hold 15 kg, not more or less. Each vegetable is the same size, about 1kg, with two green leaves and two centimetres of roots. When the root grows, the customer is not happy; When the cauliflower is short, the cauliflower will disperse.

—Wrong again. According to the old concept of farmers, the bigger the dish, the heavier the better. In order to sell more in packaging, Zunyi people seem to be very enthusiastic and sincere. The deceptive behaviors pressed on. The more solid the result is, the higher the temperature rise and the greater the loss. Zhou Ling shouted, 'vegetable logistics is piecework. Who has time to weigh each box? The more things you load, the more compensation you will have!' the villagers realized that 25 kg per box is a lost. Third, in order to maintain low temperature during long-distance transportation, a bottle of chilled water should be put into the box and sealed. When loading, lay a layer of quilt on the bottom plate of the carriage and tie a layer of quilt around it. After loading, it shall be covered with a quilt. Then, wrap the whole carriage tightly with rainproof cloth. According to this strict operation, when cauliflower arrives in Chongqing or Shanghai, it not only maintains a fresh appearance, but also the loss can be reduced to about 5%.

—The villagers have problems again. Zhou Ling caught a cold that day. The transport starts at two in the middle of the night. He moved the box and put everyone in the car until about 1 o'clock. He can't stand it. He said you should load the car and drive. I'll go first and then go back to take my medicine. In this step, in order to speed up the speed and have an early rest, after loading the truck, the local comrades threw the big quilt onto the high car like a fisherman casting a net, then tied the rainproof cloth, waved to the driver and shouted 'go'. With such a small action, they threw out the quilt covered on the vegetable box. After cauliflower arrived in Shanghai, the loss reached 25% and the sales volume was greatly reduced. Only then did local comrades understand that vegetables need quilts in summer, just as people need quilts in winter.

Later, Zhou Ling specially took a group of local officials to visit the wholesale market of Shanghai and Chongqing. They wanted to see how the food delivered from other regions were standard selected, how to standard cold storage, heat preservation and transportation. The local officials were shocked and exclaimed, 'the outside world is really difficult to deal with.'

Fourth, the local villagers went to plant a lot of vegetables, especially the minority women in the village, who looked like fairies. They twisted their waist in the field and gently moved the lotus steps, with a bamboo basket in one hand and seeds in the other. It was more beautiful than the stage performance. As for how many branches a vegetable could grow, only God knew that Zhou Ling should learn to sell it now. In order to raise the temperature of the earth and keep the water, the greenhouse had to raise the seedling in advance, and the variety was divided into four periods, early, middle, late and late. It was easy to plant with remained stubble, so that cauliflower could be sent to the market in batches all year round, in case of the peak season accumulation and the price jump.

As the Deputy Secretary of the Municipal Committee, Zhou Ling was going to have a meeting to visit. In particular, he planned to build several unprecedented large-scale vegetable bases, transfer the land, arrange the employment of the poor, draft and sign all kinds of agreements and contracts in Shanghai, Chongqing, Guiyang and other markets. Things were complicated and busy. He couldn't carry boxes and load cars with everyone every day. One day, a female vice head of the village walked into Zhou Ling's office and sat there crying. Zhou Ling asked why? The female cadre said, 'Since the director started the vegetable export, according to the administrative division of labor of the leading group of the town government, I was responsible for it. Because I would get on the bus every night and leave at midnight. I took it alone for several months. I had to work normally during the day. My husband was also very busy. My children were ill, the old man was ill, and no one took care of me. I didn't even have time to wash clothes. I was too tired to do anything I really want to quit. But what you want is to get rid of poverty and get rich for the people of this county. It's not easy for you to start this business. When I'm half done, I can't see it break, but I really can't do it...' She said, covering her face and crying again.

This was the first time that the gentle Zhou Ling became furious. He summoned leading cadres of the whole Township and said, 'Building a large vegetable base for big cities is a major undertaking related to the poverty alleviation, prosperity and sustainable development of Dao town. It is not a simple administrative order and division of labor. The whole team should take action, actively participate and dare to take responsibility. I will issue orders, and your secretary and township head will also issue orders. A female deputy mayor works alone during the day and loads cars at night, Even the iron man can't support the shaft rotation! Don't you people have any compassion?' Can't you be the pillar of this career?

The Secretary and the township head blushed and reflected on themselves. He said that his understanding was not in place, so he did it according to the general administrative division of labor. 'Now we understand,' the township head said sincerely, 'we are willing to give Secretary Zhou a military order and go all out from now on!' then he firmly held the female deputy township head's hand and expressed apology and condolences. Many cadres present shed tears.

Since then, the township leading group has implemented the rotation duty system.

3. Let cauliflower go with 'story'

The modern career and the cloud data era were becoming more and more scientific and accurate. The former labor mode of 'coaxing', the mode of 'radish fast not washing mud', and the mode of selling with bags on the market had been eliminated by the new era and new life. No matter who still did so, they would be eliminated by a basket of cabbage, scallion and radish mud. It was not because life was too ruthless, but because you have been 'buried'.

'I launched the first car selling vegetables in the history of the underworld,' Zhou Ling said with a smile. Her eyes twinkled with the unique 'tone' of Shanghai officials, which was very elegant.

'Now, our white cauliflower, purple cauliflower and Romanesco broccoli have 'registered permanent residence' in high-end supermarkets,' he said. This is a small billboard hanging on the stems of vegetables. When customers scan the above QR code with their mobile phone, they can see a video, a 'story' about cauliflower: Grandpa white beard or a beautiful peasant girl dressed in gorgeous national clothes, sweating and waiting attentively (indicating that they have never seen chemical fertilizer and agricultural medicine); Grandpa white beard or a beautiful village girl, dressed in gorgeous national clothes and sweating, waited carefully (indicating that he had never seen chemical fertilizers and pesticides); When the cauliflower is ripe, pick it from the slope (which proves that it was born in green mountains and green waters, not in a greenhouse); Then trim the leaves, cut off the stems, gently put them into a white plastic packaging box, just like a little bride sitting in a sedan chair, and then put a bottle of crystal chilled water (to prove that it is noble and free of dust)

In this way, tens of thousands and 100,000 high-quality cauliflowers on Daozhen mountain have achieved the victory of the 'great leap forward': jump down from the villagers' vegetable baskets and creaking tables, pour thousands of places in the valley, then dance two green leaves and fly to the magnificent Shanghai, high-rise buildings in the clouds, Chongqing, flower sea Guiyang, and the spring breeze flies to Chengdu to carry the 'Chinese dream'

In order to realize the healthy, orderly, stable and reliable sustainable development of the vegetable industry in Dao Town, Zhou Ling proposed to set up a state-owned head office at the county level to take the lead and focus on the sales market; 14 Township branches linked sales and orders with village collectives; 83 villages set up collective cooperatives to organize people to grow vegetables and be responsible for quality supervision; All poor families join cooperatives and become shareholders. Zhou Ling knows that with such a large base and system in the county, relying solely on official operation and administration, it is easy to lose development power and personal vitality. He suggested that the state and collectives should account for 51% of the shares, and the remaining 49% should be distributed to managers and shareholders from top to bottom. Profit is linked to performance. They get something for nothing, stay up late for no reason, burst out of enthusiasm and creativity, the more they do, the better, and realize a benign operation.

After three years of hard work, Zhou Ling summed up three simple things: selling vegetables in the first year, growing vegetables in the second year, and standardization in the third year. With the joint efforts of Zhou Ling, Daozhen County Party committee and county government, the local broken fields have been integrated into a large base, cauliflower, pepper and mushrooms from farmland have converged into a large industry, and the self-employed have become the 'group army'. At present, the county base has 140,000 mu of vegetable land, forms seven relevant industrial chains, sells more than 6,000 tons of vegetables on a large scale, helps poor households increase their net income by more than 18 million yuan, benefits more than 8,000 poor people, and realizes an output value of more than 100 million. In the past, it was just a piece of white paper. The locals on the mountain can't remember his name. Women and children are aware of the reference to 'vegetable secretaries'. Relatives and friends in Shanghai are also very strange. White faced scholar Zhou Ling is absent-minded. He hasn't seen it for three years. He became a 'vegetable expert' with a nose and eyes. Zhou Ling said, 'I have no other ability, only one ability is 'serious.' therefore, he ran more than 160000 kilometres in three years, equivalent to more than four times around the earth. The State Council Poverty Alleviation Office sent a delegation to Daozhen county to evaluate the results of poverty alleviation, which is the most severe and difficult 'big test' for Chinese officials today. Zhou Ling reported: 'through the construction and development of vegetable bases, a total of 8,147 poor people in the county have benefited.' the evaluation team politely said, 'shall we conduct a spot check?' they asked your name through field investigation or random telephone interview? How many people are there in the family? What are you doing? What is the annual income? What is the proportion of labor and dividends in the vegetable base? The farmers answered one by one. They spot checked 11 families in total, and then compared them with the basic order. The basic order is exactly the same!

In places assisted by Shanghai, we should, of course, actively absorb Shanghai's abundant human, financial and material resources in accordance with the policy of 'adjusting measures to local conditions and acting according to our ability', take advantage of the situation, go to sea by boat, and make every effort to create a new development model and trend of local 'version 2.0'. But I think it is the most important and basic to study the working spirit and innovative spirit of 'science, accuracy, seriousness and persistence' in Shanghai. The world is afraid of the word 'serious'.

In the autumn of 2019, Zhou Lingyuan's assistance to Guizhou will expire in three years. Before leaving, he spent three months writing and painting, elaborately drew a long 'strategic map' of the production and marketing integration standard of the vegetable industry, and folded it into a booklet. The whole process of healthy, orderly and sustainable development of vegetable industry base, from initial seed selection to final sales, all links, technologies, standards and quality requirements are clearly written. He gave this 'strategic map' to local cadres.

This is Zhou Ling's painstaking efforts and experience in poverty alleviation and entrepreneurship in the past three years, as well as his deep feelings for Zunyi people and real people.

V – 'Silver Age Action'

They created their own 'third youth.'

They are all old people. Their childhood and adolescence were spent in poor and weak old China. Their mother told many sad 'stories of the past'. They all experienced the passionate youth of 'everything for the party' during the founding of new China. They also experienced the influence of the political movement and three years of suffering. They are hungry, angry, loyal. The tide of reform and opening up has come, and so has their 'second youth'. The cross century 'China miracle' and 'Shanghai miracle' are shining with sweat and sweat everywhere. They turned themselves into paving stones and made the Chinese nation rise in the east of the world. After retirement, they struggled all their lives. They are really tired. They should enjoy the quiet, rich and happy life in their old age and let their children and grandchildren kneel on their knees. However, the pure heart is still beating strongly, and passion is still flowing in the blood. So, with white hair, they resolutely bid farewell to their children and grandchildren, relatives and friends, the flowers and plants on the windowsill, the walk in the shade, stood up like a generation of recruits in the motherland and regrouped under the banner of the party. With the knowledge, wisdom and skills accumulated in his life, he swaggered to the desert Gobi, endless sandstorms and the yearning and yearning of the people of all ethnic groups in Xinjiang.

There, they created their own 'third youth.'

Perhaps only China has such an elderly 'volunteer army.'

They are the seeds of history.

1. The beauty at that time laden with sorrow

Patches were everywhere in that era. People's clothes, trousers and shoes are sewn with patches, broken roads are sewn with patches, and broken classroom windows are pasted with notes. Everyone's thought, life and destiny are scarred.

At that time, the river was deep and lucid. There were many waterways like a huge fishing net cast over the Water Town. The deep and long river resembled the long prospect that Liu Hongdi and her motherland were looking for.

A covered ship swayed gently in the depths of history. In spring, the wind is still very tight. She sat on the bow and luggage. He was wearing a patched blue cotton padded jacket, which his mother left when she was young. A pair of big eyes and two braids. Think about the tears when my parents sent me and the tears when I said goodbye. My little face is still full of tears. 18 years old, what a beautiful flower of youth! What a weak Shanghai girl! She had to leave school, teachers and textbooks and queue up to settle in a distant place. At the same time, the same fate, as a high school student, I carried my luggage from Harbin to Beidahuang, and Liu Hongdi from Shanghai to Jiangnan Water Town. It has been a difficult journey for eight years. Wind, frost, rain, snow and poisonous sun paint our youth black, like pieces of steel. The voice of speaking and walking is loud, like hitting the earth. Liu Hongdi became a teacher in the 1930s in the countryside. In the third grade, thatched huts were installed for runny children and worked in turn. In today's memory, Liu Hongdi said with a smile, 'I am a junior high school student, teaching primary school students. This is really wrong for people's children.' 'No!' I said, 'at that time, people tried to teach children to read. This is the continuation of the cultural blood of the Chinese nation. The firewood of the Chinese national spirit has been passed down from generation to generation. It seems insignificant, but it is of great significance! 'Here, I have to give a foreign example. When I visited Bulgaria, people there told me that

Bulgaria was occupied by the Ottoman Empire (the predecessor of Turkey) .The occupation has a history of 500 years. In order to occupy and destroy Bulgaria for a long time, the Ottoman Empire banned Bulgarians from using their own language and characters. Even if children just reached school age, they were sent to local schools in Ottoman for education. Generation after generation, such colonial education has been carried out for 500 years! However, Bulgarians risked being beheaded and secretly organized countless 'underground reading clubs', which silently passed on their language and culture from generation to generation. Finally, the Ottoman Empire collapsed, and the Bulgarian people perfectly preserved their national culture and national character. Similarly, during the Anti-Japanese War, the Japanese aggressors conducted 14 years of colonial education in the so-called 'Manchukuo'. After the victory of the Anti-Japanese war in 1945, Chinese national culture regained its dignity and vitality overnight.

History has proven that everyone is a seed from history. When they all grow up, they still sow the same seeds. In the era of going to the countryside, how many educated youth have become rural teachers? Only this time, they have made great contributions.

In 1976, local villagers raised their hands to 'recommend'. In 1977, Liu Hongdi, who had lived in the countryside for eight years, entered the medical department of Shanghai University of traditional Chinese medicine and became a college student, worker, farmer and soldier. Where is this? She has never had the slightest interest in the profession of doctor! But finally returned to Shanghai from the countryside, that's all! Unexpectedly, the tears of joy have not dried up. The next year, the state resumed the formal university entrance examination. Liu Hongdi's intestines are green. She wants to drop out, take the exam again, choose her favorite career and become an ordinary college student. But in this way, she had to move her account back to where she cut in line. Her parents said, 'if you are a junior high school student, what if you can't pass the exam?' just admit it – study hard! He graduated from Shanghai Institute of ophthalmology in 1980 and retired in 2006. Liu Hongdi became the chief ophthalmologist and won the scientific research achievement award for many times. When she was a girl, her clear and bright eyes became a little dizzy, but she made countless eye patients 'get rid of the dark clouds' and 'see the sun again.'

In the new century, with the opening of the western development, all walks of life across the country have taken action. At that time, China had more than 5 million retired scientific and technological personnel, which was undoubtedly a large scientific and technological 'group army' with knowledge, ability and patriotic enthusiasm. The national Aging office immediately launched the 'silver age action' with elderly intellectuals as the main body and assisting the West. Since 2003, Shanghai has officially organized senior scientific and technological personnel to carry out the Shanghai Singapore counterpart 'silver age action' and Xinjiang voluntary service. By 2019, it has been carried out 18 times with the participation of more than 380 old experts, covering more than 10 fields such as medical treatment, education, agriculture and animal husbandry, greening, culture and tourism planning. These old experts have a strong 'technical authority' in the industry and units. They are all grandparents in the family. They should be able to enjoy the happiness of their children and grandchildren in their old age. However, they signed up enthusiastically again and again, and came to the foot of Tianshan Mountain, desert and Gobi again and again, leaving heavy footprints in 151 units in 16 counties and 5 cities, including Kashgar, Aksu and Karamay. Their white hair was like silver, shining with moving brilliance under the light of the snow peak.

Over the past 18 years, Shanghai has always insisted. No, with the passage of time, the people left and gradually returned to silence. Success lies in persistence, dedication lies in persistence, and character lies in persistence. This is one of Shanghai's urban genes. They don't need slogans. They always study silently.

After retirement, Liu Hongdi opened an 'expert clinic' in the eye disease prevention and treatment center, which attracted a steady stream of patients. In 2010, when she learned that the Shanghai Civil Affairs Department had organized the 'silver age action' to assist Xinjiang in the medical sector, she immediately signed the agreement. This means that her personal income will be greatly reduced and her patient resources will be lost. But Liu Hongdi did not hesitate, and her wife and children also supported her. Liu Hongdi said that when I was 18, I went to the countryside in the mountains and worked in the countryside for eight years. I can't forget the sad eyes I left in the old photos, or the sad and helpless eyes of the local villagers who lack food, clothes and medicine. Now I have the ability, why not help the people of Xinjiang?

Since then, she has signed a contract every year and went to Xinjiang eight times in 2019 for two and a half months each time. Everywhere they went, people of all ethnic groups lined up and heard that 'Shanghai experts' came to the free clinic. First, they believe in the technology of Shanghai doctors. Second, they can save a lot of medical expenses. Every time I see a long line in the hospital hall, her sad eyes and strong nostalgia in her girlhood return to Liu Hongdi's eyes. Although the white hair on her temples had appeared at this time, she did her best to let the patients with eye diseases see the light again. In the Western rehabilitation activities of the bright journey, it has become her most desired desire from morning to night. From a child with eye trauma to a 79-year-old grandmother undergoing cataract surgery, she guides local doctors to operate carefully and assists surgeons (mainly training teams). After the operation, the old lady's eyesight recovered very well. A few days later, according to the wishes of the old lady, the family specially helped the old man go to the hospital to see Liu Hongdi, and said that this was the Shanghai doctor who let you see the sun again! The old lady warmly hugged Liu Hongdi and stuffed her with a basket of Xinjiang red dates. She murmured, 'Nuerluparexita!' Liu Hongdi couldn't understand. Her little grandson translated and said, 'grandma said you were the goddess of light!'

When he was a doctor, Liu Hongdi's enthusiasm, care and meticulous care for patients deeply moved Hashiyeti, a sixth grade Uighur girl hospitalized for otitis media in Zepu County. That day, when Liu Hongdi was walking around, the little girl suddenly ran over, stuffed a note into her white pocket, and then ran away shyly. Liu Hongdi opened the letter and read it in Chinese: 'aunt Shanghai: after reading this letter, please don't laugh at me because I love you! I ask you to take a picture with me tomorrow morning, okay?'

Liu Hongdi's eyes suddenly wet. The next morning, she and Hashiyeti took a photo at the gate of the hospital. Since then, the girl has become Liu Hongdi's 'Uighur daughter' and Liu Hongdi has become Hashiyeti's 'Shanghai mother'. Later, Liu Hongdi went to Xinjiang many times. No matter how far she went, Hashiyeti came to see her by train or coach. With the help and guidance of Liu Hongdi for many years, Hashiyeti is now a college student.

2. A hero colored by another hero

Yao Meifang, whose online name is 'grandma Yao', is a well-known old military doctor and a little-known heroine. She was born in 1943 and is 77 years old. Her laughter is louder than mine!

—Yao Meifang said that she happened to be a 'combination of workers, peasants and soldiers' with her parents. In his early years, my father wandered from his hometown to Shanghai to pull rickshaws for a living. After liberation, he became a shoemaker. Her mother is a farm girl. She worked for the landlord when she was farming. The couple were often bullied in the old society. After the land reform, the whole family was divided into 4.3 mu of cultivated land. Yao Meifang, 9, graduated. Her parents and she joined the party one by one. Therefore, the whole family loves the party and the country to the bone. If anyone dares to say an unpleasant word to his face, his father can drive him out for three miles with a rolling pin.

—Yao Meifang said that for all his life her father was 'left' very cute. When she was looking for someone to marry, her father put forward an insurmountable red line: Government official families can't be a family with us, because they cannot eat together. At that time, Mei Fang was surrounded by elegant intellectuals dressed in expensive white suits. In the old society, it was obvious that when she could study all the way to college, she had a high status. She can only treat each other warmly and coldly. In the late 1960s, the father of a child patient was a military cadre. When he heard about the head nurse's blind date, he said, 'I have a company commander who is very similar to her! I asked him to go on vacation to meet her!' as he said, company commander Wang, a 'poor middle and lower farmer' in Baoding, Hebei, came. He was tall and big, not so stylish. He couldn't be found on the ground. He walked with a thud. On the blind date, company commander Wang lowered his head and blushed without saying a word, because he had never seen a big girl in the army, let alone a Shanghai girl. It's said that company commander wang hasn't been home for seven years. Yao Meifang instructed him like a 'leader' and said, 'go home and see the old man first. Maybe your family has found you a daughter-in-law. If not, come back to me.' A few days later, company commander Wang replied, 'in addition to parents, brothers and sisters, there is a pig and several chickens.' in this way, they were engaged. But his father didn't keep his promise. He regretted that Lao Wang's family was too poor and said, 'how can you find someone to eat scallions and garlic?' Mei fang said, 'don't you want me to find a poor middle farmer? Two from poor to poor, no one can say who they are.' so they live to this day.

—Yao Meifang said that like my parents, I love the party and the country. My parents don't know any words. I can't go to school without new China. Because there are five brothers and sisters, life is very difficult, tuition is free, whether it's school or vacation, they will help their mother farm when they get home. Sometimes I'm so tired that I can sleep on the waterwheel. But my homework is excellent. I used to be a team leader and a class cadre, because I know that only with culture and ability can I repay the country. In 1961, Mei Fang graduated from high school and because of his good family background and academic performance, she was sent to study in Shanghai Foreign Studies University directly, without taking the exam. She was born in Zheng Hongmiao with excellent character, but the headmaster was very worried about her, because the teacher knew that her family could not afford it and it was difficult to persist until graduation. At this time, the school of nursing of Shanghai Second Military Medical University came to recruit female soldiers. Mei fang successfully passed the exam and became the third platoon leader after entering the school. This is a difficult period for the country for three years. People are generally hungry. Mei fang lacked nutrition and grew as thin as bean sprouts. Fortunately, the army is a melting pot. Three months later, Mei fang was 1.59 metres tall and weighed 60 kilograms. Her comrades in arms ridiculed her as 'big and thick, like a water tank'. But when he was full, he had strength. The whole school held a student Wushu competition. Mei fang won the first place in the project of 'rescuing the wounded'. His name was published in *Jiefang Daily* on November 11, 1967.

—Yao Meifang said that she also shouted a slogan: 'let Chairman Mao have a good sleep!' at that time, in order to 'oppose imperialism and fight the United States and the Soviet Union', the construction of the third line in Southwest China began, and railway soldiers and engineers also went up. At the mobilization meeting, the head of the army said that Chairman Mao was particularly concerned about the construction of the third line. He said that the construction of the third line was not good and I couldn't sleep. Mei fang and her comrades in arms who joined the railway medical team shouted: 'Chairman Mao must have a good sleep!' Mei fang really worked hard for this determination. A Shanghai girl became a black ball. At that time, the construction equipment was poor, semi mechanical and semi primitive. The tractor was added with shovels and pickaxes. The soldiers were ill and injured a lot. In order to practice intravenous injection and infusion techniques, she practiced all day and all night and finally the needle technique became the first. Once, during construction on the Yunnan Guizhou Plateau with an altitude of more than 3,000 metres, the cave collapsed and was filled with toxic gas, and more than a dozen soldiers fainted inside. The commander quickly organized a stretcher to rush in, but a pair of stretchers must be carried by two people. Meifang shouted, 'what other stretcher? Rush in!' she was the first person to rush into the cave. It is more than 1,000 metres away, dark and full of stones. She was the first person to carry a comatose soldier. The soldier was saved and she fainted. The headmaster praised her as a hero. Mei fang is straightforward and not modest. She said, 'I am a hero dyed by a hero!' she also volunteered to donate blood to the wounded and helped doctors carry out emergency surgery for the wounded in a non-standard environment. Mei fang has rich nursing experience and put forward many ideas and methods to save lives. After returning home, the army awarded her third-class merit. During the 'Cultural Revolution', the military hospital was also involved in factional war, and she was dragged to Beijing. Mei fang shouted angrily in the corridor, 'how can you leave the patient? I won't go!!!'

—Yao Meifang said that after a long time of nursing, she is actually half a doctor. A colleague suggested that she become a doctor. She was a nurse when she was old. Her treatment is not good, and her cry is not good. She said, I'm not an expert. Being a doctor is always a '250' doctor. Only when I am a nurse can I become a reassuring nurse. After more than 40 years of struggle in the military nursing industry, Yao Meifang won the third prize three times. He later served as the director of the nursing department of Changhai Hospital and master's supervisor until he retired. In the spring of 2009, she heard that Shanghai was organizing a new round of 'Silver age action' to assist Xinjiang and signed the contract immediately. 'I like the title of volunteer most in my life,' she said. On July 5, she and her teammates held a free clinic for the local people of all ethnic groups in Kashgar hospital. In the evening, news came from Urumqi that a group of thugs were frantically beating, destroying, robbing, burning and killing in the street. For some time, the situation was very tense. The local power grid was once shut down, but doctors in Shanghai insisted on completing the free clinic.

From 2009 to 2014, Yao Meifang went to Xinjiang for five consecutive years to participate in the 'silver age action'. I asked, why don't you leave after 2014? Yao Meifang smiled and said, 'I'm old. They don't want me!'

However, after various efforts in 2019, Yao Meifang, 76, came to Zunyi old area.

It seems unnecessary to elaborate on her story of assisting Xinjiang. We can all imagine. Everyone believed that she would do well and very touching. In fact, it is difficult to count the number of acute and severe patients she participated in the rescue, including an infant who weighed only 860g at birth and whose skin has not yet fully developed; She helped poor villagers everywhere, including two Uighur girls and a Han girl who successfully went to college with her support. At the national commendation Conference for 'the most beautiful old man and the most promising person', the host commented on Yao Meifang in the name of 'Plum blossom bone Zhichun, fruitful medical assistance in Xinjiang; She has healed many people and is still young. Let's support Xinjiang together.'

Today, the 77-year-old 'grandma Yao' is still active in the medical front line of Shanghai Hospital. The laughter was loud and the style remained unchanged.

3. White hair turns green and extends to the desert

In the 18 years since the 'Silver age action' was launched in Shanghai, the old experts involved have left with responsibility and come back with stories.

Lin Dawei is the old director of the flower quality inspection department of Shanghai Forestry Station. He is a garden expert specializing in tree and flower breeding and seedling cultivation. Before taking part in the 'silver age action' for the first time in 2013, he did his homework on the Internet and found that Zepu County, Xinjiang is an oasis in the Gobi, most of which are saline alkali lands, the climate is dry, and ordinary plants are difficult to take root and grow. He bought more than 60 fast-growing white elms and American Red Maple at his own expense and planted them in Zepu County. When I left two and a half months later, the original 15 cm tall saplings had grown to 2 metres high! Two years later, it has reached 5 metres high and is full of depression. The local villagers have never seen trees grow so fast, even shouting miracles! With good tree species, large-scale promotion is imperative, and cultivating a large number of seedlings is the basic project. Soon, Lin Dawei brought his scientific research achievement 'plant tissue culture technology' to Zepu County. Through the agreement between the two sides, Shanghai has helped build a scientific research base, which can cultivate and produce 3 million seedlings every year. Its core institution is called 'plant tissue culture room'. In 2013, hearing that the base had started construction, Lin Dawei, his old colleague and senior engineer Xu Lizhong rushed to the construction site in Zepu County and looked at the drawings. His face changed greatly. Because the architectural design unit has no understanding of the production process of plant tissue culture, let alone strict special requirements in all links from sterilization, inoculation, culture to test tube seedling transplantation, the whole project is designed according to the general biological laboratory. Lin Dawei immediately shouted, 'stop working! Stop working! Start again!' people were stunned, and the rumbling construction site was as quiet as dead water. Quickly negotiate with the design unit, and the other party spread out his hands: 'we don't understand and can't draw.' Lin Dawei had to fight in person and spent a week drawing the sketch of each training room for the construction unit to rebuild according to the new drawings. The next year, he got off at Zepu County and went directly to the 'plant cultivation base'. All the culture rooms were built as required, but the rooms were empty and dusty. Because there are no facilities, equipment, drugs, reagents and technicians, the base is an empty shell. Lin Dawei is very sad. He immediately reported to the county leaders. On the third day, the Secretary of the county Party committee personally led the heads of relevant departments to work on the site, which was implemented one by one. Some technicians and college students were transferred, a batch of bottle seedlings and drugs were airlifted from Shanghai, and a lot of equipment was also transported in. Two months later, after Lin Dawei's hard guidance and training, the 'plant tissue culture base' was fully put into use. Today, many years later, thousands of bottle seedlings have been transplanted to the earth and become a vast shadow.

In 2012, there were more than 260 newly introduced French Wutong trees in Zepu County, because they were poorly wrapped in transportation and soon suffered dry and hot weather in summer. The locals were very worried, so they invited Xu Lizhong, an old friend of Lin Dawei, a landscape planning expert and senior engineer in Shanghai. Xu Lizhong took the 'tree nutrient solution' developed by himself for many years. After mixing according to a certain proportion, hang a bottle on a tree and drop the liquid medicine into the predrilled hole, just like giving an infusion to a patient. Half a month later, Wutong planted green leaves again, with a survival rate of 98%.

Today, Zepu County, which grows on saline alkali land, is rated as 'national greening model county' and 'autonomous region garden county'. The white hair of two old people in Shanghai has become an oasis in the desert.

—Holding my son's hand and growing old with my son is a moving picture. What is more moving and admirable is that an old couple in Shanghai joined the 'Silver age action' from a distance.

In 2009, Yang Laqing, a surgeon at the military rest center of Yangpu District, Shanghai, retired and asked to join the volunteer team to assist Xinjiang. She asked her wife Lu Shiqiu for advice. Lu Shiqiu said with a smile, 'I didn't expect my wife to become more and more sober with age. Go there and wait for me!' that year, Yang Laqing came to Korla County hospital and opened a breast surgery clinic outside the door, which said 'men are not allowed in'. The news spread, and a long line lined up outside the clinic. They were all Uighur women dressed in gorgeous national costumes. Many early breast cancer patients were found to receive timely treatment. Three years later, in 2012, Lu Shiqiu, deputy chief physician of Otolaryngology Department, also retired. He immediately signed up for the 'Silver age action' and went to Xinjiang Karamay hospital and Yecheng County People's hospital with his wife Yang Laqing. The conditions and life there are obviously much more difficult than those in Shanghai, but they say: 'old age is meaningful and worth it. No matter how old you are, becoming a useful person to the people and society is the greatest happiness.'

Similarly, in Korla County Hospital, a pair of old doctors who helped Xinjiang formed 'colleagues'. Her husband Bao Xueying works in the radiology department and her wife Yuan lunping works in the pathology department. At noon, the two met in the canteen. They're like new friends. One said, 'Hello, old Bao, how are you recently?' the other said, 'Hello, old Yuan, can you adapt to working in Xinjiang?' made the local colleagues laugh. No one knew that before participating in the 'Silver Age Action', a large private hospital in Zhejiang had offered them a high paying job invitation, but they politely declined, and both came to Xinjiang.

Zhang Junfa, Professor of Tongji University and chief physician of Obstetrics and Gynecology of Affiliated Hospital, participated in the first 'silver age action' at the age of 67 in 2003. In 2008, his wife Li Jinwen (Professor and chief ophthalmologist of Tongji University) also retired. They became volunteers of the Xinjiang medical team together. In 2012, the old couple created the oldest volunteers in the 'silver age action', 76-year-old Zhang Junfa and 70 year old Li Jinwen.

In the team of the old doctors include Wei Chaosheng and Shenyang, psychologists Xu Jinyao, Teng Meiwen, Xin Zhenhua and Shen Yanping, Old doctor Luo Keping, senior economist Yue Lu of Tongji University, singer Ye Yin (Xinjiang called 'Nightingale'), educator Fu Danjiang, Wu Hongjian, Huang Lixin, Zhang Jinghai, Lu Guowei, Jin Nan, Liu Hong, Chen Guofu, etc.

On the way to Xinjiang, they were full of white hair and passionate and sang the group song of 'silver age action':

> White hair like silver, dedication like gold,
> Silver age action volunteers love boundless.
> Firewood inheritance, wisdom and mutual education,
> With talent, the sunset is like brocade

The white hair of these Shanghai old people glittered against the high snow peaks.

From the launch of 'silver age action', until today, 3-*/73 today, it is probably only Shanghai. This is Shanghai. It not only beautiful and talented, but also has a heart of gold.

LONGJIANG CHAPTER
Hot blood flows South

I

WITH A BANG, the red sunset fell into the village's earth chimney!

Blue cooking smoke rises and crisp birds are everywhere.

Heilongjiang, once known as the 'world porridge shed', should now be called 'China's granary'.

Now, like a drop of sweat, I slide across the dark and wide land of Longjiang again.

At the age of 21, I was still a high school student. I put on a yellow cotton padded jacket, picked up my luggage roll and shouted the slogan of 'anti-imperialism, anti -revisionism, reclamation and guarding the border'. Starting from Harbin, I took a group of students (formerly known as the 'independent regiment of Heilongjiang production and Construction Corps') to Jiayin farm on the Bank of Heilongjiang and began an educated youth career of up to 8 years. After work in the evening, I often string three or four steamed buns with branches (I ate nine in a meal when I was most tired), holding a box of tasteless cabbage soup, sitting on the stone bank by the river, quietly looking at the vast and silent land of Russia opposite. In summer, I often swam to the nameless island in the river to bask in the sun. I happened to meet Natasha, a Russian girl swimming from the other bank. Her father is an agricultural machinery engineer on the other side of the red flag collective farm. I read Pushkin's poem 'if life deceives you' to her in Russian. We also talked about Turgenev and Chekhov. More than 20 years later, she came to Harbin with her daughter and became a poet. As the president of Harbin Federation of literary and art circles, I took a bunch of roses to meet her at the airport. She covered her face with a straw hat and gave me a deep kiss. The whole audience laughed and startled her 16-year-old daughter. Interestingly, in the summer of the battle of Zhenbao Island in 1969, there were millions of soldiers on both sides of Wusuli River and Heilongjiang River. The atmosphere was very tense. Seeing a Soviet patrol boat suddenly passing by this nameless island, I suddenly jumped up on a whim and shouted in Russian: 'Hello, comrades!' the Soviet officers and soldiers on board were surprised and shouted: 'Hello, Chinese boy!' I absolutely believe that this is the first friendly greetings from the military and people of the two countries on the Sino Soviet border covered with war clouds! At that time, I suddenly had a beautiful idea: why do people on both sides of the border fight? If mankind learns to live in peace and friendship, the boundary line will no longer be the fuse, but as beautiful as the lace of a woman's skirt. How beautiful the world should be! Later, I wrote my debut work *Lace of The Earth*, which was later published in *Lijiang magazine*. In this way, I lit my literary dream under the oil lamp and by the campfire in the northern wilderness.

Thanks to The Great Northern Wilderness, she forged a generation of educated youth. She let me understand the real national conditions and public feelings completely different from theoretical knowledge. She let me choose an impassioned and perseverance song, which is: 'every tear of the people is a scar of the country.' Now, I devote myself to the field investigation and writing of this book. This kind of affection and sincerity for rural land actually began from the mountain road beside Heilongjiang and Xiaoxing'an Mountain. At that time, I bravely stood on a carriage full of wheat bags, wearing a dog skin hat, a flower-patterned sheep fur jacket and a walking stick. Holding the likes of a Zhangba snake spear, he waved it in the air and loudly proclaimed, 'let's ride!'

So, the mountains receded and the golden waves surged, and that's how I came.

II

From The Great Northern Wilderness to The Great Northern Warehouse, and then to the heavy industry base of new China, this is a tragic epic engraved on the black soil.

Here, under the high sky, there are thousands of miles of fertile land. Grab a handful of soil and hold it in your hand. It was dark and hot. When you insert chopsticks, they will sprout. The men here are born with a strong disposition, likewise, the women are also embodied with strength. The 'little bastards' born here run around with energy and mischief. I have seen such scenes: in the thick wall of the earth house, the stove is burning with a high fever, red and strong, surrounded by water mist and heated Kang. The mother with a big belly felt that the time had come. She put down her three feet long copper tobacco pouch, she jumped onto the Kang with wide and free strides. Mother's scream, a red meat ball like a shell blew out of the uterus, and a scream woke up the whole world. Father squatted in the outside room and suddenly looked very proud. Like a knife, he pinned a short tobacco pouch on the waist of his cotton trousers and asked the old and young men to scald wine – I'm one of the 'bastards'. Thus, when Longjiang people were born from generation to generation, the first was Kanto tobacco, the second was sorghum wine, and the third was breast milk as white as snow, fragrant as flowers and sweet as honey.

These three constitute the character and nature of the sincere Longjiang people.

From the ancient aborigines who drank blood, killed tigers and leopards, to the roaring minority who pulled the flag and became the king, which disturbed the peace of the central region; In addition, those who couldn't be controlled in the mainland, such as traitors, bandits, bandits, murderers and looters, and even bandits, were all distributed to the wilderness of Heilongjiang province for labor and reconstruction; In the future, the 'dragon vitality land' of the Qing Dynasty was opened. For generations, bold exiles who refused to starve to death in their hometown led their families into groups to break into the east of the wild heaven pass; In the end, one hundred thousand soldiers landed on the ground and made swords into plows; Millions fought against the grand desolation mountain with great passion. All in all, the genes of a group of reckless heroes, heroes, gallant men, strong men and strong women, armored men, hot blooded young men and even the hunky men made the whole Longjiang blood group. As far as she could see, they were all men and women who were able to do everything in one go, help each other, three bowls of wine, four limbs developed, facial features were dignified, six gods were in charge, seven orifices were bright, eight sides were powerful, and everything could be in one.

They call themselves 'Northeast tigers' when they succeeded, when they fail at something they will laugh at themselves 'reckless'.

The War of Liberation, which swept thousands of troops, first began in the northeast. Without the grain and grass, cotton cloth, military shoes, bloody men and hot women in the great northeast, millions of heroes could not cross the river to resist US aggression and aid Korea. After the founding of new China, the eldest brother of the Soviet Union lent a hand. A large number of heavy industrial factories and mines have emerged in Harbin, Qiqihar, Jiamusi and even major cities such as Liaoning and Jilin, establishing a strong industrial foundation for poor new China. These historical achievements and contributions will never be forgotten. At that time, the upsurge of industrialization and mechanization swept through, the northeast recruited workers everywhere, and stories of farmers becoming workers overnight were everywhere. You see, in the red sorghum field like the sea, Wang Tiezhu blocked the village girl Xiaofang's path and said with serious eyes, 'I'm going to work in the city. Go pack and come with me!'

'Xiao Fang stared at a pair of almond shaped eyes and said,' There are so many beautiful girls in the city. 'What should I do if you regret your decision?'

Wang Tiezhu said: 'If I regret, I'm a son of a bitch!'

Xiaofang said, 'It's a deal. Forever?'

Wang Tiezhu said, 'Well, all my life!'

They spent three quarters of an hour entangled in bed together, Wang Tiezhu gave birth to a plump boy, like a dream come true. The next day, Xiaofang eloped with Tiezhu. Her father looked at his daughter's empty boudoir and sighed, 'This girl is really impetuous!'

The Tiezhus and the Xiaofang's therefore dedicated their youth and life to our country. They built a smoke filled northeast industrial base with a lifelong sweat. The sound of the machine rumbled during the day, and the sparks from welding were like the sea at night. Among the thousands of Wang Tiezhus, one is an outstanding representative of the Chinese working class, Wang Tieren. At the pep rally, he threw his wicker hat on the table and shouted, 'When the oil workers roar, and the earth will shake three times!'

He shouted the blood and tears of northeast industrial workers for more than half a century.

Since then, the great northeast was open and exported everything to all parts of the country generously and selflessly. They are called 'the eldest son of the Republic', Angang is called 'the capital of steel', Daqing is called 'the capital of oil',

Hegang is called 'the capital of coal', and The Great Northern Wilderness is called 'The Great Northern Warehouse.' The forests on Xing'an Mountain shouted 'Timber!' Thousands of ancient pines fell like martyrs and became tall buildings, bridges and sleepers all over the country.

I remember when I was a student, I carried my schoolbag and went across Jihong bridge in Harbin every day. I often look down holding the ornamental work of iron, bridge railing. Trains hauling coal, logs, crude oil and raw grain spewed out white steam and thick smoke, drove south along pairs of shiny tracks, and drove to all parts of the motherland year after year, day and night.

I remember when I passed Daqing in the educated youth era, I saw stretches of white saline alkali land, rows of dry base dormitories, silent 'kowtow machines' (oil extraction machines), and oil workers with greasy faces and cotton padded jackets. They created the heroic 'Daqing spirit' with 'hard struggle and selfless dedication', which brought the roar of the motherland and thousands of lights.

After I graduated from school, I returned to Harbin as a reporter. I visited the famous 'three driving forces' and 'ten military industries', which refers to the three large factories on the original road in Harbin, Harbin Electric Machinery Factory, Harbin Steam Turbine Factory and Harbin Boiler Factory. Both places filled by tens of thousands of people. The sound of the huge workshop was deafening. Machines labeled 'made in China' were transported to all corners of China.

From the beginning of the founding of new China to the middle of reform and opening up, the three generations of industrial workers in the great northeast have unreservedly dedicated everything to whole country in order to support national construction. With their creations, their blood flows throughout China. The good news of their success went all the way south. They left wind, snow and cold, difficulties and hardships to themselves, and sent infinite light and heat to the South and all over the country.

Wang Tiezhus are worthy of being the 'pillar' of the Republic.

III

Alas, more than half a century has passed. The great northeast is old, Heilongjiang is old, and Wang Tiezhus are old. Today, Daqing oil field is almost dry, there are few virgin forests left, the old coal mine has basically become an underground empty city, the black soil is no longer fertile and greasy, most of various resources are exhausted, and the scenery of some large state-owned enterprises slowly declined. In the middle and late 1990s, with the arrival of a new round of scientific and technological revolution, the old and drained manufacturing industry became the so-called 'sunset industry', and tens of millions of industrial workers, some of them two or three generations, were laid off at the same time. The once tall and bright workshop fell into silence overnight, becoming empty and dusty.

Arranging the life of old employees and organizing the reemployment of young and middle-aged employees once became a heavy task in large cities such as Harbin and in Heilongjiang Province. Many years later, many idle old factories have become places where real estate developers make a lot of money.

History must advance, must pay the price, and life must continue. With the great changes of the times and the rapid progress of science and technology, people in Northeast China are at a loss. The pain of reform and the difficulties of development are hurting them. However, no one has the right to laugh at the northeast, and no one has the right to forget the years when the northeast people once burned with passion. The CPC Central Committee and the State Council have decided to take all necessary measures to revitalize the old industrial base in Northeast China. This is the aspiration of the people and the time!!

We must polish the 'rusty northeast' and let it shine again!

In order to write this book, I traveled all over the country and finally came to my hometown Heilongjiang. Looking at the Songhua River flowing eastward and the green fields with spring breeze, I think the moon here is rounder than other places, and the cooking smoke here is more fragrant than other places.

I The Huachuan plow

The original aspiration is still beating fresh and powerful here.

Every morning, a beautiful and warm eyes rises with the rising sun and shines on the vast black land. She was a young female soldier with her strong gaze. Wearing a gray blue military uniform, she walked into the morning exercise crowd, the dancing crowd and the scenery by the river with a smile. She has also become the most beautiful scenery in the scenery. Looking back on the past, she was filled with emotion. She told us affectionately that after the September 18th Incident, she set out quietly at the bloody dawn of the Wancun tragedy, as known as the 918 incident, which led to the fall of the northeast into the hands of the Japanese army. She was born in a rich peasant family and studied in a women's normal school. She may have gone to the inside Shanhaiguan Pass or rear area. But she didn't. In the decisive battle, she resolutely went to the Anti-Japanese alliance team, to the hail of bullets, until she walked into the bloodstained Ouse River. She is a girl who can play harmonica and love singing, but at that moment, she raised her arms and shouted, 'Never surrender! Never imprisoned!' and then sank into the rolling waves with her seven comrades in arms. Now she has returned to her hometown. On the Bank of the Songhua River in Huachuan County, Jiamusi City, she was transformed into a huge half body white statue. Facing the turbulent waves, she held a steel gun and looked determined. She is Leng Yun, the instructor of 'eight heroines who drowned themselves in a river'. Twenty-three years old, what a beautiful flower season it is, just like the sunrise shining on us every day.

1. A man worthy to be praised

In May 2015, Guo Guangfu, 45, new Secretary of Huachuan County Party committee, set foot on this land. It is said that there is a Lengyun Village here. Soon after he took office, he arrived at Lengyun Village without pomp. He wants to find a kind of memory, a kind of sublimity and an incentive, which is the eternal spiritual torch for him and the cadres and masses of the whole county. When he entered the village, he was silent and his mood was a little down. We can't find the village branch secretary and village director here, nor can we find the trace of Lengyun. No, He found a small picture on the wall behind the door, as small as a children's drawing. There was a mess inside and outside the house, and the ground was full of dust and paper scraps. A group of villagers made a loud noise, petitioned around the accountant, demanded arrears of wages, haggled over land acquisition, and quarreled with neighbors. They yelled and scolded, with the momentum like a plow, which could dig the ancestral graves of 18 generations of village cadres to the end.

Where are the village cadres? They ran away. Years of accumulated resentment, endless disputes and many accounts in a mess have made nearly half of the villagers in Lengyun Village petitioners. Therefore, the village cadres have to leave the chaos and fly away. Guo Guangfu knew that the branch of Lengyun Village had collapsed and the people had dispirited. On the way back, he was silent for a long time and said to the comrades accompanying him, 'If she had lived to this day, we would all be sinners' How sacred a party branch secretly gathered under the oil lamp was at the moment she went into battle!

Guo Guangfu was born in the countryside. After graduating from university, he became a cadre and later became Secretary of Youth League Committee of Jiamusi City. He is well aware that the current situation of Lengyun Village may represent the weakness and looseness of some rural grass-roots party organizations in Huachuan County. China's rural reform has experienced a glorious course for more than 40 years. The labor enthusiasm and creativity of hundreds of millions of farmers are like a volcanic eruption, emitting endless light and heat. However, with two or three generations of young farmers working in cities, the problems of empty nests and aging in rural areas are becoming more and more serious, the construction of grass-roots party has been greatly affected, there are few members in village committee, and the role of branch of fighting fortress has been seriously weakened...

In the next two years, Guo Guangfu visited 105 administrative villages in whole county and made investigations and adjustments to the two-village committee one by one. Those old people who couldn't keep up with the times, lazy and idle returned to homes, and a large number of ambitious young people stepped onto the stage. Among them, there were college students, small bosses, shop assistants, grain merchants and returned workers. In short, there were all kinds of people from all walks of life in society. The only requirement was to dare to think, dare to do and dare to promise. Liu Ziyu, a college student who opened a coffee shop in the county, was frightened. He said, 'Can I sign for half a year and be an agent village party secretary?'

In 2017, the poverty alleviation work in Heilongjiang Province entered a new stage of 'targeted identification and targeted poverty alleviation'. The county Party committee and the county government decided to 'deep ploughing' Huachuan in terms of spirit, politics, economy and culture through this unprecedented great movement. We should not only fully complete the task of poverty alleviation, but also comprehensively 'upgrade' the grass-roots party construction in 105 administrative villages. In Guo Guangfu's words, it means 'selecting tough people and completing tough tasks'. They believe that the ruling foundation of the Party is at the grass-roots level. Only by laying a good foundation can we 'draw the latest and most beautiful paintings'. Otherwise, everything will be empty talk, the results of poverty alleviation will be difficult to consolidate and develop, and some people may fall back into poverty.

A large iron and steel plow of the new era was started ploughing in Huachuan.

On May 19, 2017, the county held a mobilization meeting for poverty alleviation. There were 45 village-based teams assigned by provinces and cities and 253 selected by the county. At the same time, 2609 assistant cadres paired up in the village (including Guo Guangfu and all county-level leaders).

Guo Guangfu was gentle and calm. He seldom spoke loudly or lost his temper, and so did this time. But when people heard him, they felt awe inspiring, broad-minded, and decisive. In his speech, he announced several unique moves and laws, which were refreshing and exciting!

First, he had no other choice but to select talents as elite as he could. He said that the 253 members of the poverty relief team selected from all the units in the county this time were outstanding officials and reserve officials! How many outstanding talents could a county have? It could be said that some cadres who are old or lack fresh perspectives, I strongly required that they be returned and the bureau reselect people. Some of bureaus said there was no suitable candidate. Well, it proves that there are no outstanding officials in your organization and no one is allowed to be

The second point was to fight till the end and to advocate 'two-year contracts are absolute, there's no turning back.' he said that from now on to 2020, the poverty alleviation would come to an end in less than 4 years. Two years later, it would be difficult to change a group of people. Moreover, the new candidates belonged to the second tier, and might not be better than you. You are the only child in the Huachuan talent library. It's time for you to repay our parents and villagers. 'If not you, then whom?' (Laughter) of course, if you are sick or have difficulties in your family, we will consider taking good care of you. But you have to be mentally prepared and work hard until reach a well-off society. This responsibility is once in a lifetime, and it's your honor to be selected.

The third one is that 'no one left behind'. According to the superior's requirements, every poor village should be assigned a team. We think even if it is not a poor village, there are still some poor families. In order to fully implement the requirements of 'targeted poverty alleviation and 'no one left behind', we decide to assign a team to each of the 105 administrative villages in the whole county to achieve full cover.

Fourth, we won't do it for nothing. For those who are willing to follow the orders of the Party and complete the task of poverty alleviation, we will promote and put them in an important position, and we will do what we say!

After the meeting, the cadres said that although Secretary Guo is usually reserved and quiet, he is really an 'able person'!

The battle began, and nearly 3,000 cadres rushed to the front line. Huachuan County has a population of 220,000. After complex, detailed and accurate identification, the chaotic situation of striving to be a 'poor household' has been eliminated. A total of 5,804 poor families and 11,710 people have established files and cards. The village is filled with cadres that come from all walks of life, including government cadres, doctors, teachers, bank staff, college students, police, etc. Most of them are not familiar with rural work, but during that time they lived like the villagers. Although they have trained, they are not involved in poverty alleviation policies, border determination and how to calculate farmers' income and sources. For a time, the telephone of the county Poverty Alleviation Office rung 24/7. The county party committee Guo Guangfu gave Zhang Yuxi a special task, named 'member of the Standing Committee of Zhang'. You just have to focus on poverty alleviation no matter what happens, even when the sky may fall. At that time, Zhang Yuxi shouted into the phone every day, his throat even bled. It got to the point that the other side couldn't hear his voice, he was completely voiceless. Gao Zhiwei, deputy director, has been engaged in poverty alleviation since 2010. He has studied relevant policies and actual situations in depth. The databases of the whole county are in his computer so people gave him the nickname 'information wizard'. He answered the phone calls from village cadres and poor households, hundreds of times a day. They asked all kinds of questions:

'How much alimony children give to the elderly every month? How to define it?'

'A farmer's land was expropriated last year. How to calculate his income?'

'My husband died in a car accident a month ago. I am a widow. Am I a poor family?'

'Eight of my fruit trees died the year before last, and 5 died last year. How to calculate my income?'

According to the policy, Gao Zhiwei gave answers and tried his best to persuade the other side. If he made a call for 5 minutes, more than 100 calls would be more than 500 minutes, which meant that he would answer the phone for 8 hours a day. Once he participated in a meeting, he muted it for 20 minutes. When the meeting concluded, he saw that there were 48 missed calls. My head was buzzing after a busy day. I was in a daze. I couldn't even comprehend my wife and children's words.

In order to complete this great cause, Huachuan County has made great efforts. There are 358 poor people in 197 households in Xida Village. There are 3 resident teams, 3 village cadres, 88 paired helpers and 6 village committees in the village. The total is exactly 100. They come from Bureau of Culture, Radio and Television and Tourism, the Development and Reform Bureau, the traffic police force, Huachuan No. 4 middle school, the aquatic product station, Rongxing Bank and the Chuangye township government. My God! Hundreds of elites and backbones from all walks of life gathered in this village and contributed their wisdom and money. Not to mention poverty alleviation, it is not difficult to turn Xida Village upside down.

This is the decisive will of Huachuan County.

After more than three years of hard work, up to now, the goal, measure and iron law set by Huachuan County had been achieved:

—All resident teams completed the task of poverty alleviation ahead of schedule. In May 2019, all 45 poverty-stricken villages were out of list and Huachuan County officially shook off its poverty. Now, the finishing touch of very few poverty-stricken households is accelerating their pace. In the performance evaluation of poverty alleviation in the province, Huachuan County ranked among the top of class A for three consecutive years, and won the Organizational

Innovation Award for poverty alleviation in the province in the same year.

—The two-year resident team in the village was like nails. They had been working in the village until today. There were only more than 10 members who had to be replaced because of illness, family difficulties and work. They had been away from their families for a long time, living in the countryside, visiting the poor and suffering, and fighting hard. It was conceivable that they had worked so hard.

—Generally, the leaders of the village had undergone a 'upgrade'. A large number of young, promising and righteous new officials took office, and they worked on duty every day. The phenomenon that villagers found the village officials when they worked at home had completely changed.

—Among the 253 staff, 45% have been promoted and put in an important position so far (most of them still stick to the front line of poverty alleviation). Gao Zhongliang, director of the county poverty alleviation office, a 'workaholic', was promoted to village group leader for his excellent performance and familiarity with policies. In order to fully understand the progress and achievements of China's poverty alleviation projects, I began to travel around the country in October 2019. Heilongjiang is my last stop. In terms of promoting and appointing outstanding poverty alleviation cadres, compared to other counties Huachuan County had the biggest movements and the most fulfilled commitments.

—I stayed in Huachuan for 10 days, and the public inspection and private visit from the city continued every day. (In order to strictly control the epidemic situation, there were 'check points' at the entrance of every village, and all the people had to show their identities.) 'Wherever we go, there is no one who will drop the ball.'

All this proves, 'The strong have the ability to accomplish difficult tasks.' When the Party is happy, the people are happy. Personally, I am proud and most definitely happy.

2. Humble family does not determine humble future

Huachuan County had a clear party conduct and a good public conduct. Is not considered a wealthy county, but there hasn't been any pernicious case in more than 10 years. It had been evaluated as a national level 'safe city' for 3 consecutive years, which had almost reached the degree of 'no one picks up lost things on the road and doors are unbolted at night'. The era of locking the door was gone.

Everything comes from the gene of hero, the gene of original aspiration and the gene of traditional virtue.

Yuan Yanmin, born in Hegang City, is good looking, gentle and timid. After graduating from normal school, due to the fierce competition in the talent market, she secretly made a wish: I will marry whoever can implement the authorized strength. In 2006, the state formulated relevant preferential policies to support rural education. Yanmin, 21, does not have such a high consciousness, but she believes that it is a roundabout way to achieve her goal. If she does well, she can be an authorized strength, so she signs with great enthusiasm. She won the first place in the final interview through layers of selection examination, so she came to Wanfa Village Primary School in the suburb of Jiamusi to support teaching for two years.

As soon as she entered the school, she felt extremely disappointed in the face of the clattering iron gate. There was a shabby building with three floors, full of wild grass, seven or eight old teachers with grey hair, long wooden tables and chairs in disorder, and students with unwashed faces could not sit steadily and fell down in a row. The headmaster let Yuan Yanmin be the head teacher of grade four. It was her first day to clean the classroom, but she didn't have any cleaning cloth, so she had to take her old one and turn it into pieces. After the class, the names of the students hadn't been memorized, but they were constantly changed one after another, because they were all children of rural labors. When their parents left, the children had to follow them. When she lived in a lonely dormitory at night, she often heard the screams of the owl. The school only provided lunch, for breakfast and they just had bread and instant noodles. There were no bathrooms in the dormitory, and they had to walk to the far corners of the playground. She was afraid, so she seldom drank water in the afternoon. 'People's spirit is sometimes forced out, and all these difficulties have been overcome. When I walk on the three-foot platform again and again, I think, no matter what kind of plan I have for the future, I must be responsible for these children, and can't miss their future.'

Gradually, because of the progress of students, she understood the happiness of teachers; because of the innocence and simplicity of students, she fell in love with these children. Her working spirit was highly praised by the school, colleagues and students' parents, from which she saw her own life value and meaning. Two years of support teaching time was coming, and her students were about to enter grade six. Somehow, the news of her departure spread among her students. When she entered the classroom that day, all the students in the class stood up as usual. She asked them to sit down, but all the children stood still, with tears streaming down. Yuan asked them what happened. The children were all talking about, 'We heard that you're leaving, but we don't want you to go. We won't sit down until you promise us you won't leave.'

Xiao Yuan didn't expect that her students would miss her so much. She also shed tears. She explained: 'this is a national regulation, and the period of supporting education can only be two years.' but she did not further explain: during the period of supporting education, the country paid 600 yuan a month. After the expiration, she had to leave to find another way out. However, the children's tears and calls deeply moved her. She didn't want to leave the children. So, she thought hard about it. She decided to stay for another year, hoping to help students in the key year before graduating from primary school.

Yuan Yanmin had no money for a whole year. She didn't tell Hegang's parents, worried that her parents would miss her and affect her determination. As usual, her parents gave her a monthly subsistence allowance, but she didn't eat enough, had to change three meals into two or one, and eat some cucumbers and tomatoes in the evening. Her colleagues wanted to support her, but Xiao Yuan resolutely refused and lied that her parents had sent enough money. She has lost more than 10 kilograms this year. Finally, the students graduated from primary school. At the graduation ceremony, students' parents heard that Miss. Yuan had no income for a whole year. They rushed up and surrounded Xiao Yuan, and put money on her pocket. Some gave her 100 rmb, some handed her 5o rmb. At this moment, she is deeply aware that teaching is the best profession in the world. All dedication is worth it for love, children and the future. After that, Xiao Yuan returned all the money to students' parents through the school. The next year, she was admitted to the Central School of Hengtoushan Town, Huachuan County as a head teacher with excellent results. This time, she has an authorized strength. Xiao Yuan is very happy: her personal life has a clear direction in the future. She can give all her love to rural children!

Love is the foundation of all undertakings.

—Xiaoda was a silent child. One day when she checked he homework in class, she found that she hadn't finished any question. She was very angry and asked him why? She lowered her head and asked him 3 times, but he still didn't say anything. She was angry and shouted, 'Why don't you answer the teacher's question?' he suddenly raised her head and shouted, 'Herd cattle!' Yuan Yanmin was shocked and felt a dull pain in her heart. The child was forced to give up study because of life. After that, she learned that his parents had rented hundreds of acres of land far away and couldn't go home for a long time. His grandfather raised a few bulls at home. Because it was uncomfortable for him to walk, he often asked the boy who came back from school to herd cattle. When the bulls were full, it was already dark. Yuan Yanmin went to persuade Xiaoda's parents several times and expected them to take turns to go home to take care of Xiaoda and give more love to their child. Xiaoda's parents accepted Ms. Yuan's advice. Since then, Xiaoda has been cheerful and lively, and his academic performance has improved significantly.

—Wenqiu, the daughter of migrant workers, is very lonely. Her parents have been working in Shenzhen and fostering her to local relatives. Yuan called them many times, hoping that they can give little Wenqiu more love. Her parents are annoyed. They said that we were very busy working. As a teacher, you should care more about our child. Then, they don't even answer the phone. Once I reviewed the students' composition 'What is happiness?' some children wrote 'happiness is 100 points' and some wrote 'happiness is a new dress'. Seeing little Wenqiu's composition, Yuan began to cry. Late at night, she immediately called Wenqiu's parents and said, please listen to your daughter's diary, 'What is happiness?' Happiness is when a family gets together! I look forward that my parents' can return every day. I dream about them, but I don't remember what they look like...' There was no sound on the phone, and then cry. Two days later, Wenqiu's parents came to school and told Yuan Yanmin that they decided to come back to work and never leave their daughter again. Xiao Wenqiu liked to laugh and won the 'Model student' when she graduated. In rural schools, there were many left behind children, single parent children and students returning to school. Yuan Yanmin comforted many children and families with her warm heart.

—Jiahua, a boy, used to be very active in the class and have excellent grades. But after the mid-term exam, scores dropped sharply and people became silent.

Xiaoyuan had a heart-to-heart talk with him about his declined grades. Jiahua said nothing but shed tears. After getting information, I learned that Jiahua's father was depressed after being laid off and gradually became an 'alcoholic'. When he was drunk, he either beat his wife or scolded his children. A few months ago, Jiahua's mother finally couldn't stand it. She ran back to her mother's house and insisted on divorce. The family is on the verge of separation, and nobody is looking out for the boy, of course he will feel somewhat fragile. Yuan Yanmin found an opportunity to invite Jiahua's father to school. From the change of Jiahua, she spent the whole afternoon trying to persuade her father. He said in teary eyes that he would change and stop drinking from now on. But the tall man was proud, so he felt embarrassed to take the initiative to pick up his wide. After work the next day, Xiaoyuan accompanied Jiahua's father to his wife's house and asked him to apologize to his wife and make a promise. In this way, the couple made up as before. After the autumn harvest, the couple drove a tricycle to school to pick up their children. Seeing this sweet moment, Xiaoyuan was also deeply warm. A year later, Jiahua was admitted to Huachuan No. 1 middle school with excellent results.

Guo Guangfu, Secretary of the county Party committee, went to Hengtoushan Town Central School for investigation. When he heard Yuan's story, he shed tears and personally invited her to deliver a speech at the county education conference. He said that in the 'Three Guarantees' for poverty alleviation, there is a promise about education. Go ahead and encourage everyone. When Yuan Yanmin stepped onto the podium to speak, the audience burst into tears and thunderous applause. The Ministry of Education said that teachers in special positions are the 'blood changing generation' of rural education. She has been rated as an excellent representative among 750,000 teachers in special position in China for several consecutive years. She has participated in the national lecture tour twice. She is the only candidate in Heilongjiang Province and has been warmly received by General Secretary Xi.

Liu Ziyu, black suit and white shirt, he looked like an important person. He was born in Zhujia Village, Huachuan County in 1985. After graduating from university, he opened a cold drink shop and western restaurant in the county. Hipsters and couples flocked to his stores. He became the youngest well-known successful person in the county. In the spring of 2014, he suddenly received a call from the town leader, saying that Zhujia Village should be changed the term of the office. We expect you to go back to the village and take up responsibility, Liu Ziyu was startled and said seven or eight 'no'. First of all, his two stores are very popular. They make a lot of money every day, they could afford to sit still and do nothing. (Chinese parable, it refers to consumption rather than production, even if there is a mountain of wealth). Don't worry too much. Second, the Zhu village was his home. He well knew that the village leaders were weak and the economy was extremely backward. The village was heavily in debt, and even the house of the village commissar was mortgage to private people. The sanitary condition is very poor, even the taxis in the county don't want to drive there. A large number of villagers complained, and one year they surrounded the county government for two days, which became a mass event shaking the whole province. County and town cadres were surrounded and scolded when they went to work, so they had to hide. They knew it was going to be hard, but they jumped in anyway. Cadres call him every day to persuade, and Liu Ziyu answers 'no' every day. One day when he came home and mentioned it, his father said, 'it's all about the villagers. You can do it. My only request is that you do it to the best of your ability.'

Liu Ziyu understood, but he was still very worried, so he said to the leader of town 'let me try for half a year first. If you don't do well, you can choose another wise man immediately.' The superior was worried and gave him the name of 'Acting Secretary of the village Party committee'. If he is as good as he sounded, then let's see what he can do. They didn't expect that he quarrel with the villagers on his third day in office. That day, he accompanied the leaders of the town to visit the village. There were some lazy villagers sitting by the side of the road. They said, boy, you want to come to the wrong place for undeserved reputation. Everyone in this place is self-centered. What can you do? It is waste of time!

In the face of the leaders of the town, these words were so insulting. Liu Ziyu was upset and said uncles, I had planned to work for half a year. After listening to you, I plan to stay and work for three years instead. Let's see if Zhujia Village can change by then.

There are thousands of difficulties in the world. The hardest thing to overcome is your fear that stops you from starting it.

In the first step, Liu Ziyu took 30,000 yuan from his own pocket to repay the electricity bill, turned on the tap water which is cut off for more than a year, and started the drainage pump in the low-lying lands. .

Second, the core issue of collective petition in Zhujia Village is that most villagers believe that the former village cadres concealed the amount of cultivated land and regarded it as their own cultivated land. Liu Ziyu was determined to find out the truth. He invited the cadres in relevant departments of the county, all the officials of the town, the representatives of the villagers and the leaders of the petition to participate in the investigation. They were divided into three groups to make a comprehensive measurement, and they wouldn't miss the edges and corners of fields. The measurement result was exactly the same as the record! Thousands of villagers suddenly realized. They had been deceived by those petition leaders for petitioning these years!

The third step was to change the harsh environment of the Zhu's village. Liu Ziyu called on all the villagers by loudspeaker to clean up the toilet and garbage around the houses. No one moved. Liu Ziyu walked out with three village cadres, rolled up their trousers, jumped into the road ditch with bare feet, dug out mud and garbage with shovels, and threw them out on four-wheel vehicle until it was dark. There were still four people on the second and the third day. When they arrived at a villager's house, the middle-aged men sat in front of the gate of the courtyard, smoking, and remained motionless. Not long after, an old Party member of more than 70 years old came out leant on a stick and roared at his son, 'you bastard, do you have any conscience? The Secretary has swept ground in front of the door. Haven't you seen it?' This was the first one to come out to clean, followed by more than 10 old party members, dozens of Party members and their relatives, and then hundreds of families. Every morning, the loudspeaker didn't ring. For more than half a month, the whole village's garbage, bathroom, courtyard, and road were clean. Everyone felt fresh and comfortable!

The fourth step is to build a beautiful countryside. The engineering design, government investment, materials and greening seedlings are all ready, and Secretary Guo Guangfu came to supervise. The villagers of the Zhu has a reputation of complaining about everything. When a couple fight, they will announce it to the village committee. Every little thing was reported to the county government. Guo Guangfu asked Liu Ziyu 3 times: Will you promise that no one will file a complaint? The villagers can volunteer to work? The whole village is well funded (100 yuan for each adult villager)? Liu Ziyu said, I guarantee! Finally, the whole village agreed to work together. 'Dirty bathrooms' has become 'Dance halls' for girls with high heels. The grass stacks have become green belts, and the mud houses have become large tile houses.

Fifth, there are 49 people in 25 poor households in the village. In 2017, Liu Ziyu got rid of poverty by developing courtyard economy, industrial economy and vocational training, and became one of the first batch of advanced Villages in the county. In the past, the villagers did not care about the ponding of their cultivated land. It seems that the remote Hainan Island was flooded, so they are waiting for the government's rescue. In 2019, Zhujia Village will suffer from serious waterlogging again, and the pump house needs to be drained day and night, resulting in huge fuel consumption. That morning, Liu Ziyu went to the village committee to work. When he came to the square, he was stunned. Hundreds of plastic barrels are everywhere in the square. The barrel is full of diesel. The family name is written on the bucket. All the villagers made voluntary contributions. At that moment, he burst into tears.

The style of the whole village has changed, and corrected. He worked hard and completed his three-year contract. 'Complaint village' became an advanced village, but his own western restaurant in the county had to shut down. His wife asked him to leave his post, but the villagers wanted him to stay. A sick old man in his 70s told the assessment team, 'Anyway, before I die, secretary Liu must continue his work.'

Since Liu Ziyu worked, the Party branch has become the most respected and trusted leadership core of the whole village, and Zhujia Village has become the banner of the whole county.

Similarly, Lengyun Village, led by Fu Hong, deputy secretary of the Youth League Committee stationed in the village and Deputy Secretary of the county Party committee, was once a 'village in the city' and came to the village with an infant in her arms, now she has led the whole county to the red base for revolutionary education. Poor families left behind poverty one after another. The village history hall and the deeds of martyrs are arranged along the street. Their aerobics performance team is very famous in the whole county.

3. Let the red star and the red flag illuminate the whole county

Susu Village has a great reputation. It was known as a weak and lazy village, a poor village and a trouble village in Huachuan city. The village branches had been vacant for a long time, and the people were full of resentment. There were a lot of debt disputes, land disputes, and social disputes. People often saw people with bloodshot eyes, and they were like 'deep grudges'. They often swung their shovels, which made their faces full of blood and turmoil.

On May 19, 2017, Lv Weibin, leader and first Secretary of the village working group, led the team members to the village. He is the deputy manager of the provincial agricultural development bank. He is very thin, nearly 60 years old, with half white hair, elegant behavior, and his smile seems to be his only expression. On the first day of entering the village, the iron lock on the door of the village committee greeted him, on the second day, the sad face of the village cadres greeted him, and on the third day, the sparse number of party members greeted him. It was not until Lao Lv in good faith went door to door that he to convened most of the party members. On June 30, Lao Lv invited all 39 party members to the village. A bright red party flag hung on the wall. Everyone were given a party constitution, an oath and a party emblem, and then stood in order. He led them to reexamine his pledge to join the party. The eyes of some old party members were wet, and the blood of many young Party members was stirred. Lao Lv was also very excited and his voice trembled. He said, 'Lengyun joined the party with this oath. Shouldn't we take the road she didn't finish?' Everyone was silent and everyone was reflecting.

Soon, Lao Lv creatively carried out the selection of 'ten-star party members': hang the Party member's name cards at home, wear the party emblem on his chest, divide the Party member's work and obligations into 10 items of 'learning demonstration', 'organizational discipline', 'observing discipline and law', and 'taking the lead in poverty alleviation', each of which was awarded a red star and announced. The central street of the village is called 'Party member Street'. Party members are responsible for poverty alleviation, health, mediation and ideological work. The members that received many red stars had stars in their eyes that they felt good about their standing and walk with positive steps – are they still called party members when they deviate from the direction and not decent. Needless to say, even if the villagers stare politely and smiling, they will feel a little ashamed.

But six months later, great changes have taken place in Susu Village. Targeted poverty alleviation was carried out in an orderly manner and the environment was clean. If there was a small quarrel between husband and wife, father and son, and several nearby party members will come to solve it majestically.

After listening to Lao Lv's entrepreneurial experience, Guo Guangfu immediately brought several scholars to sum up the experience. Seeing that this village has serious problems that are difficult to solve, Lao Lv's greatly impacted this village, turning mud into gold. He was very excited and inspired, said that the 'Ten Star selection' has inspired party members. To mobilize the work of Party branches, we should also carry out the 'The Ten Star' selection format, that is, the work of Party branches should be divided into five items: 'grass-roots party construction', 'beautiful countryside' and 'collective economy'. Each item should be done well, and a small red flag should be issued. He also made a decision on the spot, saying that hard-working people can't do hard work in vain, and good people can't do good deeds in vain. Reward!

In 2018, 105 administrative villages in the county vigorously carried out the activity of 'winning flags and stars'. The Party branch worked hard to become strong, Party members are scrambling, , red flags are flying, and red stars are flashing on the bulletin boards of each village. At the end of the year, the county Party committee took out 1.94 million yuan to reward the advanced in 'winning flags and stars'. The party members with the best performance and the strongest dedication will receive a bonus of nearly 10,000 yuan!

The Party has always been the mainstay of realizing the great 'Chinese dream'. The activity of 'The Ten Star' has become a powerful driving force for Huachuan County to successfully complete the great cause of poverty alleviation. Heilongjiang has a vast territory, rich resources, developed transportation and huge grain output. Basic life is not a problem. 90% of poor families are poor due to disease and disability. Therefore, healthy poverty alleviation has become the top priority of the province. Today, Huachuan County has fully implemented the 'Three Guarantees' of housing, medical treatment and education:

—The grass, mud, dangerous and poor houses of 3396 households have been renovated, the village roads have been hardened, and there is a cultural square in the village.

The severe cretin patient of Jixiang Village, nicknamed "stunning beauty"

—The itinerant medical team signs one-to-one insurance, file and card contracts with poor households. Each household is equipped with a 'love medicine box' and checked every two months. There are family doctors for minor diseases and green channels for serious diseases. The village clinic is responsible for all formalities and reimbursement. So far, the medical expenditure of poor families has been reduced by nearly 30 million yuan.

—None of the rural children in the nine-year compulsory education dropped out of school.

—By developing industries, arranging employment and absorbing social forces to help the poor families, the income of poor households will increase by 4,216 yuan in 2019.

—Water quality inspection is organized twice a year, and rural residents in the county meet the water use standard

Huachuan in the new era is like a plow. The Steel plow was shining, bravely bringing changes to the thousand-year poverty, once scattered with blood and dead branches now renewed and great. The warm 'Chinese Dream' embraced every village, every wisp of smoke and every dream.

The Party is the ploughman!

II 'The number one fool in the world'

There is such a village in Heilongjiang. For more than half a century, the former village Party Secretary has worked for 28 years, and the current village Party Secretary has worked for 22 years. They have created two great changes, which may be the only change in the country. Coincidentally, from the early stage of reform to the new period, I came to this village twice – 'fool's village'.

1. Under the Devil's Wings

On the fifteenth day of the first month, the moon was covered with dark clouds, the cold wind roared, and the crowded snowflakes seemed to freeze at night. A ghostly team walked on the snow with torches in hand, making terrifying noises.

The captain is Chen village party secretary, with a white beard and a rotten cotton-padded jacket. He knocked on the gong and shouted, 'God, show me mercy!' hundreds of ragged villagers behind him looked timid and shouted, 'let the Dragon go!' They held a can of kerosene mixed with rice bran and scattered rice bran along the village road. After walking a mile away, Chen village party secretary shouted, 'light the streetlamp and let the Dragon go!' the man who was holding the torch quickly lit a long pile of chaff. Soon, a hundreds of metres long fire dragon rose on the road. The villagers crawled on the ground and kowtowed towards the distance.

Almost every year, at midnight on January 15, Jixian Brigade (Village) of Huachuan County secretly holds the activity of 'let the Dragon go'. When the leaders of the commune knew about it, they pretended to criticize it. In fact, not taking it seriously. They knew that Chen village party secretary would do the same thing because God made the village crazy. Chen said there was nothing he could do.

Jixian Village is not so much a place to raise people as a place to bury people. In 1938, in order to prevent the activities of the guerrillas of the Anti-Japanese, the Japanese forced these villages to merge. The Japanese started fires that destroyed all the villages in four fields. They used bayonets and barbed wire to surround a group of ordinary people in the wasteland originally known as 'Dongba Weizi'. People slept in the cellar of the hut for many years. After liberation, it was renamed Jixian Village. The villagers plough in spring and harvest in autumn, not taking the sickness seriously. In the late 1950s, the villagers found a strange thing in the village: being poor is not a big deal, but how can the women in our village gives birth to some disabled children? How do men and women grow up with thick necks?

Old Zhang's family has five children, either disabled or deaf mute. Lao Li, a one-eyed carpenter, once survived by crawling out of the death pit made by the Japanese invaders. At the age of 50, his mute wife gave birth to a son. Lao Li said happily, 'The enemy couldn't bury me, and now I have a son at fifty. My son was born at noon on the fifth day of May in the year of Jiawu (Every 60 years on the

Lunar Calendar). Even the emperor (the supposed son of the dragon) was not as lucky as me!' so he named his son Baoyu (Precious Jade). Two years later, he found out that his son was a fool who could only cry. Not just the Li or Zhang family. With bitter wind and rain, cold moon and cold star, mysterious and terrible fate strangled Jixian Village, and Jixian brigade became a notorious village of fools far and near. There was a ballad spreading far and wide: 'Fools walk all over the village, the deaf and dumb gesticulate, everyone has a big neck, and his lateral lobe is swollen like a wicker pitcher.' According to statistics in 1978, there were 1313 people in 255 households in the village, 859 patients afflicted with endemic goiter and 150 patients with cretinism (dementia). The data present a bloody, tragic and terrible scene, forming a disordered 'black soil tribe'. When I came to the village, I saw an unmarried girl naked in the pigsty, the disabled boy laughing and eating the dead chicken, and a child of seven or eight years old crawling around on the ground. Neither could girls be married off, nor could boys marry wives. Poverty, stupidity, tears and death grow rampant on this land. The old secretary found a geomancer who said that there was a dragon buried at the entrance of Jixian brigade village. All this is made by the demon. It must be fed with bran on the 15th day of the first month so that it would go away. After this ceremony, the children were still born with disabilities. It was then said that there was a big stone like a monkey in the east of the village, which destroyed the Fengshui of the village. The old party secretary had the monkey-shaped stone blown up in a rage, but children were still born dumb. During the Spring Festival, the relatives of villagers were afraid to visit them, because they believed that the village was cursed. Fool's village had become an 'isolated island' that no one dared to go.

In 1970, the old secretary abandoned the village. The group of idiots had no head and was in a mess.

The commune leaders were in a hurry to select someone to replace the secretary. The Secretary said, look at the junior high school student Xu Zhenzhong. He is sane. Let's choose him. The news spread, and Xu Zhenzhong decided to run away. Early in the morning, he put on a luggage roll, two corn cakes and a cotton-padded jacket, sat on the noisy rural passengers and went straight from the county to Jiamusi railway station. On the opposite side of the train station street, there was a magnificent yellow building, known as 'the headquarters of Heilongjiang production and construction regiment'. One and a half years later, I went from an independent regiment to (Jiayin farm) the Secretary office. If it was a coincidence, I would have seen a thin and black young farmer was caught by two militiamen with red armbands. This guy was Xu Zhenzhong. His scheming had already been calculated by the Secretary of the commune. He wanted to escape but no matter how powerful he was, he couldn't leave.

Depressed, Xu Zhenzhong was 'escorted' back to the village. The Secretary of the commune had been waiting there for a long time. He tried his best to persuade Xu Zhenzhong to take over the responsibility of the Secretary of the commune, but Xu Zhenzhong didn't answer. He was impatient and upset, he blurted out, 'Sir, you know my situation. I am a fool and will always be a fool. You are asking me to do the devil's work – he's asked you to collect me!' The secretary was furious and pounded the table. 'If you dare to say that the Secretary of the commune is the devil, do dare you say that?' It was during the period of the 'the Cultural Revolution', and the 'traitor' will be arrested. But Xu Zhenzhong craned his neck and said, 'Send me to jail as soon as possible. I don't want to be scolded by the members and beaten by idiots in the village. 'For the whole afternoon, the secretary had ordered him braised pork with vermicelli, but when it came to midnight, he was still a stubborn stone. The secretary finally got angry. 'We're trying to save you face and give you some grace? Little bastard, stand up!' he took out a little red notebook from his pocket of his shirt and raised it to ask, 'What's this?' Xu Zhenzhong stood straight and said, 'Party Constitution'. The secretary said, 'according to the Party Constitution, individuals obeys the organization and you can go to work tomorrow.' Then the door slammed and he was left there alone. In the boundless night, several disabled shrill cries came from a distance.

Xu Zhenzhong had a hard life. His father was nicknamed 'Mr. Xu stubbornness', and he was a famous brave man in the village. In the autumn of 1946, the northeast land was in turmoil of war. Local bandits took the opportunity to burn, kill and plunder, and committed all manners of crime. The Dongbaweizi Village (Jixian Village). A young woman, who had been a liaison woman of the Northeast United Resistance Army, was kidnapped by a local bandit. He said that she would kill the hostage if her family didn't pay 100 dollars. The whole family was crying. Mr. Xu said stubbornly, 'I'll go get her.' Then he took his hand made gun and walked away with fury. When they found Li on the mountain, the two disagreed so Xu Lao stubborn pretended to turn back, but suddenly took out the gun and shot off Li Dazi's ear. Several gangsters jumped up, stabbed Xu Dazi through a blood hole and dragged him to the ground of Gaoliang. Two months later, the land reform team of the Communist Party of China destroyed Li. The villagers dug out the body of old Xu stubborn with five holes in his head. This year, Xu Zhenzhong is 3 years old. His mother couldn't support it, so she had to lead Xu Zhenzhong to remarry in another country. But his stepfather had a hard time adapting to Xiao Zhenzhong. Three years later, he left his mother and returned to his uncle's home in Jixian Village alone. Shortly after the liberation of both sides of the Songhua River, Xu Zhenzhong went to school, but due to family difficulties, he could not afford the tuition. When he was in the second grade of junior middle school, he had to drop out of school and go home and concentrate on agriculture. Because he was born well and belonged to a farming family, he is willing to work so he joined the party three years later. In 1971, a relative in Hegang wrote that he had opened another state-owned coal mine and was recruiting workers so that Xu Zhenzhong could leave as soon as possible. Unexpectedly, at this time, the commune Secretary detained him.

Xu Zhenzhong is as passionate as his father. The commune leader named him as the brigade secretary. He understands that this is a personal honor and the trust of the organization. However, there is a large group of the deaf, mute and fool in Jixian Village. There is not enough healthy labor force. The land was planted in a mess. The output per mu (a unit of area) is one third less than that of other villages. Even if the leader is a living immortal, he still couldn't change the situation. When he got home depressed, he opened the door and sat with five or six villagers and family members around the Kang, there was a smoke fog. Old party secretary Uncle Chen immediately asked, 'Do you accept it?' Xu Zhenzhong didn't say a word. The old man sighed: 'To tell you the truth, I recommend you to be the brigade secretary of the commune. In recent years, the fool village seems to be cursed by ghosts and gods, the monkey stone is blown up and the dragon is sent away. It was useless. You are well educated, you'd better bear this burden, and the villagers are in your hands...'

Granny knocked the cigarette packet on the side of bed and said, 'Your father has been a hero all his life. In the end, he broke into the bandit occupation alone and let the bandits pierce him to death in the farmland. Don't be a coward.'

His wife Ning Guizhen is a graduate of Jiamusi normal school. In her early years, she worked as a substitute teacher in primary school in the commune for several years. She said, 'You live in your uncle's house since childhood.' In the time of suffering, the villagers lend a helping hand to help him.

Xu Zhenzhong said in a dull voice, 'Most of the villages are fools. How do we do it?'

His wife said, 'I think you must first find out the root cause of the disease. Several villages within a radius of dozens of miles are very normal. We gather all the children in Jixian Village. I don't believe in feudal superstition, but if the root cause of the disease isn't fixed, then everything will be useless.'

That night, the commune secretary made Xu Zhenzhong stay up all night confused. His wife is highly educated. A word woke him up: Yes! First check the root cause. The root cause no longer exists, everything else will be easy.

2. Pegs bloom

Xu Zhenzhong, 28, took office. During the Spring Festival, Xu's junior high school mate working in other villages went home to visit their relatives and took Xu Zhenzhong to drink. After drinking many rounds of wine, a guy drank too much and said, 'Zhenzhong, no man is wise at all times. When you become the fool leader of the fool's village, you are the silliest fool in the world! If you can govern the fool's village, I'll stand upside down around the county and see if I can stand upside down for you now!' He stood upside down on the ground for less than half a circle, then he fell down with a bang. Xu Zhenzhong and his classmates burst into laughter. Xu Zhenzhong said, 'You can't even walk a full circle, looks like you can be a half fool in our fool's village!'

After that, whenever he went to a meeting in the commune or county, whether 'learning from Dazhai' or 'learning from Daqing', Xu Zhenzhong didn't care what others thought, when he met someone who was educated, he would ask, 'comrade, what reason can make a man have big and thick neck or give birth to a child who is a deaf or mute or fool?' The other party was stunned, and no one could answer. He then asked the health department of the county government and the county hospital again. They either can't answer or ignore him. China was busy with the 'Cultural Revolution' that month. Everyone was angry and timid. It's better to save trouble. Who is in the mood to take care of fools? Six months later, Xu Zhenzhong finally ran into an enthusiastic person – Zhou Yufu who works in the county epidemic prevention station. He said: 'people from different places have different physical qualities and even their ways of thinking are different. The surrounding villages are all right. Only your village has this disease. When I look at the test, some important qualities are either missing or too many.' Xu Zhenzhong was stunned and ran away. The next day, he took a bottle of well water from the village and rushed to Jiamusi. He asked around and found the endemic disease prevention and control center, and paid someone to help detect it. Two hours later, an old man in a white coat took out the test form. He asked Xu Zhenzhong to sit down and patiently explained to him that the water in your village was seriously iodine deficient. Every liter of normal drinking water should contain 10–200 micrograms of iodine. If it is less than 5 micrograms, the people who drink water everyday will suffer from endemic goiter, that is, his neck is large and thick. Less than 1 microgram will suffer from cretinism, that is, dementia or deafness, bone deformation, difficulty walking and loss of labor ability completely. The water in your village contains less than 1 microgram of iodine per liter, and even livestock are not suitable for drinking.

My god! Xu Zhenzhong suddenly realized. The mystery of decades has finally been solved: no wonder many old residents in Jixian Village have thick neck in the first generation, but their intelligence is still normal; to the second and third generations, they became disabled and deaf-mute, because iodine deficiency is becoming more and more serious. He didn't become like this because he lived in other places with his remarried mother for several years when he was young, and stayed in the commune for two years when he was in middle school, so he escaped. He stared at the half bottle of yellow water left in the bottle. It turned out that it was the evil created by this thing. Decades of drinking this water made everyone fools.

This is not water, it's death water!

Xu Zhenzhong asked what to do? Zhou Yufu said, first, dig a deep well; second, move. It was impossible to move thousands of people, and there was no place to move. There was only one way out: dig a deep well. But where to get money to drill the well?

Since then, Xu Zhenzhong has written dozens of hundreds of rescue reports on carbon paper. His fingers were dyed blue. Then spread the rescue reports from Huachuan County to Jiamusi, from the provincial capital Harbin to Zhongnanhai. The village couldn't afford eight-cents stamps, so he had to use his own money. Every time Xu Zhenzhong went to a county or city to attend meeting, he would stop the leader and hand him a copy. After the meeting, he stayed behind and chatted with the leader. Year after year, there were many reports sent out and the shoes were worn out one by one. The little fools were born into the world one after another, without any response. In the era of the 'the Cultural Revolution', people fell into panic. Who is in the mood to do business? All the answers are compassionate. The final conclusion is: 'no money'. The leader of the 'rebel' origin became upset and asked him to go back and 'seize the revolution'. Xu Zhenzhong said, 'We are a group of fools. Who will stand up and launch revolution?'

In 1975, a blue sky finally appeared in Huachuan County shrouded in dark clouds. Under extremely difficult conditions, the County Water Conservancy Bureau allocated 9,000 yuan to dig wells in Jixian Village. For four years, they finally saw hope! The drilling team invited by the Water Conservancy Bureau drove into the village with equipment and hulls. Villagers gathered around the construction site to watch how the towering derrick raised transparent hope and listen to how the rumbling rig called a sweet spring. The drilling rig chugged, 30m, 50m and 70m...

'Secretary Xu, hurry up and transfer the money. You have to buy materials immediately...'

'Don't worry. 9,000 yuan will arrive soon.'

'My God!' the drilling captain patted his thigh, 'this money is not enough for drilling. We have to go down the pipeline, install a water pump and build a water tower. Stop drilling quickly!'

In an instant, the whole village was silent, and Xu Zhenzhong rooted to the ground. The drill stopped, just as his breath stopped. He took the captain's sleeve and said, 'This is not drilling, this is saving lives!'

The captain said, 'I'm not responsible for saving lives. I just dig wells!'

Xu Zhenzhong was so angry that he waved his hand and shouted at the villagers, 'Go! Release all the idiots of your family!' During the days the drilling team was in the village, he was afraid of losing face in front of the young men from the city. He repeatedly told the villagers not to let their children go out of their houses. At this moment, He decided to show all the suffering of fool village to the drilling team!

The villagers came out one after another, followed by their own big and small idiots. Some were naked, some were twisting, and some were shouting and playing... This is most miserable scene in the world!

The drilling crew was shocked. They had never seen such an abnormal life and it is a human tragedy!

The captain was shocked. 'Okay, just 9,000.' he said in a hoarse voice, 'we are responsible for digging the well and running the pipe down. Let's forget the money they owe us this time, but you still have to ask for money to buy a water pump and build a water tower.' The pipe was pulled down and the drilling team was removed. What Xu Zhenzhong could do was to insert a wooden stake into the pipe mouth. In order to prevent the pipe from being blocked, he fetched a small pile of soil and buried the wooden stake. At night, he sat beside the pile for a long time, as if he was guarding a tomb of his own flesh and blood, with endless sadness in his heart.

The way out of the village is under this stake. He has to run, appeal and ask for money! Immortal black earth casts immortal soul. He ran for three years, shouted for three years, and didn't respond. A deep-water pump configured by relevant provincial departments for Jixian Village was also approved by the county leaders and sent to the epidemic prevention station.

In the spring of 1978, a great idea of changing China and shaking the world was quietly brewing in Zhongnanhai. It was a very hot day, a military plane broke through the clouds and landed at the airport of Jiamusi City, Heilongjiang Province. The hatch opened and General Li Desheng of the old red army hurried down the gangway ladder. At that time, Li Desheng was a member of the Standing Committee of the Political Bureau of the CPC Central Committee and commander of the Shenyang Military Region. He just attended a militia working meeting in Mudanjiang City and turned to Jiamusi to stay. What on earth is the general going to do? Why does he frown and look cold? All the local party, government and military dignitaries who came to meet them were speculating nervously. The general walked into the waiting hall and immediately called an emergency meeting. He took a piece of material and said seriously, 'I came here to settle down for one of your fool village. As you know, I am also the leader of the leading group for the prevention and control of northern endemic diseases of the CPC Central Committee. I invited you today. I want to ask, do you know that there is a Jixian Village in Huachuan County, where endemic diseases are very serious?'

No reply, silence.

'Comrades, you are all local governors!' The general was angry, If the people are in difficulty. Who they can we find? They can only find you. If a family has a patient who is suffering from an endemic disease, if two or more than three people can't work, how will this family live? Our revolution was raised by the common people with millet, if we don't care about the people's suffering, how can we be called the Party? We have to hurry up to solve this problem and report the result to me. A month later, on August 28, 1978, the party sent a team of endemic disease prevention and treatment to Jixian Village and checked every house. That night, the whole village gathered together and held the 'preceptor's meeting of delivering pestilence'. The leader of the team went to the platform and the first sentence was, 'villagers, we are late!' he cried. Xu Zhenzhong cried. Everyone on and off the stage cried.

On September 8, 1979, after eight years of running and shouting by Xu Zhenzhong, the deep well in Jixian Village was finally built. A water tower with a height of 10 metres and a water storage capacity of 42 tons is standing, decorated with red and green. It is engraved with two lines of bright red characters proposed by Xu Zhenzhong: 'With the fresh water the Party sent, the withered tress came back to life in the sick village. In the laughter of the villagers, as soon as Xu Zhenzhong pressed the switch, 40 water taps in the whole village flowed out of water. This is a sweet spring, bringing spirituality to life and hope to the earth! All the men, women and children in the village laugh, cry, shout, jump and drink. Even fools are infected and run around. Since then, September 8 has become the annual water improvement festival in Jixian Village.

The wood stake finally burst into brilliant spray. In the absurd history, there is a shining hope.

It never occurred to Xu Zhenzhong that he and the fools' village had made a great contribution to the people of the country. Because of the miserable lesson of the village, later the relevant department of the state parliament made a rule that all the salt entering the market must be added with a certain amount of iodine.

3. 'God's mistake.'

Now that the water is safe, but what about the life of 79 children? You can't leave them sit around and wait to die. They can't grow up normally, go to school or support themselves, which has become a heavy burden on their families and a heavy pressure on Jixian Village. One day, Xu Zhenzhong heard that there was 'mentally retarded education' abroad. He was moved. The village can run an intellectual education class. On the one hand, the county can send a medical team to treat these disabled children. On the other hand, teachers can teach them to read and learn some self-reliance skills. The appearance of Jixian Village will be greatly improved. Xu Zhenzhong was very excited. He hired teachers everywhere in and out of the village, but the result could be imagined: every door was slammed in his face.

There was no way out. He thought of his wife Ning Guizhen. Ning Guizhen's family immigrated from another place, she graduated from Jiamusi normal school. She could have stayed in the city to work, but because her brother died and her sister married again, her mother forced her only sweetheart to return to the village primary school as a teacher. At that time, Guizhen's family had half a thatched cottage idled. As an orphan, Xu Zhenzhong grew up. It was inconvenient to live at her uncle's house for many years. There was no boy in Guizhen's family. Seeing that Xu Zhenzhong was honest, hardworking and educated, her mother made her own decision to let Xu Zhenzhong be a 'live-in son-in-law'. This is a 'win-win' choice: Ning's family has added a strong labor force, and Xu Zhenzhong has married a good wife. Ning Guizhen was very delicate when she was young. She tossed her braids around. She said, 'OK, just you, I don't need to think any longer, you are who I want to be with.' Xu Zhenzhong said, 'White Swan, I also don't need to hesitate any longer.' After the Cultural Revolution, the primary schools in the village were looted, and Ning Guizhen became a housewife. Xu Zhenzhong thought about her and decided to invite her to come back to run an education class. But when she thought of those children with muddy faces and full of shit,

Guizhen was afraid and didn't want to do so. Xu Zhenzhong said: 'In fact, I don't want you to suffer, but which of those disabled children is not their parents' blood and flesh? If we had a child like this, would you strangle them to death? You support me to take over the burden of the brigade secretary. I just have to do well! Even if you don't feel good about this, you have to help me out this time.'

Ning Guizhen was a reasonable person. In the autumn of 1979, she attended the parenting class for the idiot children. Since it was set up, it must be the first one in the countryside. Every morning, parents dragged disabled children here one by one. The youngest one was 9 years old, and the oldest one was 17 years old. Each of them had a runny nose and tattered clothes. They couldn't sit still for 3 minutes and rolled into a ball from time to time. Sometimes they peed, sometimes pulled the pencil into their legs and laughed. They couldn't help but tear their trousers apart. Showing his animal instinct to girls... A few days later, a young man invited from the outside village threw up his work and quit. Guizhen can't deal with so many little fools alone! Xu Zhenzhong made up his mind and asked her daughter Xiaofeng, who taught in the village primary school, to help her mother. In order for mentally retarded children to remember a word or an action, they must repeat it thousands of times. In order to make them remember the location of the toilet outside the door, the mother and daughter dragged them in toilet hundreds of times, helped them untie their belts, wiped their hips their pants. Later, the two women vomited in the corner, hoping to spit out their internal organs. They were taught to count numbers, the two women even talked, wrote and taught hundreds or thousands of times. Their mouth parched and tongue scorched and they were too tired to lift their arms. At the same time, they must comb children's hair, wash their face and take medicine three times a day. They must see them swallow the medicine with their own eyes. When winter comes, the water outside turns into ice. Mothers and daughters should be careful not to get frostbitten and mend their cotton-padded clothes and trousers – because disabled children don't know whether the weather is cold or hot...

Day after day, year after year, the two women became close members of disabled children, understood their gestures, and learned their vague language and special emotional expression. Love is a great and magical power, which can arouse the same reaction in the hearts of fools. In order to collect firewood for the education class, some disabled children don't let Mrs. Ning work. They got on top of her and which almost made her pass out. Xiaofeng went out for a meeting for two days, and the disabled children waited at the intersection for two days. When she got out of the car, the children surrounded her with cheers, and more than a dozen hands stuffed the candy they had taken for two days into her mouth...

Most people are born with intellectual disabilities like 'God's clerical mistakes'. These good children are integrated into the world before they are designed. After six years of hard work, many disabled children in the intellectual education class have changed. Among them, 28 people can recognize and write about 1,000 words and perform 4-digit addition and subtraction. They have entered ordinary primary schools and deaf-mute schools. Most of the others can take care of themselves and join the production team. According to news reports, fools' village has attracted the attention of UNESCO. One year, they sent an international expert group to investigate. When these foreigners saw a disabled child solving a one-dimensional equation mathematical problem in education class, they were very suspicious. Dr. Holtz from Australia stood up, wrote a new one-dimensional equation on the blackboard and asked the disabled child to solve the answer. The boy stared at the blackboard in amazement. Xu Zhenzhong and Ning Guizhen, the Chinese entourage present, were all sweating. Later, the boy thought, and his face showed a very angry expression. He picked up the blackboard eraser, erased the scrawled letter X written by the doctor, rewritten a letter neatly, and then glared at Dr. Yang. That is to say, why are you slow? Can't even write an X! Then he quickly came up with the right way to solve the problem. All the people present laughed. The head of the delegation said: 'Thank Ms. Ning Guizhen for correcting the 'clerical error of God' in an outstanding humanitarian spirit.' Dr. Hertz sighed: 'Jixian Village in China has created a miracle of intellectual disability education!'

The National Commendation Conference for advanced workers in special education was held, and Ning Guizhen boarded the podium in front of the sea of applause.

4. Raise up fool Village

The flood control has been completed, the cure of ignorance is in progress, and the cure of poverty should be carried out on a large scale.

In 1981, Xu Zhenzhong led the villagers to work hard. The whole village ate 300,000 kilograms of resold grain, and each work point was only 4 cents. At that time, some rural areas such as Anhui and Sichuan were vigorously promoting family contracting and land household division, but there were many disputes in political and ideological circles, and the action of Heilongjiang Province was still very slow. What can the people in Jixian Village do? Can we find a cure for poverty? Xu Zhenzhong has traveled all over the world in recent years and broadened his horizons. He told the villagers that we had been busy for a year and couldn't even afford public food. We must rely on state relief. It seems that we can't turn it over just by growing food. He suggested that an industry and a brick factory be established through loans and raising 200,000 yuan. He said that now the country is carrying out reform and opening up, and life is getting better and better. In the future, more and more people will upgrade from grass houses to brick houses, and red bricks will sell well.

The people in fool's village have never been out of the village. They work in the fields during busy season. In slack season, they squat at the foot of the wall to bask in the sun. The main reason is that everyone is afraid of losing face because of his thick neck. In addition, they are illiterate and can't understand the road signs clearly. They don't know that great changes are taking place in China. They heard that Xu Zhenzhong wants to take out a loan of 200,000 yuan. This is a mountain they can't stand! All cadres and villagers are strongly opposed. They are afraid of losing some of their surplus. Only Xu Zhenzhong himself agrees. Xu Zhenzhong forced the old branch secretary: 'Count you in! When you recommended me to be the brigade secretary, you had to support me!' The old party secretary said, 'That's only two percent.' Xu Zhenzhong said, 'If you mobilize your son and daughter to come in, I'll pull two more households in, which will be six. Don't worry, I'll sacrifice myself to the kiln if I lose the money!'

Through the 'snowball' system, the villagers are ready to give their children the money to get married, the money to repair their houses, and the money to visit relatives for the New Year's festival. After the bank loan was paid, the construction of the furnace began. Without paying service charges, the party members lead a 'free service' team.

Xu Zhenzhong devoted himself to the work in the village and left everything at home to his wife Ning Guizhen. That spring, he accompanied his superior leaders to check the situation of seedlings and found that some parts of the land has a few seedlings or grass. It was a shame! He asked angrily, 'Find out whose land this is? They are not taking this seriously. I won't give it to him next year!' The cadres next to him quickly pulled his sleeve. As soon as Xu Zhenzhong shrunk his neck, he knew that this was his own land. Another time, he came home from work in the middle of the night. He opened the door and saw a big flower pig weighing 200 kilograms arching cabbage in the garden. While chasing the pig out, he shouted to the house, 'Whose pig has come to our house for free food?' Ning Guizhen smiled and said, 'Whose pig? It's yours!'

180 days later, the magnificent 24-holes brickkiln rose from the ground, making a profit of nearly 130,000 yuan that year.

Later, Xu Zhenzhong took advantage of the situation to establish a 'fool winery'. He proclaimed the following advertising line, 'The first fool in the world. He doesn't adulterate.' 'Fools are honest and fools are handsome, Fools have Love for the world!' Because everyone knows about the fool village, coupled with good advertising, 'fool's white wine' soon became popular all over China. The economic situation of Jixian Village has improved sharply, becoming the first village in Huachuan County to 'get rid of poverty and get rich'. In 1998, Xu Zhenzhong, 55, was promoted to Deputy Secretary of the county Party committee. He wore farmland shoes and sat in the office building for a few days. In addition to attend meetings, he read documents. He's not used to it. It doesn't make sense for a farmer to not do any farm work. His feet were stinking. 10 days later, Xu Zhenzhong left without saying goodbye and returned to Jixian Village. The Secretary of the county Party committee called him many times to urge him to go back to work. Xu Zhenzhong said, you can decide. I agree with everything. There were so many calls that Xu Zhenzhong simply stopped answering.

Wang Xilin, in his early 20s, took over as secretary of the village Party committee. He announced in public: 'The old Party branch secretary led everyone to cure ignorance and poverty, which is called 'The first fool in the world.' I firmly promise that in the future, 'I won't adulterate.' The audience laughed. Wang Xilin realized that with the progress of the times, low-level maintenance development is far from meeting the aspirations of the masses. He put forward 'Three leaps in the new century' and changed into 'Three measures in the new era' after the 18th National Congress of the Communist Party of China – which keenly focuses on keeping pace with the times.

First, the fool village has a good reputation, and more and more people come to visit and study. We must build a 'beautiful home' to show to the world.

Second, vigorously promote villagers' 'entrepreneurship' – this is a bold new idea. What he means is to change the traditional image that farmers can only cultivate land, so that they can either become enterprise workers or enter the market to do business.

Third, use the business card of 'fool village' to vigorously attract investment.

The villagers objected in unison, saying that you won't let us work on the farm. What do we eat?

Wang Xilin said that you used to eat 'food' and grow whatever you want to eat. Since you have made a lot of money in business, you will eat 'business food' from now on. You can eat whatever you want!

The villagers laughed and said it was reasonable!

The leap of history is to wait for opportunities. In the past, these three measures were promoted by the village's own strength, and the progress was relatively slow. After the 18th CPC National Congress, the policy of 'Revitalizing the countryside', 'Building a beautiful countryside', 'Poverty Alleviation', 'First secretary' and village groups have come down. Millions of investment came from Heilongjiang Province, Jiamusi City and Huachuan County. Wang Xilin said happily, 'This is called 'big interests controls small interests.' The conditions are there, the only thing left is work.' He fully carried forward the glorious tradition of the old Party branch and organized the second 'free service' in the history of fool village with village cadres and Party members as the core. Broaden hardened roads, plant green belts around villages, promote enterprise restructuring, introduce photovoltaic industry, and strive to expand villagers' employment. By 2019, the per capita income of villagers will exceed 10,000 yuan. At the end of May 2020, I came to fool's village again. The 77 years old Secretary Xu Zhenzhong and the current branch secretary Wang Xilin received me. Looking around, the cement road extends in all directions, with beautiful flower beds on both sides of the road, beaded solar streetlamps, flat and open Central Square, rows of villager's new houses with pink walls and red tile... Wow, the old impression I left in that interview more than 30 years ago has disappeared!

The town leaders told me that Xu Zhenzhong, the old secretary, had worked for 28 years and solved the problem of 'cure the disease, cure the fool and cure the poor' in fool's village; Wang Xilin has worked for 22 years and basically solved the problem of 'getting rich, beautiful and strong' in the whole village. To add their time together, it would be half a century. The villagers were grateful for the two secretaries. They specially composed a couplet and wrote it on the wall of the village committee courtyard: 'Half a century to get rid of poverty, the torch passed for two generations.' Wang Xilin quickly waved and said: 'This is mainly a good basis for the old secretary's arrangement! In order to let future generations always remember Secretary Xu's contribution, we specially retained the half bungalow of Secretary Xu. However, he is still alive, and we can't do too much.' the audience laughed.

Xu Zhenzhong said: 'Now the villagers are most proud of their children!' It is reported that the central endemic disease prevention and control team tests the IQ index of primary school students in the village every few years, and the results rank first among primary schools in the county. So far, there are 70 college students, the highest number in the county. There are also three masters and three Ph.D. Many of them have become executives or think tanks of well-known large enterprises in China.

I am filled with emotion, from fool village to Jixian Village (Jixian means gathering talents). The village earned its name!

III Harbin, fire in snowflakes

1. One year in advance
In Heilongjiang Province, it was a season of ice and snow for thousands of miles. It was a day to tell stories in the countryside.

Every household opened the curtain of white frosted cotton, and the story filled the whole room!

In Harbin, the famous Central Street is a world-famous spot to visit. Every summer, it is the longest catwalk in the world. An online review said that Harbin girls are the most beautiful all over the country. Beauty cannot be idled, it must be expressed and displayed. You must come out and let the world admire you! So, looking all the way along central street, there are beautiful times and beautiful carvings and endless beautiful women, colorful and charming. When I was president of the Federation of literary and art circles in Harbin, I made a joke that painters who had not been to Harbin could only learn from Picasso and draw beautiful women into pipes and geometric figures; Writers who haven't been to Harbin can only learn from Kafka's *The Metamorphosis* and write people as insects; Poets who have never been to Harbin can only learn from Eliot to write hazy poems, everyone can't understand them, nor can they understand them.

This is the lethality of Harbin.

Harbin created the first symphony troupe, the first ballet troupe and school, the first cinema, the first brewery, the first music festival 'The Summer of Harbin', the first large generating unit, the first helicopter...

This is the creativity of Harbin.

However, Harbin didn't forget its own countryside. Looking from afar through the lofty church and towering buildings into the clouds, it was the broad and vibrant Songnen plain that the city relied on to survive. The urban area of Harbin was not very big. It was a vast countryside after passing through the white birch forest on Sun Island a few years ago. After the reform and opening up, Harbin opened its arms and merged 9 districts and 9 counties to drive them to get stronger motivation and faster development. Now the north side of the Songhua River had become a prosperous city center, university town and tourist resort with Sun Island as the center. After the 18th National Congress, the poverty relief war was fully carried out. As one of the central cities of the old industrial base, although the financial resources were limited, Harbin still invested a huge amount of money, it spared no effort to fight against the poor and achieved a decisive victory.

In 2018, Mulan County and Bayan County, two provincial-level poor counties, were out of the list. In 2019, Yanshou County, a national key poverty alleviation and development county, was listed. A total of 163 poor villages have been rid of poverty in the city. In Yanshou County, Dong Shaotao, director of the municipal Poverty Alleviation Office, told me: 'At present, only 847 of 514 families have not been lifted out of poverty. They are all in Yanshou County and are carrying out dynamic poverty alleviation. The city's poverty alleviation task has been basically completed and absolute poverty has been basically eliminated one year ahead of schedule.' I noticed that Dong Shaotao drove alone when I went to the county and village. He was like the Lone Ranger. He was visiting the county openly and secretly. He's skin is very dark, looks like a village cadre, probably no one tries to stop him.

Harbin is cold and hot, because there are flames in every snowflake. As long as you rub your head with snowflakes, you will be covered with milky 'steam'. Along the way, when I visited the village and walked into the house, I really felt the heat. This heat permeates the smoke in the village, the stove of the villagers, the green rice fields, the smiling faces of poverty alleviation cadres, poverty alleviation farmers and aunts in the square, and the Kaoliang spirit in glasses... Comrades from the Poverty Alleviation Office of Heilongjiang Province told me that the problem of 'Two not worry and Three Guarantees' (That is, to ensure that the rural poor do not worry about food or medical care). For the majority of farmers here has been basically solved. I smiled and said that this did not depend entirely on the struggle of cadres and the masses, nor was it so 'arduous'. After all, unlike Guizhou, Xinjiang, Gansu, Zhongyuan, Jiangnan and other provinces, Heilongjiang has a vast land, rich resources and fertile land, with a per capita cultivated land of more than 8 mu, ranking first in the country! As long as the policies, work and diligence are in place, the vast majority of farmers can make lots of money; their happy lives will be reflected on their sun kissed dark complexions. It is worth noting that due to objective factors such as natural and cultural environment, there are few poor families in history, most of which are poor due to diseases and disabilities. People say, 'Once the ambulance rings, the wages earned from raising pigs for one year will be gone; once they arrive at the last hospital, they will need to work three years.' Therefore, medical security has become the top priority of poverty alleviation in Heilongjiang Province and Harbin city. Therefore, the counties (cities) I visited have fully opened a 'green channel' from hospitals to poor households. It is normal for doctors to go to the countryside for treatment and medicine delivery. Insurance, reimbursement and other procedures shall be handled by the village health office. The travel expenses, registration expenses, medical expenses, accommodation expenses and meals saved by the sick villagers are by no means decimal!

I seldom get sick. Even during the epidemic, I often braved the hail of 'virus' and bravely marched forward wearing a mask. Therefore, I don't know much about the policy of medical insurance and the love and warmth it brings to people. Therefore, on June 5, 2020, I went to the largest drugstore in Harbin – the store conducted a survey on the new medicine. That's where I bought medicine for my parents when I was a child. Because Harbin had imported cases from abroad, so epidemic prevention measures became stricter. When entering the spacious warehouse, it is necessary to scan the code for temperature measurement without 'leakage'. All counters were hung with vertical isolation transparent plastic sheets. Cheng Xiuyun, the retail manager, thought I was here to buy medicine and warmly welcomed me. She said that according to the requirements of the municipal party committee, the municipal government and enterprise leaders, preventing the epidemic and using national policies to help patients are the two key tasks of the pharmacy. She gave me two examples of her own experience:

The patient surnamed Li from Tieli city (county-level city) found gastrointestinal tumors and needed to take specific drugs. Two boxes per month and every box is about 718,200 yuan. Buying such expensive medicine naturally attracted her attention. After careful discussion, the other party said that according to the national medical insurance policy and work unit regulations, he can reimburse 70% of the total amount and personally responsible for 30%, that is, 2,154.60 yuan / box, which greatly reduces his burden. Cheng Xiuyun is worthy of being a retail manager and knows the relevant national policies and the situation of the pharmaceutical industry like the palm of her hand. She immediately provided Mr. Li with an important message: when you buy the drugs, you must keep the relevant bills well. After taking it continuously for 4 months, you can apply for China Cancer Foundation. With approved help, you can get free drugs for eight consecutive months starting from the fifth month. Cheng Xiuyun's words have reduced the profits of the drugstore, but Mr. Li can save more than 34000 yuan of personal expenses! He jumped up and said happily, 'I'll make you a silk banner now!' Two days later, Mr. Li came with the silk banner.

Mr. Lv is an old farmer in Fangzheng County and is also an extremely poor family. He only charges a minimum premium of more than 100 yuan a month. His spouse is a second-class disabled person. A few years ago, he found himself suffering from cancer. According to the doctor's advice, he took a specific drug, 13,100 yuan per box, 7 days per box, 4 boxes per month, with a total monthly cost of 52,400 yuan. For more than three years, he has been taking more than 300,000 yuan of foreign debt to buy medicine, but he stopped taking medicine which means he would lose his life. Fortunately, the two children working outside helped him more than 2,000 yuan a month, so they survived. Not long ago, Mr. Lv came to Xinte drugstore to buy medicine. Cheng Xiuyun told him that as long as you buy 8 boxes of this medicine continuously, you can enjoy it for free for life. Some of profits of the drugstore were lost, but Lao Lv saw the hope of survival. Since then, every time Lao Lv went to the city to do business, he would take a bag of fresh vegetables to see Cheng Xiuyun, his 'good daughter'.

The government's 'Put people and life first' policy had greatly reduced the burden of the masses, and had indeed entered every household and peasant.

On June 4, 2020, according to the introduction of the person in charge of the Poverty Alleviation and Development Office of Heilongjiang Province, Heilongjiang Province, as a major province in agriculture, had 20 national level poverty-stricken counties, 8 provincial level poverty counties, and three counties were severely impoverished. As of February this year, five poor counties and cities, Yanshou, Baiquan, Lindian, Hailun and Qinggang, finally shook off their poverties, and all poor counties in Heilongjiang Province were 'cleared'.

A great historical monument stands on this memorable time node.

2. Yanshou County once had a great county magistrate

Yanshou County is the only national key county for poverty alleviation and development in Harbin.

On the day of arrival, I ate in their cafeteria. I grabbed a handful of scallions and ate three bowls of mayonnaise. You can imagine how much I miss the taste of my hometown! The cook was very interested in my edacity, so he sat down and chatted with me. When I heard that I was from Beijing, he proudly said, 'Although I look like a confused man, I was once on CCTV news! But it passed in the twinkling of an eye, and my wife didn't see me!' Zhang Fengping, director of the Publicity Department of the County Party Committee, smiled and said, 'If you wrap your face tightly, who could recognize you!' I have known this director for less than two hours, and she has called me brother-in-law – I don't know what to say.

It turned out that since the poverty alleviation campaign was launched, in order to unite people and boost morale, Zhang Fengping and her deputies Zhang Hongmei and Jin Jinling, these women have characteristics of Northeast, tough and brash. The annual 'Make dumplings activity' in the county and called on volunteers to participate in the Spring Festival every year. On the cold New Year's Eve, the square was full of laughter. Everyone dressed up like a big cotton ball. When they got together, their hands and feet were frozen stiff. The only requirement for making dumplings is to be fast, otherwise the dough, meat and people will freeze hard respectively. Seeing the dumplings flying out like flowers scattered by heavenly maid, twenty or thirty thousand white dumplings soon covered the whole square, as vast and spectacular as the sea! Needless to say, after that, all these dumplings were sent to poor households and villagers' homes respectively. This activity has become a traditional program in Yanshou County for many years. This is a report from CCTV Network News Broadcast. The cook seized the opportunity to squeeze in.

It is particularly worth mentioning that in the Songjiang Provincial Museum of Historical Sites of Yanshou County, I met Liang Mingde, a great but seemingly unknown old county magistrate in the early days of liberation. In the photo, his eyes are bright, his short hair is gray, he is tall and steep, and he stands like a stone carving in the depths of history. If we do not carefully explore his origin, it is difficult to know that his soul stirring actions largely determine the fate of the Party Central Committee and the Red Army in the Central Soviet area. History cannot be assumed, but without him, the history of Chinese revolution and the history of the Long March will be rewritten.

Liang Mingde, formerly known as Xiang Tingchun and Xiang Yunian, was born in 1894 in a wealthy farmer in Pengkou Township, Liancheng County, Fujian Province. He secretly joined the Communist Party of China in 1925. After the failure of the Great Revolution in 1927, he transferred to the Central Intelligence Agency founded and led by Zhou Enlai in Shanghai. In 1933, he was a spy for the Kuomintang government under the pseudonym Liang Mingde and served as the confidential secretary of the Fourth Security Command of Jiangxi

Province. It was in this year that Chiang Kai-Shek mobilized one million troops to launch the fifth 'Encirclement and Suppression' against the Central Soviet Area of Jiangxi Province. At this time, Wang Ming's 'left' dogmatism dominated the Red Army and advocated positional warfare instead of guerrilla and mobile warfare. Mao Zedong's correct proposal was completely rejected, causing the Red Army to suffer heavy losses and be in a passive position. In early October 1934, Chiang Kai -Shek, who was determined to win, held a top-secret military conference in Lushan and formulated the 'Iron Bucket Encirclement and Suppression Plan' in the Central Soviet Area, in an attempt to completely eliminate the forces of the Communist Party of China and the Red Army at one fell swoop. After the meeting, Mo Xiong, then Commissioner and Security Commander of De'an District of Jiangxi Province, handed the top-secret documents to confidential secretary Liang Mingde, who further formulated relevant action plans. Mo Xiong, a Cantonese, joined the United League of China in his teens. He took part in the Huanghuagang uprising, National Protection Movement, the crusade against Chen Jiongming and the northern expedition. He was promoted from soldier to general. He was called 'Brother Mo' in the Kuomintang military circles. He had a close relationship with the Communist Party in private, so Chiang Kai-Shek never trusted him. After liberation, he lived in Hong Kong. In 1956, he was invited to Beijing to attend the National Day ceremony and then settled on the mainland. Liang Mingde was shocked to see the 'Iron Bucket Encirclement and Suppression Plan' handed over to him by Mo Xiong. He immediately conveyed the main points of the plan to the Party Central Committee through the organization. However, the local party organization believed that this could not fully explain the crisis of the situation. Therefore, Liang Mingde, 40, was appointed to rush to Ruijin and sent the confidential documents directly to the Party Central Committee. Liang Mingde used encryption to write the file into a student dictionary overnight. The next day, he dressed as a schoolteacher. But at this time, Jiangxi was covered with war clouds and smoke of gunpowder. On the way from De'an to Ruijin, the Kuomintang army set up checkpoints everywhere and carried out very strict inspection. It's hard not to pay attention to the image of the teacher. He is often stopped to investigate, which makes Liang Mingde very afraid. On the third night, he decided to change his appearance, then he knocked off four front teeth with a brick, cut his hair, tore his clothes and soaked in the mud, then turned black and dressed up as a disabled mute beggar. There will be no checkpoints to stop him then. After six days and six nights, Liang Mingde crossed the heavy blockade, passed through eight counties and cities, and finally arrived at Ruijin. He gave the secret to his old superior Zhou Enlai. The CPC Central Committee immediately adjusted the withdrawal deployment. Before the Kuomintang army formed the situation of 'Iron Bucket Encirclement and Suppression Plan', the Red Army successfully jumped out of the encirclement and began the world-famous 25,000 mile Long March. At this time, Mao Zedong had to lie on a stretcher because of his serious illness. After breaking through the natural danger of Wujiang River, the pressure of the Red Army chased and intercepted by its tail was greatly reduced. Mao Zedong said with emotion that if our comrades engaged in intelligence work can live, they will make contributions!!

During the Long March, Liang Mingde was sent to Hong Kong to engage in underground activities. After completing the task, he returned to Yan'an and served as member of the Standing Committee of Suide prefectural Party committee and Minister of United Front work. Xi Zhongxun is secretary of the prefectural Party committee. In July 1996, comrade Xi Zhongxun recalled Liang Mingde's outstanding contribution to the Party in the preface to *Boundless Winds the Mountain Pass*. His most brilliant page is that he and his comrades in arms obtained the important information of the suppression plan aimed at the Communist Party. 'During the Lushan conference, in order to deliver it to the Central Soviet Area in time, he knocked off his front teeth, disguised as a beggar, passed through many blockades' day and night, sent this important information related to the overall situation of the revolution to Ruijin in time and handed it to Zhou Enlai face to face. At that time, the Red Army was making a major strategic turn the night before the action.'

The great cause of the Chinese revolution is actually hanging on the dangerous line related to survival and determining the future in six days and six nights! Liang Mingde paid the price of four front teeth. Think about the night he hit his front teeth with a brick in front of the hotel mirror. He twisted his eyebrows and stared, suffering pain with his mouth full of blood. It was a heroic battle, like being shot by the enemy.

After the victory of the Anti-Japanese War, Liang Mingde and his wife Wu Jian followed 100,000 troops to the northeast. On January 24, 1946, Yanshou County in Songjiang, occupied by the remnants of the Kuomintang, was captured by the advance force of the 359 brigade and became the first county magistrate elected democratically in April. Due to the outstanding performance and stable situation of the county in suppressing bandits, land reform, establishing a new political power and mobilizing the masses to support the front line, the Songjiang provincial Party committee moved to Yanshou County for a time. So far, Yanshou people still won't forget the scenery at that time. When Liang Mingde was in power, it was called 'Big Yanshou County, little Harbin' Liang Mingde was transferred to the provincial government in April 1947 and then worked in Liaoning Province. He died in Longyan, Fujian in 1978 at the age of 84.

Today, the two slogans shouted by the old county magistrate Liang Mingde at the county farmers' association still twinkle on the memorial wall of the exhibition hall: 'Suppress bandits and abolish poverty!'

In February 2020, after comprehensive inspection and assessment, Yanshou County lifted out of poverty-stricken counties

3. Determined to carry out the plan to the end

In order to interview and write this book, I entered dozens of villages which are near the mountain and by the river and amidst red flowers and green trees in the northwest, southwest and south of the Yangtze River. When I arrived in Heilongjiang Province, the villages with the tile roofed houses jumped in front of me like playing chess one by one. The word 'Tun' (which means village) is not the local language, but the leftover appellation of station troops in the 'Land of the Dragon Rising' in the northeast of the Qing Dynasty. It is similar to that of the current militia company. They rode horses during the war and returned to their fields after the war. In the past, the men here were tall and stoutly built, and the women would shout loudly. The young lady will twist their slender waist and ripple in the waves. I left my hometown nearly 30 years ago, but now Longjiang is really different. It used to be covered with big wheat and corn. Now most of the plains are glittering rice fields. The fragrant northeast rice has become the favorite of the people all over the country. Walking into villages, wide roads, large squares and big houses are everywhere, big pots, big stoves and big fire pits in every family. All these are intimate for me, because I was born in the whole family under the Yellow Banner. But now everyone is wearing masks. The girls only show affectionate faces with a pair of arched eyebrows and almond eyes make her more charming.

Driving from Harbin to Yanshou County, the Poverty Alleviation Office of county recommended a typical disabled person who successfully got rid of poverty through self-struggle: Li Yanxi, a villager of Xinmin Village, Qingchuan Township. When I left, Li Yanxi welcomed him out happily. He is dark and thin. He has ankylosing spondylitis. His body is too stiff to bend deeply. One leg is a little short. He walks very bumpy. When I walked into the house, I sat cross-legged on the Kang, just like the old village head. Li Yanxi couldn't sit still, but leaned against a special high back wooden stool. After talking all morning, everything was ordinary and plain. No story, no twists and turns, no stimulation, no typical 'great deeds' and 'great achievements'. This is the daily account of an ordinary farmer. But I have a strong desire to write him down. Why? Answer found later.

The first account: from 10 thousand yuan to heavy debts

In 1973, Li Yanxi was born in a village in Bin County with a brother and a sister. Because of the poor local water quality, many people suffering from Kashin Beck disease. The whole family moved to Xinmin Village, Yanshou County in 1984 (here, the village is called Tun). His father had a good handcraft skills in beekeeping. The extracted honey was pure and sweet, and the selling price was very high. Therefore, his father was very bullish at that time. When drinking, no matter how much, there was a heroic look in his eyes. He looked down on ordinary people were not in his league, because the old man had a 10000 yuan saved in his bank, it was rare '10000-yuan household' in the countryside at that time. Li Yanxi graduated middle school without any stress, during the preparation for entrance examination for high school; he rode his bike to the school 10 kilometres away every day. There was a rainstorm. He had a fever and caught a cold. At first, he didn't take it seriously. He just took some medicine, but later his condition became more and more serious and his waist couldn't straighten up. His family sent him to Harbin's hospital, he was diagnosed by the hospital and found out he had ankylosing spondylitis. The doctor said, you don't have to spend money on it, because this disease can't be cured, you can only recover slowly. You should do more exercise, or you will be paralyzed. 17-year-old Li Yanxi fell ill and his family became a poor household with heavy debt. Throughout the country, many poor households are poor because of illness. In fact, they are also sick because of poverty – after all, it's too tired to work hard to support their families in the wind, rain and snow. Since then, Li Yanxi has become taciturn, but he is very sensible. He couldn't work on the farm, so he raised a few pigs at home to ease the burden on his parents. A few years later, relying on his silent diligence and perseverance, his body slowly recovered and reached an age for marriage.

The second account: from repaying a debt of 100,000 yuan to owing 260,000 yuan.

In the winter of 1998, Li Yanxi married Ma Shufeng, a girl from a neighboring village. He rose on a tractor to take the bride in a red cotton padded jacket into a dirt house. The doors and windows were covered with frost, and only the Kang was hot. To this end, his parents and he raised 50,000 yuan (private usury), plus the previous 'famine' (debt), a total of more than 200,000 yuan. For an ordinary farmer, this is a big mountain on his head! Chinese farmers have a good quality, that is, no matter how hard it is, they can bear it. Li Yanxi is like this. He looked a little dull after his serious illness. He didn't smile or frown all day. His expression was clear at a glance. No one knows what's on his mind and how to repay the 'famine' with compound interest. The villagers saw the thin Li Yanxi go up the mountain with a machete, then rent a carriage and carry back bundles of wooden poles as thick as arms – these wooden poles were bought from the forestry department with the newly raised money. Then he erected wooden poles in his field, bought a large bundle of plastic cloth and fastened it in the shed with a belt. This was the first greenhouse in Xinmin Village. It was very novel at that time. The couple began to grow vegetables in it. I asked, did you do the math? Can you pay off your debt by selling vegetables alone? Li Yanxi said faintly that he had no calculation, but found a way of life. In fact, his taste was very accurate. The land of the surrounding villagers is full of food. They depend on their own small garden for food. After a while, as soon as the season for planting passed, they stopped planting. Vegetables in the greenhouse can be supplied at any time across seasons. In addition, he always adheres to green planting and does not use chemical fertilizers and pesticides. The villagers saw clearly and breathed a sigh of relief. Early in the morning, the couple woke up earlier than the chicken and immediately went into the greenhouse to pick vegetables. When the sun came out, several villagers in the surrounding villages lined up outside the greenhouse to buy eggplant, sweet pepper, tomato, potato, radish and cabbage, paid money and brought vegetables. Some people say they have no money, so they owe money first. Ma Shufeng said 'well', all the veggies were sold out in the morning. Some people, who owed less than one hundred yuan, forgot that they owed him money. After three years of hard work, the couple still owes more than 100000 yuan, but their lives has slowly become better. Li Yanxi came and went silently, without a smile or a sad face. He looked determined to carry out the numbness to the end. In winter, the wind and snow roared and the ground was as hard as steel. The villagers sat on the hot Kang and 'winter at home' and gossiped about the ins and outs. This is the habit of farmers in Northeast China who have been idle for half a year. In this way, they talked about a group of laughing stars such as Zhao Benshan and Fan Wei, which made the people all over the country laugh. Li Yanxi couldn't sit still or sit down. He was crippled in his legs, but he worked in the greenhouse to and did the dishes every day. He often didn't say a word all day. His wife Ma Shufeng was busy working at home, taking care of the children and the elderly, and no one spoke to Li Yanxi.

He became the first greenhouse vegetable farmer in Qingchuan.

As soon as the winter of 2011 was over, the 'famine' was repaid over half. The couple is more confident and is ready to expand another greenhouse next year. That day, Li Yanxi drove agricultural tricycles and took his wife to carry goods. On the freeway, a large truck full of load sped up. There was an unlocked door in the back compartment, which was open for a while and closed for a while. Li Yanxi neither saw nor took preventive measures. He drove by the roadside and was slammed by the door. The whole tricycles roared through the highway ditch. His wife was throwed out. Li Yanxi was pressed in front of the car and couldn't move. Seeing the bad situation, the big truck sped away. Ma Shufeng shouted 'Help'. The two passers-by on the motorcycle were very friendly. They came down to help break the three wheels and pulled Li Yanxi out. Ma Shufeng stopped a taxi and took Li Yanxi, who was bleeding on his face, to the hospital. After investigation, he broke his clavicle, a leg bone and seven ribs, but fortunately, his life was saved.

Suffering from the disaster, Li Yanxi had been lying for a whole year, and his bones gradually drew closer, but ankylosing spondylitis were found in his upper body. What's more, one of his leg was longer than the other, his waist was stiff, and he couldn't sit or lie, he was crippled and couldn't do anything. The greenhouse was left unattended and had to be abandoned. Without income, plus treatment and medicine, he owed another 260,000 yuan for 'famine'. For most people, the whole family would suffer from his illness. Li Yanxi is an ordinary person, even worse off than ordinary people. Finally, there wasn't any edible food for him to eat. A bowl of mayonnaise is the food of the whole family all day. But he did not complain, nor did he shout firm slogans to his wife and children. He just grinned and endured silently, waiting for his recovery. In order to help his parents, his son cried and dropped out of school to work in Harbin. He sends a lot of hard-earned money to home every month. Not much. It is a good thing for parents to feel their son's filial piety and care. The family is so simple that it won't lend a helping hand to anyone except borrowing money.

The third account: from paying off debt to the richest man in Xinmin Village.

Slowly, Li Yanxi was able to stand up on crutches and walk around. He forced himself to do something, or he couldn't pay his debts or support the family. At that time, it was the time when video halls were popular in urban and rural areas all over the country. Li Yanxi had a brainwave. He bought a player and a pile of DVDs and played them at home every night. Each villager charged thirty or fifty cents. Later, many people had players, but they had to rent DVDs in the town or county. Plus, the travel expenses, it was not worth it. Li Yanxi made up his mind to buy a motorcycle. He left his crutches at home every day, then carried a large bag of DVDs on his back, rode the motorcycle around more than a dozen villages door to door, rented the discs first, then charged, and came to pick them up in three days. The family cinema of eight villages, from Hongkong martial arts movies to America thrillers, was booked by Li Yanxi. He could earn about 300 yuan per month. There was a winter night when snow was falling strong, he bravely took a car and flew across the road ditch, crossed the opposite fence, and fell into the farmhouse with a bang. Fortunately, the thick snow saved him, but his face and hands were scratched a little. When he returned home, his wife asked him what was wrong. Li Yanxi said indifferently, 'shit, it seems that the scene of a car robbery in America movie is fake!' In this way, Li Yanxi fell and got up again and again, and once again, he silently saved himself. However, his thin face was still the same, without smile or sadness, unchanged for a long time.

With the popularity of television in rural areas, the trend of video discs soon passed. Li Yanxi's body was stiff so he couldn't work on the farm. He came up with another way of life: raising geese. In 2012, he bought 300 goslings. I asked again, did you calculate it? Can you make money? What if the geese catch the disease and die? Li Yanxi's disposition was as stiff as his body, he said he didn't calculate the cost. In his mind, he thought it didn't have to be big, start small by selling one or two. As long as the family can live off it, there's no need to count. He might have been thoughtless about it, but he knew that geese are always more valuable than goslings. Free-range geese are always more valuable than assembly line feeding and captive breeding, and goose eggs are also more valuable than eggs and duck eggs. Then, Li Yanxi waved double crutches and Ma Shufeng waved bamboo poles. From dawn every day, she set free a group of geese. This black soil is rich in water resources and lush vegetation, which can save costs of a lot of feed. In addition, it belongs to natural pure green breeding, we hit two birds in one stone, why not? After autumn, the snow-white big fat geese stood up with their heads held high and honked loudly, becoming another scenic spot in Xinmin Village. The goose is more than 10 yuan per kilo. The female goose has an egg for two days, and each egg is 3-5 yuan. The numbers keeping rising! This year, Li Yanxi earned more than 20000 yuan. In 2013, he raised 500,800 in 2014, 1,200 in 2015 and 2,000 in 2016... His geese sold out rapidly, he didn't even have to step out of his house. In 2019, he raised 3,500 geese. By the end of the year, it was difficult to sell because of the epidemic. Dong Zijian, leader of the village-based poverty alleviation team sent by the public office of the Heilongjiang provincial Party committee, led a team to help him sell more than 1,000 (it can be seen that the village based team is really effective and do practical things). Li Yanxi finally showed a rare smile on his dark face!

Life was so difficult and life was so rough. It was really difficult for Li Yanxi to smile!

Because Li Yanxi was on crutches every day and couldn't keep up with the march of thousands of geese, the magnificent and angry geese kept yelling up to the sky and repeatedly issued mass 'protests', forcing him to abandon his crutches.

Li Yanxi's business is booming, and there are many people in the market every day. Many villagers who raised chickens and ducks around village moved boxes of eggs and duck eggs and asked him to help sell these goods. Li Yanxi promised happily and didn't get paid. If there are broken eggs in the transportation, he will pick up the small gosling eggs to make up. When shipping, he will also buy cartons and pay the transportation fee. Everything was paid by him. Ma Shufeng, his wife, is very unhappy. She said, it's none of your business; you shouldn't manage your business like this. Li Yanxi said plainly that the villagers should help each other. Besides, helping everyone sell eggs, duck eggs and goose eggs can be sold. As soon as Ma Shufeng heard that, she thought it was reasonable, so she didn't say a word.

In 2017, the great cause of poverty alleviation in China was carried out in an all-round way. Han Fengqi, Secretary of the village Party committee, was a township leader. He is loyal to the people and has high prestige. After retirement, he took the initiative as the Secretary of the village Party committee and was willing to build a well-off society in an all-round way. He knew Li Yanxi's pain and that Li Yanxi had a lot of foreign debt, so he took the initiative to visit and said that he had reserved a place for poor families. Li Yanxi said, I'm doing better now, please allocate quotas to those more needy villagers. The two of them inspired each other.

By 2019, relying on his hard work, Li Yanxi had fully repaid more than 200000 yuan of foreign debt and transformed two adobe houses into red brick houses. Entering his home, the window is bright and clean, the floor is shiny, you need to change your shoes to enter the house, and there are all kinds of modern household appliances. It's not like my house – the Beijing Evening News has published about the poor situation of my family – as I said: 'the thief doesn't know what to steal when he comes in, and it is hard to tell what the thief took. 'The wall is also decorated with glittering metal plates such as golden phoenix, horse painting and pastoral scenery, which are cut and inlaid by Li Yanxi with zip-top cans. You can imagine that behind the dull expression, Li Yanxi is actually full of vitality and has extremely rich inner world. Last year, Li Yanxi established a cooperative with six poor families and took the initiative to help 14 disabled families every year. I asked him the ins and outs; he wouldn't have shared if I didn't ask. He was plain, didn't show any emotions on his face. When he spoke, it felt as though he was talking about other people's things. He had a determined disposition – just like my rigid body didn't give in and never bent to difficulties.

This is why I must write down the life of Li Yanxi. A normal farmer, who is very ordinary, worked very hard all his life and has no big achievement or failure. For the past five thousand years, the Chinese nation cultivated these farmers.

Li Yanxi's quality is very representative in China. I must salute him with this article.

The county did not provide me with any information about Li Yanxi. He has no material. On the way back, I knew he was the Harbin Model Worker.

Li Yanxi never said a word.

4. Home is where the heart is

In history, Heilongjiang has no culture, because the bandits sent by the Qing Dynasty in the early years and the 'Shandong Bangzi' who later venture to northeast have no culture. This can be seen from the place names. Everyone has heard about the Yuexiu Mountains in Guangzhou, Lijiang in Yunnan, as well as Chuxiong. Huaxi in Guiyang, Xianju in Zhejiang, Lijiang River in Guangxi and so on. The places with beautiful scenery, like poetry. The places and names in Heilongjiang: Heixiazi Island, Zhangguangcai Mountain, Lazi rock, Harbin's earliest Yangma shelf, Pian Mianzi, Three-tree, the 'crotch street' in the early days of Daowai District of Harbin. The name doesn't sound too pleasant. They say that no culture is also a culture. It is as vibrant and unique as crotch cotton pants.

I went to Xinhua Village, Xinmin Town, Mulan County. At first glance, the name comes from the new society. There are three villages affiliated it: Yangshulin Village, Yueyapao Village and Yu Shizhang (division commander) Village. 'Division Commander Yu'? Who is he? None of the villagers can tell.

Jiang Sheng, village group leader and first secretary, is 49 years old. You can tell that he was a handsome young man. In 1971, he was born into a peasant family in the suburbs of Chongqing. His father worked as a railway soldier for seven years and served as the Secretary of the village Party Committee for decades after returning home. After graduating from high school, Jiang Sheng also signed up to join the army. A boxcar train carried him and his comrades from the southwest to the northeast. Seeing his gentle appearance and careful work, the military leaders appointed him an aided man. After demobilization, he stayed in Harbin to study medicine. His job was ordinary, but he won the only female classmate, a beautiful girl from a well-off business family. The relationship was strongly opposed by the woman's family and all her relatives. They said that a poor boy in rural area of Chongqing had nothing, and our 'beloved child' was not made for just anyone. We don't agree! Sichuan boy was born stubborn; Jiang Sheng became upset and stopped contacting the girl. Harbin girl was born thoughtless; she presented her heart to Jiang Sheng. A few years later, Jiang Sheng won the love of the whole family and the appreciation and trust of the leaders of Harbin health committee with his diligence and filial piety. Later, he was promoted to deputy director of the municipal 120 emergency center.

In May 2017, the unit received the task of poverty alleviation. The superior leaders talked with 46-year-old Jiang Sheng and pointed out that he had three advantages: first, he was born in the countryside, second, he knew medical treatment, and third, he was in his prime of life. Then the leader solemnly proposed that he should be the first Secretary of the village and take the team to the countryside to help the poor for three years. Jiang Sheng's expression is very deep. He is neither excited nor enthusiastic. He said calmly that his family had some difficulties. It's best to let the leader choose another person. As for the specific difficulties, he left without saying.

It is estimated that after careful investigation, Jiang Sheng's 'three advantages' are still irreplaceable. Half a month later, the leader found him again. His attitude was very kind and his position was very firm. He said you were still the most suitable candidate! Jiang Sheng didn't say anything more. He changed his senior suit and Italian leather shoes given by his father-in-law, pulled up his luggage roll, and took two young subordinates to Xinhua Village, Xinmin Town, Mulan County. Later, the authorities found out that that Jiang Sheng declined the leader's will not because he was unwilling and afraid, it was because his wife had cancer and has just had a major operation. His son who attains the age of twenty has also suffered from an incurable disease. He is the only healthy person in the family. He focused on his work, both in the office and at home. However, when soldiers go to the battlefield, they must not hesitate at any cost. A few months later, Jiang Sheng took his sick wife to Xinhua Village and took care of her while working, so that love and loyalty can be taken into account. From then on, Jiang Sheng's heart was completely placed in Xinhua Village. His heart was here and his home was here. They lived in the village together. When his wife's condition was slightly relieved, she also went to villages and households with him to do villagers' ideological work. Jiang Sheng advised her not to be tired. His wife said, 'Just take a walk.' This moved the Municipal Health Commission and the people of the whole village.

Nearly four years later, Jiang Sheng and his wife are still in the village. The couple became tan. They ate green onions and garlic sauce. In winter, they slept on the hot Kang. When they talked about this and that with the villagers, the villagers could tell they were really close. For a long time, Jiang Sheng, a native of Chongqing, learned the authentic northeast dialect, full of 'um' (that) 'ganha' (what's up?) and 'this geda and that geda' (this place and that place). At the seminar, he recalled that when he first entered the village, he said: 'There has been no village branch secretary in the village for many years, and the villagers are unorganized, belonging to no group. The three villages looked dirty, trash were everywhere and the wind made it worse. The village was scattered and unorganized. The walls were painted with all kinds of mess. Looking at this village, one could easily be stressed. Three days after entering the village, I saw three villagers fighting one by one. They are crazy and their eyes are red. After some exchange, they started fighting each other. I thought, how can we help this village? Went to the Party members' homes and talked about the situation. Because of old age, their eyesight was blurry. They all said that there was no hope in the village. Some old women made some sarcastic remarks, said someone wants to be promoted in the government ranks, don't think about Xinhua Village. Leave quickly. Everyone were inconsistent with their remarks. What am I supposed to tell my superior when I get back?

I couldn't help laughing when Jiang Sheng rattled a native dialect, but the ending often threw out a long tune like singing in Sichuan dialect.

Chinese farmers always believe seeing is believing. What are happy life, beautiful yearning and Chinese dream? For them, it means the meat in the pot, the rice in the pot, the road in the village and the warm house! The 'three fires' lit by Jiang Sheng: first, collect garbage and pave new roads; second, clean up dilapidated houses and build new houses; third, help the poor and create new enterprises. Of course, this is not a one-person job. A large amount of money and courage followed 'The Four big Strength' poured in. The first is the poverty alleviation policy of the party and the government, the second is the strong support of the Municipal Health Commission, the third is the determination of Mulan County, and the fourth is the counterpart assistance of cadres. All the energy was focused on Jiang Sheng's determination and action. The stagnant Xinhua Village soon became a roaring construction site. Wearing a helmet, Jiang Sheng shouted to the whole village in the local dialect. For the first time in nearly half a century, Xinhua Village has carried out large-scale villagers' volunteer work, which proves that unity is strength...

More than three years later, the original Xinhua Village has become the Xinhua Village of the new era. At a glance, there are new houses, new roads and new scenery everywhere, including infirmaries, libraries, party and mass activity rooms and projectors. The villagers showed their skills, participated in the construction of photovoltaic industry, processed 'Xinhua fragrant rice' and local specialty dandelion tea (its root is called 'little ginseng'), and opened tofu shops, small restaurants and small supermarkets. On a good season night, all the aunts in the village danced in the square. It was very lively.

In 2019, all poor households in Xinhua Village lifted out of poverty-stricken.

At the symposium, Lin Fuyou, a villager with a gray beard, said that before the team entered the village, he had cancer and was heavily in debt. His wife is also very weak and ill. The old couple was almost desperate. Jiang Sheng heard that he has ancestral brewing skills. He came many times to persuade him to return to his original industry and help him raise money to build a brewing workshop. Six months later, a small pot of wine registered as 'Lin's beard' soon became popular. Local 'breweries' generally commented that this kind of wine 'is not drunk, not appreciated and not high'. The old man made more than 20,000 yuan that year. The next year, he paid off the loan and earned more than 40,000 yuan. Now Lin Fuyou is ruddy and strong. He doesn't look ill at all.

In the past three years, in addition to the new appearance of Xinhua Village, Jiang Sheng had also made a great contribution. With the support of the Municipal Health Commission, he had installed a large electronic scale of 100 tons for the village. In the past, in the autumn, when the grain merchants came to the village to collect grain, they would ask the villagers to use the large scale they had brought to weigh the food. The villagers gritted their teeth and swallowed it. They didn't dare to say it, because they couldn't afford it and couldn't understand. Since the village was installed with a check scale, the situation had reversed. The food traffickers could only recognize it, and said nothing. Only in this way, Jiang Sheng had reduced the loss of nearly a million dollars for more than 2,000 villagers every year. How can the villagers not be happy?

The poverty relief program in the village had been completed for 3 years. Jiang Sheng and his wife still lived in the village. Every time there was a meeting, Jiang Sheng shouted through the loudspeaker. When the villagers heard his northeast words and the sound of Chongqing, they would arrive at the village at the same time, laughing and cheering all over the square.

5. 'Seven fairies'

At the critical moment of the national poverty relief and decisive battle, the coronavirus disease broke out in Wuhan and Hubei and quickly spread throughout the country. The importance of life was a standard of national civilization. The love for the people was a symbol of a country's fundamental nature. General Secretary Xi Jinping immediately issued a strong mobilization order, and the whole country was affected by the news and responded in unison.

It was nearly 4 o'clock in the afternoon of February 18th in Yanshou County. All the medical staff was busy at their own positions and hospitals. Some of them had just walked out of the operating room, some were still receiving patients, and some had completed the donated treatment task of poverty relief that day, and were on their way back. Suddenly, their mobile phone rang. At the same time, they received a message: according to the requirements of relevant national departments, Heilongjiang Province needed to send the seventh batch of medical rescue team to Wuhan, a total of 171 people. There were 7 vacancies in the Yanshou County, mainly nurses. Please sign up voluntarily and leave tomorrow!

They all had professional knowledge. They all knew that the virus was spreading rapidly in Wuhan, Hubei and all over the country, and they also knew the danger and aggressiveness of the virus that spread all over the country in an instant. Did they hesitate for a few seconds or a minute? Maybe not. But in an instant, with the sense of responsibility of 'save lives and rescue the wounded' as a natural duty, and with 'When difficulties arise in one place, aid comes from everywhere' as sense of mission ignited their hearts. At the first time, hundreds of generous and excited replies rushed to the leader's cell phone. 'I'll sign up. I'll go!' 'Write down my name right away. I'll go!' 'I promise to complete the task. I'll go!' At the same time, they told this news and their decision to their family.

At 6 pm, the names of the 'Seven fairies' were determined. They were Song Shuxia, Wang Jing, Tao Ye, Li Qiao, Yu Xiaoling, Gong Yue and Ren Shuang (with photos for each).

Song Xiaoxia was the vice chief physician of the County People's Hospital, 50 years old. Her husband had just received an operation, and the child was a little reluctant to let her leave and said, 'Dad needs you. There are so many doctors in county, and you don't have to go.' Xiaoxia replied, 'The country is in danger, and Wuhan is in danger. They need mom to go!'

Wang Jing, the head nurse, was 47 years old. The 16-year-old daughter was afraid that her mother would not come back, so she cried. Her husband said, 'If you don't go, you will regret for the rest of your life!' She didn't tell her aged parents that she had been pretending to be still in the city during her trip to Wuhan. Anyway, no visits are allowed during the epidemic.

Gong Yue, a nurse, was 30 years old and the only daughter in her family. When she saw the news that the medical staff and the People's Army in some big cities all over the country rushed to Wuhan a few days ago, she was eager to go, but she knew that it was a big event of the whole country. It was organized and directed, and it was difficult to turn to a remote town. When she received the promotion order of the leader, she was excited, and immediately signed her name up. Her father was driving a big car for transportation, he said, 'you have to go! Even if our daughter doesn't go, other girls also have to go!'

Li Qiao, a nurse, was 32 years old and the only child in her family. She said to her husband, 'My life is dedicated to nursing, it would be an honor to be a nurse in the front line.' Her grandfather, who was 80 years old, said, 'My granddaughter has been a good child since she was a child. If she doesn't go, who will?'

Ren Shuang's application for fight only wrote one word: 'Go!'

The news spread and shocked the whole city. Everyone was proud of the 'Seven fairy' who had volunteered to go to the epidemic area. From that moment on, their mobile phone exploded, and a wave of questions, exhortations, and wishes came from their WeChat moments, 'Safe!', 'Salute!', 'Come on!' and 'Victory!' 4 main theme words were overwhelming. Some relatives called, she cried if she couldn't speak.

Zhang Fengping, member of the Standing Committee of the county Party committee and Minister of publicity, believed that she and the publicity department should do something for them. A woman's heart is always fragile. She knew the task was urgent and the time was short. These brave white soldiers don't need flowers and slogans. What they need is some of the most practical necessities of life on the battlefield in wartime. She thought of the wet and cold climate in Wuhan in early spring, and it was important to keep warm, so she rushed into several small shops still open on the street. She chose a red velvet scarf and a 1.5-metre-long velvet blanket, but there were only two or three in the store. Zhang Fengping usually keeps a low profile. This time, she said to the female shopkeeper, 'I'm a member of the Standing Committee of the county Party committee and the Minister of publicity. To prepare daily necessities for the medical staff going to Wuhan, you must prepare seven sets for me before dawn! I won't go, just wait here!' The female shopkeeper's eyes were wet and immediately got on the motorcycle. It was frantically looking all over for business partners. At about 11 pm, seven sets of scarves and blankets arrived at the scene. During this period of time, Zhang Fengping, who was sitting in the shop, was not idle. She ordered the subordinates to quickly make a slogan, which meant, 'Yanshou County, will wait for you, and come home safely!' Later it proved that these scarfs and blankets were the favorite and most needed necessities of the seven fairies. At night, the hotel room was very cold. It was strictly forbidden to turn on the air conditioners. During the interval of the battle, when they were very tired and it was difficult for them to support her strength. They lay on the bench or floor, wrapped in a scarf and blanket from head to foot, as if they were lying in the arms of their hometown.

That night, 'Seven fairies' cut their beloved long hair. In the twinkling of an eye, they became 'tomboys'! Parents or husbands are very distressed and dare not look. They hid in other rooms in tears. After cutting their hair, they also smiled at the strange image in the mirror. In fact, they are ready for everything, including sacrifice. How many chance can there be in life? Go to the battlefield! The wife told her husband to take good care of the family and her children to study hard; when her daughter told her parents to take care of themselves, two of the girls completely 'entrusted' their private money card number. At last, they're ready.

On the morning of February 20, that is the next day, Yanshou County was cold and snowy. The seven fairies got on the bus in round clothes and set off. According to the regulations during the epidemic, there were not many people to see them off, and cadres such as the Secretary of the county Party committee, the county head, the propaganda minister and the leaders of the Ministry of health were also present. They are full of love and care and say that if they encounter any difficulties, they must call their hometown. The people of the whole county are your strong backing! 'Seven fairies' had a firm and powerful expression and repeatedly said 'Please rest assured' and 'We promise to complete the task and win glory for the people in our hometown', but the girls didn't dare to look back to their loved ones. Facing the warmth and affection of the people in their hometown, they are afraid that they will cry.

On the same day, they went to Harbin airport to meet the whole team, a total of 171 people, and flew to Wuhan in the afternoon.

Yu Xiaoling wrote in her diary: 'When I first came to Wuhan, I saw this beautiful and long-standing city. The streets were silent. The once prosperous city became a huge empty city. I couldn't see any pedestrian. I could only occasionally see vehicles carrying goods and ambulances passing by. I was very sad. I unconsciously felt my nose sour and my eyes wet.'

In the morning of the second day, they immediately entered the Houhu District of Wuhan Central Hospital, which was one of the most serious hospitals at that time. It was the hospital where the 'Whistler' Li Wenliang had worked as a hero. The medical staff here had been fighting all the time and were very tired. Now the medical rescue team of Heilongjiang took over, and they could finally have a rest. After the short-term training of 'memory enhancing' for taking off the high-intensity protective clothing, they put on large masks and goggles, wrapped in diapers, and entered the tightly closed 'front line', starting a selfless, patient and tragic battle. When this young girl participated in such a dangerous 'war' for the first time, she felt uneasy. When I put on the protective clothing and walked into the ward, I was very calm. I wasn't afraid? With 1.4 billion compatriots supporting us and countless comrades in arms around us, I believe I can do it!'

Here, 23 doctors and 60 nurses are assigned to each inpatient ward. Doctors work two shifts a day, 12 hours per shift. Nurses are divided into four groups, each working for 6 hours per group. The patients they are responsible for are grandparents in their 80s. Some are confused for a while. Most of them can't take medicine on time and can't leave bed. Because there are no relatives to accompany, the mood is very irritable and pessimistic; some are children from Wuhan welfare homes, all surnamed Wu. Many nurses from Heilongjiang are 'post-90s' or 'post-00s'. They are children, but now they play the role of parents and take good care of every child. They whispered softly, trying to comfort people who were full of fear and anxiety; as long as the patient's hand did not release, as long as there was no other urgent task, they would always sit there, looking to talk to them about happy things, encouraging them to build confidence, defeat the pestilence and evil, and welcome a better tomorrow. They said that such a big pestilence had infected tens of thousands of people. All the medical expenses will be paid by the party. Tens of thousands of medical staff are urgently transferred from all over the country. Which country in the world can do that? You can rest assured. With the strong power and kind care of the party and country, with our efforts, your disease will definitely be cured!

The patients were moved. Some of them wiped their tears, and some showed a smile of relief. Knowing that they were from the medical team of Heilongjiang Province, many patients said, 'Thank you for coming to help us in Wuhan from so far.' 'Thank you for saving my life...'

In March, the temperature in Wuhan suddenly rose, and the protective clothing was sweating profusely. But they often didn't dare to drink water all day long, because the diaper was limited. It was too troublesome and dangerous to wear the protective clothing again. 'Angel' Their faces were covered with protective goggles and a large mask, along with blood and sweat. It hurt so much that even the back of their ears was bleeding. As soon as they spoke, they were heartbroken.

In a WeChat message, Taoye wrote, 'During my work in Wuhan, I have received constant care from leaders and colleagues from my hometown, and my heart is full of gratitude. From protective equipment, living goods, to snacks and fruits, they are all so considerate. If I had prepared this myself, I wouldn't have thought of so many things. It's on goddess day (Woman's Day). Tears streamed down my cheeks as soon as I received the flowers. The carnations warmed my heart and made me feel like a child who has been married thousands of miles away. The leader and some of my colleagues are all from my family. At home, our families took care of us. We didn't have to care about anything, spent leisure time shopping. As soon as we put on the white coat, we seemed to have become brave women in armor. The power and mission given to us by the white clothes are the call of professional spirit and the great love of the angel in white.'

Li Qiao wrote, 'When I recall the days and nights of fighting in Wuhan, I am still very excited. Fighting at the forefront of the epidemic has not only experienced training, but also gained growth, which makes me have a new understanding of nursing work. What I have experienced in Wuhan will always inspire me to remember the responsibility and mission of doctors and do my best to help more people in need.' Every time she and her family watch a video, she wants to see her 5-year-old daughter, but her daughter always disappears from the screen at a glance because she doesn't want her mother to see her tears.

Gong Yue's grandmother has been bedridden for a long time, Every time she talked to her family through phone or video, she would ask when her beloved granddaughter would come back. The old woman finally couldn't wait for her. At night, Gong Yue cried in Wuhan hotel.

On March 11th, the head nurse, Wang Jing wrote in her diary, 'It's a nice day today. Wuhan is a rainy and cold place, and it's rare to have such a good day. When I opened the window and heard the singing of birds, the quiet city was filled with joy, and I was particularly happy. Recalling the work these days, I'm very grateful. I'm lucky to meet every member of the group. They are so excellent, and they work so hard every day. No one refused or slacked off when the work was arranged. They used their sense of responsibility, love and superb technology to interpret the duties of the angel in white, and their great love was fully reflected on them. Our group's goal is unite and cooperate, help each other, complete the task, and go home safely.' Once, Ren Shuang, the youngest sister in our group, was locked in the ward because of a sudden problem with the door lock. When we heard the phone, we quickly opened the lock and let her out. When she came out, she was afraid and cry. I comforted her and said, don't be afraid, we are all here. Don't cry. Tears will wet the mask and affect the protective effect. Ren Shuang is very obedient. She held back his tears, then said that my work had not been completed, and then silently returned to the ward. Looking at her back, my eyes were moist. What a good child! They are little princesses and babies in their families. I wonder if their parents would be surprised that their daughter is so strong in her position. Facing the difficulties of the country and Wuhan, they shoulder this responsibility with fragile shoulders... When I was writing here, I cried again. Yes, from the moment we put on our protective clothing, we are not children!'

In Wuhan, the most popular song they sang was 'Me and my country', which made them cry.

On April 6th, the 'Seven fairies' of Yanshou County returned with victory. All their patients survived. The doctor Song Shuxia wrote on the WeChat, 'Others say that I'm a hero, but in fact, I'm just an ordinary person. I just did what I should do when the motherland and the people need most.' Little Ren's writing was more passionate, after our united efforts, perseverance, the situation of COVID-19 in Wuhan has improved greatly. From the full hospital beds, all of them recovered. We are full of sense of achievement! The cherry blossoms in Wuhan, which blossomed as usual, roared with the spring work song and machines on the ground of the divine land, revealing a vigorous vitality and hope. The heroic people are unyielding, the heroic city is as solid as a rock, and the heroic China is indestructible. History will prove once again that the Chinese nation has gone through a lot of hardships, but we have never been crushed. Instead, we are getting more and more valiant, constantly growing from trials and tribulations, and rising from them!

On April 8th, Wuhan ends the lockdown.

IV Ma Xu entering Epilogue

The room was dark, but she was radiant.

She is a warrior made of fire, a woman made of steel, a woman made of miracle. However, few people knew her before she was 'detained and advised' by a bank and police in Wuhan. Time flies, distant history is gone, and the city is brightly lit at night. Award certificates from more than half a century ago faded and wrinkled. The newspaper that published her story had long turned yellow and entered the historical archives. I don't know whether the highly modern airborne troops are still in use today, and there are not many old comrades in arms who are familiar with her. She quietly hid in a remote corner of Wuhan and was quietly busy with her own affairs. When she occasionally goes out, her husband always entwined his fingers with hers, like leading a child.

1. Sensation after being 'detained and dissuaded'

One day in March 2018, Xu Xiangfeng, deputy secretary of Mulan County Party committee, his phone rang. A stranger-a veteran Jin Changfu. During the war to resist US aggression and aid Korea, this unit was one that Huang Jiguang wrote about, Xu Xiangfeng showed respect. Jin Changfu said, I finally got your phone number. What I want to say is that at the beginning of the war of liberation, a little girl named Ma Xu in Mulan County became a soldier. Later, she served in the army until she retired. She is 85 years old and now lives in Huangpi District, Wuhan. I used to be an old teacher of her. For decades, she has saved a sum of money and wants to donate it to her hometown, so she asked me to contact the leaders of the county to discuss how to deal with the money and where to use the donation?

Xu Xiangfeng was very happy and moved. He asked how much the donation was. Jin Changfu said, Old Ma didn't say, I don't know.

Xu Xiangfeng is a young cadre. He graduated from Heilongjiang Agricultural University. He is a graduate and doctoral student. He is full of enthusiasm and gratitude for education. Mulan County is a provincial poverty-stricken county. At this time, the county is fully implementing the goal of 'Two Reassurances and Three Guarantees', and developing and improving education is a top priority. Xu

Xiangfeng immediately thanked Mrs. Ma for her love and care for her hometown. All donations will be used for Mulan County's culture and education. After that, he arranged Ji Desan, director of the County Education Bureau, to do it and contacted Old Ma directly.

On September 12, the county Party committee and government appointed Ji Desan to take two subordinates to Wuhan to receive donations from old Ma. On the way, he always wanted to know how much money the Old Ma donated. He guessed it wasn't little, otherwise it wouldn't be this serious; at the same time, it's probably not too much. If a veteran lives frugally, he won't save a lot of money. After getting off the plane, Jin Changfu and Huang Jiguang's niece came to pick him up and take him to Old Ma's hometown. Facing everything in front of him, Ji Desan was stunned. This is a small house in the corner of a village located in the outskirts of Huangpi. The bricks and tiles are old, the house is low to the ground, didn't let in too much light. It is said that the villagers used this uninhabited broken house as a morgue a long time ago. It was also said that earlier, it was an abandoned old military camp in the Republic of China. Most of them were demolished by the villagers, leaving only this one. Ji Desan walked into the small yard. There were several orange trees in the yard. Vegetables such as eggplant and green pepper were planted in the open space. Farm tools such as hoes, shovels and manure forks are leaned against the wall outside the barn. Obviously, the family is too poor. Listening to the movement in the yard, an old lady with short stature and silver hair came out. Jin Changfu pulled Ji Desan to the old man and introduced him. This is Ji Desan, director of the Education Bureau of Mulan County. Then he introduced the old woman: 'This is Ma Xu, Mulan veteran. He talks about every day when you will come.'

Then, old Ma's husband Yan Xueyong came out to greet us.

It seems that the old Ma is less than 1.5 metres tall and looks very small. The upper body is wearing grass green short sleeved military uniform and the lower body is wearing camouflage military pants. The leather shoes fall off in many places and there are many holes in the vamp. The old woman enthusiastically took Ji Desan's hand and said to her husband, 'Great! People from my hometown have come to my house for decades. This is the first time that people from my hometown have come to my home...' Ji Desan completely didn't expect that Ma was 85 years old, but she danced like a child. Her speech was bright and clear, her thinking was flexible and agile, and her every move still showed a military style.

Ji Desan walked into the room and looked around carefully with the help of the dim light. The old sofa was covered with black cotton, and a lot of wall sheets fell from the mottled wall. The old furniture was worn out to reveal wood texture. There were two bowls on the small wooden table, and there were still some unfinished porridge with sweet potatoes and potatoes. The old bookshelf standing against the wall was stuffed with books, and there were piles of newspapers and magazines on the ground. What surprised Ji Desan most was that there were small pieces of paper everywhere in the room, which were full of Japanese words. It could be seen that the old woman was still learning Japanese

Seeing all this, Ji Desan was a little confused. Was this the house where the vice division-level cadres lived? Seeing his surprise, Mrs. Ma explained with a smile, 'A few years ago, the cadre's sanitarium was decorated, and we temporarily moved here. When the decoration is finished, the things in this house won't be moved, just the two of us, we want to live peacefully.'

Ji Desan couldn't help but mutter in his heart, this thin and small old comrade seems to be poor. How much savings can she have? If the donated money is very little, although the old woman's spirit is very respected, the whole matter can only be treated as a general work.

After a short exchange of pleasantries, the old man came back to the point, and his expression became particularly serious. She put on her presbyopia glasses and proposed to see Ji Desan's ID card, work card, official letter and printed blank withdrawal agreement. All the terms of the agreement were unclear. The old woman raised a question, and Ji Desan explained it. After all the examination was passed, the old woman took off her glasses and calmly said, 'That's it. I'm very satisfied. I've donated 10 million dollars to my hometown in total. This is all my savings...'

Ji Desan hardly believed his ears. Such a huge number was beyond his imagination! Jin Changfu, who was sitting beside him, knew well the difficulties of Ma's life. Hearing this number, he was also greatly shocked, and tears poured out. Mrs. Ma then said, 'Tomorrow, a financial product of 3 million yuan will expire. Send it to the hometown first. There will be another 7 million yuan given in May next year.'

Ji Desan was so excited that his blood was boiling. In the dim light, Mrs. Ma, who was sitting opposite to him, was thin and small with deep wrinkles on his face. If he didn't wear a military uniform, he would look like an ordinary old woman from the countryside. At this moment, he felt that she was a God, a military soul, a monument, and pearlescent!

As soon as they walked out, Ji Desan immediately reported to Xu Xiangfeng, the Deputy Secretary of the Municipal Committee. The leaders of the county soon knew that. They were not in high spirits, and their eyes were wet. The Municipal Committee decided to donate all the money from Mrs. Ma to build a 'Ma Xu Art Center'.

The next morning, according to the agreement, Ji Desan and his colleagues first came to the Airport River branch of Wuhan Industrial and Commercial Bank of China and waited for Mr. Yan and Mrs. Ma. At about 9 o'clock, Mr. Yan and Mrs. Ma arrived. Together, they explained their intentions to the bank staff. But listen, the bank staff thought it's too rare and strange. The old couple must have been cheated. It's not easy to save more than 10 million yuan in a lifetime! Therefore, he repeatedly advised Ma not to believe the words of some people. Ji Desan immediately showed the official letter of Mulan County government, the letter of introduction from the Education Bureau and his ID card, but the bank staff still didn't believe it and resolutely refused to transfer money. They also sent security to detain Ji Desan and others, and report to the local police and ask him to further 'cooperate with the investigation'.

The case involved a huge sum of 3 million yuan. This is a shocking case! The director personally led four fierce policemen to rush to bank. They not only isolated Ji Desan and his subordinates, but also isolated Ma Xu, Yan Xueyong and Jin Changfu for detailed questioning. After that, the police called the seventh cadre sanitarium in Wuhan, Mulan County Government, County Public Security Bureau and County Education Bureau respectively for verification, and repeatedly asked Mrs. Ma about the origin of 10-million-yuan deposit, the reason for donation, and so on. As things got more and more complicated, Mrs. Ma finally couldn't help but get angry and said loudly, 'I saved my savings as a soldier all my life. I volunteered to donate to my hometown. What reason do you have to doubt me?' When it comes to the emotional place, the old woman even jumped up, beat her head with both hands and shouted: 'I'm willing to donate my money for my hometown even if I'm cheated. Don't worry! Don't make difficulties for the people in my hometown!'

Old Ma's pure heart and deep affection for her hometown were so sincere and intense in her screams and anger, which made Ji Desan cry again and again. Until 4:47 p.m., the bank and the police checked everything clearly. Finally, they believed Mrs. Ma's generosity and transferred 3 million yuan to the account of Mulan County Education Bureau. For nearly eight hours, when things were done, Ma was exhausted and couldn't stand up.

Mulan County was in an uproar. Wang Xuefei and Jiang Yuanyi from the publicity department wrote the news release at the first time; *Harbin daily*, the place where I once worked, and then released the report that *Ma Xu donated 10 million to support cultural and education*. The news soon spread all over the country, and major media swarmed up

2. Flowers in the army

After the tragic night of the September 18th Incident, 300,000 northeast troops were ordered to 'resistance not allowed' and all withdrew into the Shanhaiguan Pass. Officials of the national governments at all levels of the three northeastern provinces, like frightened birds, ran off with money one after another, leaving the people behind. The people of Northeast China have been plunged into a sea of blood ever since. In 1933, Ma Xu was born into a poor peasant family in Libaozhong Village, Mulan County. Two years later, she had a younger brother. Soon, his father died of illness and hunger. Without a place to live, the mother had to entrust her infant son to her elder family. She led little Ma Xu around, begging and earning some sorghum, rice and corn flour by singing the traditional big drum song. However, under the Tie Ti (iron heel) bayonet and tight blockade of the Japanese aggressors, who is in the mood to listen to the big drum song? After returning home, the two women had to go to someone else's field and dig some residual potatoes or corn grains to satisfy their hunger. The hungry little Ma Xu grew to more than 1.4 metres and never grew again. Sometimes, the mother and daughter go to a familiar village and find that there is only a large area of black ruins and ashes. Because the devils burn, kill, loot and forcibly merge the village, the villagers die and escape, and the village disappears from now on. Ma Xu was frightened to cry. When they moved to another village, the mother sang the story of Mulan joining the army, his mother and the Yang family's general resisting Jin Dynasty. He made special efforts with emotion and enthusiasm, singing herself, her daughter and those listeners in tears. This is the voice of immortality. After the victory of the Anti-Japanese war in 1945, Japan surrendered unconditionally and the whole country was jubilant. The villagers of Libaoguo Village collectively asked the mother to sing the traditional Big Drum song. The first two sentences were: 'The devil is gone, China has won!' This is a word compiled by their mother. After that, the villagers invited 12-year-old Ma Xu to eat her first full meal in her life, and she and her mother burst into tears.

In 1946, the fourth field army (then known as the Northeast Democratic Coalition Army) attacked major cities such as Heilongjiang and Harbin, and all counties were liberated one after another. Land reform began immediately, and the poor smiled happily. Little Ma Xu got several acres of lands and some clothes at home. She saw the comfortable smile on her mother's face and fell in love with the Communist Party and the people's Liberation Army. In March 1947, when heard that the fourth field army would expand southward and liberate the whole China. Ma Xu jumped with joy to the recruitment office and asked to join the army. The recruiting cadre said, 'Look, you look like bean sprouts. You're not as tall as a gun. You're still a little girl. Go home!'

Ma Xu said stubbornly, 'I'm only 14 years old. I'll grow up!'

The recruiter laughed, 'But the army can't wait for you to grow up!'

The section chief, who was working in the back room, walked out and looked at Ma Xu, asked her, 'Aren't you afraid that you will bleed and die in the battlefield?'

'If I am afraid of death, I won't come! And I can heal myself. My family is an ancestral traditional Chinese medicine.'

The section chief's gaze sharpened: 'The army is going to fight a big battle down to south. Let's take you as an aided woman.'

The little girl wore a big gray blue military uniform. After half a year's training, she followed an invincible army into The Liaoxi-Shenyang Campaign, and followed the fifteenth army of the Chinese people's Volunteer Army, which was Huang Xuguang's troop, into the battlefield of resistance and reinforcements. She was small and agile, walking around in the rain of bullets, binding up the injured and bringing food and water to the soldiers in the Triangle Hill. The enemy fired a shell and she buried herself in the soil, moved hard, poked out her little head, and then pulled out her military cap. On the night of October 19, 1952, the Battle of Triangle Hill was extremely fierce and stalemated. The boy charged in front was seriously injured, and several grenades had been used up. In order to stop the crazy shooting of the enemy's bunker, he threw himself on, blocked the muzzle of the bunker with his body, and made a heroic sacrifice. He was only 21 years old. Volunteer officers and soldiers jumped out of the trench and shouted, 'Revenge for Huang Jiguang!' They rushed to the enemy position all over the mountains and fields. Little Ma Xu was in the team of the decisive battle. After the war, she won the commemorative medal for resisting US aggression and aiding Korea, the commemorative medal for safeguarding peace and the Third-Class Merit Medal awarded by the Korean government. After returning home, Ma Xu was escorted to the First Military Medical University for further study, and his cultural knowledge and medical level were comprehensively improved. In her later years, recalling the war years of life and death, she said excitedly: 'Compared with my comrades who died on the battlefield, my survivalist the greatest happiness!'

In 1956, Ma Xu, 23, was assigned to the General Hospital of Wuhan military region. After years of baptism of war, further study and practice by the hospital bed, the 'little girl in the army' became a highly skilled military surgeon. Although she is small and wears two pigtails, she speaks loudly and works vigorously. He often stands by the operating table for more than ten hours. She was praised by her colleagues as 'A knife in the army'. General Chen Zaidao, who was enlisted in the old Red Army, once had an operation, and Ma Xu was specially named to take the lead.

In 1961, the Central Military Commission ordered the formation of the airborne force of the Chinese people's Liberation Army with Huang Jiguang's heroic force as the main body. This is a new branch of our army. Everything starts from scratch. Ma Xu is a 'veteran' of this force, so she was ordered to participate in medical security work with the team. Strict training began. Chinese soldiers flew into the sky for the first time and learned to fly and land. The weather is unpredictable, and the terrain of the landing site is unpredictable and dangerous.

The initial training starts from the ground and boarding practice can only be carried out after all subjects are pass. The soldiers parachuted from the air with weapons and ammunition. Many people hung on trees, rolled down the hillside, fell into the river, fell head down to the ground, they were injured and blood was visible, their noses and faces were scratched, and their arms, ankles and ribs were broken. It took a lot of time to find them in the mountains, deep valleys and dense forests, and then send them to the site of the field medical team. As a result, the treatment of the wounded was delayed, resulting in much depletion of numbers. Ma Xu is in a hurry. She found the commander and urged: 'I want to learn skydiving with the soldiers! I will go wherever they go, so that the wounded can be treated in time!' The commander shook his head again and again: 'Parachuting is a very difficult action, not to mention that there is no precedent for female soldiers parachuting in China. Look at your height, you are so small and weighs less than 70kg. If you encounter a strong wind in the air, won't you be blown away?'

Ma Xu roared: 'As a military doctor of airborne soldiers, if I can't parachute with the soldiers to the battlefield and rescue the wounded at the first time, I'm equal to a waste!'

After returning to the field dormitory, Ma Xu spent two days digging a big pit nearly two metres deep behind the house. There was a layer of fine sand under the pit and several steps on the slope – otherwise she would not be able to climb out if she jumped in the pit. Then she took out the tables and chairs and built them into a high platform. Since then, she continued to treat the wounded in the field medical station every day. She came back to practice skydiving in the evening and jumped off the platform again and again. When she fell and got up again, she paid attention to the movements and feelings when she landed. Her body is highly tightened and completely relaxed to maintain the elasticity of her waist and legs... Then she jumped with her luggage and medical bag, irritating herself again and again.

Six months later, the army made a major assessment of the landing operation, and Ma Xu asked to participate many times. Considering the low risk, the chief reluctantly agreed. After the soldiers jumped down, it was Ma Xu's turn. Surrounded by hundreds of officers and soldiers, little Ma Xu jumped down from the high platform like a swallow gently landed on the bunker. Her actions are standard and sharp! The head was blinded. He didn't believe she jumped so well. He said, 'Have you been making wild guesses?' Ma Xu said with a smile, 'Then let me jump twice more!'

Ma Xu jumped twice again, lighter and lighter than before, and accurately landed in the center of the bunker. The surrounding officers and soldiers cheered and applauded.

In the autumn of 1962, Ma Xu boarded the plane and parachuted with the army for the first time. In order to reach a certain weight to maintain a stable landing, she must increase the load. In addition to weapons and ammunition, she also has more medicine boxes and heavier clothes. At that moment, she was the only female soldier among hundreds of blooming like flowers under the blue sky. In the next 20 years, Ma Xu parachuted more than 140 times, from her 20s to her 50s. Due to her superb skydiving skills, she was also selected as the vanguard of 'wind skydiving' with the greatest difficulty and risk. In this way, Ma Xu, in the spirit of 'not afraid of hardship, difficulty and death' created three Chinese soldiers in the history of airborne troops: the first female parachutist, the female parachutist with the most parachuting times and the oldest female parachutist.

Ma Xu is known as 'A flower of Chinese airborne troops'. She is so small that she really looks like a flower.

3. A completely selfless choice

In the process of practicing skydiving, Ma Xu met Yan Xueyong, a tall and gentle instructor. Yan Xueyong is the same age as Ma Xu, from Chongqing. He was obviously convinced by the heroic and brave Ma Xu. Ma Xu was also attracted by his elegant temperament. They soon fell in love and got married. Seeing that China's airborne troops are growing, Ma Xu thought a lot and made a major decision. She said to Yan Xueyong: 'I am thin and small, and it must be difficult to have child. Besides, once I have child, I can't work for at least three years and can't train with soldiers. As a military doctor, I will be abandoned, and the paratroopers won't allow her to be on the parachute force. I don't want to leave the soldiers, and I don't want children because I don't want them to affect my career.'

Yan Xueyong's love for his wife is absolute and unconditional, and his love for the army is also absolute and unconditional. Chinese servicemen take obedience to national interests as their highest duty and do everything at their own expense. He agreed with emotion. It was a quiet night. The husband and wife made the only 'mistake' 'of' concealing major personal matters from the organization' in their life – they were afraid that the leaders would disagree. At home, Ma Xu closed the curtains, locked the door and secretly sterilized her husband. They made an appointment with each other. From then on, they walked and grew old together. This is how loyal, selfless, firm and noble love!

Old Ma said to me on the phone, 'It's nothing, because we are Chinese soldiers.'

In 1983, after years of research, repeated tests and improvements, Ma Xu and her husband developed a lightweight and strong 'inflatable ankle protection', which greatly reduced the impact of paratroopers on landing and reduced the injury rate of soldiers to almost zero. After examination and approval by relevant departments of the Central Military Commission, the product is widely used in airborne troops and has obtained a national patent. This is the first time in China.

In 1996, Ma Xu and her husband in their 60s invented and developed the 'single soldier parachuting plateau oxygen supply vest' The *PLA Daily* carried out a special report on this, and the product obtained the national patent again. This is a large part of the couple's huge savings. In addition, for decades, Ma Xu has made in-depth exploration on family traditional Chinese medicine prescriptions. Through years of practice, she has creatively prepared many good drugs for the treatment of gastrointestinal diseases, which are welcomed by the majority of patients. There are long lines outside her clinic every day. In the past few decades, Ma Xu has also published more than 100 academic papers, filling some gaps in national and military scientific research. Therefore, she has won many awards at home and abroad, such as 'Edison International Invention Gold Award' and 'Bauhinia International Invention Gold Award' along with other international rewards.

Ma Xu never stopped studying, struggling and creating in her life. In 2011, Ma Xu, 78, made another amazing decision – take postgraduate entrance examination! Tongji Medical College of Huazhong University of Science and Technology was deeply moved by the old woman's resume and contribution and made an exception to admit her. After years of hard study, she passed most subjects successfully, only Japanese failed. So far, Japanese notes have been pasted everywhere in her home, even on her vamp for some time. In a phone call, Lao Yan smiled and said to me that once Ma Xu went out to buy vegetables and forgot to take down the small note on her vamp, 'the old lady walked down the street in her military uniform and received a lot of admiring glances.'

In March 1976, Ma Xu returned to her hometown, Mulan County, where she left for 30 years to commemorate his parents. She also set up a new monument with her parents' names engraved on the front and her motto engraved on the back: 'Contribute everything to mankind and the revolution will last forever'. After returning home, she experienced the storm of the 'Cultural Revolution' for ten years, and the dead villages and poor villagers left her unforgettable pain. Perhaps at that moment, she had the desire to do her best to help the people in her hometown. Since then, Ma Xu and her husband have maintained a hard-working and simple style for decades, and they are harsher on themselves. Mrs. Ma never bought new clothes again. When the right cuff of the sweater was wore out (worn when writing), she cut it off to make the two cuffs long and short. The TV, refrigerator, sofa and desk at home are old. They look even older than her. There is only one newspaper every day, and the vegetables planted in the yard are new...

In this way, the old couple who always wore a military uniform squeezed out 10 million yuan from everything they had.

In September 2017, the 45 division of the fifteenth army in Wuhan held a series of activities to celebrate the 65th anniversary of the death of Huang Jiguang. Mrs. Ma was invited to attend the meeting, and she met by accident with Jin Changfu, the coach of the original army. She expressed her willingness to donate money for her hometown. Jin Changfu was deeply touched, and said that he was willing to help her contact her hometown.

In March 2018, Ji Desan, director of education on behalf of the county Party committee and the county government, arrived in Wuhan and walked into the humble house of Mrs. Ma. A great and selfless act of kindness and feat has moved more than 200000 people in Mulan and quickly spread throughout the country.

On June 28, 2019, Ma Xu and Yan Xueyong in blue camouflage were invited to fly to Harbin and were cordially received by Zhang Qingwei, Secretary of the provincial Party committee and other leading comrades. On the bus to Mulan County, Ma Lao stared at the land of her hometown through the window. For a long time, she kept raising his hand to dry the rolling tears, as if looking for the memory of her childhood. Passing by the Songhua River Bridge, she specially called off, looked at the fence for a long time, and murmured, 'This is my mother river. I know her and remember her, but the scenery on both sides changed a lot, more beautiful...'

Upon arriving at the construction site of 'Ma Xu Cultural and Art Center' in the county seat, Mrs. Ma opened her arms and enthusiastically shouted to the local people and builders who welcomed her: 'villagers, the daughter of Mulan County is back!' The atmosphere was exciting with people cheering: 'Welcome Mrs. Ma home!' But many women just kept crying and couldn't say a word. Then, Mrs. Ma waved her arms vigorously and commanded everyone to sing 'There would be no new China without the Communist Party', and their loud voice resounded through the world...

She back her home, Libaoguo Village, where dozens of her relatives live. From Ma Xu's father Ma Yongshan, the genealogy has multiplied to the sixth generation, and the youngest has just entered primary school. The villagers said that with the care and support of the county Party committee and the county government and the help of the team stationed in the village, the whole village has been lifted out of poverty and lived a comfortable new life. The old woman shed tears of relief.

In February 2019, Ma Xu was rated as 'Ten of China's Inspirational role models 2018' by CCTV.

Fortunately, the heroic old woman Ma Xu has become the glorious end of this book!

RECOLLECTIONS

Comparison and Thinking

IF THERE WAS only one kind of flower in the world, even if they were roses, it would extremely horrible.

Therefore, there is a shining, ubiquitous, invisible and colorless knife in the universe that is comparison. In comparison, the universe has and presents a magnificent diversity. Every star, every creature, every leaf and every grain of sand are different. In comparison, from nebulae to black holes, from nature to human society, from civilization to life, there are warm and cold. Through comparison, human beings can learn to think, understand truth and choose, so as to continuously open up their own way forward and create colorful flowers of civilization. Comparison can create truth, civilization, path and emotion.

Every heart beats in comparison.

In the past year, I have been devoted to the interview and writing of this book. The observation and comparison of history, world, country, system and culture have given me a steady stream of passion and strong motivation. Tears are a kind of temperature, moving is a kind of temperature, and happiness is a kind of temperature. Hunger, cold and satiety, thatched houses and new houses, dirt roads and avenue, each has their own temperatures. Therefore, no matter where I go, my heart is close to those villages and farmhouses, listening to the tearful past, the warm present and the steps of great changes. Isn't it a miracle in the history of world civilization that this oriental power that was once poor, weak, and slaughtered all over the place rose up with socialist power? Becoming wealthy and strong, now it is opening its warm arms to embrace its people. Leading everyone to a more comfortable life and a well-off society. This is a historical miracle.

This is the national temperature of China!

The temperature was a standard of national civilization and a thermometer of values. Writing the rise of temperature, more free, more realistic and authentic. Writing the temperature of China, the whole world could see that China was here. China was like this, except for those who would never wake up, and those who had been sleeping in the cold war.

Lying, deception, attack, and smear were another kind of temperature, a cold and despicable temperature. Put it in the sun, it will be thoroughly exposed and disappear. The only thing left is 'The emperor's new clothes'. It's too ugly!

Walking into the battlefield of poverty alleviation in China, I was moved, excited and proud all the way.

I believe that this unprecedented 'First livelihood project' in China has profound and long-term multiplicity, creativity and constructive significance:

First, with the greatest determination, strength and speed, we have completely eliminated the long-standing phenomenon of absolute poverty in Chinese history, lifted the last part of the poor population out of poverty since reform and opening up, and completely solved the problem of food and clothing of the Chinese nation for thousands of years. Income continued to grow rapidly, the 'Three Guarantees' were fully implemented, and living standards were generally improved. The most gratifying thing is that in the past few decades, I have traveled all over the country and the vast rural areas and found that generation after generation of children is generally taller than their parents. The fact that the average height of the Chinese women's volleyball team ranks first in the world is a strong proof. Therefore, netizens jokingly call them 'All legs below the neck'. Children is the nation's future. This is the greatness cannot be underestimated.

Second, the new rural construction has achieved strong and rapid development. In the past few thousand years, the dirty and chaotic appearance of China's rural areas has changed. Mud houses, thatched cottages and shacks have been cleaned up, and rural infrastructure has been comprehensively improved. 'New houses, wide roads, large squares, planting and breeding cooperatives, water supply and ventilation networks, rural supermarkets and farmhouses' are becoming common landscapes in rural areas. The wave of new homes, new lives and new weather has indeed come. As a Yikoudao villager who moved to new community in Tongren, Guizhou, said, 'I didn't expect that a happy life should come to me so soon!'

Third, in places where 'one side of land and water cannot support one side of the people', most scattered households living in deep mountains and valleys have moved into new resettlement areas, realizing the citizenization of farmers. China's landscape and ecological environment have changed. The great idea of 'clear water and green mountains are as valuable as mountains of gold and silver' has become the consensus of the people all over the country, and our motherland is becoming more and more beautiful.

Fourth, poverty alleviation cadres went to villages and households to eat, live and work with farmers, which deeply baptized the thoughts and feelings of the majority of Party members and cadres. In the beginning, it was for 'responsibility' later it become for 'family', the hearts of the party and the people are getting closer and closer, and the relationship between the party and the masses, cadres and the masses has greatly improved. The cadres came to village bringing meat, and the farmers give vegetables when cadres leave. The two families are like one family. Along the way, I walked into every village. The accompanying cadres stationed in the village and poverty alleviation cadres knew every villagers' names. Villagers working or chatting on the roadside affectionately call 'Secretary Wang', 'Captain Li' and 'team member Zhao', full of family affection. The cadres said that the 'fish water relationship' between the army and the people in the war years has returned; the villagers said that the style of 'The Eighth Route Army' (Honorable name for army) has come back. Lu Yongzheng, publicity Minister of Guizhou provincial Party committee, told me that since the launch of the poverty alleviation project, the relationship between the party and the masses has entered the 'best period', which means that the ruling foundation of the Communist Party of China is becoming stronger and stronger, and the grass-roots management level and governance ability are significantly improved.

Fifth, Guided by the great banner of socialism with Chinese characteristics and under the leadership of Xi Jinping, China has achieved decisive victory in the struggle against poverty. Through national strict prevention and control, defeating COVID 19 was possible and successful. And the superiority of the socialist system with Chinese characteristics is reaffirmed. The national institutional advantage of concentrating on major events has greatly enhanced the 'confidence in the path, theory, system, and culture' of the whole Party and the people of the whole country, and greatly improved the party's core position of leadership, combat effectiveness, cohesion and attraction. A western scholar exclaimed 'China is the most disciplined country, and no other country can compare with it.'

Sixth, World Bank's data show that China's contribution to world poverty reduction exceeds 70%. By 2020, China organized and planned large-scale targeted poverty alleviation to get rid of poverty. It not only enable Chinese people to enter a well-off society, but also provide Chinese experience and Chinese textbooks for poverty alleviation to the world. China's comprehensive reform and innovation in poverty alleviation system, policies and methods have undoubtedly made great contributions to promoting the progress and development of world civilization and building a community of common density.

I made a detour to the whole country and went deep into the village for an interview. There were also some work steps worth thinking and vigilance that needed to be particularly noticed:

First, treat laziness. Lazy people have existed since ancient times. 'Laziness leads to poverty' is also common in rural China. Although within 2% or 3%, it cannot be underestimated. How to 'Laziness leads to poverty' should become an important topic in the national poverty alleviation work? We should take administration, management, governance, incentive, reward and punishment and other measures according to law. We must have a set of methods to 'force people to go to Liangshan' (a metaphor for taking action because of oppression) resolutely change the living habits of 'lazy people', stimulate their endogenous motivation and let them become self-reliance men. Relying solely on the government to solve the 'Two worries and Three Guarantees' is not a permanent solution. At the same time, it will also create an unbalanced and unconvinced negative effects among the people.

Second, prevent the phenomenon of 'homogenization and collectivization'. This is a big problem that has plagued us for a long time. From north to south, I have been to many places where the government encourages and supports the development of industry, such as apples, walnuts, red dates, tea, etc. I think the market capacity is limited after all. Many years later, the crisis of agricultural and sideline products piling up and oversupply will be a very real threat and challenge. What should we do when farmers' labor and cooperatives invest a lot of money, but the products are difficult to sell and even rot in the fields, leading to the return to poverty of farmers who has been out of poverty?

Third, establish a long-term mechanism for poverty alleviation and act in accordance with the law of market economy. For poor households, we should unswervingly solve their 'two worries and Three Guarantees' in accordance with policies and regulations, which is determined by the party's purpose of 'taking the people as the center' and the National Nature and system of socialist China. In order to achieve the party's Centennial goal, let the people of the whole country share the fruits of reform and development, and enable the people of all ethnic groups to build a well-off society in an all-round way by 2020, we must completely realize it one by one! Some people call these policy measures 'duck feeding'. You must fill in when you should and give when you should. At the same time, I believe that attaching great importance to the establishment of a long-term poverty alleviation mechanism and supporting farmers to develop industries in accordance with the law of market economy are major events and principles worthy of study in poverty alleviation. It is particularly noteworthy that most of the cadres who go to the countryside to help the poor come from cities, and most of them are cadres of Party and government organs. They are not familiar with the countryside and are not familiar with the operation and law of the market economy. Anyone can 'duck feeding ', but it takes some wisdom and ability for them to push farmers onto the track of market economy and obtain strong self-generating power. Section 17 of this book, 'new Tending the Roots of Wisdom: cauliflower 'great leap forward' is a successful example. Another vivid example is that at a provincial poverty alleviation seminar, a poverty alleviation cadre reported a major project he was actively promoting. Because he helped the village get close to the provincial capital, he called on the farmers of the whole village to plant vegetables on a large scale, and then rent a large market in the city as the 'export' of villagers' vegetables. Sounds good, but he was refuted by a farmer on the spot: can you earn 160,000 yuan of rent a year? Can farmers recover the cost of renting cars and driving vegetables? What if there are no vegetables in the off-season? If you lose, you will leave a lot of trouble in the future. The farmer came up with an idea on the spot: you can contact and combine the canteens of several large enterprises and companies to jointly operate an e-commerce platform with the village cooperative. Both sides have a car. What and how many dishes do you need per unit per day? On the platform, the vegetables are sent to the door by special bus, and the villagers can sell vegetables without going out.

All the people present agreed with him. This was the difference between a government official and a farmer who knew the rules of the market. It could be seen that in the work of poverty relief, only by learning to use the rules of the market economy could we stimulate the inner motivation and achieve a long-term system.

The final victory of the war made the whole country happy. The future had come, and the dream came true.

From time to time, in the country wide village, I would drink with the poverty relief officials and villagers. We would talk about the ancient and modern times, talk about changes, pour out our hearts, and drink happily. Because of the new era and new life, every day is worth celebrating!

Today, no one could stop the magnificent March of the 'dream of China', just like no one could stop the sun rising from the East!

Today, no one could prevent the great revival of the Chinese race, just like no one could prevent the Yangtze River and Yellow River from heading east!

The party, the motherland and the people united into one, which was the united will and astonishing great power of the country made of steel!

My country is very impressive!

Harbin, June 10, 2020

POSTSCRIPT
From 'five force'

In September 2019, I started from Beijing and went to Yulin, Hotan, Urumqi, Xinjiang Uygur Autonomous Region, Tongren, Guizhou, Shanghai, Jiamusi, Heilongjiang and Harbin. By June 2020, I have spent a full 10 months basically making a circle around China. Go deep into many counties, townships and villages, climb mountains, organize groups to enter households, visit poverty alleviation cadres, village cadres, paired cadres and villagers, talk about the changes in their hometown, listen to their stories, see the beautiful new immigrant new areas, new villages, new industries, enterprises, schools and kindergartens, and then immerse yourself in local writing. After the manuscript is basically completed, go to the next stop. Tired, a little tired. Is it bitter? A little bitter. Are you happy? Very happy. Because every day I face a new environment, a new life, new characters, new stories, lofty and great love, passion and moving, as well as the comfortable smile of poor villagers, from which I can feel and appreciate the temperature of the party, the country and the people's life. Whose life vision is so broad and information content is so rich? Only writers, and must be diligent writers, I am.

I'm a small regret. In Tongren, Guizhou, a local friend gave me a small pot of flowers called the fragrance of touching. They smelled very fragrant, and even more fragrant when I touch them. I would touch it when I get tired of writing, it was a source warmth. Try to imagine, I was alone everyone in that little room, facing a lonely computer, constantly on those keyboards, no one to talk to, this flower plant was there with me through it all. You can imagine how fond I grew of it. Later, I moved to a different place. Took the plant with me on a bus, a high-speed railway, a plane, and carefully carrying it. When my wide found out about it, she joked and said that she was my second girl——what she said got to me. Later in Shanghai, I put it on the plant outside the hotel for some sun. I went to see it every day on my walks. Three days later, it was stolen, which made me sad for several days.

In June of 2020, the book was finally finished. The Party Center and the

Chinese Art Association encouraged me to write a masterpiece by means of 'strength, insight, wisdom and writing ability'. I needed finish the book with 'strength', if the 'five forces' were expressed in this book, then it has to be a book of 'strength'. No matter what criticism I might get from readers, this book records the greatest, the most extensive and effective livelihood project in human history. Thousands of years of absolute poverty have been historically solved in our generation. This is an initiative of the Chinese government and a vivid embodiment of the great purpose of 'people-oriented' of the Communist Party of China. I'm proud of it.

I would like to thank the Poverty Alleviation Office of the State Council and the Chinese Writers Association for their trust in me, which not only gave me the honor to participate in this major writing project, but also baptized me in spirit and thought.

I would like to thank Liu Lihong of Yulin Poverty Alleviation Office, Hu Xudong of Hotan Poverty Alleviation Office, Yuan Ming of Tongren Poverty Alleviation Office, Zhang Jun of Shanghai Poverty Alleviation Office, many comrades of Huachuan County Poverty Alleviation Office of Heilongjiang Province, Dong Shaotao of Harbin Poverty Alleviation Office, Qi Yan, Tang Biao and Guan Jingtao of the Municipal Federation of literary and art circles for their help in writing this book.

Thank Ms. Shi Jiali and Ms. Yan Hui of Writers Publishing House for their enthusiastic attention and support to my interview and writing. They often ask me very gently where I am. The meaning of that, I understand.

June 12, 2020